THE ORIGINS OF LOGIC
Six to Twelve Months

DEVELOPMENTAL PSYCHOLOGY SERIES

SERIES EDITOR
Harry Beilin

Developmental Psychology Program
City University of New York Graduate School
New York, New York

LYNN S. LIBEN. *Deaf Children: Developmental Perspectives*

JONAS LANGER. *The Origins of Logic: Six to Twelve Months*

In Preparation

GILBERTE PIERAUT-LE BONNIEC. *The Development of Model Reasoning: Genesis of Necessity and Probability Notions*

TIFFANY FIELD, SUSAN GOLDBERG, ANITA SOSTEK, and DANIEL STERN. (Editors).
High-Risk Infants and Children: Adult and Peer Interactions

BARRY GHOLSON. *The Cognitive-Developmental Basis of Human Learning: Studies in Hypothesis Testing*

THE ORIGINS OF LOGIC
Six to Twelve Months

Jonas Langer

Department of Psychology
University of California, Berkeley
Berkeley, California

ACADEMIC PRESS
A Subsidiary of Harcourt Brace Jovanovich, Publishers
New York   London   Toronto   Sydney   San Francisco

ACADEMIC PRESS, INC.
111 Fifth Avenue, New York, New York 10003

United Kingdom Edition published by
ACADEMIC PRESS, INC. (LONDON) LTD.
24/28 Oval Road, London NW1   7DX

Library of Congress Cataloging in Publication Data

Langer, Jonas.
    The origins of logic.

    (Developmental psychology)
    Bibliography: p.
    Includes index.
    1. Cognition in children.   2. Logic.
3. Infant psychology.   I. Title.   II. Series.
BF723.C5L364   155.4'22   79–23266
ISBN 0–12–436150–1

PRINTED IN THE UNITED STATES OF AMERICA

80 81 82 83   9 8 7 6 5 4 3 2 1

Contents

16   Structural Development during the First Year   391

Appendix   417

References   433

Preface

Little attention has been given to the origins of logical cognition during infancy. In part, this is because it has been assumed that logic requires a formal symbolic language and that infants do not even possess a verbal language let alone a formal symbolic language. This assumption has led to the further presumption that logical cognition is an advanced cultural product transmitted to prelogical children when they are ready to manipulate formal symbols, probably beginning during late childhood and early adolescence.

Similar but more cautious views have been proposed in historical analyses of the rise of logic and mathematics from their Sumerian and Babylonian manifestations onward. Here it has been assumed that the initial great advances in logic and mathematics occurred when special systems of arbitrary symbols were introduced to represent objects, quantities, variables, operations, etc. It has not been denied that the rudiments of logic, upon which these advances were built, were constructed in ordinary language. Further, the issue of prelinguistic antecedents of logic has not yet been reached in historical analyses.

The theory proposed in this work is that logical cognition does not require a symbol system at its origin. Rather, logic is rooted in actions that generate pragmatic transformations which have logical properties. As we shall see, infants possess such operational capacities at a very early age. The task we have therefore set for ourselves is to discover the precursors of formal logical cognition in infants' developing actions. This volume is only the first installment in this endeavor. The complete endeavor requires further installments, to be presented as subsequent volumes, which trace the developments in logical cognition during early childhood that are transitional to the construction of symbolic logic.

The theory makes two general predictions. The first is that at their origins infants' actions already include elementary logical and mathematical properties. These properties are precursory to symbolic logical thought which develops from late childhood to adulthood. This general hypothesis leads to a set of specific expectations. Among other expectations, it implies that infants' actions entail elementary logical and mathematical operations, such as addition and subtraction, but in pragmatic rather than symbolic guises. Consequently, their initial manifestations are much less powerful than symbolic logic. It also implies that even pragmatic operations are used to produce the fundamentals of logical and mathematical thought. These are equivalence, nonequivalence, and reversible relations within and between elements, sets, orders, and quantities.

The second general hypothesis is that infants' original logical and mathematical operations and concepts are not preformed givens. They are the constructed products of infants' interactions with their environment. Their environment, however, includes more than just its physical and social properties. Equally important parts of their environment are their own actions and observations of those actions and their results. Thus their cognitions are, in good measure, the recursive products of their interactions with their own actions and observations.

The initially constructed cognitions progress as an intersective function of two forms of interactions. The first, as always, is their interactions with their environment. The second is their interactions with the organization of their previously constructed cognitions. An expected result is that even elementary logical and mathematical operations already develop through a sequence of four stages between ages 6 and 12 months. A distinguishing feature of sequential stage development is that successor operations build upon and integrate their progenitor operations, as much as upon interactions with their environment. Sequential stages are progressively marked by constructing cognitions upon cognitions previously constructed.

Acknowledgments

This research was conducted with the assistance of Julie Gerhardt, Teresa Jacobsen, Carol Slotnick, Susan Sugarman, and Loretta Townsend while they were graduate students in the developmental program, Department of Psychology, University of California, Berkeley. It was supported, in part, by funds from the James McKeen Cattell Fund. It is particularly indebted to continuing support from the Institute of Human Development (University of California, Berkeley) and from the Institute's director, Paul H. Mussen. Appreciation is also due to Carolyn Bennett for audiovisual transcription, to Rosemary Hendrick for typing the manuscript, and to Emily Reid for drawing the illustrations.

Protologic

Logical structure, however primitive or sophisticated, characterizes all cognition. The ontogenetic origins of logical structure must inevitably be sought in inferential transformations or operations. The earliest behavioral organization featured by precursory inference structures is, as we shall see, quite extensive. It includes transformations such as pragmatic addition which generates ordered iteration and pragmatic substitution which constructs set equivalence.

The elements of logical cognition, we would propose, comprise three base structures: combinativity, relational, and conditional operations. They constitute the foundation out of which all logicomathematical cognition is generated.

Combinativity structures comprise three basic elements: composing, decomposing, and deforming operations. These combinativity operations construct elements, sets, and subsets.

Relational structures comprise four basic elements: addition, subtraction, multiplication, and division operations. Relational operations are applied to the products of combinativity operations. Thereby, they generate quantitative relations within and between elements, sets, and subsets. For instance, they transform unordered sets into iteratively ordered series.

Conditional structures comprise three basic elements: exchange, correlation, and negation operations. Exchange structures comprise replacement, substitution, and commutative operations. Correlation structures include one-to-one and one-to-many correspondence operations. Negation structures comprise inverse and reciprocal operations. Conditional operations are applied to the products of both combinativity and relational operations. Thereby, they generate equivalence, nonequivalence, and reversibility within and between elements, sets, orders and quantities.

I. Proto-operations

Protological operations are constructed from their precursory origins. At their origins, precursory logical operations are limited to pragmatic acting on concrete objects, behaviors, and interactions. Precursory logical transformations do not operate on symbols, as true inferences do in formal logic.[1]

While not initially operating on symbols, infants' transformative transactions[2] map the transformational consequences of actions upon objects. Many are predominantly physical, that is, spatiotemporal, kinetic, and causal, rather than logical. For instance, displacement transactions map the transformational spatial properties of the actions on the objects displaced by changing their placement relations. Some transformational consequences are predominantly logical and quantitative. For instance, biting transactions map the decomposing properties of the actions on the objects bitten by transforming them from singular into multiple objects.

These and other mappings[3] transform the part–whole relations internal

---

[1] For these and other reasons we have adopted the admittedly cumbersome but necessary convention throughout the rest of this volume of prefixing "proto" to all references to logic at its origins in infancy. The aim is to keep clear that advanced formal symbolic logic is not reducible to its antecedents in infants' precursory pragmatic logic, even though it grows out of protologic.

[2] The term "transaction" is used here in accordance with the analysis introduced by Langer (in press). Three forms of transformational interaction are distinguished in that analysis, namely, integrative, coordinative, and transactive interaction. Integration refers to interactions which are internal to subjects' individual functional structures, that is, between substructures of a single functional structure. Coordination refers to interactions between different functional structures comprising subjects' mental organization (e.g., logical and physical structures). Transaction refers to interactions between subjects' functional structures and the physical and social environment, that is, interactions between subjects and objects. It is hypothesized that all three forms of transformational interaction vary as a function of subjects' developmental stage.

[3] Since Kant the concept of schemes has been used to focus upon both subjects' processes and products. While sharing this concern, the focus here is wider. It includes processes and products of object transformations as well. This is the reason for introducing the concept of

to individual objects. Displacement changes a variety of part–whole relations, such as which parts and how much of the whole object is observable; which parts are the top, middle, bottom, front, and back parts of the whole. Biting an object into two pieces drastically changes the initial part–whole relation. Most significantly, it multiplies the number of discrete parts and divides the size of the initial whole. As we shall see throughout this work, a number of proto-operations develop which structure physical, logical, and quantitative transformations in part–whole relations internal to individual objects. For instance, comparative and compensatory operations develop. They produce progressively stable and consistent objects. These objects may then serve as constant protoelements subject to progressively advanced proto-operations, such as being exchanged within a set by commutativity.

Other mappings on discrete objects compose, decompose, or recompose configurations of elements. They transform the part–whole relations between two or more objects. Composing may construct structures where there were only elements, larger structures out of smaller ones, new out of old structures, integrated out of segregated structures, and structures with differentiated parts. Decomposing may construct elements where there were structures, smaller structures out of bigger ones, and subdivided structures with coordinated parts. Recomposing may construct variant structures out of initial thematic structures such that successive sets are related.

Proto-operations, such as protoaddition, protocorrespondence, and protocommutativity relate and condition discrete structures. The results are manifold but of three basic types. They produce protological and protoquantitative equivalence, nonequivalence, and reversibility, and thereby, provide the structural basis for constructing protosets featured by both extensity (quantitative relations) and intensity (predicate relations). They also provide the structural basis for constructing proto-orders of increasing, decreasing, and combinations of increasing and decreasing magnitudes.

Transformational operations upon continuous and quasi-continuous objects share some properties with those upon discrete objects. Here we will be concerned only with quasi-continuous objects, in particular objects made of malleable Play-Doh. Quasi-continuous objects may be transformed as if they are discrete. With some important exceptions, the results are not unique. It is equally possible to place rings made out of Play-Doh or of wood on top of each other to compose a stack. Proto-

---

mappings. It shifts the unit of analysis to the transformational correspondences and interactive relations between subjects' (organismic) and objects' (environmental) processes and products.

operations, such as protoaddition and protosubtraction, isomorphically transform discrete and quasi-continuous structures when quasi-continuous elements are treated as if they are discrete. Adding and subtracting rings to and from a stack is not affected by whether the rings are Play-Doh or wooden, as long as they are treated as if they are merely discrete.

Discrete objects cannot be transformed as if they are quasi-continuous. Wooden rings cannot be compressed into each other to compose a set into an element; while Play-Doh rings can be. Combinativity operations upon quasi-continuous objects, then, have some significant unique properties. A preliminary way of analyzing their special properties is to dichotomize them into (a) those relevant to the intensity (form) of elements, and not their extensity (quantity); and (b) those relevant to the extensity (number) of elements, and not their intensity (form).

A number of combinativity operations uniquely apply to quasi-continuous objects and not to discrete objects. Deforming transforms the shape of a quasi-continuous object; thereby transforming the internal part–whole relations. Breaking, too, only transforms the part–whole relations within individual objects. Breaking takes two main forms. Holes can be punched, but the number of elements does not change. The transformation is from a Euclidean-like form to a topological-like, sometimes ring, form. Rings can be broken once. Then the number of elements does not change. The transformation is from a ring into a nonring.

Reforming makes deforming pragmatically reversible. A Play-Doh ball may be deformed into a sausage and then reformed into a ball. Reconstructing makes breaking pragmatically reversible. A ball may be transformed into a donut by punching a hole in it and then reconstructed into a ball. A ring may be transformed into a string by breaking it once and then reconstructed into a ring.

All these direct and reversible operations transform the intensive or internal part–whole relations within objects. They operate upon the internal organization of individual elements. They do not transform the extensive part–whole relations within a set of quasi-continuous elements; other specialized operations do that.

The operations which transform extensive part–whole relations within a single set of elements do, of course, also transform part–whole relations between two or more sets. With precursory exceptions produced by 12-month-olds, however, they are not generated in relation to more than one set by babies in the 6–12-month-old age range analyzed in this volume. Comprehensive analyses of between sets part–whole transformations will therefore not be undertaken here, but rather reserved for a subsequent volume on older infants.

Three main combinativity operations construct extensive part–whole relations within quasi-continuous sets. Composing transforms sets (many elements) into elements (one), smaller into larger elements, and separate into linked elements. Decomposing multiplies elements (one) into sets (many), divides larger into smaller elements, and detaches linked into separate elements. Combined composing and decomposing produces a myriad of transformational possibilities. One is central: Successive negation of composing by decomposing and vice versa transforms these combinativity operations into precursory reversible operations.

Combinativity operations upon sets of discrete and quasi-continuous objects combine the properties of transformations upon each kind of object. Beyond these they include three unique properties. Attaching links together separate discrete and quasi-continuous objects into conglomerate objects. Detaching transforms linked elements into separate discrete and quasi-continuous elements. Successive attaching and detaching which negate each other transforms these combinativity operations into precursory reversible transformations between combinativity operations.

Manipulative transactions, such as these, entail mapping the structure of infants' transformational actions on the structure of objects. Of course, mappings need not be limited to one-to-one correspondences between transformative activities and transformational products. Rather, it is expected that mappings become progressively defined, consistent, and regulated in the course of infant development. As infants develop, the transformations in objects become progressive functions, albeit complex, of their maturing transformational operations.

Consistent mappings constitute the origins of constructing protosymbolization by infants by mapping the structure of their actions on that of objects, such that object transformations become lawful functions of their own constructions. These mapping functions remain protosymbolic as long as the correlations constructed are restricted to presentational relations which only include direct physical and social transformations upon objects.

Mapping functions develop into true symbolization when the constructed correlations between the structures of actions and objects also include representational relations. Representational relations begin with detaching mappings from the objects of their consistent transaction, such that various gestural mappings are created. This generates the protosymbolic structure necessary for the coordination of mapping functions to each other since mappings have become independent of their original objects of transaction. Mappings of mappings, then, constitute the transitional functional structure between presentational protosymbols and representational symbols.

Representational symbols are not limited to direct physical and social transformations on objects. They include transformations about objects with which children are not directly transacting. Infants transact with them indirectly, and thereby, transform them only abstractly by constructing mappings of mappings. Thus, the structure of their transformative actions is mapped on previously constructed, but now detached, mappings of objects. Representational symbolization, then, involves second-order functions which coordinate previously constructed first-order protosymbolic functions.

Transformational operations may also operate on mappings so as to construct protoclass, proto-order, and protoquantitative relations. Two hands can be used, for instance, to generate an iterative order. This can be done by clapping them together once, pausing, clapping twice, pausing, clapping three times, pausing, and so on.

This leads to the realization that in the real world of infants transacting with the environment the potential objects of their transformative proto-inferences are an amalgam. They are not simply things, but are also mappings. Indeed, the objects of interaction are sets of mappings, things, mappings-upon-things, and resultant transformations. Thus, a good segment of the objects of infants' transformative proto-operations is their transactions and prior transformations. Progressive coordination of multiple transactions and transformations provides much of the protoinference structures that develop during infancy.

Consider in this light our initial proposal about the base structures of logical cognition. Viewed in terms of their ontogenesis, the theory we shall be testing is that the precursory structures of logicomathematical operations (a) take three foundation forms, and (b) originate and develop during infancy.

The first base set of precursory logical structures is hypothesized to consist of elementary combinativity proto-operations. They are fundamental to infants' initial construction of elements and collections of elements. Three elementary combinativity operations are basic. These are the operations of composing, decomposing, and deforming. Infants are expected to use these three combinativity proto-operations to construct individual and multiple elements out of concrete objects, behaviors, and interactions. They are also expected to constitute the structural developmental sources of derivative combinativity proto-operations, such as recomposing and reforming objects and collections of objects. Derivative combinativity proto-operations are expected to develop later during infancy than the three elementary ones.

The second foundation set of elementary logical structures, expected to originate in infants' interactions, are precursory forms of relational operations. Four elementary relational operations are basic: precursory forms of addition, subtraction, multiplication, and division. They construct pragmatic set, order, and quantitative relations within and between individual and multiple elements.

A third foundation set of elementary operational structures are expected to already condition combinativity and relational structures. All three basic conditional proto-operations are expected to originate during infancy. They are expected to take pragmatic forms of exchange, correlation, and negation operations. These three proto-operational conditions are fundamental to infants' initial construction of elementary equivalence, nonequivalence, and reversibility within and between elements, sets, orders, and quantities. For instance, inverse proto-operations are already expected to be generated by infants in order to determine the presentational identity of individual objects when they are pragmatically transforming them.

II. Objects and Classes

This theoretical proposal about the origins and structures of protologic sets the context for determining whether, in fact, babies can and do construct precursory logical operations and structures. Structurally, this means discovering (a) the forms logical constructions take and (b) the organization of these forms, at any given stage. Developmentally, it means discovering (a) their origins and (b) their lawful progressive transformations from one stage to the next.

Classification is a prime target domain in which to initiate an investigation of protologic. Classification occupies a central, perhaps the central, position in theory and research on cognitive development (Flavell, 1970). Class logic is a basic element in the foundations of logic (Kneale & Kneale, 1962) and mathematics (Kramer, 1970). Boole (1854) went so far as to formulate an algebra of classes as the laws of thought; though nonreductionistic, constructivist versions of the universal role of class logic in all cognition, including mathematical reasoning, seem more plausible (Piaget, 1972).

As a working definition we may accept, with one addition, Cantor's (1895) characterization of a class or a set (Menge) as "a collection into one whole of definite, distinct objects of our perception or our thought [or our manipulation], which are called the elements of the set." Adding manipulation to Cantor's definition of sets is necessary to meet the structural developmental requirements of infant transformational transactions.

Agreement on the centrality of classification has led to various theoretical analyses of classificatory development. The causal-explanatory accounts vary greatly in these theoretical analyses. The descriptive–formal models derived from these theoretical analyses have important commonalities, most importantly, the formulation of sequential stage models of classificatory development. The developmental models derived from theoretical perspectives, ranging from the behaviorism of Welch and Long to the functionalism of Vygotsky to the structuralism of Piaget and Werner, are all sequential stage models. Of course, they diverge in their definitions of both sequence and stage.

Often, developmental investigators also agree, in some form, that the stage progression in classificatory structuring is along the concrete to abstract dimension first proposed by Goldstein and his followers to analyze the psychopathological degeneration of cognition (Gelb & Goldstein, 1925; Goldstein & Scheerer, 1941; Trunnell, 1964, 1965; Weigl, 1941). Three major developmental shifts along the concrete–abstract dimension have been hypothesized (Hanfmann, 1939; Kasanin & Hanfmann, 1938–1939). These are (a) from considering configurations and functions of things to considering categories of things, (b) from being bound to some particular stimulus property to general formulations of the totality of elements involved, and (c) from rigidly adhering to one kind of actual sorting to flexibly searching for other hypothetically possible forms of sorting. Vygotsky (1962) and his colleagues used these dimensional specifications not only to analyze the ontogeny of classification in Western children, but, as did Werner (1948), they also used these dimensional specifications as the basis for a comparative developmental analysis of (a) the cognitive ontogeny of animals, (b) the cognitive ontogeny of children with sensory deficits, such as deafness, (c) the psychopathology of cognition in schizophrenic and brain-damaged people (Vygotsky, 1934), and (d) the cognitive ontogeny of people in primitive non-Western societies (Luria, 1976).

Notwithstanding the major importance attached to classification, little theoretical research has been devoted to its origins. To the extent that precursors of classification during infancy are analyzed by structural theorists they are assimilated to sensorimotor schemes of action and circular reactions (Inhelder & Piaget, 1964; Piaget, 1952; Werner, 1948). Vygotsky's (1962) functionalism led to the conclusion that the origins of classification consist of children constructing "unorganized congeries" or heaps of objects. However, it was assumed that these precursory forms could not develop until the onset and early development of the directive function of speech during late infancy. Consistent with behavioristic theory, Welch (1940) assumed that the antecedents of classification develop during the first 2 years. The antecedents were hypothesized to be nothing more than discrimination and generalization of stimulus features. Infants learn the similarities and differences between the predicate properties of objects. However, the criterial attribute of classification, according to Welch, is the ability to group class hierarchies, and even the most rudimentary hierarchization was not found to develop until at least the third year. Welch therefore concluded that infants are preabstract and cannot classify; even though to a limited extent they can discriminate between categories and generalize within a category.

An inevitable result flowed from these previous theoretical analyses. No empirical research has been directed toward investigating classificatory development during the first year of life.

Another inevitable result has been that even less theoretical attention has been paid to the origins of cognizing the elements of classes. Much research has been done on the origins of cognizing objects during the first year, but this research focuses upon objects as physical phenomena (Piaget, 1954) or as the referents of symbolic phenomena (Werner & Kaplan, 1963). No research, theoretical or empirical, has analyzed the cognition of objects in relation to classes. That is, no research has dealt with the origins of cognizing objects as logical phenomena in general, and as potential or actual elements of sets in particular.

Yet, classes are nothing if not collections of definite, distinct objects, as Cantor pointed out in his mathematical theory. Our theoretical proposal about the origins and threefold structures of proto-operational transformations provides the minimal framework necessary to account for the construction of protological classes and objects; that is, precursory sets of elements which have both extensive (quantitative) and intensive (predicate) properties.

III. Structural Development

The theoretical scope of this research is to analyze the origins and structures of logic in infancy and their developments during early childhood which are sufficient for the development of formally constructed logical thought. Elements of the logical structures which develop during middle to late childhood have already been determined, at least as far as classification is concerned (Inhelder & Piaget, 1964; Piaget, 1972). These structures constitute the transitional stage of concrete operational logic which bridges the precursory logical developments under investigation in the present research and the development of formal constructions during adolescence and adulthood.

Logically necessary inference structures are not constructed until the development of formal reasoning during adolescence (Inhelder & Piaget,

1958; Langer, in press) and adulthood (Kuhn, Langer, Kohlberg, & Haan, 1977). Formal symbolic logic is a final product of developmental interaction and transformation, not an innate given. The problem, therefore, becomes to discover the developmental interactions whereby (a) elementary inference structures are originally constructed, and then (b) sequentially and constructively transformed, such that (c) they issue in formal logical structures later in development.

Formal logical cognition is a final, not an original, a priori construction. It is constructed in and by developmental interactions. The epistemology of the most mature organization of logic generated in development thereby provides the theoretical parameters for predicting and analyzing its proper ontogenetic antecedents (Langer, 1969a, pp. 168–180). Inherent in this developmental epistemology is the notion that the final stage of constructive logic constitutes the criterial standard against which to measure the requisite original antecedent stage of transformational logical organization. It also imposes constraints on the direction and forms that developmental interaction may take stage by successive stage, so as to transform precursory into mature logical structures. The contents of developmental interaction are free variables. They are unconstrained and therefore open to the variety of circumstances which different environments, including children's own actions, present.

The problem of logical antecedents may not be glossed over. Partial isomorphisms may be appropriately formulated in order to construct a theory of the organization of different cognitive structures, that is, mathematical, logical, and physical, at each successive developmental stage. However, it is not adequate to search for the ontogenetic antecedents of formal logical cognition in related but different primitive structures, such as sensorimotor groupings of spatial relations. It will do even less to give accounts of related but primitive functions, such as sensorimotor circular reactions, perceptual discrimination and generalization, and memory encoding.

The requisite ontogenetic antecedents of formal logical cognition are the protological features of the organization of pragmatic protooperations and protosymbols generated by infants interacting with their environments. These provide the only sufficient conditions for the original construction of protoinferential relations.

Consequently, our structural developmental analyses of protological interactions include two basic components. The first is the organization of the structures of interactions which produces consequent transformations. Transaction with objects which produce changes in their part–whole structures is only one aspect of the organization of interactions. Infants also transact with actions, both their own and that of social and physical objects. They transact with the part–whole relations between objects, between actions, and between objects intersecting with actions. As they develop, infants progressively transact with and integrate the transformational resultants of all the preceding list of transactions. Together with observation and recording of the resultant transformations, these interactions are the constructive structural causes of organized cognition, including protologic.

The organization of transformational interactive structures is analyzed in extension, stage by progressive stage. To begin with, this includes antecedent biological structures inherent in transformational transactions. Consider the evolving structure of deforming the internal part–whole relations within quasi-continuous objects. Deforming is logically entailed when an organ, such as a hand, grasps a ball of Play-Doh with some minimal force. Antecedent inherent structures elaborate into precursory constructed structures of transformational transactions. Deforming becomes detached, at least in part, from its logically entailed biological structure, when a hand displaces a Play-Doh ball against a surface. Then any deformation is contingent upon the physical properties of the surface. Such deformation is contingent upon the resistance of the surface. If the surface is the top of a tub full of water, then the result may be no perceptible deformation. If it is the top of a pillow, then a minor transformation may be constructed. If it is the top of a wooden table, then a gross deformation may be constructed. Deforming is subject to progressive regulation via observation, recording, and directed variation by the subject producing deformation. Regulated deforming provides feedback and feedforward conditions necessary to progress from precursory to more developed constructed structures. Then, one deformation, such as pulling at a Play-Doh ball, can compensate for another deformation, such as pushing at it. This results in reforming the Play-Doh ball, thereby constructing a protoidentity operation.

Similar plus additional structural developmental analyses apply to all the structures comprising the organization of transformational transactions generated at each stage described in this volume. These analyses are applied to (a) protosymbolic and proto-operational mappings, (b) proto-operational transformations within the part–whole relations internal to the structure of discrete and quasi-continuous objects, and (c) proto-operational transformations in the part–whole relations between elements of a set and of an order. It is therefore necessary to analyze the total organization of transformations generated at each antecedent stage before proceeding to those of the next successor stage. They constitute the analyses presented in successive parts of this volume.

The parameters of these organizational analyses are set by both final a priori and developmental considerations. The structures of advanced cognition, toward which the initial structures are developing, determine which initial transformational interactions are centrally relevant precursors to investigate. The constraints thereby imposed upon the study of precursory transformational interactions are general to their total structural organization. These include the requirement that structures must be consistently related to each other in inferential procedures and in developmental level at each stage. In turn, these analytic organizational requirements are subject to empirical proof, stage by successive stage.

This brings us to the second and complementary process component of our structural developmental analyses. Most importantly, it provides the complementary empirical data necessary to test the sufficiency of our structural analyses of precursory transformational transactions. For instance, it provides the sequential ontogenetic data necessary to test the hypothesis that inherent deforming is an antecedent of contingent deforming and that it in turn is a precursor of protocompensatory deforming.

The basic assumption is that the organization of antecedent progenitor operations are the causes of successor transformational interactions. The requirements of the final organization of structural constructions therefore determine the criterial standards and parameters of analyses for all the preceding structural stages hypothesized. These include the original and all transitional stages hypothesized.

The basic hypothesis about the process of structural development is that progenitor interactions constructively transform initial protooperational relations; thereby they generate the origins of equilibrium between infants and their environments. However, these initial constructions are also incomplete, at times contradictory, and certainly not entirely coherent; thereby they simultaneously generate the origins of disequilibrium between infants and their environments. This self-generated dialectic, between equilibrated and disequilibrated structures of transformational interactions, is the source of development directed toward progressive cognitive equilibrium and disequilibrium (Langer, 1969b, 1974, in press: cf. Piaget, 1977).

One reason, then, for simultaneously employing organizational and process analyses is to determine when proto-operations are lawful, both structurally and developmentally. Both analyses are necessary for determining when infants are not merely generating protological transformations by chance, that is, when their transformations have so-called psychological reality. Any time a subject produces a given kind of transformative transaction, it may, of course, be nothing more than a chance variation in behavior. This problem arises at all points of development, not only in infancy. It is, perhaps, particularly troublesome in early infancy when given transformations may occur infrequently. In addition, there may as yet be no precise way to calculate quantitatively the rate at which some given transformations must be performed in order to determine whether or not they are being generated lawfully or by chance.

The components of the structural developmental resolutions of this problem which are proposed throughout this volume are manifold. The discussion here will be limited to three central complementary components. Understanding them will be facilitated by outlining one set of findings to be detailed in subsequent chapters. Equivalence between consecutive sets of objects composed by infants may be constructed by substituting equal numbers of objects within a set while holding the compositional arrangement constant. At the first stage (6 months), 4 out of 12 subjects substitute one object for another in two-object sets which they have constructed (see pages 79–82). These infants barely begin to produce equivalence between consecutive versions of two-object sets. They take away one element from an initial two-object set they have just composed and immediately substitute another object in its place. No subjects invert the exchange by resubstituting the original object taken away so as to reconstruct their initial two-object sets. At the second stage (8 months), 10 out of 12 subjects substitute one object for another in two-object sets which they have composed (see pages 156–157). Three subjects invert the exchange. These subjects resubstitute the original object for the substitute object such that they reconstruct their initial two-object sets. At the third stage (10 months), all 12 subjects substitute one object for another in two-object sets which they have composed (see pages 241–244). All 12 subjects also invert their exchanges such that they reconstruct their initial two-object sets. At the fourth stage (12 months), all 12 subjects substitute and invert one object in two-object sets which they have composed (see pages 338–341). Six subjects extend protosubstitution to exchanging one object or two objects in three-object sets which they have composed. Two subjects invert their exchanges such that they reconstitute their initial three-object sets. None of the 36 subjects tested under age 12 months ever substitute objects in three-object sets which they have composed.

The first component of the structural developmental resolution is longitudinal. As the illustrative data on protosubstitution indicate its developmental transformations are lawful. The developmental transformations are quantitative. But, they are also structural. For instance, the element of reversibility only enters into substitution beginning at the second stage. Thus, even within the relatively small ontogenetic slice of a half a year, between ages 6 and 12 months, four sequentially ordered stages develop. Taken in isolation, the protosubstitutions generated at any given age could be mistakenly interpreted as random transactions; but, taken together, their progressive quantitative and structural elaborations mark the development of a proto-operation which is lawfully transformed three times within 6 months. These lawful developmental transformations constitute an invariant four-stage sequence. In such stage sequences successor proto-operations are both structural transforms of their progenitor proto-operations and integrate their progenitor proto-operations into more inclusive structures. The first component of the structural developmental resolution, then, is the analytic requirement that given transactions must be taken in their proper developmental context to determine whether they are random or lawful. The classical precedent is, of course, Piaget (1952).

The second component is cross-sectional. The stage-by-stage findings on protosubstitution are consistent with the developments in all the other combinativity, relational, and conditional proto-operations hypothesized as comprising the base structures of protologic. Most directly, parallel developmental results are found for the two other proto-operations hypothesized to make up exchange structures (which are a subset of conditional proto-operations). The first is protoreplacement. In this exchange proto-operation, the same object(s) is (are) taken away and replaced within two- (three-) object sets which infants compose, while the compositional arrangement is held constant. The second is protocommutativity. In this exchange proto-operation the objects comprising two- (three-) object sets which infants compose are rearranged such that the order relations are varied, while the membership is held constant. Parallel developmental results are also found for all the other less directly related proto-operations. Thus, cross-sectional empirical consistency between protological structures is found at each of the four developmental stages between ages 6 and 12 months. Moreover, theoretical coherence also emerges between the proto-operations generated at each stage. It is impossible to briefly summarize the nature of the theoretical coherence in the organization of structures at each stage. Instead, the concerned reader is urged to turn to Chapter 16, this volume, in which a structural developmental model of protologic is proposed. Both cross-sectional empirical consistency and theoretical coherence, then, constitute the second analytic requirement for evaluating whether any given type of transformation generated at any given age is random or lawful. Given transactions must be taken in their proper structural context to determine whether they are lawful.

The third complementary component of our structural developmental resolution, then, is structural developmental sufficiency. For any given type of logical operation the fundamental determinations become whether sufficient antecedent or precursory conditions have been generated and what they are. For instance, considered in this way, whether or not biologically inherent deformation of quasi-continuous (malleable) objects is sufficient to the eventual development of compensatory deformation is, indeed, a problem. However, the problem does not hinge upon whether the antecedent deformations are entailed by the conditions of the transactions or not. Both may well be lawful. Rather, the problem becomes that of discovering sufficient antecedent conditions for each stage in the development of deformations. This includes determining the relevant precursory transformational transactions generated at each stage. Relevancy, as indicated above, is determined by theoretical parameters set by final a priori criteria. Sufficiency also includes determining the mechanisms and stages of transition, that is, the equilibrium and disequilibrium conditions at the initial stage and at each transitional stage, which generate further development to the next stage of deformation until the final, most mature stage develops. The sufficient conditions we have hypothesized are none other than the protological features entailed by transformational transactions. Structural developmental sufficiency, then, is the third analytic requirement for determining lawfulness. Given transactions must be taken in their proper structural developmental context to determine whether the accounts of their sufficiency are lawful.

IV. The Empirical Research Program

The scope of the empirical research was designed to begin to test our structural developmental analyses. Investigating the origins and earliest developments of protological cognition in general, and about objects and classes in particular, necessitated extensive empirical research. Only the major general features will be sketched here. A detailed exposition of the entire research design is presented in the Appendix.

To generate as fine-grained ontogenetic structural data as practical, babies were tested at 2-month intervals between ages 6 and 12 months. Each of the four groups of subjects consisted of 12 babies, 6 male babies and 6 female babies in each. A subset of the babies were tested partially longitudinally. The 6- and 12-month-old groups consisted of cross-sectional subjects, while the 8- and 10-month-olds were partially longitudinal.

The 6–10-month-olds were tested extensively on five or six tasks. Each task lasted about 5 minutes. So, the data base for each baby totaled about

30 minutes of videotaped task-oriented nonverbal behavior. For the most part, the behavior consists of manipulatory transactions with objects and sets of objects. Some semisystematic recording of visual perception of the objects was also done. Because of their increased stamina, it was possible to test each 12-month-old more extensively. They were tested on nine or ten tasks. Thus, the data base nearly doubled for each subject at 12 months, that is, close to an hour of videotaped task-oriented nonverbal behavior.

The resultant data are unique in several ways. Each baby's range of transformational transactions was sampled as widely as possible. The chances of generating behavioral data reflective of each infant's range of and optimal protoinferential capacities were maximized.

Two fundamentally different kinds of objects were presented to the babies to transact with, discrete and quasi-continuous. All were small enough to be grasped and manipulated by babies.

Three types of discrete objects were used: (a) solid, geometric objects which emphasize their Euclidean form, such as cylinders and triangular columns; (b) geometric, ring objects which emphasize their topological form, such as circular and triangular rings; and (c) realistic objects, such as spoons and miniature dolls. All the discrete objects were made out of materials which are basically nonflexible and nonbreakable (at least as far as babies are concerned) such as masonite, wood, and plastic.

All the quasi-continuous objects were made out of Play-Doh material which is very flexible and breakable, even for babies. Two forms, analogous to the discrete objects, were used: (a) solid, geometric objects which emphasize their Euclidean form, such as balls and cubes; and (b) geometric, ring objects which emphasize their topological form, such as circular and triangular rings. It was not practicable to make realistic objects out of Play-Doh, so this form of quasi-continuous object was not used.

Both the discrete and quasi-continuous objects can be (a) united together into sets, or (b) separated into unrelated elements, or (c) reunited into variant sets. Only the quasi-continuous objects can be transformed from (d) one form of object into another, for example, from a Euclidean to a topological form; (e) an object into a set by decomposing the whole into two or more parts; and (f) a set into an object by uniting the elements into a single, larger object. Transaction with discrete and quasi-continuous objects at the same time permits two additional transformations: (g) attaching separate objects into conglomerate, part discrete and part quasi-continuous, wholes; and (h) detaching conglomerate wholes into unique parts, that is, discrete versus quasi-continuous elements.

The overall objective in presenting single quasi-continuous objects and sets of quasi-continuous objects to babies was to investigate the origins and initial developments in their construction of transformations (d), (e), and (f). Three main conditions were therefore tested. In one condition, a single large Play-Doh object was presented by itself. In a second condition, one set of three identical small Play-Doh objects grouped together was presented. In a third condition, two sets of Play-Doh objects were presented. Each set consisted of three objects. The objects in each set were grouped together. The two sets were distinctly separated in space, one on the baby's left and the other on the baby's right. One set consisted of three identical small objects, as in the second condition. The other set was composed of two identical small objects with a third that had the same form but was larger, as in condition one.

Testing always began with a spontaneous phase of transaction in which the babies were encouraged, by nonverbal means, to engage in free play with the presentations. Whenever practical the first phase lasted a minimum of 2.5 minutes. However, some babies insisted upon eating the Play-Doh, which caused them to gag and forced an early end to the test condition.

Spontaneous transaction was followed by a second, provoked phase. This phase began with the experimenter either (a) decomposing the large object into two smaller ones or (b) composing two small objects into one larger object; but always so as to preserve the objects' initial forms, for example, square ring to square ring and ball to ball. Half the time the experimenter demonstrated the transformation in an exaggerated, visible way. Everything was presentational—the initial state, the transformational process, and the final resultant state. The other half of the time, the experimenter performed the transformation under the table—only the initial and final resultant states of the objects were visible to the subject; the transformational process was not. After the experimenter finished, the resultant set of two objects was presented to each baby. The babies were encouraged to transact with the objects for at least 1 minute. The aim was to determine the effects of the four kinds of transformations upon the babies' subsequent behavior.

A third, and final, test phase consisted of the third condition in which two sets were presented, as previously described. This condition was the most complex because it presents infants with multiple sets and elements. Presenting the most complex quasi-continuous condition last minimized overwhelming the babies and interfering with their performances in the simpler conditions. Again the babies were encouraged to transact with the presentation for a minimum of 1 minute.

The general purpose in presenting babies with discrete and quasi-continuous objects at the same time was to investigate transformations (g) and (h). Accordingly, the main condition consisted of a three-object random array: a Play-Doh ball, a wooden tongue depressor, and a Play-Doh ball with a tongue depressor firmly stuck into one end. The third, conglomerate object looked very much like a base drum beater.

As always, testing began with a 2.5-minute phase of spontaneous transaction in which the babies were encouraged to engage in free play with the presentation. It was followed by a second phase designed to determine whether modeling would provoke attaching and detaching transformations. The experimenter demonstrated both transformations in an exaggerated, visible way by detaching the conglomerate object into its constituent parts, a tongue depressor and a ball of Play-Doh; and attaching by inserting the separate tongue depressor into one end of the Play-Doh ball so as to form the conglomerate object. Then the babies were encouraged to transact with the array for another 2.5 minutes.

Presenting discrete objects to babies enabled us to study transformations (a), (b), and (c). Sets of discrete objects were presented which represented six class conditions. Three conditions embodied three well-delineated class structures, respectively: additive, multiplicative, and disjoint class structures. Three conditions served as semicontrol conditions. They embodied ambiguous class structures.

In the additive condition two classes differing only in one property, their form, were presented; for example, sets of circular and square rings. The sets are both complementary, circular and square, and subsets of a more inclusive set, rings.

The multiplicative condition presented sets of objects which make up a 2 × 2 matrix; for example, blue and red, circular and square rings. The only differences, then, are in both form and color. It should be noted that multiplicative sets also partially embody properties of additive and disjoint structures. The sets are additive by their form properties alone and by their color properties alone. Some of the intersective properties are disjoint, for example, blue circular rings and red square rings. They become additive only at the most inclusive level, namely, they are all rings.

The disjoint condition consisted of two classes which differed as much as possible when embodied in objects, rather than symbols, for example, green rectangular rings and red dolls. All the obvious properties are different, for example, the colors, the forms, and the geometric versus realistic types. Union of the two sets into one more inclusive set requires taking a very distant supraordinate perspective to the two distinct sets since they share almost no common properties.

The three comparatively ambiguous class conditions were as follows:

(a) A singular class of identical objects is presented (e.g., all blue square rings). All the objects are identical. (b) All different classes with singular elements are presented (e.g., one toy car, one girl doll, one toy plate, and one miniature toothbrush). All the objects are different. (c) One multiple-element class of identical objects is combined with singular-element classes of different objects (e.g., two girl dolls, one toy mirror, and one small spoon). Half of the objects are identical and half are different.

The 6–10-month-old babies were tested on all three distinct class conditions plus one of the more ambiguous class conditions. The number of objects used in each condition was always four. This is the minimal number of elements necessary in order to present the three distinct class conditions. The number of objects was kept to a minimum because babies this age have difficulty transacting with more than a few objects in the same spatiotemporal frame (Halverson, 1931).

Twelve-month-old babies begin to be able to handle more objects in the same spatiotemporal frame. They were tested on all the same conditions as the younger babies. In addition they were tested on more complex versions of the same conditions. In these versions the number of elements was doubled from four to eight objects.

As always, testing the class conditions began with a 2.5-minute phase of spontaneous transaction or free play with the array of objects presented. It was followed by a second phase designed to provoke sorting the objects into class-consistent groupings. Two basic procedures were used. One procedure consisted of a continuous process in which the experimenter modeled consistent sorting plus assisted and elaborated upon the subject's sorting and emphatically corrected the subject's inconsistent sortings. Thus, the procedure was a very natural process in which the experimenter was both guided and tried to guide the subject's behavior. The other procedure was standardized and therefore less natural to babies' transactions. The experimenter modeled class-consistent sorting of all the objects. The display was left in front of the subject, who was handed additional elements for matching to the presorted elements.

The provoked phase was followed by a third phase in which subjects were tested in one of three additional ways: (a) An additional singular element, odd class was presented. For instance, in the additive condition involving four circular and four square rings, one triangular ring was added to the presentation. (b) An additional intersective, anomalous element was presented. For instance, in the disjoint condition involving green rectangular rings and red dolls, one red rectangular ring was added to the presentation. (c) A countercondition was administered in which the experimenter class-consistently sorted all but two elements of the presentation.

While the babies were tested in one room their entire performances were video- and audiotaped through a one-way mirror from an adjacent room. The recordings were transcribed into comprehensive logs of subjects' performances. The system of transcription devised is designed to provide a sequential log of all the transactions. Basically, it records, in spatiotemporal order, the subjects' actions, relations between subjects' actions, object transformations, relations between object transformations, and relations between subjects' actions and object transformations.

A comprehensive system was devised to code the data logs. Reliability checks of the transcription and coding systems found agreement ranging between .77 and .98 (Sugarman, 1979). The coding systems were designed with two primary purposes in mind. One was sequential analysis of the number and types of transformational acts generated by subjects, including their relations to the number and types of transformations in objects directly resulting from subjects' transformational acts. The other was to determine the extent and type of extensive and intensive relations generated by the subjects. To illustrate, the aims included determining: (*a*) the number of elements grouped into a set; (*b*) the number of sets sorted into groups; and (*c*) the level of class consistency, randomness, and inconsistency in configural groupings.

At this point it may be useful to mention the full scope of the research endeavor; of which this volume represents only the initial part. The empirical research extends beyond the 6–12-month-old developments reported here. The structural developmental course of logical reasoning is traced through the first 5 years of childhood. The basic properties of the research design were held constant for all ages in order to insure comparability. Thus, for instance, the actual testing procedure used with the 6–60-month-olds was always nonverbal in all its relevant features. Only the numerical complexity of the sets presented varied with age. Young children were presented with more classes and more objects per class than infants.

V. The Mode of Analysis

The overall objective is to discover the organization of protologic and how it develops from stage to stage. Therefore, except for Chapter 16, this volume, the following chapters are divided into four successive parts representing the sequential stages. The chapters within each part describe the findings on the functional structures which comprise the organization of protologic at each stage.

The first chapter within each part is devoted to discovering the structures of infants' transactions at each stage. Therefore, the analyses are directed toward determining the hypothesized central structural properties of infants' transactions and their construction of equivalence and of ordered nonequivalence relations between transactions. In the order listed, these always include determining how and to what degree:

1. Infants' transformative actions are mapped onto objects;
2. Objects are transformed by mappings;
3. Mappings take general forms which have consistent consequences for the pragmatic meanings attached to their objects of application;
4. Mappings acquire precursory symbolic properties;
5. The identities of objects and sets of objects are established by comparative inverse proto-operations, such that they can be used as constant given elements of precursory logicomathematical relations;
6. The causal experimental properties of objects and sets of objects are investigated, such that they can be used as constant variables of precursory physicohypothetical relations;
7. Equivalence relations are produced by mappings which are in one-to-one correspondence to each other; and
8. Iterative order relations are produced by mappings which systematically vary in additive or subtractive properties.

The next one or two chapters within each part are devoted to discovering the structures of infants' logical and mathematical constructions with *discrete* objects at each stage. Therefore, the analyses are directed toward determining the structural properties hypothesized as central to the formation of protoinferential relations with discrete objects. In the order listed, these always include determining how and to what degree:

9. Sets are composed, recomposed and decomposed as a function of class and test conditions;
10. Sets are constructed (*a*) of different sized membership, (*b*) by direct transactions with the objects composed, and (*c*) which are consecutively recomposed into variant configurations;
11. The compositions constructed are (*a*) mobile kinetic configurations such as one object pushing another, (*b*) stable static configurations such as one object placed on top of another, and (*c*) combined mobile–stabile configurations;
12. Mobiles, stabiles, and mobiles–stabiles are featured by spatial contact, proximity, and combined contact–proximity features;
13. Mobiles and mobiles–stabiles are marked by causal features;
14. Mobiles, stabiles, and mobiles–stabiles are constructed in the horizontal, vertical, and combined horizontal–vertical dimensions;
15. Sets are composed in temporal isolation, consecutivity, partial overlap, and simultaneity;

16. Equivalence relations are constructed within and between sets by exchange proto-operations of replacement, substitution, commutativity, and coordinative combinations of exchange proto-operations;
17. Equivalence and multiplicative relations are constructed within and between sets by correlational proto-operations of bi-univocal (one-to-one) and co-univocal (one-to-many) correspondences, respectively;
18. Iterative unidirectional and bidirectional order relations are constructed within and between sets by addition, subtraction, and reciprocal proto-operations; and
19. Compositions consistently comprise similar or different objects.

The last chapter within each part is devoted to discovering the structures of infants' logical and mathematical constructions with *quasi-continuous* objects at each stage. Therefore, the analyses are directed toward determining the structural properties hypothesized as central to the formation of protoinferential relations with quasi-continuous objects. In the order listed, these always include determining how and to what degree:

20. Objects are deformed, directly and contingently;
21. Deformed objects are reformed by negation proto-operations thereby producing intensive (form) identity;
22. Equivalence relations between deformations are produced by one-to-one correspondence proto-operations;
23. Iterative unidirectional and bidirectional order relations between deformations are produced by addition, subtraction, and reciprocal proto-operations;
24. Objects are broken, directly and contingently;
25. Broken objects are reconstructed by inverse proto-operations thereby producing aspects of intensive identity;
26. Objects are decomposed, directly and contingently;
27. Objects are decomposed into (*a*) single unordered sets, (*b*) single ordered sets of elements progressively decreasing in size, and (*c*) binary unordered sets;
28. Decomposed objects are recomposed by inverse proto-operations thereby producing extensive (quantitative) identity;
29. Sets of objects are composed, directly and contingently, into single objects;
30. Composed objects are redecomposed into sets of objects by inverse proto-operations thereby producing extensive identity;
31. Combined discrete/quasi-continuous objects are detached from and attached to each other.

As already noted, the presentational format traces the developing organization of protologic, including its previously listed 31 properties, stage by progressive stage. It is also possible to follow the evolution of individual properties across all four stages by referring to the ordinally equivalent sections in four chapters. The four stages of Property 1 are always considered first in Chapters 2, 6, 9, and 12; the four stages of Property 2 are always considered second in these four chapters; and so on.

Furthermore, it is possible to obtain a preliminary idea of the structural developmental model of protologic proposed here from the following hypotheses. The 31 properties listed previously comprise the main structural features of the organization of protologic at each of the four stages investigated in this volume. The first six properties constitute essential features in generating transformational transactions and constructing constant given elements necessary to form protoinferential relations. Properties 9–15, 19, 20, 24, 26, 29, and 31 are central features of the elementary structures of combinativity operations. Properties 8, 18, 23, and 27 are central features of the elementary structures of relational operations. Properties 7, 16, 17, 21, 22, 25, 28, and 30 are central features of the elementary structures of conditional operations.

1

STAGE 1 AT SIX MONTHS:
ELEMENTARY TRANSFORMATIONS

2

Unary Transactions

Transformational acts are basic to the construction of protological inferences. We shall therefore begin investigating their origins and structures by examining how infants' manipulatory actions are first structured into transformational mappings.

This requires determining the spatiotemporal and causal parameters of transformational actions, including investigation of the forms transformational actions take, their extent of application, and their coordinative relations to each other. For instance, constructing correspondences between mappings is facilitated when transformational actions are generated simultaneously. On the other hand, constructing order relations between mappings is facilitated when transformational actions are generated consecutively.

Inquiry into how infants' pragmatic actions are initially structured into transformational mappings includes determining how they are applied to and detached from their objects of transaction. This is the structural developmental source of the transformation of a subset of mappings into protosymbolic gestures. For instance, mappings which anticipate but do not consummate transactions with objects generate the initial precursory structure necessary for the formation of virtual gestures.

Analyses of the structure of mappings provide the basis for investigating how infants transform the objects of their transactions into constant given protoelements. This includes studying the regulatory processes as well as the comparative and compensatory operations involved in relating successive states of an object to each other. Construction of given proto-elements is the minimal requirement for the formation of set, order, and quantitative relations. This chapter includes findings on order and quantitative relations generated by 6-month-old babies. However, the discussion is limited to those findings which are relevant to mappings and transactions with individual elements. All the findings on the initial construction of sets of elements at this stage, including those involving order and quantitative relations, will be taken up in Chapters 3–5.

I. Successive Mappings upon Single Objects

Unary mappings are individual manipulations successively applied to individual objects, and consist of one manipulatory transformation at a time. Long sequences of consecutive and different unary transformations are thereby generated. They are interspersed occasionally by binary transformations. Binary mappings are two partially overlapping or simultaneous manipulatory transformations.

When 6-month-olds transact with two objects simultaneously, they almost always map different binary transformations onto the two objects. Usually, one of these mappings is relatively transformative, such as "waving," while the other is relatively passive, particularly "holding," as though the object is being stored for subsequent transaction. Sometimes both mappings are relatively passive:

49.3. *RH holds Block 2 to mouth*
49.7. *LH barely touches Block 4 as looks at it*   (6NF, page 3)[1]

Sometimes, both mappings are actively transformative:

87.5. *LH hits down on Cylinder 2*
87.5. *RH pushes Square Column to the right slightly*   (6DF, page 21)

---

[1] Protocol fragments are identified by subject and log location. Subjects are indicated by their age in months and by their initials. This behavior was produced by a 6-month-old whose initials are NF. Log location is given by page number(s) following subject identification, and by line number(s) before each transaction. Consecutive transactions are numbered seriatim from one on. Two or more partially overlapping transactions are assigned ordinally averaged numbers. Thus, the line numbering of this protocol fragment indicates that first the right hand holds Block 2 to the mouth (Line 49.3). It continues to do so while the left hand touches Block 4 and while 6NF looks at Block 4 (Line 49.7). Two or more simultaneous transactions are assigned averaged numbers. For instance, the line numberings of the next protocol fragment presented, that by 6DF, are both 87.5. They indicate that the two transactions were generated simultaneously by 6DF.

Rare transactions are produced which consist of binary (two simultaneous) mappings and three objects. This is the maximum extent of a 6-month-old's transactions. These transactions take two forms: either two objects are transformed actively (e.g., pushed) while one is not (e.g., held), or one object is transformed actively while two are not.

The most advanced binary mappings produced at this stage consist of two-step sequences of simultaneous but different transformations:

33.5. *LH raises Square-Column 2 up to face level*
33.5. *RH slides Square-Column 1 to the right*
35.5. *opens mouth and LH inserts end of SC2 into mouth*
35.5. *RH pulls SC1 back toward self and releases it*   (6GG, page 28)

16.5. *RH grasps Cylinder 2*
16.5. *leans head toward Square-Column 2 again, opening mouth*
18.5. *RH pulls C2 nearer to self*
18.5. *places open mouth over end of SC2*   (6GG, page 33)

Two-step successive binary mappings represent the outer limits of contemporaneous transformations by 6-month-olds.

Some two-step binary transformations are preceded and accompanied by visual and tactual perception as if the subject is doing some comparing:

1.5. *looks at Yellow Triangular Column*
1.5. *LH touches YTC*
  3. *looks toward Green Triangular Column and Yellow Cylinder quickly, still touching YTC*
4.5. *LH pushes YTC about 1 inch away from self*
4.5. *looks at YTC*
6.5. *left thumb pushes Green Cylinder away from self—GC rolls a little on its own*
6.5. *LH jiggles YTC side to side as pushes it a little further away from self, no release; so:*

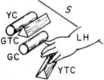

8.5. *LH releases from YTC and pushes GC about 1/2 inch to the right with LH thumb, as looks at GC*
8.5. *LH's fourth and fifth fingers simultaneously turn YTC horizontally:*

(6CL, page 30)

This fragment also illustrates that organ usage is beginning to be differentiated. Different fingers of the same hand are used to apply different transformations to different objects at the same time, twice in a row.

Overall, a 6-month-old's binary mappings consist of two different transformations performed at the same time, transacting with two separate objects of the same or different classes. The smaller subset of binary mappings are actively transformational. Rarely, binary mappings are produced twice in succession. When consecutive binary mappings are well differentiated and are generated in a comparative observational context, then it seems particularly appropriate to hypothesize the origins of transformational regulation. Consecutive binary yet different mappings reflect beginning competence to split and eventually coordinate transformational constructions in a controlled fashion. Though infrequent, precursory split transformations originate at least as young as age 6 months.

Two qualifications to this structural developmental hypothesis about the origins of split transformations should be emphasized. First, only isolated instances of such advanced binary mappings are produced by 6-month-olds in the entire half-hour session. Subjects rarely engage in repeated simultaneous but different mappings, whether immediately or subsequently. Second, the different transformations comprising binary mappings are very brief and inefficient. For instance, the fingers of 6DF's right hand (second Line 87.5) have very little transformational effect; they only move the objects slightly. Thus, while they are beginning to be generated, these simultaneous yet split transformations are not at all well regulated.

II. Predominance of Mappings over Objects

The frequency with which subjects map different transformations upon four objects ranges between about 15 to 30 per minute. These numbers should only be taken as estimates because they vary with the boundary definitions used to mark acts; for example, how one defines the boundary conditions between pushing and sliding an object will affect the count. Nevertheless, the overriding fact that emerges is that the mapping change rate is quite rapid, about every 2–4 seconds.

The number of different objects subjects transact within a minute is much smaller. The upper limit is always less than 10 per minute. This does not vary with type of discrete object (i.e., Euclidean, topological, and realistic), neither does the mapping change ratio. At most the object change rate is once every 6 seconds.

The initial fragment of subject 6AB transactions with four small blue blocks is typical:

6AB *began with a sequence of transactions with Block 2. He successively pushed, pulled, and pushed Block 2. This was immediately followed by a sequence of transactions with Block 1. He successively pushed, pulled, held, rotated, held, mouthed, and held Block 1. While continuing to hold Block 1 in his left hand, 6AB used his right hand to first push Block 3 and then push Block 2. Then 6AB returned to transacting with Block 1 by first touching it with his right hand while holding it with his left hand and then by rotating it with both hands.*

A reasonable estimate of the change ratio of mappings to objects is at least three-to-one. The preponderance of mappings over objects, represented by the change ratio, constitutes one constant of 6-month-olds' transactions. This ratio constant is marked by three features. First, subjects map a series of consecutive transformations on to a given object of transaction before proceeding to another object. A one-to-one change ratio is a rare exception. It occurs once in the summary protocol fragment. Second, a switch in object of transaction is sometimes accompanied by constancy in mapping. This, too, is illustrated in the summary protocol fragment. When 6AB switched from Block 1 to 2 to 3 to 2 the mapping did not change. Each time he switched objects the same "pushing" mapping continued, perhaps to bridge the change in transaction. In most instances, however, a change in object is accompanied by a change in mapping as well. Third, mappings and objects of transaction are usually singular. Objects are usually transacted with one at a time. Infants are only just beginning to generate binary transformations, as indicated in the previous section.

The original structure of mappings-to-objects transactions is characterized predominantly by diachronic continuity and discontinuity; that is, either mapping continuity and object discontinuity or mapping discontinuity and object continuity. Secondarily, it includes synchronic discontinuity, or both mapping and object discontinuity. The transactive functional structure is only beginning to include synchronic continuity, that is, both mapping and object continuity. This structure of transactions suggests cognition in which object and action fluctuate together but one or the other is beginning to stabilize in succession.

III. The Compactness Constant

Mappings, as already noted, are numerous and occur in rapid succession. Their transformational forms, however, are decidedly compact and repetitive; notwithstanding the already noted problem in defining their boundary conditions. Including those mappings which were produced with rare frequency still results in less than 20 transformational forms. The most frequent are push (P), pull (U), hold (H), rotate (R), mouth

(M), touch (T), hit (I), drop (D), throw (O), shake (S), raise (A), lower (L), place (C), and open and close (E). Only six of these mappings account for most transformations upon discrete objects, namely, P, H, M, T, I, and D.

> For illustrative purposes we may profitably pursue the performance of subject **6AB** that was partially described in Section II. He produced a total of 78 mappings. They represent 11 transformational forms, P, U, H, R, M, T, I, D, A, L, C. Only four forms account for 83% of the mappings, P (28%), H (21%), T (19%), and M (15%). The objects of these mappings were four identical Blocks, B1, B2, B3, and B4. Yet, the distribution of all mappings is decidedly skewed: B1 (37%), B2 (36%), B3 (19%), B4 (8%). Indeed, one predominant mapping, P, was used by **6AB** no more than once when transacting with B4; while H was not used at all.
>
> Similar patterns of behavior were produced when **6AB** transacted with four ring shapes only, four realistic things only, and two ring things together with two realistic things. The overall frequency distributions of mapping did not deviate significantly from those produced when the subject transacted with four solid shapes. Which mapping predominated did vary as a function of the objects of transaction. For **6AB** it is P for solids, I for rings, H for realistic, and T for rings together with realistic.
>
> Interestingly, M was never produced most frequently or even close to most frequently by **6AB**. It was always outproduced by another mapping by at least a factor of 2. In fact **6AB** produced M least frequently when transacting with realistic shapes only; and they consisted only of two spoons and two cups. For practical purposes, subjects were still too young to map the conventional significance of these objects. For instance, subject **6DF** mouthed every object except the spoon when transacting with two dolls, a hand mirror, and a spoon.
>
> Regardless of the object condition, **6AB** always transacted with all four shapes. Sometimes he transacted mostly with two shapes, sometimes three, and sometimes all four. He never preferred only one object or one type of shape. He always transacted with as many as four objects within a couple of minutes, but in unevenly distributed frequency.

The predominance of a small set of mapping forms imposed by subjects upon the wide range of object conditions tested, constitutes a second constant of 6-month-olds' transactions. It is as if subjects protosymbolize the semantic domain of discrete objects as mainly representing "pushables," "holdables," "mouthables," "touchables," "hitables," and "dropables." To a lesser extent, subjects also map some other transformative intensions onto discrete objects, such as U, R, O, S, A, L, and C, mentioned previously.

Compact construction of the semantic object domain has obvious cognitive advantages. It facilitates the inexperienced infant's job of interpreting the vast array of still unfamiliar objects so that they can be used as givens for further consideration. One consequence of the compactness constant is that objects are construed as having some transformative consistency across time. The very compactness and repetitiveness of mapping forms insures the recurrence of the same semantic transformations applied to objects.

The result is an initially equilibrated functional structure of semantic transactions. Transactive mappings-to-object forms are conserved. This hypothesis suggests cognition in which transformational consistency is minimally preserved over sequences of transactions; where the mappings change frequently and rapidly; and the objects are switched often but not as frequently nor as rapidly. This hypothesis, however, also suggests cognition in which proper semantic object distinctions are not made by 6-month-olds' mapping transformations.

At least two conditions of subjects' transactions provide the disequilibrium necessary for progressive alteration of this semantic functional structure. Eventually, they lead to elaborating transformative predicate distinctions while preserving transformative predicate sameness and similarities. The first condition is also integral to how the compactness constant regulates transactions with discrete objects. It will therefore be discussed in the remainder of this section. The second is a consequence of structural differences in how the compactness constant regulates subjects' transactions with discrete versus quasi-continuous objects, and therefore will be deferred to Chapter 5.

Subjects' mappings are the overriding determiners of their transactions at any particular time; objects are not. The evidence is twofold. First, the same mappings are applied to different objects. For instance, when the object condition consisted of two rectangular rings and two miniature dolls, 6AB's predominant mapping was T, by a factor of two. This factor applied to both object types. Second, the conventional predicate properties of the objects do not condition subjects' mappings. For instance, as already noted, cups and spoons do not elicit mouthing more frequently than other objects. Both findings are consistent with the hypothesis of an equilibrated functional structure.

At the same time, however, subjects' recurrent mapping transformations did not overlay exactly with each other. For instance, another major mapping produced by 6AB was D. With one exception, however, it was mapped onto dolls only, and not onto rings. Conversely, transformation E was primarily mapped onto rings. This subject differentially accommodated to the topological properties of rings by opening and closing his hands on them so that his fingers would poke in and out of the enclosed open spaces.

Discrepancies in mapping-to-objects transaction are a necessary disequilibrating condition for consistently applying different transformational properties to different objects. The findings are that the mapping discrepancies are a function of class (of object) by temporal proximity. The least discrepancy was found when the subjects transacted (*a*) with an identical object at different times but within a brief time frame (e.g., the same blue block) and (*b*) with similar objects at different times but within a brief time frame (e.g., the four blue blocks). It is as if 6-month-olds still cannot keep track of elements and therefore cannot tell apart predicate "sameness" from "similarity." The most mapping discrepancies were found when subjects transacted with different types of objects at different times within an extended time frame. For instance, the predominant transformation mapped by 6AB onto geometric solids was P (28%), onto rings was I (27%), and onto realistics was H (31%). It is as though the class (of objects) by extended time differentials was sufficient for the subjects to begin to transformationally differentiate between the predicate properties of classes of objects but not elements of the same set.

Mappings are just beginning to be detached from the objects of their transformations. Initial mapping detachment takes three complementary forms. First, mappings are continued after the transactions have been terminated, forming reproductive or "after gestures" of past transformations:

40.   *LH lowers Yellow Cup such that rim moves out of mouth, but mouth*
      stays open
47.7. *LH moves YC away from mouth to left, but mouth stays open*
                                                   (6AB, pages 23 and 24)

The second precursory form of protosymbolic detachment involves anticipatory transformations. Mappings are begun prior to the consummation of transactions, forming "anticipatory gestures" of future transformations:

110. *mouth opens as BH raise Orange Spoon*
111. *LH inserts bowl end of OS into mouth as RH releases*
112. *mouths OS four seconds held by LH*   (6AB, page 29)

The third precursory form of protosymbolic detachment involves a rupture between transformations and the objects of their reference. Anticipatory mappings are coupled with nonconsummated transformations. They form "virtual gestures" of planned but not executed transformations:

34.5. *LH picks up and inverts Yellow Cup such that its bottom is up*
34.5. *opens mouth*
36.   *LH holds YC up in air momentarily*
37.   *LH lowers YC such that its bottom touches the table*   (6AB, page 23)

68.   *RH picks up and pulls Yellow Spoon to mouth*
69.3.   *mouth opens*
69.3.   *RH starts to insert handle end of YS into mouth*
69.3.   *LH moves up close to YS handle as though to touch*
72.3.   *mouth stays open, as looks at YS*
72.3.   *RH lowers YS before inserting it into mouth such that handle end touches table*
72.3.   *LH lowers but does not touch spoon or table*
75.   *RH moves YS close to body such that handle end touches bend in left arm, as looks at YS*   (6AB, page 26)

24.   *RH picks up Cylinder 2*
25.5.   *RH starts to put C2 to mouth*
25.5.   *opens mouth as RH moves C2 toward mouth*
27.   *RH extends C2 away from self*   (6DF, page 18)

The second 6AB fragment is particularly noteworthy. It includes two simultaneously nonconsummated anticipatory mappings, that is, binary virtual gestures of mouthing and touching.

Lack of transformative consummation may be due to a variety of indeterminate local causes. Its consequence, however, is definitive. The mappings are produced when (*a*) a pragmatic goal is not achieved and (*b*) no presentational contact is established between the mappings and their referent objects. Thus, the necessary conditions for distancing between mappings and referent objects have been produced by the subject (cf. Werner & Kaplan, 1963). This is a minimal basis for the origins of mappings which are not directly and pragmatically applied to objects. Together with reproductive and anticipatory mappings, virtual mappings provide constructive bases for the origins of immediate gestural or proto-symbolic detachment.

IV. Constructing Single Objects as Constant Given Elements

Determining the existential properties of objects is well under way. As expected at this stage of unary transformations, most observations are directed toward single-object transformations. Infants coordinatively explore the part–whole relations internal to individual objects. That is, they observe what happens to objects which they are in the process of manipulatively transforming from one successive part–whole state to another.

Exploration usually involves visiomotor coordination. Successive part–whole transformations of an object are produced by continuously rotating it. Simultaneously, infants visually monitor the transformations they are constructing:

> 73. *LH rotates Cylinder 1 side to side as looks at it*   (6TT, page 22)

Coordinated visiomotor exploration becomes quite explicit, extensive and detailed, indeed, semisystematic:

> 25. *LH slowly rotates Doll 2 (held away from face) as looks at it intently for about 10 seconds*   (6AW, page 16)

Exploration is also conducted via tactilomotor coordination. While not as frequent as visiomotor exploration, it may be just as extensive and detailed:

> 9–14. *LH slowly rotates Cross Ring 2 as fingers it for about 15 seconds*
> 15.   *LH rotates CR2 more slowly as fingers it*   (6AW, page 9)

This exploratory behavior involved one-handed tactilomotor coordination. Others involve both hands so that they are based upon binary mappings:

> 18.5. *LH rotates Green Rectangular Ring a little*
> 18.5. *RH touches GRR*   (6TT, page 11)

Even at this early stage determining the single-unit extension of individual objects is beginning to be regulated. Regulated determination of object transformations is most apparent when infants construct consecutive transformations which cancel each other out so as to form object identity. The initial part–whole state of an object is altered by a first transformation. This is followed immediately by a second transformation which is the inverse of the first. It results in reconstructing the initial object state, thereby resulting in protoidentity. While engaged in constructing identity proto-operations infants perceptually monitor both (*a*) their own constructions and (*b*) the objects' states and transformations:

> 89. *looks at Yellow Spoon as LH turns it side to side in front of self*
>   (6CB, page 11)

> 26. *looks at Orange Spoon as RH turns its handle backward and forward a few times*   (6CB, page 14)

Constructing and determining individual object protoidentity is part of initially structuring the existence of elements. When structured as invariant elements, objects can be used as constants or givens for further cognitive consideration. It begins to be possible to use these givens as elements for constructing more advanced protoinferential structures. For instance, invariant elements provide the definite, distinct objects necessary to constructing a collection, that is, a set or a class of elements.

Comparative exploration of part–whole transformations in two objects is just beginning to be generated. Typically, determining the comparative existential properties of two objects is relatively brief and rudimentary:

91.3.   *LH rotates Circular Ring in air briefly as looks at it*
91.7.   *RH picks up Oval Ring*
  93.   *RH moves OR toward self a bit and then away from self as looks at it*
(6AS, page 6)

Some comparative exploration, however, is already quite advanced. The following protocol fragment, though lengthy, is but a small sample of the comparative two-object exploration generated by one 6-month-old:

    90.   *looks at Circular Ring in RH*
    91.   *looks at Triangular Ring in LH*
92.2/92.4.   *RH moves CR up and down as looks at it*
  92.4.   *LH moves TR up and down as looks at it*
    95.   *LH puts TR in mouth*
  96.3.   *RH flips CR back and forth*
  96.7.   *looks at CR*
  98.3.   *LH takes TR out of mouth*
  98.7.   *looks at TR*
  100.   *looks at CR*
101.3.   *looks at experimenter*
101.7.   *LH puts TR in mouth*
  103.   *RH raises CR as looks at it*
  104.   *LH takes TR out of mouth as looks at it*
  105.   *looks at CR in RH*
  106.   *looks at TR in LH*
  107.   *looks at CR in RH*
  108.   *looks at TR in LH*   (6KF, page 5)

These comparative observations of transformations applied to two objects are semisystematic and regulated. Subject 6KF repeatedly looks back and forth from one object to another. She repeatedly compares the objects before (Lines 90–91), during (Lines 92.2–104), and after (Lines 105–108) repeatedly transforming their states. Thereby, she generates the conditions necessary for mapping extensional transformations onto two objects and comparatively exploring invariant part–whole relations internal to each.

This protocol fragment reveals that regulated comparative determination of two objects in succession has also begun. The subject's activity is repeatedly directed toward comparing the two objects as she inversely transforms each. She observes her own construction of the protoidentity of each object. She generates these protoidentity transformations three times in succession. The first time is by moving the circular ring up and down while looking at it (Line 92.2/92.4). The second time is by moving the triangular ring up and down while looking at it (Line 92.4). The third time is by flipping the circular ring back and forth while looking at it (Lines 96.3–96.7).

Regulated comparative determinations are not only marked by repeated inverse transformations that produce identity proto-operations; they are marked by two additional features. The first is correspondence between inverse transformations. This is just beginning, that is, *6KF* moves both objects up and down (Lines 92.2/92.4 and 92.4). The second is generating more than one successive inverse transformation. This, too, is just beginning. After applying inverse transformations to the circular and the triangular ring, *6KF* applies an inverse transformation to the circular ring once again.

In sum, a precursory combinativity operation possible when transactions are limited perforce to one or two objects is to compare their corresponding part–whole structures under differing transformational conditions. We have just seen that 6-month-olds already engage in much activity symptomatic of regulated comparative proto-operations. The necessary conditions are present whenever the subjects (*a*) transform objects, (*b*) observe the transformations, and (*c*) have the ability to conserve in practical memory the transformations. Confirmation of the latter condition *c* requires evidence of at least aspects of practical preservation, such as searching after a disappearing object. Most importantly, evidence must also be manifested of a fourth condition, namely, (*d*) overt inverse transformations.

Comparative inverse transformations may be manifested by two forms. One is general to all types of objects. It relates translations internal to an object with external spatial coordinates. The other form is unique to quasi-continuous objects and will be considered in Chapter 5. It is entirely internal to the translations between part–whole relations within an object.

The first comparative form, which is our concern here, consists of inverse transformations whose long-term developmental descendant is an identity operation. Aspects of reverting, symptomatic of condition *d*, are readily discerned in rotational and in displacement–replacement transformations. Corroborating evidence is provided when subjects successively repeat aspects of reverting transformations. Much evidence has already been noted of condition *b*. Subjects often observe the transformations, including reverting transformations, which they are constructing with objects.

It remains to provide evidence of condition *c*, practical conservation by subjects of transformations in objects which they have generated. Its structure is still quite limited. Subjects search after individual objects they have dropped:

60. *LH drops* Yellow Cup *on table edge while looking in lap;* YC *rolls over edge to floor*
61. *looks over left chair arm toward floor*   (6AB, page 25)

However, subjects usually search with only one modality at a time, for example, either visually or tactually and not both simultaneously. Typically, they follow the trajectories of single objects, including objects disappearing from view, only when the trajectories are (*a*) continuous spatiotemporally with the transformations which produced them, and (*b*) readily perceptible. Also, they only search after individual objects. At its foundation, practical conservation is only a unary transformation.

The most advanced symptoms generated at this stage begin to include very minor spatiotemporal discontinuity, that is, initial mediation, between the transformation and the search:

13. *RH pulls Triangular Ring 1 off table to lap*
14. *LH pushes Cross Ring 2 forward and releases it*
15. *looks at TR1 in lap*   (6NF, page 11)

A single transaction is interpolated (Line 14) by the subject between her displacement transformation (Line 13) and her perceptual search (Line 15). Thus, she provides evidence of preserving momentarily the consequence of her own transformation, namely, the resultant location of Triangular Ring 1 in her lap while she pushes Cross Ring 2.

The presentational, pragmatic structure of preservation may be beginning to include a social dimension:

94. *LH slides Square Column 1 about 1/2 inch to the right, no release*
94a. *SC1 pushes Cylinder 2 to the right—C2 rolls toward experimenter*
95. *LH pushes SC1 toward self by doing an open-closing motion against left side of SC1, twice*
96. *LH fingers push SC1 all the way against own chest by applying pressure directly against left end of SC1:*

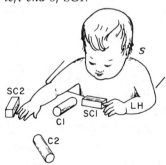

97. *looks toward C2, which is still rolling toward experimenter*
98.5. *LH fingers touch SC1*
98.5. *watches C2 roll over experimenter's table edge onto floor*

100. *looks quickly at experimenter*
101. *looks toward far table edge where C2 went over*
102. *looks at experimenter (experimenter places C2 upright on table)*
103. *looks at C2*   (6DF, page 22)

This type of behavior is subject to two interpretations which are not necessarily exclusive. The subject may be attempting to communicate with the experimenter (Lines 98.5–102). The experimenter does replace Cylinder 2. Then, the subject does look at Cylinder 2 (Line 103). More than likely, however, the subject is looking toward the experimenter merely because it is the direction where he last saw Cylinder 2 and where he saw it disappear. In that case, the behavior may reflect nothing more than immediate and spatiotemporally continuous practical conservation, that is, nothing but a unary proto-operation.

V. Transitions to Regulated Causal Experimenting

Causal transactions plus observation prerequisite to protoexperimental investigation of object transformations are being prepared. However, causal transformations are still not regulated. They are rarely reproduced consecutively. Exceptions do occur:

39. *RH bangs Block 1 on table two times, letting go of B1 after second bang; B1 flies off to experimenter, RH lands on top of Block 3*
39a. *B1 displaces B3 on first bang*
39aa. *B3 displaces Block 4 on first bang*
40. *RH removes from B3 and quickly replacing RH on top of B3, pushes it forward a little*
40a. *B3 displaces B4*
41. *RH lets go of B3 and touches table space in front of it; B3 "jumps" a little in place when RH releases it*
42. *RH touches B3 again, pushing it a little to left, no release*
42a. *B3 displaces B4 a little (B4 rotates a little in place)*   (6AB, page 11)

In this sequence of replications, causal transformations are generated three times in a row. More typical is repeated causal transformations interspersed, but not consecutive, in long sequences of transactions.

Some measure of control over causal transformations is being achieved. Occasionally, this includes observation of the independent variable (agent object) and dependent variable (patient object) prior to and after causal transactions.

85. *RH removes Doll 2 from mouth, looking quickly at it*
86. *looks down toward Doll 1*
87. *LH fingers (extended) touch D1*

88.5. *RH hits D2 down on D1*
88.5a. *D1 rolls off to the left out of subject's reach*
88.5. *LH partially rests on top of Mirror*
90. *RH hits D2 on table, in succession from No. 88.5.*
91.5. *looks toward D1*
91.5. *LH fingers clench on top of M—momentarily grasps mirror end of M*
      between fourth and fifth fingers   (6DF, page 6)

Control over the dependent (patient) object transformation is also just beginning. When it occurs, it suggests the hypothesis that subjects are beginning to anticipate or predict some aspect(s) of the causal transformative results:

   (experimenter rolls Cylinder 2 back to subject on left side of table)
1. *subject watches C2 roll as BH hold Cylinder 1 in air*
2. *as C2 approaches table edge, BH lower C1 onto table in front of it*
    (horizontal)
2a. *C2 stops against C1, and then rocks in place*
3. *LH releases C1 and lifts C2*
4. *LH lowers C2 on table in back of and touching C1:*

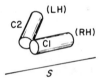

                                               (6TT, page 24)

Targeting her "catching" transformation to the dependent variable, such that it is stopped, indicates some prediction of the object's spatial trajectory.

The hypothesis of precursory causal prediction at this stage is reinforced by the finding that causal transformations are just beginning to take on a social dimension. This occurs rarely and only with causal transformations which subjects are already in the process of generating:

31. *LH shakes down in air—then fingertips lightly push down on*
     Cylinder 2—C2 rolls toward experimenter
31a. *C2 pushes Cylinder 1—C1 rolls toward experimenter also (two cylinders*
     separate and roll as in drawing on next page)
     (experimenter slides the cylinders back to subject; see drawing)
32. *simultaneously with experimenter's move, RH lowers Square Column 1*
     to a horizontal position, still grasping it (see drawing)
33. *LH fingers push down on C1 (left arm is extended at full length)—C1 rolls*
     to experimenter
     (experimenter rolls C1 back to subject; it bounces off of extended LH
     fingers and rolls a few inches back toward experimenter)
     (experimenter rolls C1 back again—it stops against subject's LH fingers)

34. *LH fingers touch C1—only fingertips reach C1*
35. *contracts and extends LH fingers against C1—C1 rolls fast to experimenter*
    (experimenter rolls C1 back to subject—it hits against LH fingers and rolls back towards experimenter a little, out of subject's reach)
    (experimenter rolls C1 back—it stops against LH fingers)
36. *contracts fingers against C1—C1 rolls away from LH (only about 2 inches out of reach)*   (6DF, page 25)

When cooperative causal transformations are successively replicated, as they are three times by 6DF, then there is some indication that they are beginning to be regulated. Moreover, the replications suggest some initial control over the dependent variable. In order to repeatedly target the object toward experimenter, the subject must anticipate the results of his own causal transformations, at least minimally. Otherwise, 6DF is not likely to succeed in rolling the cylinder to the experimenter three out of four times, as he did.

VI. Single-Unit Protocorrespondence between Successive Mappings

Equivalence relations between mappings and between their transformational results are beginning to be constructed by one fundamental proto-operation. Correlation relations between magnitude transformations are generated regularly. Moreover, the structure of protocorrespondences is already rich in the variety used to condition equivalence relations between magnitude transformations.

Protocorrespondences are beginning to condition the extent of mappings. This includes constructing equivalences between frequencies and intensities of mappings even when the objects of the transformations vary:

11.   *LH hits down on Doll 1 lightly, 2 times*
11a.   *second hit flips D1 up and over to the left side of table*
12.   *LH places on top of D1, with mostly wrist part of hand touching D1*
13.   *removes LH from D1, and hits LH lightly on table in front of self, 2 times*

(6DF, page 11)

Both protocorrespondences in number and force of hitting are achieved even though the repetition of the mapping (Lines 11 and 13) is interrupted by the subject (Line 12) apparently to negate the causal effect of his initial mapping (i.e., to stop Doll 1's movement).

Nor are protocorrespondences constructed by 6-month-olds limited to conditioning a single consecutive reproduction:

36.5.1.   *LH hits Spoon onto table, 1 time, then raises it in air again immediately*
36.5.2.   *RH continues to cover mirror part of Mirror*
38.   *looks at the experimenter*
39.   *repeats No. 36.5.1.*
40.   *RH removes from M and pushes fingers into Doll 2—D2 falls flat*
41.   *RH index turns D2 approximately 90°:*

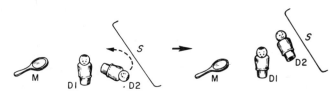

42.   *repeats No. 36.5.1.*   (6DF, page 13)

Equivalence transformations, hitting the spoon once on the table (Line 36.5.1.), are reproduced twice (Lines 39 and 42). Moreover, the protocorrespondence is constructed across two interruptions. The first is rather unobtrusive, looking at the experimenter (Line 38); but, the second is an active transformation of another object (Lines 40–41).

Most transformations which provide necessary conditions for proto-inferential correspondences at this stage span consecutive mappings. Successivity imposes an additional time factor that infants must handle if they are to cognize protocorrespondences within their own transformations. Successive mappings are not in direct temporal correlation even when their extensity properties are in correspondence. Bridging temporal asynchrony requires some, at least limited, representation to reconstruct consecutive into coordinate transformations. Reconstructive representation, however, is not necessary for coordinating protocorrespondences produced at the same time:

11.5.   *RH pushes Orange Cup over*
11.5.   *LH (holding Orange Spoon) pushes Yellow Cup over*   (6AB, page 21)

Protocorrespondences between temporally simultaneous mappings are generated infrequently by 6-month-olds, but, precursory individual instances, such as this one, are produced by almost all subjects. They also produce protocorrespondences that partially overlap in time, and that are occasionally reproduced twice in a row. Replication indicates that the construction of equivalences is beginning to be regulated:

16.3. *RH drops and retrieves Cross Ring 1*
16.7. *LH drops and retrieves Cross Ring 2*
18.3. *LH drops and retrieves CR2*
18.7. *RH drops and retrieves CR1*   (6AW, page 9)

Protocorrespondences, as shown, are constructed between discrete magnitudes. Most produce single-unit equivalences. Subject 6DF (p. 13) successively hits the spoon one time onto the table; 6AB simultaneously knocks over the cups one time; 6AW partially overlappingly drops the rings one time. The limit at this stage is two-unit equivalences. Subject 6DF (p. 11) hits his left hand down twice and then hits his left hand down twice again.

In addition to their rarity at this stage, two-unit equivalences manifest no symptoms of being regulated; are never reproduced more than once; and are always successive, never simultaneous or partially overlapping. Single-unit protocorrespondences are beginning to be regulated. They are occasionally constructed simultaneously (e.g., 6AB) and in partial overlap (e.g., 6AW). When successive they are often reproduced more than twice in a row. For instance, shortly after generating the partially overlapping single-unit protocorrespondence, presented previously, 6AW produces a successive single-unit protocorrespondence. It consists of picking up and dropping Cross Ring 2 onto the table six times in a row.

Protocorrespondences are also constructed between continuous magnitudes. The only instance reported so far is in force or intensity of hitting. Subject 6DF (p. 11) successively reproduces hitting *lightly*. Indeed, it is to be expected that continuous magnitude protocorrespondences should be generated less frequently than discrete protocorrespondences. It is more difficult to gauge or measure the continuous than the discrete magnitudes of mappings. Therefore, production of continuous equivalences is less likely in early pragmatic transactions.

Some protocorrespondences clearly involve both discrete and continuous magnitudes, for example, this same 6DF (p. 11) sequence produces number and intensity equivalences at the same time. Others are less clear-cut, and seem to be predominantly about continuous magnitude transformations. Yet they may also be about discrete magnitudes:

4. *RH pushes Block 2 out to right*
    (experimenter taps and places Block 3, center)
5. *RH pushes B3 to right*   (6NF, page 4)

   12. *RH fingertips push Doll 2*
12a. *D2 spins in 1/4 circle towards right*
   13. *RH fingertips push D2*
13a. *D2 rolls forward toward experimenter*
   14. *RH, two fingertips only, pushes D2*
14a. *D2 rolls forward toward experimenter slightly before coming to rest*
                                                   (6NF, pages 16 and 17)

Invariably, protocorrespondences are self-initiated at this stage. When initiated by the experimenter, the subjects never participate. One illustration, in which the experimenter repeatedly taps objects, will suffice since it is totally representative of the negative results obtained regardless of the mapping form the experimenter modeled:

    2. *LH grasps Green Cylinder*
       (experimenter taps Yellow Cylinder on subject's LH)
    3. *LH releases GC and withdraws from table*
       (experimenter puts YC with GC and holds up Yellow Triangular Column to subject)
       (experimenter taps YTC on table near subject's LH)
    4. *LH grasps YTC and holds it briefly*
    5. *LH releases YTC*
       (experimenter taps Green Triangular Cylinder on table in its original place)
    6. *watches GTC being tapped*
    7. *RH picks up GTC*
    8. *mouths GTC*
       (experimenter taps YC and YTC in place on table)
    9. *looks toward YC and YTC after experimenter has removed her hands, as still mouthing GTC*
  10. *RH removes GTC from mouth*
  11. *LH grasps GTC (so BH hold it on table) and looks at it* (6AS, page 28)

If anything, modeling inhibits the production of protocorrespondences. The subjects observe the experimenter's behavior, but, they do not imitate, rather they followup with different mapping forms. The only instances in which modeling evokes reproduction, and they are infrequent, occur when the mappings involved are first produced by the subject and then imitated by the experimenter:

36.7. *RH bangs Block 1 on table three times*
       (experimenter imitates, banging Block 4 on table twice)
  37. *RH bangs B1 on table twice*
       (experimenter knocks fist on table twice)
  38. *RH raises B1 about 2 inches above table while experimenter knocks fist*
  39. *RH bangs B1 on table twice more letting go of B1 after second bang; B1 flies off to experimenter, RH lands on top of Block 3*   (6AB, page 11)

Both trials yield positive results. The subject's reproductions constitute exact frequency correspondences of the experimenter's knocking. The experimenter's first copy, on the other hand, does not correspond to the frequency of subject's banging. The instrument of reproduction is not the same as that used by the experimenter. The experimenter knocks with her fist while the subject bangs with a block. Nevertheless, there is even one indication of the subject anticipating reproducing the experimenter's activity. While observing the experimenter's activity in administering the second trial, the subject raises his hand as if preparing to construct the correspondence (Line 38).

A third trial was administered later in the testing:

13. *RH bangs Orange Spoon on table 4 times*
14. *RH holds OS on table*
    (experimenter imitates, banging Yellow Cup on table)
15. *LH grasps bowl end of OS (which is held by RH on table)*
16. *RH raises OS and pulls it out of LH grasp*
17. *RH inserts bowl end of OS into mouth and mouths it approximately 5 seconds*   (6AB, page 33)

The result is negative. The subject responds by doing something else having nothing to do with frequency.

Taken together, the findings indicate that the social environment may occasionally play a role in the construction of precursory correspondences. However, when the social environment has a part to play the initial mappings and protocorrespondences are constructed by the infants. Even when the subjects reproduce the experimenter's actions, the cooperative protocorrespondences constructed followup the subjects' initial transformational constructions.

VII. Two-Step Additive and Subtractive Mapping Series

Mapping iteration sufficient to establish ordinal series of magnitudes is beginning to be generated. Two fundamental proto-operations are involved: protoadditions which produce ordered increases in magnitudes, and protosubtractions which produce ordered decreases in magnitudes. Protoaddition and protosubtraction are also beginning to be related to each other at this stage. Consequently, the foundations are being laid for structural integration of magnitude increases with magnitude decreases. When achieved, the resultant products of such reciprocal nonequivalences are logical equivalences.

Protoaddition applied to discrete transformations results in unidirectional orders of increasing magnitudes:

63.5. LH *hits Yellow Rectangular Ring on table 1 time*
63.5. RH *raises Yellow Cross Ring high in air—fingers through center of it*
  65. LH *hits YRR on table 2 times, releasing it after second hit*
                                                                 (6DF, page 31)
  67. LH *hits Cross Ring 1 on table 3 times*
  68. LH *raises CR1*
  69. LH *hits CR1 on table 4 times*   (6NF, page 13)

At this stage most orders of increasing magnitudes are limited to two-step couplings, but as the protocol fragments also reveal, the increase may be quite precise. The nonequivalence or increase is exactly one mapping unit. Moreover, the largest magnitude may consist of as many as four mapping units.

Three-step unidirectional orders of increasing discrete magnitudes are generated infrequently:

  18. RH *hits Block 3 on table 1 time, lightly*
  19. RH *thrusts B3, no release, such that back of RH displaces Block 2 to right*
  20. RH *hits B3 on table 2 times, hard*
  21. RH *moves B3 in air above table a few seconds*
  22. RH *hits B3 on table 6 times, then subject laughs hard*
  23. LH *grasps B3, BH hold it on table a few seconds while watching experimenter's action and laughing*
       (experimenter bangs Block 4 on table twice)
  24. LH *releases grasp on B3, RH raises B3 slightly off table*
  25. LH *grasps B2*
26.5. RH *lets B3 go*
26.5. LH *turns and releases B2, B2 turns 180° and falls flat on table, partially over the edge*   (6AB, page 8)

Frequency of hitting the block on the table is increased from one to two to six times. The first magnitude increase, as expected of ordered couples, is a precise addition of one unit. Additional increases, as also expected at this stage, are imprecise. The three-step ordinal frequency scale of $\langle 1, 2, 6 \rangle$ constructed represents the order relation $\langle 1, 2, \text{many} \rangle$.

As with the construction of equivalences by protocorrespondences, social intervention by modeling does not have a positive effect. Subject 6AB's response is entirely typical in this regard. He observes the experimenter's behavior (Line 23), but, if the experimenter's modeling has any effect it is to derail the subject. It is followed by 6AB ceasing the orderings in which he was engaged and switching to totally different mappings (Lines 24–26.5).

Protosubtraction applied to discrete transformations results in unidirectional orders of decreasing magnitudes. The findings are the same as those just described on increasing orders. To illustrate:

9. LH *taps Triangular Ring 2 on table five times*
10. LH *touches TR2 three times, lightly on edge of Cross Ring 2*
11. LH *lifts TR2—it falls out of LH*
12. LH *lifts TR2*
13. LH *touches TR2 one time, lightly on CR2*   (6NF, page 14)

A three-step decreasing scale of ⟨5, 3, 1⟩ is constructed by 6NF. Thus, the
scale represents the order relation ⟨many, less, little⟩.

Protoaddition and protosubtraction are also applied to continuous
transformations. Indeed, as revealed in some of the protocol fragments
already presented, continuous unidirectional orders may be produced
together with discrete unidirectional series. Subject 6NF (p. 14) generates
a decreasing continuous order while producing a decreasing discrete
order. Subject 6AB (p. 8) generates an increasing continuous order while
producing an increasing discrete order. Thus, the directions of the simultaneous continuous and discrete orders constructed always covary. At
this stage the subjects do not produce reciprocal, discrete, and continuous orders. They do not generate simultaneous series in which one order
increases while the other decreases.

Of course, continuous like discrete orders are generated by themselves
as well. Usually, they are also limited to two-step continuous orders.
Protoaddition produces increasing unidirectional orders:

25. RH *taps Green Rectangular Ring lightly in place, 1 time*
26. RH *taps GRR a little harder, 1 time*   (6GG, page 17)

Protosubtraction produces decreasing unidirectional orders:

28. RH *taps Spoon on table hard, 1 time*
29. RH *taps S on table lightly, 1 time*   (6TT, page 7)

Two-step continuous orders, such as these, involve fairly precise protoaddition and protosubtraction. Three-step continuous unidirectional
orders are generated infrequently. Unlike three-step discrete orders, they
tend to be limited to increasing magnitudes. Like three-step discrete
orders, at most, only one protoaddition is precise:

13. RH *pushes Block 2 a little to left*
14. RH *pushes B2 a little more—it gets displaced a bit more to the left*
15. LH *pushes B2 an arms length to the left in one quick swoop—rests hand
    on it there for about 8 seconds*   (6AW, page 1)

The first increase in the pushing transformation is small while the second
is as big as this baby could achieve. Thus, 6AW generates the continuous
unidirectional order relation ⟨little, more, much⟩.

Consecutive protoaddition and protosubtraction resulting in bidirectional order relations are generated infrequently. When limited to the
minimum of one protoaddition and one protosubtraction required to

create a bidirectional series, the order relations may be precisely constructed:

13. LH *hits down on Square Column 1, two times, pushing it to the left*
14. LH *hits down on SC1 three times, pushing it further to the left*
15. LH *hits down on table two times*   (6DF, page 26)

The bidirectional order relation is $\langle 2, 3, 2 \rangle$.

Bidirectional order relations which exceed the minimum of two protooperations, one protoaddition, and one protosubtraction, fluctuate internally between precise and imprecise differences:

63. RH *taps Block 3 on table to right, 2 times*
64. RH *taps B3 one time lightly on table, also touching it to Block 2 in process*
64a. B3 *touches against B2, very slightly displacing it*
65. RH *taps B3 on table, 3 times*
66. RH *inserts B3 into mouth for a moment*
67. RH *taps B3 on table to far right, 2 times, first lightly then hard*
68. RH *inserts B3 into mouth briefly*
69. RH *taps B3 on table to right, 4 times*
70. LH *hits down on B2 one time—B2 slides far to the right*
71. RH *taps B3 on table 3 times, releasing it after third tap—B3 stays in front of him*   (6CB, page 4)

Two bidirectional order relations are produced within this sequence. One is the discrete order $\langle 2, 1, 3, 2, 4, 1, 3 \rangle$. Each direction is limited, as expected, to two-step relations. Protosubtraction alternates consecutively with protoaddition. The other bidirectional order relates continuous magnitudes. The magnitude decreases then increases in force of hitting on the table.

This sequence also reveals that as the ordered series become long, covariation between continuous and discrete orders begins to break down. The possibility is thereby opened for detaching continuous and discrete orders from each other even when they are produced simultaneously by the same behavioral sequence. Thus, an initial necessary condition for elaborating reciprocal relations between continuous and discrete orders is beginning to be constructed.

VIII. The Constitutive Form of Elementary Transactions

These findings on how pragmatic transformational actions are originally structured into proto-operations and protosymbols lead to several conclusions. They constitute the framework within which the results to be presented in Chapters 3, 4, and 5 should be viewed.

Long sequences of consecutive transactions are generated. Some sequences consist of individual transformational manipulations applied to single objects. While the transactions are sequential, individual transformations and objects transformed remain structurally segregated. They are unrelated to each other in any inferential way. Their main bonds are mapping repetitiveness and compactness coupled with relative invariance of the objects to which the transformations are applied.

Other sequences which include precursory structural relations between consecutive unary transformations necessary to inferences about object transformations are also beginning to be generated. Central to the formation of these protoinferential structures are rudimentary transformational coordinations, including causal transformations necessary to precursory comparative determination of objects. In like manner, elementary inverse transformations are necessary to the application of precursory identity proto-operations to objects. Initial structures of proto-inferential relations between transformations are ingredients in the construction of known objects. As such, protoinferentially known objects can then be elaborated into established givens or invariant elements for progressively coordinated logical differentiation and integration.

Precursory structural relations necessary to cognition about the extent of small magnitudes are beginning to be generated regularly. Central to the creation of initial protoinference structures of extent are transformations which condition mappings, such as protocorrespondences. These proto-operational conditions are necessary in order to produce equivalence relations between quantities. Also central are relational transformations, particularly protoaddition and protosubtraction, necessary to form precursory ordered series of magnitudes.

3

Labile Construction of Mobiles and Stabiles

Lability marks all combinativity transformations. It marks composing discrete elements into sets. Labile composing is the predominant combinativity proto-operation applied to discrete objects at this stage. Lability also marks decomposing and recomposing discrete sets of elements. These two combinativity proto-operations are generated less frequently than composing.

Numerous and varied features mark labile combinativity. These features will be discussed as they arise throughout this chapter. As a preliminary to our analyses we may categorize lability along extensive, temporal, spatial, and kinetic dimensions (cf. Werner, 1948).

Combinativity proto-operations are applied to the minimum number of objects necessary to compose, decompose, and recompose sets. Most applications are limited to one two-element set. Application to three-element sets is infrequent, and application to four-object sets even rarer.

More revealing of the primitive structure of combinativity at this stage is that it usually involves direct contact and manipulation by subjects of only one element of the sets; for example, composing by dropping or hitting one object on top of one or two objects sitting on the table. Consequently, composing one two-element set is not integrated with composing another two-element set. On rare occasions they compose one segregated four-element set; usually involving direct transactions

with only one element of the set. Ingredient to these primitive combinativity proto-operations is asymmetry. Asymmetrical transformational
processes and configurational products predominate.

Composing, decomposing, and recomposing are transient. They are
momentary combinativity proto-operations which dissolve as subjects go
on to their next transactions. Many are formed in isolation, they are
unary combinativity relations. Partially overlapping and simultaneous
combinativity proto-operations are so rare as to suggest that when they
occur they are probably accidental productions.

Combinativity is structured in one spatial dimension. Two-dimensional
constructions are rare. Compositional configurations tend to be imprecisely aligned. Other configurations, such as elbow-shaped forms or
triangular forms, are rarely produced. Most also require the support of a
surface, such as the tabletop. Combinativity is not usually generated in
the air, even by holding two objects together in one or two hands.
Exceptions are, however, just beginning to be generated:

> 19. *RH brings Doll 1 and LH brings Spoon together in air, such that they*
>   *touch about 2 inches above table*   (6TT, page 2)

Movement is an integral part of the processes and products of pragmatic combinativity. The products constructed include more mobile than
stabile forms. Unlike sculptural mobiles, most mobiles produced at this
stage are causal as well as kinetic. They are usually the product of causal
relations, such as hitting one object into another so that they are displaced together. They are kinetic relations involving spatial contact and
temporal partial overlap; rather than spatial proximity and temporal
simultaneity which characterizes most sculptural mobiles. Like their
sculptural analogues, most stabiles relate elements via static spatial contact. Unlike sculptural stabiles, most do not endure beyond the moment
of construction.

I. Uniform Composing Productivity

Composing is produced regularly. Two or more objects are joined to
form a variety of compositional relations. Frequent composing is already
a well-established spontaneous combinativity proto-operation (Table 3.1).
Subjects generate many compositions in all class and semiclass conditions. The rate of productivity is uniform, around five per minute, across
class conditions when the duration of transaction is taken into account
(Table 3.1, Row 3). The variance by ranks between class conditions is
random (Friedman $\chi_r^2 = 1.50$, $df = 3$, $p > .50$). Composing frequency
varies less than 20% between all conditions.

TABLE 3.1
Spontaneous Phase I: Mean Frequency by 6-Month-Old Subjects of Compositions, Mean Duration of Phase I, and Mean Frequency of Compositions per Minute

		Class conditions		
	Semicontrol	Additive	Multiplicative	Disjoint
1. Compositions	14.25	15.42	12.33	10.50
2. Time	3 min 13 sec	2 min 51 sec	2 min 33 sec	2 min 8 sec
3. Productivity per minute	4.43	5.41	4.84	4.93

Consistent rates of production are all the more remarkable given that the object types also varied. For instance, the disjoint condition always involved both topological and realistic types of objects while the additive and multiplicative always involved only one kind of object, that is, either Euclidean, topological, or realistic. Moreover, a breakdown by class and by object conditions reveals that productivity rates do not vary as a function of object conditions (see Section II), nor do the productivity rates vary consistently as a function of the interaction of class-by-object conditions.

High and consistent rates of productivity have significant implications. First, they imply that composing is not merely the accidental result of random transactions with objects. Fortuitous constructions of relations between objects are not likely to be generated with such consistency in rate across varied class and object conditions plus a half-hour time span of transactions. Second, they serve as additional reliability measures of the transcription coding. They corroborate that frequency of compositions is a highly reliable measure of combinativity proto-operations.

The frequency with which compositions are generated varies as a function of test phase. Most frequent and complex compositions are produced when the subjects have to do relatively little to produce such results. Any presentational array of objects to infants may already appear like or be suggestive of a composition. Moreover, the suggestive properties may vary as a function of the age of the children. In short, there is no way of insuring that the initial presentation is totally neutral in its combinativity properties.

Most compositions are generated during the first (spontaneous) test phase when the subjects are initially presented with four objects randomly assorted in close proximity to each other so that they form a single-dimensional alignment:

Array:

1. *LH pushes Square Column 1 to the right, into Cylinder 1, fingers also touching C1*
1a. *SC1 pushes C1 next to Square Column 2:*

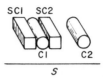

2. *LH turns SC1 over onto adjacent side—movement of SC1 pushes against C1*
2a. *C1 pushes SC2 against Cylinder 2—all objects touch:*

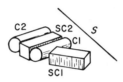

3. *LH pushes SC1 slightly more to the right—all the objects move to right slightly:*

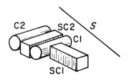

(6GG, page 26)

The least frequent and simplest couplings are produced when the initial presentational array is relatively resistant to the formation of compositions. This happens at the beginning of the second (provoked) test phase when the experimenter intervenes in order to help the subject group the objects. The experimenter sets up an array of two objects not aligned in close proximity to each other and the subjects are handed a third object. Sometimes this results in no couplings:

> *(experimenter places Cylinder 1 on the subject's right and Square Column 1 on subject's left):*

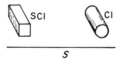

> *(experimenter hands Cylinder 2 to subject)*

1. *RH takes C2*
2. *RH inserts one end of C2 into his mouth (the other end touches table)*

3. *mouths C2 briefly*
4. *RH takes C2 out of mouth, holding it upright on table*
5. *RH pushes C2 toward experimenter, upright position*
6. *RH turns C2 flat*
7. *RH pushes C2 to the right and toward table edge in an arc, then over edge, not letting go*
8. *RH raises C2 in upright position to mouth*
9. *RH lowers C2 to table, holding it upright, as simultaneously leans head forward*
10. *RH holds C2 in an upright position on table as mouths the top end of it briefly*
11. *leans head back from C2, thus removing it from mouth, as RH continues to hold it upright on table*
12. *leans head forward again and mouths end of C2 momentarily, held upright by RH*
13. *removes mouth from C2 as RH holds C2 at table edge (almost over edge)*

(6GG, pages 32 and 33)

Compositions of intermediate frequency and complexity are produced in phase three of the testing. The presentation consists of two separated mixed sets of two objects, where the objects within each set are in close proximity to each other:

Array:

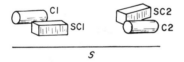

1. *RH lightly hits down on the right ends of Cylinder 2 and Square Column 2*
1a. *C2 and SC2 move to left slightly*
2. *RH grasps C2*
3. *RH slides C2 right and to edge, in an arc*
4. *RH slides C2 along table edge to the left*
5. *RH hits C2 down on table edge once*
6. *RH slides C2 away from self*
7. *RH slides C2 to the right and back to the left, quickly*
7a. *left end of C2 hits Square Column 1 to the left slightly*
8. *RH slides C2 to the right again*
9. *RH slides C2 to the left again*
10. *RH slides C2 away from self and to right a little, in an arc*
11. *RH slides C2 about 2 inches toward table edge*
12. *RH slides C2 back to the left and in front of SC1*
13. *RH slides C2 against SC1, displacing it slightly*
13a. *SC1 pushes slightly against Cylinder 1—C1 rolls away*

(6GG, pages 34 and 35)

It is the condition of spontaneous transactions (first protocol fragment), rather than that of either provoked spatial sorting (second protocol fragment) or preexistent groupings composed by the experimenter (third protocol fragment), which results in the most frequent and complex compositions. Subjects do not cooperate with the experimenter in producing compositions during phase two. If anything, the experimenter's assistance and modeling inhibits composing by the subjects.

It should be understood that the differential rate of composing is not simply a function of the spatial proximity between the objects presented in phases I, II, and III. The reasons are several. First, after subjects have transacted with the objects for a while in phase I they usually become as spatially separated as in phases II and III. Yet this does not reduce the rate at which compositions are produced. Second, in phase II the objects are gradually elaborated by the experimenter into alignments or matrices marked by close spatial proximity as the experimenter attempts to assist the subjects in sorting the objects. Third, in phase III the objects are always initially presented in compositions marked by close spatial proximity.

As compared with spontaneous composing (phase I), decomposing and recomposing well-formed preexistent compositions constructed by the experimenter (phases II and III) constitute decidedly subordinate combinativity proto-operations. Decomposing is infrequent. Invariably, when it occurs, decomposing is limited to isolated subtractions of only one object from preexistent compositions. Subtracting single elements is not generated in any systematic way. For instance, the subjects do not even subtract one element consecutively, twice in a row.

Recomposing preexistent compositions constructed by the experimenter is rare. Transforming preexistent compositions is generally disorganized. Subjects do not reorganize preexistent compositions into related well-formed variant configurations. Rather, they simply subtract an element and transact with it in unary isolation many times in sequence, as characterized in Chapter 2. When they do couple one subtracted object with another the resultant compositions are the usual transient labiles. The new compositions evidence no regulated relations to the preexistent compositions.

II. Two-Object Compositions and Recompositions

Most labiles (85%) comprise two objects only (Table 3.2, Column 1). Three-object compositions are generated infrequently (Tables 3.2, Column 2). Only 12% of the compositions include three objects. Four object

TABLE 3.2
Spontaneous Phase I: Mean Frequency of Two-, Three-, and Four-Object Compositions
by 6-Month-Old Subjects

	Set size			
	1 Two-object	2 Three-object	3 Four-object	4 Total
1. Total semicontrol	11.00	2.50	0.75	14.25
2. 1 × 2; 2 × 1 Realistic	13.75	1.75	0.00	15.50
3. 1 × 4 Euclidean	5.75	1.25	0.75	7.75
4. 4 × 1 Topological	13.50	4.50	1.50	19.50
5. Total additive	13.42	1.67	0.33	15.42
6. Realistic	18.50	1.00	0.25	19.75
7. Euclidean	12.00	3.25	0.75	16.00
8. Topological	9.75	0.75	0.00	10.50
9. Total multiplicative	11.17	1.00	0.17	12.33
10. Realistic	8.25	1.00	0.00	9.25
11. Euclidean	9.25	0.50	0.00	9.75
12. Topological	16.00	1.50	0.50	18.00
13. Total disjoint	9.00	1.33	0.17	10.50

compositions are even rarer (Table 3.2, Column 3). They constitute just 3% of the compositions. The protocol fragment from 6GG (p. 26) array—Line 3, reproduced on page 54, actually consists of two successive four-object labiles. The first is reported in Lines 2–2a and the second in Line 3. Such rare four-object labiles are probably intersective products of the fortuitous circumstances of the subject's mappings and the initial presentational placement of the objects. Thus, 6GG directly manipulates only one object; yet the causal results are two consecutive four-object compositions.

The relative frequency of two-, three-, and four-object compositions does not vary as a function of either class or object conditions. Minor exceptions occur when the subjects transact with four differently shaped topological rings (Table 3.2, Row 4, Column 2) and two classes of Euclidean objects (Table 3.2, Row 7, Column 2). These minor exceptions are based upon data from only four subjects each. There is therefore little reason to believe that they are anything but random deviations.

The extent of elements within compositions which are directly manipulated by subjects is extremely limited. Two-thirds of all the compositions generated are the result of unary transactions (Table 3.3). Only individual objects are manipulated; but in such a fashion as to couple them with other objects not directly transacted with.

One-third of the compositions are generated as the result of subjects

TABLE 3.3
Spontaneous Phase I: Number of Objects Directly Manipulated by 6-Month-Old Subjects
to Produce Compositions in All Class Conditions

	Number of objects		
	1	2+	Total
1. Frequency of compositions	404	226	630
2. % Compositions	64	36	100

directly transacting with two or more objects. Even when the resultant compositions relate three of four objects, almost all are the products of direct transaction with only two objects. Nevertheless, direct transaction with two objects producing one-third of the compositions generated is an indication that composing sets, albeit small sets, is beginning to be a regulated combinativity proto-operation.

Recomposing preexistent compositions constructed by the experimenter has barely begun (see page 56). In comparison, spontaneous recomposing by subjects of their own compositions is already a well-advanced combinativity proto-operation. A good measure is the proportion of initial or thematic compositions which are followed-up by subsequent variant compositions.

The criteria for measuring followup variants are stringent. Only four forms of recomposing are tallied. They are contact, proximity, replacement, and substitution variants. Contact variants transform initial contact relations composing objects continuously in space, but not necessarily in time, into derivative compositions. Some or all of the initial physical contact must be preserved by the transformation. For instance, an initial horizontal array of two objects may be transformed into a variant vertical stack of the same two objects. Objects may be added or subtracted as long as the initial contact relation is maintained. Proximity variants transform the proportions or dimensions of initial proximity compositions but preserve their form relations or Gestalt properties. For instance, an initial triangular arrangement of three objects in which the apex element is furthest from the subject may be symmetrically transformed into a variant by bringing the apex element closest to the subject. Objects may be added or subtracted as long as the initial Gestalt is preserved. Replacement variants occur when one or more elements are removed from initial compositions and then put back into their original places. Substitution variants are the same as replacement variants with one difference: One or more new objects are substituted for original elements in the initial compositions.

Variants are produced by all the subjects. They constitute one-fourth of the compositions generated (Table 3.4, Column 3). The proportion of variants does not vary as a function of class condition. It is remarkably constant for the semicontrol, additive, and multiplicative conditions (Table 3.4, Rows 1, 5, and 9). It drops off a bit only for the disjoint condition (Table 3.4, Row 13). Nor does the proportion of variants vary as a function of object conditions (Table 3.4, Rows 2–4, 6–8, and 10–12). The range is extensive, though, as a function of Class × Object conditions interaction. The proportions vary from a low of 5% variants in the multiplicative realistic condition (Table 3.4, Row 10, Column 3) to a high of 42% in both the semicontrol topological (Row 4, Column 3) and multiplicative topological (Row 12, Column 3) conditions.

Inspecting carefully once again the brief protocol fragment from 6GG, (p. 26) array—Line 3, is instructive in this regard. The initial composition relates three objects (Lines 1–1a). It is followed by two consecutive four-object recompositions (Lines 2–2a and 3). Both four-object recompositions are variants of the initial thematic composition. Both involve causal relations of pushing objects into each other. In this way 6GG constructs a series of three successive labiles. The series begins with a three-object thematic composition. It is recomposed immediately into a four-object variant. It, in turn, is recomposed immediately into a four-object variant.

Now, as already noted, the unusual extent (three- and four-object compositions) of this series of three consecutive labiles is probably due to

TABLE 3.4
Spontaneous Phase I: Mean Frequency of Composing and Recomposing by 6-Month-Old Subjects

	1 Thematic	2 Variant	3 % Variant
1. Total semicontrol	10.25	4.00	28
2. 1 × 2; 2 × 1 Realistic	13.25	2.25	15
3. 1 × 4 Euclidean	6.25	1.50	19
4. 4 × 1 Topological	11.25	8.25	42
5. Total additive	10.17	4.20	27
6. Realistic	13.00	6.75	34
7. Euclidean	9.75	6.25	39
8. Topological	7.75	2.75	26
9. Total multiplicative	9.17	3.17	26
10. Realistic	8.75	0.50	5
11. Euclidean	8.25	1.50	15
12. Topological	10.50	7.50	42
13. Total disjoint	8.75	1.75	17

particular, and possibly accidental, circumstances of transaction. However, there is no reason to believe that the recompositions are not beginning to be regulated productions. Indeed, it is not unusual for subjects to produce more extended series of variants than these. The extent of recomposing series is as high as a thematic followed by five or six variants:

61. *RH extends Green Rectangular Ring looped over thumb to the right, touching it against table edge directly in front of Yellow Cross Ring, as RH fingers extend toward YCR as if to grasp it:*

62. *RH fingertips (excluding thumb) slide YCR to the left towards self, while GRR is still looped over thumb*
63. *RH pushes YCR back to the right, as thumb touches table such that GRR lowers flat onto table and thumb touches table space in center of GRR:*

64. *RH pulls YCR and GRR together toward self and off table edge*
65. *RH holds YCR and GRR together in air on his right briefly*
66. *RH partially inserts GRR into mouth, as holding YCR*
67. *RH lowers GRR and YCR to table, while still mouthing GRR by leaning head forward*
68. *removes (raises up) mouth from GRR as RH tips GRR and YCR away from mouth and looks up at experimenter*   (6GG, pages 19 and 20)

Here, the same subject, 6GG, couples two objects, a Green Rectangular Ring and a Yellow Cross Ring into a thematic composition by placing one directly in front of the other (Line 61). In order of production the subsequent recompositions consist of: (Line 62) pushing both left; (Line 63) pushing both right; (Line 64) pulling both toward self; (Lines 65–66) holding both in air and partially inserting the rectangle in mouth; and (Lines 67–68) displacing both and removing rectangle from mouth. This series, then, includes inverse spatial transformations which we will have occasion to consider in Chapter 4.

Equally extended and complex recomposing series are generated which include reproducing some compositions:

15. *RH grasps Triangular Ring 2 and Cross Ring 1 together*
16. *RH raises TR2 and CR1 as LH touches TR2*
17. *RH holds TR2 on top of CR1 and hits them down on table, such that only CR1 hits table*
18. *RH raises TR2 and CR1 such that CR1 displaces Cross Ring 2 to the right*
19. *RH hits TR2 and CR1 on top of CR2 such that only CR1 contacts CR2*
20. *RH hits TR2 and CR1 on table in front of self*
21.5. *RH holds TR2 and CR1 in air*
21.5. *LH pushes Triangular Ring 1 over left table edge; it hits floor (noise)*
23. *RH bangs TR2 and CR1 on table twice such that only CR1 hits table; after second hit, CR1 falls out of RH onto table* (6AB, pages 15 and 16)

The series proceeds from an initial two-object thematic composition (Lines 15–17) to a three-object (Line 18), to a three-object (Line 19), to a two-object (Line 20), to a two-object (first Line 21.5), to finally a two-object (Line 23) variant labile. Some of the variants are replicas of each other. Compositional reproduction between variants tends to corroborate the hypothesis that regulated recomposing is beginning to be generated with some frequency at this stage.

III. Predominance of Mobile Compositions

Compositions and recompositions are fundamentally labile constructions at this stage. Lability is underlined by the finding that the majority (55%) of the momentary constructions are mobiles. Forty percent are stabile, although still momentary, labiles. The remaining 5% are combined mobiles and stabiles.

Mobiles are the most frequent labile form generated in all class conditions (Tables 3.5–3.8, Row 11). They are overwhelmingly predominant in the multiplicative (Table 3.7, Rows 10–12) and disjoint (Table 3.8, Rows 10–12) conditions. Labiles are almost evenly split between mobiles, on the one hand, and stabiles plus mobiles–stabiles, on the other hand, in both the semicontrol (Table 3.5, Rows 10–12) and additive conditions (Table 3.6, Rows 10–12).

This difference is about the only result indicating that the level of composing and recomposing may vary as a function of class condition. All other measures of combinativity level, such as frequency and extent of compositions and recompositions generated, do not vary as a function of class condition. Therefore it is highly unlikely that this exception is significant. All other measures indicate that combinativity is equally labile, that is, primitive across all class conditions.

TABLE 3.5
Semicontrol Conditions, Phase I: Mean Frequency of Compositional Forms by
6-Month-Old Subjects

		1 $1 \times 2; 2 \times 1$ Realistic	2 1×4 Euclidean	3 4×1 Topological	4 Total
1.	Contact stabile	3.50	3.25	6.50	4.56
2.	Proximity stabile	0.75	0.25	3.50	1.50
3.	Contact–proximity stabile	0.00	0.25	0.50	0.25
4.	Total stabile	4.25	3.75	11.00	6.33
5.	Contact mobile	7.25	3.25	4.75	5.00
6.	Proximity mobile	2.75	0.00	1.50	1.50
7.	Contact–proximity mobile	0.50	0.50	0.25	0.42
8.	Total mobile	10.50	3.75	6.50	6.92
9.	Mobile–stabile	0.75	0.25	2.00	1.00
10.	% Stabile	27	48	56	44
11.	% Mobile	68	48	33	49
12.	% Mobile–stabile	5	4	10	7

Predominant mobile production does not vary as a function of object conditions (Tables 3.5–3.7, Rows 10–12, Columns 1–3). If anything, there may be a small tendency to produce less mobiles and more stabiles when subjects transact with topological-like objects, but, even this result is mixed. For instance, the smallest proportion of stabiles is generated when topological objects are presented together with realistic objects in the disjoint class condition (Table 3.8, Rows 10–12).

TABLE 3.6
Additive Condition, Phase I: Mean Frequency of Compositional Forms by
6-Month-Old Subjects

		1 Realistic	2 Euclidean	3 Topological	4 Total
1.	Contact stabile	3.75	4.25	3.00	3.67
2.	Proximity stabile	6.75	0.50	2.00	3.08
3.	Contact–proximity stabile	0.25	0.25	0.00	0.17
4.	Total stabile	10.75	5.00	5.00	6.92
5.	Contact mobile	4.75	9.25	5.50	6.50
6.	Proximity mobile	3.50	0.75	0.00	1.42
7.	Contact–proximity mobile	0.25	0.00	0.00	0.08
8.	Total mobile	8.50	10.00	5.50	8.00
9.	Mobile–stabile	0.50	1.00	0.00	0.50
10.	% Stabile	54	31	48	45
11.	% Mobile	43	63	52	52
12.	% Mobile–stabile	3	6	0	3

TABLE 3.7
Multiplicative Condition, Phase I: Mean Frequency of Compositional Forms by
6-Month-Old Subjects

		1 Realistic	2 Euclidean	3 Topological	4 Total
1.	Contact stabile	1.00	1.75	7.00	3.25
2.	Proximity stabile	0.50	1.00	1.75	1.08
3.	Contact–proximity stabile	0.25	0.00	0.00	0.08
4.	Total stabile	1.75	2.75	8.75	4.42
5.	Contact mobile	6.25	6.00	7.00	6.42
6.	Proximity mobile	1.00	0.25	1.00	0.75
7.	Contact–proximity mobile	0.25	0.25	0.00	0.17
8.	Total mobile	7.50	6.50	8.00	7.33
9.	Mobile–stabile	0.00	0.50	1.25	0.58
10.	% Stabile	19	28	49	36
11.	% Mobile	81	67	44	59
12.	% Mobile–stabile	0	5	7	5

Most mobiles are based upon direct contact between the elements composed (Tables 3.5–3.8, Row 5). This relation is general. It does not vary as a function of either class or object conditions.

Two kinds of contact mobiles are constructed. One type involves causal properties. We have already come across many instances when, for example, subjects use one object to push and thereby displace another object. One or more objects serve as actor (instrument) and one or more as patient. Only rare causal couplings produced by 6-month-olds are

TABLE 3.8
Disjoint Condition, Phase I: Mean Frequency of Compositional Forms by
6-Month-Old Subjects

		Realistic and topological
1.	Contact stabile	1.58
2.	Proximity stabile	1.25
3.	Contact–proximity stabile	0.25
4.	Total stabile	3.08
5.	Contact mobile	4.83
6.	Proximity mobile	1.67
7.	Contact–proximity mobile	0.08
8.	Total mobile	6.58
9.	Mobile–stabile	0.83
10.	% Stabile	29
11.	% Mobile	63
12.	% Mobile–stabile	8

symmetrical; that is, where all objects function as both actors and patients. This can be accomplished, for example, by grasping one object in each hand and banging them into each other to cause a collision or sound.

Most causal relations are constructed in the horizontal dimension. Exceptions are generated in the vertical dimension:

> 44. *LH removes Doll 1 from mouth and taps it down on top of Rectangular Ring 2*
> 44a. *RR2 moves back about 2 inches on table*   (6GG, page 38)

By tapping the doll on top of the rectangular ring, 6GG causes the rectangular ring to move. The composition, then, is a contact mobile enacted in the vertical dimension.

The other kind of contact mobile does not involve any causal relations between the objects composed:

> 56. *RH places on top of Cylinder 2 and Square Column 2*
> 57. *quickly, RH pushes C2 and SC2 together a few inches away from self, as looks away toward mirror*
> 58. *RH fingers slip off of C2 and completely grasp SC2*   (6GG, page 30)

The objects displaced are in direct contact with each other. This is typical of most spatial mobiles constructed by 6-month-olds. They consist of aggregate elements displaced together.

This spatial mobile is typical in another way as well. The placement of the objects is symmetrical and their displacement is in parallel. The presentational spatial correspondence is total, but exceptions do occur. Consider once again the protocol fragment (6AB, p. 15–16) presented at the end of the previous section. Object placement is asymmetrical while their displacement is symmetrical (in parallel) in five spatial mobiles (Lines 17–20, and 23). Spatial mobiles are not generated by 6-month-olds in which the placements are symmetrical while the displacements are asymmetrical. Spatial mobiles always involve correspondence in the displacements, even if the placements are not symmetrical.

Composite symmetrical spatial relation of both placements and displacements constitute original spatial correspondence proto-operation constructed by babies. It typifies the spatial mobiles which do not involve causality. Even in those rare compositions where the objects placements are asymmetrical, their displacements are symmetrical, that is, in correspondence.

A small but substantial fraction of mobiles are based upon proximity spatial relations between the objects composed (Tables 3.5–3.8, Row 6). The range is from a low of 10% in the multiplicative condition to a high of

25% in the disjoint condition. Combined contact and proximity mobiles are rarely produced (Tables 3.5–3.8, Row 7).

At this stage, proximity mobiles are based upon inherent protocorresponding trajectories between the objects composed since they are displaced together by one organ. Therefore, whatever independence the trajectories have from each other is minimal:

81.5. *looks at Mirror 2*
81.5. *places RH on top of Brush 2 and M2 (palm is on top of B2, fingers are on top of M2)*
83.   *RH quickly slides M2 and B2 simultaneously to the right about 2 inches:*

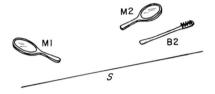

(6CL, page 20)

The same hand slides the two objects at the same time (Line 83) while keeping them spatially separate. The only contact between the objects is indirect via the hand. Proximity mobiles are rarely generated with two hands by 6-month-olds. Proximity is maintained only briefly. It gives way immediately to increased separation. Nevertheless, mobiles of this form provide necessary precursors for the formation of symmetrical displacements; although limited by the restrictive usage of only a single hand. As such, they form an initial inherent basis for constructing protocorrespondences between relatively independent trajectories simultaneously generated by two organs. This has structural developmental significance for the formation of both spatial and movement proto-operations.

The most rare mobiles involve consecutive aggregate spatial displacements and causality:

14.   *LH slides Square Column 2 and Cylinder 1 to the left, turning them vertically as does so*
14a. *C1 turns Square Column 1 vertically also*   (6GG, page 27)

At this stage, the subjects never produce mobiles in which separate but parallel spatial displacements are simultaneously constructed with causal relations. This form of protocorresponding combinativity, as we shall see, does not develop until age 12 months.

Spatial displacement mobiles in which objects acquire trajectories independent of the motions of subjects' organs are also rarely produced. Occasionally two cylinders are pushed such that they roll away as independent trajectories. These independent trajectories are probably more due to the lack of object resistance than to subjects' mappings. The usual productions involve a single organ maintaining contact with at least one of the objects, such that the organ completely directs its trajectory.

Stabile, as opposed to spatial mobile, compositions usually involve asymmetrical placements:

1. *LH moves to the right—thumb knocks Doll 1 over into Green Rectangular Ring 1:*

(6CL, page 46)

Occasionally they involve symmetrical displacements plus both symmetrical and asymmetrical placements:

1. *RH touches Rectangular Ring 2 as LH touches Rectangular Ring 1*
2. *BH simultaneously move the rectangles in toward Doll 2 such that the three objects are almost touching and BH also touch D2 as well as the rectangles*   (6AB, page 36)

73.5. *LH pushes Doll 1 to the right, flat onto table, as looks at D1*
73.5. *RH pushes Rectangular Ring 2 to the left, flat on table, such that RR2 and Rectangular Ring 1 touch, as looks at D1:*

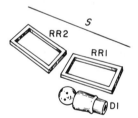

(6CL, page 49)

Here the symmetrical displacements are not in parallel; rather, they are the inverse of each other. The objects are displaced in opposite directions, toward each other. Their resultant placements are symmetrical to each other. They are asymmetrically placed in relation to the object which they surround. Subject 6CL immediately recomposes the initial labile into a variant spatial stabile:

75.5. *LH grasps Doll 1*
75.5. *RH palm places on top of Rectangular Ring 2 and Rectangular Ring 1, as looks quickly toward rectangles*   (6CL, page 49)

Now the placement relation has become totally symmetrical. This is unusual since 6-month-olds tend to compose asymmetrical stabiles.

Also unusual is that these latter two stabiles are composed in two dimensions. Typically stabiles are single-dimensional constructions; as are the first two examples (6CL, p. 49 and 6AB, p. 36). As unusual as they are at this stage, two-dimensional stabiles open up the precursory possibility of including one object in two parts of a composition. In this composition, Rectangular Ring 1 ends up being both an element of the couple [D1, RR1] in the mesial (anterior-posterior) plane and of the couple [RR2, RR1] in the medial lateral plane, even though RR1 is not directly transformed.

Potential inclusion of one element in two parts of a larger whole provides the necessary initial, if most rudimentary, structure for multiplicative proto-operations. Protomultiplication is a necessary transformation for the production of intersecting predicate properties of individual elements. Protomultiplication is also a necessary transformation for the union of subsets of two or more elements.

As in the construction of mobiles, most stabiles are based upon contact between the elements composed (Tables 3.5–3.8, Row 1). Unlike mobiles, more stabiles are based upon proximity relations (Tables 3.5–3.8, Row 2). Contact plus proximity is as unusual in the formation of stabiles as it is in mobiles (Tables 3.5–3.8, Row 3). These findings do not vary in any consistent way with class or object conditions. One exception stands out. Almost twice as many proximity as contact stabiles are generated in the additive realistic condition where the objects are miniature hairbrushes and hand mirrors (Table 3.6, Column 1, Rows 1 and 2).

Proximity stabiles always involve some separation between the placements of elements. Yet the placements are such that corroboratory evidence of, at least, momentary stabile composition is provided:

227. *LH places Brush 1 on table to the left of Mirror 2:*

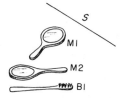

(6CL, page 27)

23. *RH places Triangular Ring 2 behind Cross Ring 2, no release*
24.5. *RH continues holding TR2 in place* (6AB, page 16)

In both stabiles, proximity and separation between object placements is established. In addition, 6CL's proximity stabile is marked by symmetrical placement of the objects. Subject 6AB's stabile does not evidence any additional spatial configural features, but it is expanded temporally a bit so that it lasts longer than most labiles.

A small fraction of compositions combine mobile with stabile forms (Tables 3.5–3.8, Rows 9 and 12). The frequency with which mobiles–stabiles are generated does not vary in any consistent way with class or object conditions. It should be noted, however, that none are generated in the additive topological condition (Table 3.6, Column 3, Row 9) and in the multiplicative realistic condition (Table 3.7, Column 3, Row 9).

This coordinated form of combinativity is only beginning to be constructed at this stage. It requires transforming one compositional structure (which itself is a transformation of object relations) into another compositional structure (itself also a transformation):

61.5. *RH moves Square Column 1 forward slightly*
61.5a. *SC1 pushes Cylinder 2 forward, such that C2 almost touches Square Column 2:*

(6DF, page 20)

2. *LH turns Square Column 1 over onto adjacent side—movement of SC1 pushes against Cylinder 1*
2a. *C1 pushes Square Column 2 against Cylinder 2—all objects touch:*

(6GG, page 26)

The requirement of binary consecutive composing accounts for the fact that only the simplest combined mobile–stabile labiles are constructed at this stage. Almost all begin with a mobile which is transformed into a stabile. Few begin with a stabile which is transformed into a mobile. Beginning a dynamic composition and then letting it be at rest requires less effort or offers less resistance to pragmatic construction than beginning with a static composition and then putting it in motion.

Occasional combined mobile–stabile compositions are more complex:

59. *RH withdraws to chest, pushing Green Cross Ring up against chest such that GCR is completely on top of Green Rectangular Ring, and simultaneously sliding Yellow Cross Ring closer to self such that YCR touches GRR:*

60. *LH picks up Yellow Rectangular Ring*
61. *LH withdraws YRR close to chest such that edge of YRR knocks GCR and GRR to the right slightly—GCR and GRR remain stacked* (6DF, page 31)

This composition is marked by three structural features rarely found together in constructions by 6-month-olds. First, all four objects are composed. Second, the composition is constructed in two-dimensions. The green cross and rectangular rings are stacked vertically while the yellow cross and rectangular rings contact the stack horizontally. Third, the composition is both a mobile and a stabile. Particularly unusual is that the composition begins as a stabile (Line 59) and ends as a mobile (Line 61). As just noted, this order of consecutive combinativity transformations—a stabile transformed into a mobile—is probably more difficult to construct than the reverse order.

Other compositions are more typically constructed in the order of mobile followed by stabile:

42.5. *looks toward Rectangular Ring 2 and Doll 1*
43. *LH pushes Rectangular Ring 1 against D1 such that RR1 displaces D1 closer to RR2 and then releases RR1 next to D1*   (6AB, page 39)

Such combinations are unusual in another respect. Consider 6AB's composition. The final product is marked by proximity between three objects (RR1, D1, RR2) such that D1 is between RR1 and RR2. The process involves causal contact; RR1 is used as an instrument to propel D1 closer to RR2. Such labiles, then, compose causal mobiles with stabiles.

IV. Vertical as Well as Horizontal Construction

Physical placement relations between objects built in the horizontal plane require less knowledge, and perhaps less perceptual-motor skill, than those constructed in the vertical plane. Building a stable tower by stacking blocks on a table, for instance, is a comparatively difficult task. Presumably, constructing an array of blocks by aligning them on a table is relatively easy to do. So, children under age 18–24 months seem to build arrays in the horizontal while those over 2 years begin to construct vertical structures such as towers.

This generalization seems appropriate if we compare building vertical structures, such as towers, with any horizontal configuration, such as a bunch. To preserve a tower requires that the objects composing the tower be relatively well aligned vertically; otherwise the tower will tumble. No such physical constraints are imposed upon the construction of a bunch of objects placed in a horizontal plane.

A more apt comparison, however, is that between vertical towers and horizontal alignments. The more appropriate horizontal standard of comparison consists of compositions of objects in physical contact making up straight–line projections. Children cannot construct straight-line projections out of discrete objects until around age 4 to 5 years (Piaget & Inhelder, 1967). This standard of comparison makes similar structural requirements for the construction of horizontal compositions and for vertical compositions. Using this standard requires modifying the generalization that infants construct compositions in the horizontal plane before they do in the vertical plane.

TABLE 3.9
Spontaneous Phase I: Mean Frequency by 6-Month-Old Subjects Constructing Horizontal, Vertical, and Combined Horizontal-Vertical Compositions

		1 Horizontal	2 Vertical	3 Horizontal–vertical
1.	Total semicontrol	7.75	4.25	1.33
2.	1 × 2; 2 × 1 Realistic	9.25	4.50	0.50
3.	1 × 4 Euclidean	4.50	2.50	0.50
4.	4 × 1 Topological	9.50	4.75	3.00
5.	Total additive	11.25	3.08	0.17
6.	Realistic	13.00	4.25	0.00
7.	Euclidean	14.50	1.50	0.00
8.	Topological	6.25	3.50	0.50
9.	Total multiplicative	8.42	2.75	0.08
10.	Realistic	6.25	2.50	0.00
11.	Euclidean	8.00	1.50	0.00
12.	Topological	11.00	4.25	0.25
13.	Total disjoint	8.00	1.50	0.00
14.	Total all conditions	8.88	2.90	0.43
15.	% All conditions	73	24	4

Labiles, as shown, are momentary compositions. They are fleeting regardless of the plane in which they are constructed. Most labile structures are built in the horizontal plane (Table 3.9, Column 1). Cursory rereading of some of the above protocol fragments should provide adequate illustration of labiles constructed in the horizontal plane.

At the same time, one-fourth of 6-month-olds' labile compositions are constructed in the vertical plane (Table 3.9, Column 2). Even though sufficient examples are to be found in the protocol fragments given so far, two brief additional illustrations may be helpful:

20. *RH touches end of Cylinder 2 to top of Square Column 1, momentarily:*

(6DF, page 18)

13. *RH places Cross Ring 1 on top of Cross Ring 2, hard*   (6AB, page 15)

These and the previously presented fragments make clear that vertical constructions are not permanent compositions. However, they are no less permanent than horizontal constructions generated by 6-month-olds. Vertical constructions certainly are not well-articulated structures. But, then, neither are 6-month-olds' horizontal structures.

The main difference between the vertical and horizontal labiles constructed at this stage is that the latter are generated three times as frequently. Even this differential rate of production requires qualification. Predominance of horizontal constructions varies by class condition. The ratio of horizontal to vertical compositions ranges from a high of 5-to-1 in the disjoint condition to a low of less than 2-to-1 in the semicontrol condition (Table 3.9, Rows 1, 5, 9, and 13). Moreover, the ratio is highest when compositions are constructed with Euclidean objects. It drops off considerably when the objects composed are realistic and topological.

Labiles constructed in both horizontal and vertical dimensions require composing a minimum of three objects in two dimensions. It is therefore not surprising that they are constructed infrequently at this stage (Table 3.9, Column 3). As with the infrequent production of two-dimensional horizontal compositions, they do begin to open up precursory possibilities for multiplicative inclusion of individual elements in two parts of a whole.

Transitory Combinativity

4

The analyses so far of initial combinativity structures found that composing, recomposing, and decomposing by 6-month-old subjects are ephemeral. They are limited in time rarely lasting more than a moment. They are limited in space, usually involving rapidly changing displacements. They tend to be impermanent, most not involving placement relations between objects which are conserved or which are changed but in a constant or systematic pattern. They are limited in causality; when labiles involve causation they are not well-controlled transformations, rarely involve intermediaries, and have haphazard goals.

These constructions constitute a shifting panorama of combinativity. Labile organization of combinativity generated by 6-month-olds provides them with a sparse structural foundation upon which to reflect and build more advanced structures. This primitive organization is correlative to the fluctuation due to the change ratio constant (Chapter 2, pages 30–31). Just as with the change ratio, the shifting and fleeting character of combinativity at this stage provides minimal opportunity for presentational equilibrium. It should be difficult for the subjects to focus upon the labiles they have constructed.

For this reason, it should, by hypothesis, take many months for subjects to progressively transform the combinativity relations they construct. Yet, and also by hypothesis, labile composing, recomposing, and decomposing provide the main structural foundations upon which post-6-month-old children build more advanced combinativity, culminating years later in classificatory as well as other logical and quantitative structures of reasoning. Here a likely structural source of support is another constant of mappings, namely, compactness (Chapter 2, pages 31–35). If anything, the range of mappings used in combinativity proto-operations is even more compact than that which characterizes 6-month-olds' overall transactions. For instance, one mapping form, "push," by itself accounts for almost half the production of compositions by subject 6AB. Two others, "hit" and "touch," accounts for most of the remainder.

Thus, while the products of combinativity might be extremely labile, the means of production are relatively compact or constant over the succession of transactions. By itself this is sufficient to insure that at least the physical form of the products is also relatively uniform. Most are asymmetrical, causal, or mobile two-element couplings based on contact in a single dimension, the horizontal.

This sparse organization of combinativity proto-operations is augmented by other equilibrating combinativity features described in this chapter. For instance, most compositions are generated as parts of sequences of two or more compositions. Thus, these original, labile combinativity structures are nevertheless sufficient to begin to form equivalence and ordered nonequivalence relations within and between consecutive constructions. Coordinations in the extent and predicate properties of combinativity structures are beginning to be constructed by relational proto-operations which we have already seen at work in Chapter 2, such as protoaddition. They are also beginning to be conditioned by proto-operations which are unique to combinativity structures, and which we have not encountered so far, such as protocommutativity and protosubstitution.

I. Predominance of Sequential Composing

Isolated compositions, by definition, are neither preceded nor followed immediately by other compositions; nor are they recomposed into any variant configurations. Even at this early stage, isolates are already subordinate forms of composing. Only a third of the compositions are produced in isolation (Table 4.1, Column 1). The range is quite narrow; from a low of 30% in the additive and 31% in the semicontrol conditions to a high of 39% in the disjoint and 41% in the multiplicative conditions (Table 4.1, Rows 1, 5, 9, and 13). The proportion of isolates does not vary as a function of object conditions (Table 4.1, Rows 2–4, 6–8, and 10–12).

TABLE 4. 1
Spontaneous Phase I: Mean Frequency by 6-Month-Old Subjects Generating Isolate, Consecutive, Partially Overlapping, and Simultaneous Compositions

		1	2	3	4
		Isolate	*Consecutive*	*Partially overlapping*	*Simultaneous*
1.	Total semicontrol	4.42	9.58	0.25	0.00
2.	1 × 2; 2 × 1 Realistic	5.25	8.25	0.00	0.00
3.	1 × 4 Euclidean	3.75	4.00	0.00	0.00
4.	4 × 1 Topological	4.25	14.50	0.75	0.00
5.	Total additive	4.58	10.83	0.00	0.00
6.	Realistic	5.25	14.50	0.00	0.00
7.	Euclidean	4.50	11.50	0.00	0.00
8.	Topological	4.00	6.50	0.00	0.00
9.	Total multiplicative	5.00	7.08	0.25	0.00
10.	Realistic	5.25	4.00	0.00	0.00
11.	Euclidean	3.50	6.25	0.00	0.00
12.	Topological	6.25	11.00	0.75	0.00
13.	Total disjoint	4.08	6.25	0.00	0.17
14.	Total all conditions	4.52	8.44	0.13	0.04
15.	Percentage of all conditions	34	64	1	0

Isolate compositions provide minimal opportunity for structuring part–whole relations between sets. Yet, even though they are constructed in segregation from other compositions, they do provide opportunities for structuring some essential part–whole relations internal to individual sets. To begin with, a small but substantial proportion of isolates are extended beyond the moment of their' construction (e.g., holding one object on another for several seconds before lifting it away). Preserving compositions for substantial durations is a necessary condition fundamental to the process of equilibrating labiles as initial sets. Only then can these initial sets begin to be treated as constants or given elements upon which to elaborate progressive combinativity protooperations.

Regulated anticipation and observation further extend the boundaries and constancy of isolated compositions:

27. *looks at Doll 2 standing on table, as LH holds Doll 1 in air*
28. *LH hits D1 into D2, knocking D2 over*
28a. *D2 rolls about four inches to right*
29. *looks at D2, as LH holds D1 just above table*   (6TT, page 2)

Subjects are beginning to look at objects prior to composing them. They are also beginning to monitor what happens to the objects after they have been composed. These precursors of regulated prevision and postvision extend the life span of labiles beyond their momentary constructive boundaries.

These precursory regulations, and other structural components which cannot be constructed in isolated compositions, are embodied more robustly in consecutive compositions. Consecutive compositions predominate (Table 4.1, Column 2); virtually no compositions are generated in either partial overlap or in simultaneity with other compositions at this stage (Table 4.1, Columns 3 and 4).

The negative import of not generating partially overlapping or simultaneous compositions is manifold. At heart these constructive lacunae impose restrictions on the possibilities for structuring differentiated yet coordinated sets. They eliminate the easiest avenues for integrating and recombining compositions. Consequently, the level of formulating and reformulating sets necessarily remains rudimentary. This significantly constricts conceptualizing classes and extents in practical transactions.

Consecutive labile compositions are, as we shall see in subsequent sections, sufficient to begin generating precursory part–whole relations internal to single sets. These include constructing various precursory equivalence relations depending upon the proto-operations in play. Fundamental here are replacement, substitution, commutative, and correspondence proto-operations. They also include constructing precursory nonequivalence and order relations. These, too, vary as a function of the proto-operations producing the relations. Fundamental now are addition, subtraction, and reciprocity proto-operations. Finally, they are sufficient to the precursory formation of predicate relations within a set. These are not random. They are dominated by negation proto-operations.

II. Partial Exchange Proto-operations upon Single Two-Element Sets

Three proto-operational structures of exchange, which originate at this stage, construct equivalence relations within sets. All three involve pragmatic transformation and reconstitution of an initial composition. Protoreplacement consists of subtracting an element from a set and then adding it back, thereby recomposing the extent and the intensity of the initial set. Protosubstitution consists of subtracting an element from a set and then adding a different element back, thereby recomposing the extent, but not the intensity, of the initial set. Protocommutativity consists of transforming the placement relations between the elements composing a set, thereby recomposing the extent and the intensity of the initial set without ever subtracting or adding.

Protoreplacement and protocommutativity hold both the elements and the set constant. Protoreplacement exchanges one element of a set for itself such that its initial and final placements are identical. Protocommutativity exchanges the placements of all the elements of a set such that the initial and final placements of all elements are different. Protosubstitution holds the set constant but exchanges one of the elements.

All three proto-operations are restricted to consecutive recompositions of one set since two temporally overlapping or simultaneous sets are rarely generated. Consequently, their resultant equivalence relations only apply to consecutive part–whole relations internal to single sets. Until applied to two contemporaneous sets, these three proto-operations remain essentially first-order transformations.

Replacement proto-operations are generated by 5 of the 12 subjects. Protoreplacement is fundamental to constructing both (*a*) predicate or intensive equivalence and (*b*) extensive or quantitative equivalence, within individual sets of elements. However, protoreplacement fuses predicate with extensive equivalence. Both are generated simultaneously by the same sequence of consecutive recompositions. Protoreplacement does not provide any structural possibilities for differentiating and coordinating predicate and extensive equivalences.

Initial protoreplacement begins with unary recompositions of two-element compositions. One element is subtracted once from an initial composition, then the same element is added back immediately. Thereby, protoreplacement recomposes the two-element set such that both the initial and variant groupings are equivalent in both predicate properties and extent of elements.

Protoreplacements are applied to stabile recompositions:

20. *RH touches Spoon on top of Mirror*
21. *RH raises S*
22. *RH lowers S on top of M*   (6AM, page 2)

Replacement proto-operations are also applied to mobile recompositions:

56. *LH pushes Cylinder 1 against Square Column 1*
56a. *C1 pushes SC1 about three inches away*
57. *LH withdraws C1 from SC1 and then pushes it against SC1 again, pushing SC1 slightly further away*   (6TT, page 21)

Protoreplacements are even targeted:

42.7. *RH drops Rectangular Ring 1 on top of Doll 1*
44. *RH picks up RR1 off of D1*
44a. *RR1 pushes D1 toward subject slightly*
45. *RH twists RR1 around in air*
46. *RH drops RR1 next to D1, just about touching it*   (6KF, page 28)

Targeting indicates that replacement is beginning to be a regulated equivalence proto-operation. Another indication is that protoreplacements are occasionally reproduced several times in a row:

11.5.   RH *lowers Doll 2 and holds it on top of Doll 1, touching:*

13.   RH *raises D2 about 2 inches above D1 and looks at it* (*experimenter retrieves Spoon from subject's lap*)
14.   RH *lowers D2 to table—touches head of D2 to table space just in front of D1:*

15.   RH *raises D2 about 4 inches above table* (*experimenter replaces S in front of subject*)
16.   LH *touches D2 held by RH*
17.   RH *lowers D2, touching its head to head of D1—forearm turns S handle in process*
17a.   D2 *turns D1 slightly*
18.   RH *raises D2 a couple of inches above table*
19.   RH *lowers D2—hand rests on top of D1:*

20.3.   LH *hits table, twice*
20.7.   RH *slides D1 to right, approximately 1 inch*
22.   RH *raises D2 about 3 inches above D1*
23.   RH *waves D2 forward and back in air briefly, with short strokes*
24.   RH *hits D2 on top of D1*
25.   RH *raises D2 in air again immediately after hit* (*experimenter wiggles S on table a little*)
26.   RH *lowers hand on top of D1 again, this time D2 head touches table space just in front of D1*
27.   *looks at experimenter a few seconds, maintaining position in No. 26*
(6DF, pages 14 and 15)

The initial two-object composition (Line 11.5) is recomposed five times (Lines 14, 17, 19, 24, and 26). All recompositions are constructed by successively subtracting and replacing the same element. The sequence includes visual (Line 13) and tactual (Line 16) inspection of the element being replaced. It ends in a recomposition relatively extended in duration (Lines 26–27).

Substitution proto-operations are generated by 4 of the 12 subjects. Protosubstitution, like protoreplacement, is a fundamental equivalence operation. It constructs extensive equivalence within sets, that is, between consecutive recompositions of the same number of elements. Unlike protoreplacement, protosubstitution need not generate predicate equivalence since it always involves exchanging elements. The quantity of elements subtracted and added are equal, but the predicate properties of the elements exchanged need not be; they may be identical, complementary, or disjoint. Consequently, protosubstitution opens up the additional possibility for differentiating and coordinating the extensive and intensive properties within single sets.

At its origins, protosubstitution is also limited to unary transformations applied to two-element compositions. A single element is subtracted from an initial two-element composition and another single element is substituted to recompose a two-element set. The elements exchanged may be directly transformed while the constant element is not:

 2. *LH lifts Cross Ring 1 and Triangular Ring 2*
 3. *LH releases CR1 which falls to lap*
 4. *LH grasps Cross Ring 2 with TR2*   (6NF, page 11)

14.7. *RH drops Doll 2 into Rectangular Ring 1, as looking at D2*
16.3. *RH quickly lifts D2 out of RR1*
16.7. *LH drops Doll 1 into RR1*   (6AW, page 13)

Alternatively, the constant element may be directly transformed while the exchanged elements are not:

31.5.   *LH pushes end of Yellow Triangular Column against Yellow Cylinder*
31.5a. *YTC knocks YC flat*
33.5.   *LH pushes YTC against Green Cylinder*
33.5a. *YTC pushes GC flat*   (6SA, page 11)

Protosubstitution is beginning to be regulated. Some indications can be found in 6AW's (p. 13) production. At least one of the exchanged objects is monitored visually (Line 14.7). The exchanged objects are targeted to the exact same location; thereby, achieving the same relation to the constant element. Protosubstitution, then, is a directed exchange of single elements.

The most advanced protosubstitution generated at this stage extends to three element exchanges:

62. LH touches Cross Ring 1 upright on Cross Ring 2
63. LH raises CR1 and drops it partly on Triangular Ring 1
64. LH lifts CR1
65. LH touches CR1 on Triangular Ring 2 in sweeping movement to left
66. LH draws CR1 back and touches it on TR1   (6NF, page 13)

The manipulated object, CR1, is held constant while the exchanged objects, CR2, TR1, and TR2, are not directly transformed. The initial composition and the three recompositions are all two-element labiles. Only single elements are exchanged, but the protosubstitution includes exchange of three elements for each other. In addition, TR1 is exchanged for both CR2 (Lines 62–63) and TR2 (Lines 65–66).

Repeated protosubstitution of one for two elements is a further indication that the extensive equivalences generated are beginning to be extended and regulated. Elements are exchanged without regard to the different predicate properties of the objects substituted for each other. Thus, extensive equivalence is produced at the same time as intensive nonequivalence; thereby generating the necessary conditions for differentiating between them.

Coordination of protosubstitution and protoreplacement originates at this stage. Sequences of consecutive recompositions are beginning to be generated by two subjects which combine both forms of producing equivalence relations within two-element sets:

43.   LH pushes Rectangular Ring 2 into Doll 2
43a. D2 rolls across table to left
44.   LH pushes RR2 into Doll 1
44a. D1 rolls across table to left
45.   LH pushes RR2 into D1
45a. D1 rolls across table to left   (6NF, page 19)

12.   RH hits Yellow Cup bottom end into Yellow Spoon
12a. YS is pushed away on table
13.   RH hits YC into Orange Cup
13a. OC is knocked over
14.   RH hits YC into OC
14a. OC is pushed away
15.   RH hits YC onto table
16.   RH hits YC into YS
17.   RH hits YC into YS
      (experimenter replaces OC upright in front of the subject)
18.   RH hits YC into OC
18a. OC is knocked over   (6AW, page 5)

Subject 6NF combines one protosubstitution (Lines 43–44) with one protoreplacement (Lines 44–45). Subject 6AW produces the most advanced coordination of these two equivalence proto-operations generated at this stage. Protosubstitution (Lines 12–13) is linked to protoreplacement (Lines 13–14), which is linked to protosubstitution (Lines 14–16), which is linked to protoreplacement (Lines 16–17), which is linked to protosubstitution (Lines 17–18).

The sequence of consecutive composition and five recompositions forms an extended equivalence structure:

$$(YC > YS) \approx (YC > OC) \sim (YC > OC) \approx (YC > YS) \sim (YC > YS)$$
$$\approx (YC > OC) \tag{4.1}$$

The elements are neither arbitrary nor specified and are therefore symbolized in Eq. (4.1) by the initials of the actual objects used. They are pragmatic agents or patients. The relations between elements do not consist of logical constants; rather, they are transformational, unidirectional causal relations of hitting one object against another single object ($>$). Nor are the classes or sets arbitrary or specified. They are nothing but labile couplings of two individual objects. Their lack of arbitrariness is revealed in many ways, most notably, by not holding for more than two-element compositions. The relations between recompositions do not consist of logical equivalence. They are beginning to be regulated protological equivalences based upon pragmatic protoreplacement ($\sim$) and protosubstitution ($\approx$) relations.

Transformational relations ($>$) and equivalence structures of protoreplacement ($\sim$) and protosubstitution ($\approx$) are combined in Eq. (4.1). They are the result of initial coordination between these two proto-operational forms of generating equivalence. Most sequences of composing and recomposing are limited to generating either protoreplacement ($\sim$) or protosubstitution ($\approx$) equivalences within a single set. These constitute the structures of the proto-operations considered at the outset of this section.

Even at this initial stage the organization of protoreplacement and protosubstitution operations include three preliminary structures. The first structure is that of protoreplacement in which extensive and intensive protoequivalence are fused. The second is that of protosubstitution which constructs extensive protoequivalence and ignores, at this stage at least, the predicate properties of the elements exchanged. The third structure begins to coordinate protoreplacement with protosubstitution operations. This precursory coordinative structure of protoequivalence is most rudimentary. It does not even involve unification at the same level of quantification. It certainly does not involve any hierarchic integration or subordination of either structure to the other. At most this structural coordination consists of partial correlation limited to temporal overlap between the production of protoreplacement and protosubstitution equivalence.

Complementing these three structures of exchange proto-operations is equivalence by protocommutativity. Like protoreplacement, protocommutativity does not exchange any elements within sets. Its uniqueness resides in varying the order of placement relations between elements while preserving both extensive and predicate equivalence. Protocommutativity is generated by 5 of the 12 subjects.

The most primitive protocommutativity does not even include mapping constancy:

9.   RH *drops Green Cross Ring from high in air onto and partially overlapping Yellow Rectangular Ring*
10.   RH *immediately lowers on top of YRR*
11.   RH *pushes YRR to the right, such that YRR slides to the right while staying under GCR*
11a.   GCR *moves right with YRR*   (6AM, page 16)

Nor is the exchange of elements repeated.

Thus, if

$$\langle \text{GCR} > \text{YRR} \rangle \ \rightsquigarrow \ \langle \text{YRR} > \text{GCR} \rangle \qquad (4.2)$$

then the relations between placement orders ($\langle \ \rangle$) remain unregulated and irreversible equivalences ($\rightsquigarrow$). Note also that the mappings are minimal, that is, unary transformations of individual objects. So are the compositions, that is, two-object labiles in which only one object is directly manipulated. The elements are concrete objects (GCR and YRR). Compositional relations between elements are pragmatic ($>$). They are certainly not yet logical conjuncts or disjuncts; although they are their progenitors.

The most advanced protocommutativity generated at this stage includes partial mapping constancy:

55.   LH *drops Brush 2 about 1/2 inch behind Mirror 1:*

56.   LH *lifts and immediately drops B2 about 2 inches behind and parallel with M1, as looking at experimenter*

57. *LH lifts M1 as looks at it*
58. *LH holds M1 in air briefly*
59. *LH drops M1 on top of and approximately parallel with B2*
60. *LH lifts B2 and M1 together*
61. *LH drops M1 onto table*
62. *LH drops B2 about 4 inches behind M1:*

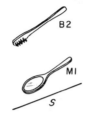

63. *LH pulls M1 over table edge, releasing it such that it falls to floor via lap*
64. *LH lifts B2*
    (experimenter replaces M1 on table; slides Brush 1 in front of subject):

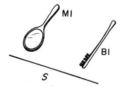

65. *LH releases B2 onto table about 5 inches to left of M1*   (6SA, page 19)

With the exception of the last recomposition (Line 65), all the preceding relevant compositions and recompositions involve the same mapping, that of "dropping" (Lines 55, 56, 59, and 61–62). More significant is the single repetition in exchanging the element transformed in three of the compositions (Lines 56, 59, and 61–62). The protocommutative series is extended to equivalence relations between three ordered sets, such that

$$\langle B2 > M1 \rangle \rightsquigarrow \langle M1 > B2 \rangle \rightsquigarrow \langle B2 > M1 \rangle \qquad (4.3)$$

Reproduction, if only a single replication, is the first precursory indication of regulated protocommutativity. It also bespeaks the origins of pragmatic reversibility between placement orders which is to become protoreciprocal equivalence ($\leftrightsquigarrow$).

One other structural relation between two exchange proto-operations is generated by only one subject at this stage. It coordinates protocommutativity with protoreplacement. Even its precursory production remains infrequent and limited. Consider the entire sequence of labiles generated by 6SA (Lines 55, 56, 59, 61–62, and 65). It successively interweaves protoreplacement with protocommutativity, such that it expands Eq. (4.3) into

$$(B2 > M1) \sim \langle B2 > M1 \rangle \rightsquigarrow \langle M1 > B2 \rangle \rightsquigarrow \langle B2 > M1 \rangle \sim (B2 > M1)$$

$$(4.4)$$

Protoreplacement equivalence between unordered sets ($\sim$) immediately precedes and succeeds once-repeated protocommutative equivalence between ordered sets ($\rightsquigarrow$).

This fifth structure completes the precursory organization of first-order exchange proto-operations between unordered and ordered two-element sets. Three structures are direct equivalence proto-operations of replacement, substitution, and commutativity. Two structures are coordinated equivalence proto-operations combining replacement with substitution and replacement with commutativity. A third, potential structure coordinating protosubstitution with protocommutativity is a second-order exchange structure which does not develop for several months.

III. Partial Protocorrespondences within Single Sets

Two protocorrelational structures originate at this stage. Their operations construct equivalence relations within sets by producing one-to-one (bi-univocal) or one-to-many (co-univocal) correspondences. Correlation proto-operations are already generated, often numerous times, by all subjects. However, bi-univocals are generated much more frequently than co-univocal protocorrespondences.

Frege (1884/1974) first proposed that a correlation operation constructs numerical equivalence: "The expression the concept F is equal to the concept G is to mean the same as the expression there exists a relation $\emptyset$ which correlates one to one the objects falling under the concept F with the objects falling under the concept G [p. 85]." Cantor (1895) expanded this formulation of numerical equivalence to the proposition that two sets have an equivalent cardinal number or extent of objects if and only if every member of one set is in unique one-to-one correspondence with an element of the other set such that all elements are matched. Frege (1884/1974) provided a pragmatic embodiment for his formal symbolic proof which is particularly apt for the study of protologic:

> We will consider the following example. If a waiter wishes to be certain of laying exactly as many knives on a table as plates, he has no need to count either of them; all he has to do is lay immediately to the right of every plate a knife, taking care that every

knife on the table lies immediately to the right of a plate. Plates and knives are thus correlated one to one, and that by the identical spatial relationship. Now if in the proposition

"*a* lies immediately to the right of A"

we conceive first one and then another object inserted in place of *a* and again of A, then that part of the content which remains unaltered throughout this process constitutes the essence of the relation [pp. 81–82].

Constructing an identical spatial relation is only one of many ways in which protocorresponding equivalence is generated at this stage. However, two protocorresponding sets are not generated until the fourth stage when precursors of Frege's example begin to be produced. Protocorrespondence is limited at this stage to producing equivalence relations between elements within single sets:

48. LH *places Triangular Ring 2 adjacent to Triangular Ring 1:*

(6NF, page 13)

59.5. RH *touches table edge to right of Block 3*
59.5. LH *touches corner of Block 1 to left of B3:*

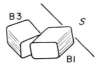

61. RH *pushes B3 to upright position, such that B3 touches B1:*

62.5. RH *holds B3 upright, such that RH supports it but B3 never quite reaches a fully upright position*
62.5. LH *holds B1 upright briefly*
64. RH *removes from B3 and B3 falls flat*   (6AB, page 4)

Symmetrical correspondence in the orientation of object placements is constructed by both subjects. The second involves groping and adjustment. The initial composition consists of an asymmetrical placement (second Line 59.5, plus diagram). Block 1 is placed in an upright position such that it is in physical contact with Block 3 which is in a flat orientation. The subject constructs a correspondence by uprighting Block 3 against Block 1 so that their orientations are symmetrical (Line 61, plus diagram). He maintains the correspondence by holding Block 1 and Block 3 upright (Lines 62.5). However, the fragility of the correspondence structure is made quickly evident. Subject 6AB lets go of Block 3 and it falls flat (Line 64). He makes no further attempt to reconstruct the correspondence; rather, he shifts to another object and mapping.

Groping adjustment of matching between objects is an initial indication that protocorrespondences are beginning to be regulated. Still produced infrequently their constructions are notable:

> 58. *LH touches Cylinder 1 on top of Square Column 1*
> 59. *releases C1 in front of and touching SC1, not quite aligned:*

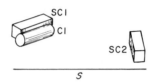

> 60. *LH slides C1 to right, so it sticks out 1 inch on right of SC1*
> 61. *pushes C1 back to left slightly, thus aligning them perfectly:*

(6TT, page 21)

Such spatial correspondences are between two elements within one stabile composition. Spatial correspondences are produced at least as frequently within mobile compositions:

> 35. *RH slides Cross Ring 2 toward left as LH slides Cross Ring 1 toward right, very slowly, such that they touch*   (6AW, page 10)
>
> 92. *LH touches Cylinder 2 and Square Column 1*
> 93. *LH grasps and turns C2 and SC1 clockwise about 20 degrees, such that they remain together*   (6DF, page 22)
>
> 124. *RH raises Circular Ring*
> 125. *looks at CR*
> 126. *LH takes Triangular Ring out of mouth*
> 127. *looks at TR*

128. *RH and LH simultaneously flip TR and CR, such that they touch together for a moment* (6KF, page 6)

Some protocorrespondences, such as that generated by *6KF*, are preceded by visual observation of the objects to be composed. This is a further symptom of beginning regulation. Yet another is that protocorrespondences are beginning to be extended beyond the moment of their construction:

209. *LH removes Triangular Ring from mouth*
210. *LH holds TR upright, just above table*
211. *RH lowers Oval Ring upright onto table*
212. *LH lowers TR in diagonal upright position onto table*
213. *BH simultaneously turn their respective objects to a nearly flat position*
214. *BH grasp objects through their respective centers in nearly horizontal position* (6CL, page 11)

The composition starts out with the two objects in vertical correspondence (Lines 209–212) and is transformed in rotational correspondence (Line 213) into horizontal correspondence (Line 214).

One-to-one (bi-univocal) protocorrespondence between two objects is constructed in these compositions by continuous mappings of spatial displacements and placements, and by kinetic trajectories such as rotation. Continuous mappings allow for the construction of global correlation within sets between equivalent numbers of objects. Discrete mappings, in contrast, permit constructing precise equivalence in both mappings and objects. The potential for quantitative correlation within sets between equivalent numbers of mappings and objects would thereby be generated in precursory form.

Discrete bi-univocal protocorrespondences even of this precursory level are not yet generated. An antecedent form is generated:

17. *LH taps Doll 1 on top of Mirror, three times* (6TT, page 1)

14. *LH touches Cross Ring 2 onto Cross Ring 1, three times* (6AW, page 9)

42.7. *RH drops Rectangular Ring 1 on top of Doll 1*
44. *RH picks up RR1 off of D1*
44a. *RR1 pushes D1 toward subject slightly*
45. *RH twists RR1 around in air*
46. *RH drops RR1 next to D1, just about touching* (6KF, page 28)

Repeated discrete mappings, hitting, touching, dropping, and so on, are used to compose two objects. Reproducing single-unit discrete mappings provides sufficient conditions for elaboration, at a later stage, of precursory into elementary discrete protocorrespondences (e.g., simultaneously hitting two objects against two other objects one time).

Co-univocal (one-to-many) protocorrespondences are invariably discrete. The mapping protocorrespondences are single-unit but the object protocorrespondences are multiplicative and range from one-to-two (6TT) to one-to-three (6KF) objects:

8.   LH *taps Doll 1 on top of Rectangular Ring 1*
8a. *RR1 moves slightly to right*
9.   *LH taps D1 against Doll 2*
9a. *D2 falls over and lands in front of and touching Rectangular Ring 2*
                                                                        (6TT, page 31)

57.   *RH sweeps Doll 1 across table from left to right, knocking into Rectangular Rings 1 and 2 and Doll 2 in that order*
57a. *RR1 and RR2 displaced to right slightly; D2 falls and rolls to right*
58.3. *RH touches D1 to RR2*
58.7. *RH touches D1 to RR1*   (6KF, page 28)

The protocorrespondence generated by *6KF* is particularly notable in two respects. The first is that the composition evolves from globally knocking one object into three to differentiated touching of one object into two. The second is that the differentiated co-univocal one-to-two protocorrespondence partially replicates the global one-to-three protocorrespondence. In both these respects the construction is beginning to be regulated.

Other productions suggest that co-univocal protocorrespondences are extended beyond the limits of the presented objects:

15. *RH holds Block 2 to head*
16. *RH touches B2 to Block 3*
17. *RH holds B2 up to cheek*
18. *looks up at experimenter*
19. *RH touches B2 lightly on B3*
20. *RH extends and withdraws B2*
21. *RH holds B2 to mouth*   (6NF, pages 1 and 2)

40. *RH touches Block 1 on Block 2 and looks at them*
41. *RH holds B1 to right; looks at experimenter*
42. *RH touches B1 to her hair as turns toward mother*
43. *RH holds B1 to her nose*
44. *RH lowers B1 and touches it on B2, as looks at Blocks 3 and 4*
                                                                        (6NF, page 3)

Indeed, the first fragment suggests that co-univocal protocorrespondences are just beginning to be extended to matching one-to-four objects. Block 2 is successively matched to Block 3, her head, her cheek, Block 3, and her mouth. Both protocorrespondences also include one reproduction of matching blocks to each other; further indicating that protocorrespondences are beginning to be regulated.

All co-univocal protocorrespondences generated at this stage match one-to-many objects. None match many-to-one objects even though their formal structures are isomorphic. Many-to-one protocorrespondences, such as consecutively touching two objects to one, are not produced until a later stage. This is a clear indication that the structure of co-univocal protocorrespondences generated is primitive and precursory to that which incorporates and ultimately integrates both one-to-many and many-to-one multiplicative correlations.

IV. Predominance of Additive Iteration within Compositions

Quantifying sets is only partly a matter of producing equivalent extents by exchange or correlation operations. Another essential component is generating ordinal nonequivalent extents. This requires ordering operations which construct iterative series such that successor sets compose ordinally increasing or decreasing numbers of elements directly after their predecessors.

At this stage subjects are not able to construct more than one composition at a time. Therefore, they cannot construct ordinal relations between sets (e.g., a two- and a three-element set at the same time). Ordinal constructions, then, are limited to the number of elements within compositions or recompositions. That is, they seriate elements within sets. They do not yet iterate sets of elements.

Ordinal series within compositions or recompositions begin to be constructed by three first-order proto-operational structures. Protoaddition produces progressions such that successive compositions increase by the same number. Protosubtraction produces progressively decreasing compositional extent. These two direct proto-operations are beginning to be combined into a coordinated protoreciprocal structure. They construct bidirectional series in which successive sets alternate between increasing and decreasing extent.

Composing two-element sets predominates. The very act of constructing two-element compositions consists of transforming one-element sets by protoaddition into two-element sets. Inherent, then, in multiple two-element composing is repeated and varied construction of 2-point ordinally increasing series within compositions. Directed decomposition is not as prevalent as composition. But when generated, most consist of transforming two-element sets by protosubtraction into one-element sets. Inherent, then, in two-element decomposing is repeated and varied production of 2-point ordinally decreasing series within compositions.

Protoaddition is the most frequent generator of ordinally seriated elements at this stage. Most, as just noted, consist of the bare minimum necessary to construct a precursory series of increasing extent. Some two-element compositions are increased into three-element compositions by the addition of one element. These form three point ordinally increasing series of elements within compositions (i.e., ⟨1, 2, 3⟩ element sets). This level of protoaddition is generated by 6 of the 12 subjects. Some subjects already do so repeatedly.

Only one element is directly transformed in constructing the initial two-element compositions. Only the added single element is directly manipulated in further amplifying two- into three-element compositions:

    1. *LH pushes Cylinder 1 to right so it touches Square Column 1:*

    2.5. *LH touches C1 and SC1*
    2.5. *RH pushes Cylinder 2 to the left so it touches SC1; so has three objects together:*

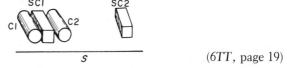

                                                            (6TT, page 19)

The complementary form of protoaddition by directly manipulating the initial compositions such that these two elements are added to a third is just beginning to be generated:

    66. *LH pushes Green Rectangular Ring next to Green Cross Ring (i.e., to right slightly)*
    67. *LH places on top of GRR and GCR and slides both to the right*
    67a. *GCR pushes Yellow Rectangular Ring to the right*   (6AM, page 19)

    20. *LH moves to Cross Ring 2 and holds Triangular Ring 2 on CR2*
    21. *LH draws CR2/TR2 to left until they barely touch Triangular Ring 1*
                                                               (6NF, page 14)

Series in which compositional extent increases ordinally from one- to two- to three- to four-element sets are never generated at this stage. Just beginning to be generated are rare instances of adding two elements to initial two-object compositions resulting in four-object compositions:

121.5.   *RH lowers Circular Ring and Rectangular Ring to table—CR falls off of hand on top of Oval Ring:*

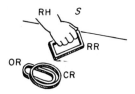

121.5.   *looks toward CR*
123.5.   *LH immediately lowers Triangular Ring to table such that only one corner touches table*
123.5a. *TR displaces CR partially off of OR*
123.5.   *RH holds RR upright to right of and touching OR, so:*

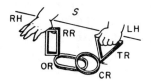

(6AS, page 8)

41.3.   *LH touches Block 1 to Block 2:*

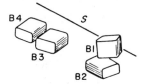

41.3a. *B1 slips off to right of B2*
        (LH still touching B1):

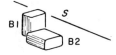

43.   *fourth and fifth fingers of LH push B2 to right*
      (other fingers of LH touch B1)
43a. *B2 moves right into B1, moving B1 right also:*

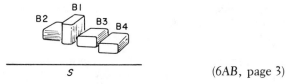

(6AB, page 3)

These are the first constructions which may reflect precursory integration of two parts into whole, albeit still highly labile, compositions. Subject 6AB's composition is as advanced and comes as close to integration of two differential parts as is generated at this stage.

Protoaddition within compositions already begins to take a magnitude form as well:

58.   *touches Doll 1 to Doll 2*
      (experimenter holds onto D2)
59.   *taps at D1 with D2, two times*   (6TT, page 3)

4.   *hits Doll 2 on table in front of Rectangular Ring 2*
5.   *taps Doll 1 on D2, three times*
5a. *third hit knocks D2 over table edge to floor*   (6TT, page 31)

The number of objects composed is not increased. Only the mapping units are increased. Sometimes the increase is a precise addition of one unit forming the pragmatic iterative series $\langle 1, 2 \rangle$. Sometimes it is imprecise and results in the order $\langle 1, \text{many} \rangle$. In either case, these ordered magnitude series do not exceed a 2-point scale.

Protosubtraction from three-element compositions is less prevalent. It is generated by 5 of the 12 subjects. Some involve constructing 3-point ordinally decreasing series of $\langle 3, 2, 1 \rangle$ elements within sets:

22.   *LH fingers push over Doll 1 such that it rolls to the right and stops next to*
      Rectangular Ring 2:

23.   *RH drops Doll 2 in front of D1, almost touching*
24.   *immediately RH pulls D1 and D2 simultaneously toward table edge*
25.   *RH slides D2 over edge such that it falls to lap*
26.   *RH places on D1*   (6CB, page 23)

3.   *LH touches Cylinder 1, Square Column 1, and Cylinder 2 simulta-*
     neously
4.   *BH lift C2 and SC1 simultaneously*
5.   *drops SC1 onto table as simultaneously BH insert end of C2 into mouth*
5a. *SC1 partially rests on table edge and against stomach*
6.   *mouths C1 several seconds held by BH*   (6AM, page 9)

Other protosubtractions only construct 2-point ordinally decreasing series of $\langle 3, 2 \rangle$ (6AM) and $\langle 4, 3 \rangle$ (6AW and 6AS) elements within sets:

20.   *RH pulls Yellow Rectangular Ring toward self*
20a.   *Green Cross Ring moves toward subject:*

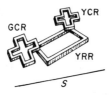

(6AM, page 17)

8.   *RH grasps–pushes at Block 4 which pushes the whole line of four blocks a little to the left*
9.   *RH pushes Block 3 which pushes Block 2 and Block 1 a little more to the left*

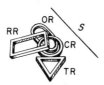

(6AW, page 1)

136.   *RH immediately rests on top of Rectangular Ring*
137.3.   *RH pushes stack of three (RR, Oval Ring, Circular Ring) toward self—in process RR moves in front of other two objects, resting partially on table:*

(6AS, page 9)

These protosubtractions are particularly interesting. The first two are the result of unary transformations, that is, singular mappings in direct contact with one object. The last involves pushing three objects. All are produced by direct or indirect subtraction of the larger part from the whole; rather than subtracting only a single element.

Coordinated protoreciprocal structures of addition and subtraction are just beginning to be generated by 3 of the 12 subjects. At the outset they are limited to one alternation of a single-step increase followed immediately by a single-step decrease. One element is added to a two-element set resulting in a three-element set. Then one element is subtracted from the three-element set resulting in a two-element set once again:

15. *places Triangular Ring 2 on table behind Cross Ring 2, touching:*

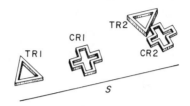

16. *RH grasps Cross Ring 1 and slides it to the right*
16a. *CR1 pushes TR2 and CR2 to the right*
17. *RH slides CR1 further right, then lifts it*
17a. *CR1 slides CR2 to the right*   (6CB, page 15)

45.5. *LH holds Triangular and Clover Rings as mouths CR*
45.7. *RH raises Circular Ring to below chin and grasps CR and TR, such that
       RH holds all three rings*
       (experimenter replaces Rectangular Ring onto table)
45.8. *looks at RR*
48. *LH releases CR*
49. *RH extends TR, CR, and CircR together forward and immediately drops
       TR such that it lands on top of RR*
50. *RH holds CircR and CR together in air to the right, as looks at TR/RR;
       RH is only grasping CircR as CR is caught within CircR* (6SA, page 3)

The bidirectional series generated by 6SA is the most advanced found
at this stage. The sets are preserved for a few moments. At least some
objects are observed visually, and, the final construction results in two
simultaneous two-element labiles (Lines 49–50).

The precursory status of reciprocal ordering is also apparent in these
productions. Bidirectional series are limited to single shifts from increasing to decreasing numbers of elements within a set. Alternation is not
reproduced. Protoaddition and protosubtraction are restricted to a single
element. Bidirectional series are always constructed in the sequence
protoaddition followed by protosubtraction. They are never the products
of protosubtraction followed by protoaddition even though these two
forms of constructing protoreciprocal orders are formally isomorphic.

V. Predication by Differences

Most compositions, as we have seen, consist of two elements constructed in isolation or consecutively. Insofar as this makes it difficult to
represent additive, multiplicative and disjoint classes in practical transac-

tions, 6-month-olds do not classify according to the predicate class structure embodied in the objects of their transactions. They do not compose
objects into groups which accord to these three class conditions on which
they were tested.

Isolated or consecutive labiles are sufficient to compose only one set. A
singular composition, even when limited to only two objects, neatly does
the trick. In the additive class condition it only requires composing two
identical elements, and not the two other objects belonging to the complementary class. In the multiplicative class condition it only requires
composing two objects identical in either form or in color. In the disjoint
class condition it only requires composing two identical objects, and not
the two other objects belonging to the disjoint class. All the requisite
material objects and compositional skills are therefore at the disposal of
6-month-olds to classify only one set at a time. All that is necessary is to
compose two identical objects in the additive and the disjoint condition,
and two similar objects in the multiplicative condition.

Three structural articulatory features can serve to instantiate by practical grouping the predicate properties of additive, multiplicative and disjoint conditions. These features are general, such that they even apply to
isolated compositions.

The *order* in which objects are transacted with to compose them into
sets may be consistent with the predicate properties of the class conditions. Of course, order as a structural feature of compositions can only be
determined when two or more objects are directly transacted with. Most
compositions generated at this stage only involve unary transactions.
Therefore order is only a determinable structural feature of the smaller
subset of compositions generated by 6-month-olds.

As an illustration consider order of grouping in the additive class
condition. Let a1, a2, b1, b2 stand, respectively, for the two blue cross
rings and the two blue triangular rings when the objects presented are
topological-like. Then two objects composed in the orders $\langle a1, a2 \rangle$
or $\langle b1, b2 \rangle$ are unmixed in order of predicate properties. Unmixed
predicate grouping order, then, is defined as class consistent order of
usage such that (a) all objects in one class are composed before (b) any
objects in a second class are composed; and so on. Any $\langle a, b \rangle$ combination is mixed in grouping order. Three objects composed in the orders
$\langle a1, a2, b1 \rangle$ or $\langle a1, b1, b2 \rangle$ are unmixed. Order $\langle a1, b1, a2 \rangle$ is
mixed. Four objects composed in the order $\langle a1, a2, b1, b2 \rangle$ is unmixed.
Four objects composed in the order $\langle a1, b1, b2, a2 \rangle$ is partly unmixed.
Four objects composed in the order $\langle a1, b1, a2, b2 \rangle$ is mixed. As just
illustrated, partially unmixed predicate composing order only becomes
possible when four or more objects are directly transacted with.

Enclosure features of composing may be consistent with the predicate properties of the class conditions. Unmixed enclosure is defined as compositions in which all elements of each class grouped are (*a*) enclosed on each other and (*b*) not on any element of another class. Two-object compositions of (**a1, a2**) or (**b1, b2**) are unmixed in enclosure of predicate properties, while any (**a, b**) combinations are mixed. Three-object compositions of (**a1, a2, b1**) or (**a1, b1, b2**) are unmixed, while (**a1, b1, a2**) enclosures are mixed. Four-object compositions of (**a1, a2, b1, b2**) are unmixed, of (**a1, b1, b2, a2**) are partly unmixed, and of (**a1, b1, a2, b2**) are mixed in enclosure.

It should be noted that order and enclosure are totally independent structural features of compositions. To illustrate, subjects can compose in the unmixed class order ⟨**a1, a2, b1**⟩ but place **b1** between **a1** and **a2** such that the neighboringness is (**a1, b1, a2**) and the enclosure is mixed. Conversely, subjects can compose in the mixed class order ⟨**a1, b1, a2, b2**⟩, but place the objects such that **a1** is proximal to **a2** and **b1** is proximal to **b2**. Then the enclosure (**a1, a2, b1, b2**) is unmixed in predicate properties.

Proximity and separation features compositions which meet requirements for enclosure plus (*a*) proximity between members of each class and (*b*) separation between classes. In order to be applicable at least three objects must be composed. Also it should be noted that proximity and separation is independent of order and partially independent of enclosure. The basic finding is that proximity and separation does not yet mark compositions at this stage. Therefore, we will reserve a more detailed analysis of this structural feature until it becomes developmentally relevant.

The two structural features of composing generated at this stage, order and enclosure, were almost perfectly correlated. When one was unmixed, partly mixed, or mixed, then the other was correspondingly unmixed, partly mixed, or mixed in 93% of the compositions. Only 16 out of 226 compositions deviated from this pattern. This is consistent with the hypothesis that these two structural articulatory features are not yet differentiated at this stage. It is as though these structural features have no independence from each other as far as 6-month-old's constructions are concerned. They are syncretically fused features of pragmatic composing.

The findings on predicate order and enclosure features as a function of class condition are presented in Table 4.2. Consider first the additive condition (Rows 5–8). Four objects were presented with two identical members of one class (**a1** and **a2**) and two identical members of a complementary class (**b1** and **b2**), such that the **a**s and the **b**s are similar but

TABLE 4.2

Spontaneous Phase I: Mean Frequency by 6-Month-Old Subjects Generating Unmixed, Partly Unmixed, and Mixed Compositions

		Order			Enclosure		
		1	2 Partly	3	4	5 Partly	6
		Unmixed	unmixed	Mixed	Unmixed	unmixed	Mixed
1.	Total semicontrol	2.63	0.00	4.25	6.88	0.75	9.88
2.	1 × 2; 2 × 1 Realistic	1.25	0.00	3.50	5.50	0.00	10.00
3.	1 × 4 Euclidean	—	—	—	—	—	—
4.	4 × 1 Topological	4.00	0.00	5.00	8.25	1.50	9.75
5.	Total additive	1.58	0.00	5.75	3.92	0.00	11.50
6.	Realistic	3.25	0.00	11.00	2.75	0.00	13.25
7.	Euclidean	0.75	0.00	2.75	3.00	0.00	7.50
8.	Topological	0.75	0.00	3.50	6.00	0.00	13.75
9.	Total multiplicative	1.00	0.08	3.00	5.42	0.16	6.67
10.	Realistic	0.75	0.00	0.75	5.75	0.00	3.50
11.	Euclidean	0.00	0.00	2.50	3.50	0.00	6.00
12.	Topological	2.25	0.25	5.75	6.50	0.50	10.50
13.	Total disjoint	0.67	0.00	2.92	2.92	0.00	7.58

different. Consequently, once a subject has transacted with one object (e.g., a1) the probability of composing it with its one identical object (a2) is 33%; while the probability of composing it with one of its two complementary objects (b1 or b2) is 67%. Taking this differential probability into account reveals that subjects do not compose by predicate identity. Their compositions are not random in terms of predicate properties, rather, they compose by predicate complementarity.

The ratio of mixed (complement) to unmixed (identity) composing is almost four-to-one for order (Row 5, Columns 1 and 3) and three-to-one for enclosure (Row 5, Columns 4 and 6). The random composing ratio, as just noted, is two-to-one. Predominance of composing order and enclosure by complements is general to all types of objects used (Rows 6–8, Columns 1, 3, 4, 6). They are corroborated by the results of sign tests by subjects for order ($N = 9$, $x = 2$, $p = .09$) and enclosure ($N = 12$, $x = 2$, $p = .019$).

In the multiplicative condition four objects were presented making up a matrix of complementary forms and complementary colors; identical objects were not presented. Consequently, once a subject transacts with one object the probability of composing it with one of its two complements is 67%, while the probability of composing it with its sole disjoint object is 33%.

The ratio of mixed (disjoint) to unmixed (complement) composing is three-to-one for order (Row 9, Columns 1 and 3) and a bit more than one-to-one for enclosure (Row 9, Columns 4 and 6). The random composing ratio, as just noted, is one-to-two. Some variation in ratio resulted as a function of object type. Disjoint predicate order and enclosure predominates for Euclidean and topological objects (Rows 11 and 12). Random predicate enclosure is approached for realistic objects (Row 9, Columns 4 and 6), while there are too few cases to determine its predicate order (Row 9, Columns 1 and 3). The tendency to compose by disjoint predicates is statistically significant for enclosure ($N = 11, x = 2, p = .033$, sign test). While not statistically significant for order features, the trend is in the direction of disjoint order predication ($N = 8, x = 2, p = .145$, sign test).

In the disjoint condition the probabilities of mixed (disjoint) predicate composing is 67% and of unmixed (identity) predicate composing is 33%. The random composing ratio, then, is two-to-one. The observed ratios are four-to-one for order (Row 12, Columns 1 and 3) and 2.5-to-1 for enclosure (Row 12, Columns 4 and 5). Only the tendency to order by disjoints rather than identities is significant ($N = 11, x = 2, p = .033$, sign test). The trend is in the same direction for enclosure, but it is not statistically significant ($N = 12, x = 4, p = .194$, sign test).

Similar analyses were applied to the two appropriate semicontrol conditions. In the $1 \times 2; 2 \times 1$ realistic condition two objects are identical (a1 and a2) and two objects are disjoint (b and c) both from each other and from the as. The random composing ratio of mixed (disjoint) to unmixed (identity) is two-to-one. In the 4×1 topological condition two objects are complementary rectilinear rings (one rectangular and one triangular). The other two are complementary curvilinear forms (one circular and one clover). The random composing ratio of mixed (partly disjoint) to unmixed (complement) is two-to-one. The results are random predication for both order ($N = 7, x = 4, p = .50$, sign test) and enclosure ($N = 7, x = 5, p = .227$, sign test) of composing (Rows 1, 3, and 4).

The general thrust of these findings is consistent. Predication is random in the semicontrol conditions where the class structures are ambiguous. Remarkably, predication of compositions is not random in the class conditions which explicitly embody logical structures. Predication is by negation, that is, by maximum possible differences in the class conditions. Predication is by complements, not identities, in the additive condition; predication is by disjoints, not complements, in the multiplicative condition; and predication is by disjoints, not identities, in the disjoint condition. Disjoints predominate over complements which predominate over identical predication in composing labiles.

Even at age 6 months, then, predication varies as a function of logical structure. Predication is random in the face of ambiguous logical structures. Predication is by negation properties, that is, complements and disjoints instead of identities, when the class structures are explicit.

These findings do not vary as a function of test phase. Attempts to help subjects construct unmixed compositions by identities during phase II were completely unsuccessful. Nor did the countercondition presented in phase III result in any reconstruction of the mixed compositional presentations into unmixed compositions. Indeed, if our hypothesis that subjects predicate by negation at this stage is correct, then phase III does not constitute a countercondition for these subjects. It merely replicates or confirms the negation structure of subjects' own predication.

5

Isolated Deforming and Decomposing

Transformations of quasi-continuous like discrete objects are predominantly unary. Long sequences of consecutive mappings are applied to individual objects before subjects switch to transacting with another object. The result is that the rate at which mappings are changed greatly exceeds the rate at which objects are switched. The change ratio in which mappings predominate over objects is as much a constant of 6-month-olds' transactions with quasi-continuous objects, as with discrete objects.

Compactness also marks subjects' transactions with quasi-continuous objects. A small set of mapping forms are applied. Many mapping forms overlap with those applied to discrete objects, such as pushing, holding, dropping, mouthing, and hitting.

The transformational consequences of similar mapping forms for quasi-continuous objects only partially overlap with the consequences for discrete objects. Some mapping forms merely transform the kinetic, locational, and other properties of quasi-continuous objects, as they do discrete objects. Others result in additional transformations possible only in quasi-continuous objects. For instance, a hand hitting an object may have the same result, such as displacing it, whether it is discrete or quasi-continuous. In addition, it may result in deforming the shape of a quasi-continuous object, breaking it open, decomposing it into two pieces, and so on.

Some mapping forms are beginning to be applied only or predominantly to quasi-continuous objects, such as digging fingers into an object or repeatedly opening and closing a hand on an object. The resultant transformations are unique, for example, indentations or holes. Overall, then, the semantic domains of discrete and quasi-continuous objects overlap partially. Proper and consistent mapping distinctions are already beginning to be made between these two kinds of objects.

The unique properties of combinativity proto-operations on quasi-continuous objects are the topic of discussion here. Two transformations dominate their original constructions. These are direct deformation and decomposition proto-operations. A third, coordinative structure of deformations and decompositions is also in its initial stage of development. Recompositions are barely emerging, and compositions are yet to develop. Thus, all the transformations generated are only irreversible proto-operations.

The result is that the total organization of transformations consists of direct and coordinative proto-operations which negate the initial part–whole structure within and between quasi-continuous objects. Moreover, they are labile and fundamentally segregated transformations, with precursory exceptions, particularly, rudimentary coordination between the negation proto-operations of deforming and decomposing. It should therefore be underlined that decomposing multiplies one into many objects in only a precursory sense. It does not construct a set of elements for at least two reasons: Decomposing is rarely generated consecutively or simultaneously, and, new elements are discarded as soon as they are created.

I. Direct Deforming

Deforming is generated frequently (Table 5.1, Row 1). The mean frequency is four per minute during the spontaneous phase I when one object is presented. This rate does not vary as a function of the objects' form; that is, whether it is a Euclidean ball or a topological circular ring. The mean frequency increases a bit to five per minute during the provoked phase II. It should be recalled, however, that this phase does not involve any experimental manipulations designed to provoke deforming. On the contrary it is designed to provoke decomposing and composing by the experimenter modeling these transformations.

The mean frequency of deforming is a bit higher when three objects are presented; six per minute in the spontaneous phase and five per minute in the provoked phase. Again the form of the objects, Euclidean or topological, does not affect the rate of deforming. It is unlikely that this

TABLE 5.1

Mean Frequency of Combinativity Proto-operations Generated by 6-Month-Old Subjects in Quasi-Continuous and Discrete–Quasi-Continuous Conditions

	One object		Three objects		Discrete–Quasi-Continuous	
	1 *Phase I*	*2* *Phase II*	*3* *Phase I*	*4* *Phase II*	*5* *Phase I*	*6* *Phase II*
1. Deforming	8.20 (2.00)[a]	5.25 (3.00)	12.50 (5.00)	5.00 (3.50)	6.00 (3.00)	4.25 (0.50)
2. Reforming	0.00	0.00	0.00	0.00	0.00	0.00
3. Breaking	0.60	0.25	0.00	0.50	0.25	0.00
4. Reconstructing	0.00	0.00	0.00	0.00	0.00	0.00
5. Decomposing	2.80 (0.1)	0.75	2.00	1.00	1.75	0.25
6. Recomposing	0.10	0.00	0.50	0.00	0.25	0.00
7. Composing	0.00	0.00	0.00	0.00	0.00	0.00
8. Redecomposing	0.00	0.00	0.00	0.00	0.00	0.00
9. Attaching	—	—	—	—	0.00	0.00
10. Detaching	—	—	—	—	0.25	0.75
11. Number of subjects	10	4	4	2	4	4
12. Mean duration	2 min 07 sec	1 min 07 sec	2 min 00 sec	0 min 30 sec	1 min 08 sec	1 min 11 sec
13. Discrete compositions	1.00	1.50	3.00	0.00	2.00	3.25
14. Rate of productivity	0.47	1.34	1.50	0.00	1.77	2.75

[a] Mean frequencies of proto-operations involving multiple transformations are given in parentheses.

small difference in rate when one or three objects are presented is significant. It is based on only four subjects tested with three objects.

The mean frequency of deforming remains constant even when the subjects are presented with conditions combining discrete with quasi-continuous objects; that is, a Play-Doh ball, a tongue depressor, and a Play-Doh ball with a tongue depressor stuck in one end. The rate is six per minute in the spontaneous and four per minute in the provoked phase. What emerges, then, is a uniform production picture of deforming rate. The range is between four and six deformations per minute.

Deforming is a totally irreversible proto-operation at this stage. It is never followed by any reforming transformations (Table 5.1, Row 2). Deforming negates preexisting internal relations between parts of a quasi-continuous object and the whole object. It transforms those relations into new internal relations between parts and the whole elements. Negation is not yet compensated at all during this stage. Initial internal part–whole relations are not affirmed by any attempts to reform them. No intensive identity proto-operations are constructed. All quasi-continuous objects presented, one or three, are deformed, never reformed.

Logically entailed deformations predominate. The very structure of (a) the mappings applied to (b) the relatively nonresistant matter of quasi-continuous objects, necessitates deformation. To illustrate, when fingers are pressed into a quasi-continuous object the only possible results are indentations, that is, deformations in the objects' internal part–whole relations.

Logically entailed deformations also entail synchronic tactilokinesthetic perception by the subjects of both (a) their own transformational proto-operations as they are in the process of producing deformations and (b) the ongoing resultant transformations in the part–whole relations internal to the quasi-continuous objects. Inherent, then, in the structure of deformation proto-operations is immediate feedback on and monitoring of the constructive process itself. Thus, the necessary conditions to begin to regulate deforming are already constituent properties of the structure of deforming.

Contingent deformation is just originating. It involves using independent objects to produce deformations. Contingent deformations are more than intersective functions of the structure of mappings by individual quasi-continuous objects. They vary as a function of the particular physical properties of another object (e.g., the surface properties of the table top when the subjects rub a ball across its surface).

The most infrequent contingent deformations are produced by using either a discrete (tongue depressor) or a quasi-continuous (Play-Doh) object to transform a quasi-continuous object. Instrumental contingent deforming embodies unique proto-operational properties when both objects are quasi-continuous:

14. *RH rubs Ball 1 very slightly and briefly on Ball 2*   (6TT, page 38)

Reciprocal deforming is a new proto-operational possibility generated by this transformational form. Both the agent and the patient objects' internal part–whole relations are transformed simultaneously. As evident from the protocol fragment, reciprocal deformation is only generated in a rudimentary, precursory form at this stage. It is momentary and not reproduced in any way.

Only half of the subjects, five out of ten, generated any contingent deformations at all in any of the conditions or test phases. Two subjects generated contingent deformations only once; two subjects reproduced one contingent deformation twice in a row; and two subjects produced numerous contingent deformations, including many reproductions (e.g., banging a ring into a deformed mass on the table top).

Deforming is primarily a unary proto-operation at this stage. Many deformations consist of isolated transformations of single objects. Yet, even these are becoming regulated. A substantial proportion of unary deformations include multiple, consecutive or simultaneous deformations in a single object (Table 5.1, Row 1, figures in parentheses). Multiple consecutive deformations involve successive reproductions of the same mapping (e.g., rapidly repeated squeezing). Multiple simultaneous deformations involve synchronic reproductions of the same mapping (e.g., poking several fingers into an object at the same time).

Even rudimentary regulated deforming is featured by the subjects observing the component mappings, objects, and resultant transformations. Objects are examined as soon as they are presented, and followed immediately by deforming them:

3. *looks at Ball as LH fingers it a little bit*
4. *LH touches B so that it rolls minutely back and forth toward self and away, several times*
5. *LH fingers depress B such that several little holes are made in it*
                                                                (6DF, page 48)

The object is examined in a variety of ways before 6DF deforms it. Only after examining it visually, motorically, and tactually does the subject proceed. It is as though the subject first determines that the object has a quasi-continuous structure appropriate to deformations. Indeed, his next full transformation of the object is to deform it in a more differentiated way:

9.5. *RH pinches Ball between thumb and index, making indentations*
                                                                (6DF, page 48)

Elaboration of differentiated reciprocal pinching between the thumb and index finger following gross depressing by the fingers is a further indication that deforming is becoming regulated.

Objects of deformation are observed as the subjects are in the process of transforming them:

13.5.   *RH makes open-close movements on Ball, producing indentations*
13.5.   *looks at B*   (6AB, page 45)

 7.5.   *LH fingers press into Ball 1 in nine separate squeeze motions, in about 15 seconds*
 7.5.   *looks intently at this at about eye level for first half, then looks toward mother for second half*
 7.5a. *as a progressive result, B1 becomes first indented from fingers, then more obviously deformed*   (6AW, page 18)

In these ways subjects monitor both (*a*) their own ongoing transformations and (*b*) the corresponding resultant multiple sequential deformations in the objects' internal part–whole relations.

Subjects also begin to observe the objects of their deformations before and after they have transformed them. This makes it possible to compare objects' initial and final internal part–whole relations. Thus, the basis for determining the transformational properties of deforming is produced:

1.   *LH lifts Ball*
2.   *LH holds B in air briefly, looking at it*
3.   *LH pushes one finger into B, making an indentation mark*
4.   *LH drops B onto table and it rolls a few inches toward experimenter*
5.   *looks at B, as rests LH on table*
     (experimenter places B closer to subject)
6.   *LH fingers grasp B such that they make slight indentation marks*
                                                                   (6SA, page 33)

1.   *looks from experimenter to Ball to experimenter to lap to B to experimenter to lap*
2.   *RH grasps B and rotates it in air as raises it slightly off table*
3.   *LH grasps B*
4.   *BH put B to mouth*
5.   *LH lets go, RH holds B to mouth as makes chewing motions on the end of it*
5a. *subject's fingers have made indentations in B*
6.   *bites B or makes like he's taking a bite out of it*
7.   *LH grasps B such that BH hold it to mouth as bites it again*
8.   *BH take B down from mouth and looks at it*
9.   *BH put B to mouth again and mouths on it five seconds, changing its shape*
10. *BH lower B down from mouth and looks at it* (6AB, pages 44 and 45)

Subject 6SA looks at the object before (Line 2) and after (Line 5) the first deformation. This is followed immediately by multiple deformations (Line 6). Subject 6AB inspects the object visually and motorically (Lines 1–2) before multiply deforming it (Lines 5–7). He looks at the resultant transformation (Line 8). He makes some additional multiple deformations in the object (Line 9) and looks at the resultant transformations (Line 10).

These behaviors indicate that deforming is becoming regulated. The transformations are beginning to be reproduced frequently in a somewhat directed, controlled, and differentiated manner. Moreover, they are beginning to be monitored before, during, and after their execution. It should not be forgotten that most deformations produced at this stage are logically entailed. Thus, visiomotor and tactual monitoring of deforming complements, reinforces, and extends the ongoing tactilokinesthetic perception of the entire process which is inherent in the structure of logically entailed deformations.

II. Rudimentary Equivalence and Order Relations between Deformations

Multiple synchronic deforming is clearly produced by at least half the subjects at this stage. These produce multiple protocorresponding part–whole transformations within the same quasi-continuous object. As a reminder it may help to repeat one line from a previously presented protocol fragment:

> 5. *LH fingers depress Ball such that several little holes are made in clay*
> (6DF, page 48)

These multiple one-to-one protocorrespondences between deformations within individual objects are produced simultaneously. They provide the pragmatic constructions necessary for comparing and determining multiple equivalence relations between single-unit part–whole transformations. They are particulary fecund in this regard. The traces of deforming are recorded and preserved in the object. So, the protocorresponding deformations are readily observable until subjects further transform the objects.

Protocorresponding equivalence relations between synchronic part–whole deformations are precursory structures at this stage. As just noted, they are clearly produced by only half of the subjects. Most of the remaining subjects do, however, produce more obscure antecedent forms of protocorrespondences. They generate multiple but asynchronous deformations at different locations within individual objects. Again, the physical structure of quasi-continuous objects is such as to promote recording and preserving even successive deformations. For instance, successive poking in different places on the surface of a ball leaves indentation marks. The result is that some asynchronous deformings become synchronic protocorresponding deformations. Thus, antecedent conditions are generated for the formation of equivalence relations between part–whole transformations.

With one exception, precursory protocorresponding deformations are limited to producing equivalences within one set of transformations. They are constructed within individual objects. Some subjects begin to produce them within two objects, but then they are generated asynchronously. Multiple protocorresponding deformations are produced within one object. The object is discarded. Another object is transacted with. At some point, within lengthy sequences of transaction with the new object, multiple protocorresponding deformations are produced within it. No attempts are made by subjects to compare, in any way, the two sets of protocorresponding deformations they produce at different times. Therefore, there is no way in which they can begin to compare and determine equivalences between these two sets of part–whole transformations. This is the case even though these subjects have actually constructed equivalences between two sets of deformations.

Nevertheless, these behaviors provide evidence that significant aspects of constructive transformations necessary to the formation of equivalence relations between sets of deformations are beginning to be generated. This hypothesis is supported by the one exception alluded to at the beginning of the previous paragraph. One of the four subjects presented with three objects produced many multiple synchronic deformations in two objects at the same time. The list of productions in order generated, but omitting intervening transactions, are:

17.5. *LH fingers continue both squeezing and depressing into Piece 1 for about 10 seconds*

17.5. *RH engages in more of a flicking of the fingers onto and into Piece 2 for about 10 seconds*

17.5a. *in BH, Play-Doh is deformed quite noticeably*

17.5aa. *after about 10 seconds, a little bit falls from RH on table in front of subject*

19.5. *LH fingers continue both squeezing and depressing into P1*

19.5. *RH makes more squeezing-like movements into P2*   (6AW, page 19)

22.5. *LH lifts Piece 1 and begins squeezing into it*

22.5. *RH fingers both squeeze and depress into Piece 2*
    (*experimenter draws attention to the other two Balls in front of subject by wagging them in air then dropping them on table in front of subject*)

24.5. *LH makes smaller open-close movements on P1*

24.5. *RH really splays open fingers, then depresses fingers, grossly transforming appearance of P2*   (6AW, page 19)

34.5. *RH fingers repeatedly open and close into Piece 3*

34.5. *LH fingers repeatedly open and close into Piece 4 (such that BH are engaged in the same, symmetrically performed actions*   (6AW, page 20)

47.5. *LH fingers maul Small Ball*

47.5. *RH fingers maul Large Ball*   (6AW, page 21)

Repeated protocorresponding sets of deformations are produced in two objects by 6AW. They extend over sizable durations and several mapping forms. Most resulting protocorrespondences in part–whole transformations, however, are global and labile. They are the products of continuous squeezing, depressing, and mauling. The most differentiated are the result of opening–closing fingers on two objects (Lines 34.5). But even these are labile. They are repeated rapidly and continuously such that the protocorresponding sets of transformations last only as long as the process of construction. Then they are erased by successor deformations. Lability of construction and impermanence of protocorresponding transformations is not sufficient to observe and record equivalence relations between two sets of deformations. It is sufficient to the formation of precursors to equivalence relations between two sets of internal part–whole relations within two objects.

Precursory ordered deforming is generated frequently. All are limited to seriated transformations in the part–whole relations within individual objects. The most frequent increasing deformations are produced by continuous mappings, particularly, continuously pulling on an object. Consequently, objects are progressively elongated, often until a piece is pulled off, resulting in a decomposition as well.

Discrete, progressively increasing deformations are generated rarely:

8.7. *RH index finger plucks twice at Ball 1 held in LH*

10. *RH pulls at B1 held in LH*

10a. *RH pulls off the major part of B1, such that it adheres to the RH thumb*   (6AW, page 18)

Discretely increasing deformations are more articulate than continuously increasing deformations. Resultant continuous increases are not at all detached from continuous deforming proto-operations producing them. Discrete increases are just beginning to be detached from discrete deforming proto-operations. The cumulative effect is different from each deformation. It is therefore to be expected that continuous deforming should predominate over discrete deforming at the origins of ordered part–whole transformations within individual objects.

The most frequently produced decreasingly ordered deformations are also continuous. Typically, individual objects are squeezed continuously such that they become progressively thinner, often until the object is decomposed into two pieces. Some even involve contingent deformation:

9. *RH hits Piece 1 twice down onto the table, releasing it after second hit*
17. *RH hits Piece 1 a few times down onto the table*   (6AM, page 24)

The object becomes progressively flattened as a consequence of being hit down successively onto the table. Successive transformations also provide the necessary conditions for articulating discrete decreasing orders. As with the production of increasing series, discrete decreasing orders are generated less frequently than continuous decreasing series at this precursory stage.

No attempts are made to coordinate increasing with decreasing orders. No sequences are generated in which progressive series of deformations even fluctuate between increasing and decreasing part–whole transformations, such as by pulling and squeezing at the same time or in sequence. Actively constructed compensations of increasing for decreasing or decreasing for increasing deformations are not generated in any way.

Yet, their antecedents are inherent in the structure of both increasing and decreasing series generated at this stage. The structure of deforming quasi-continuous objects insures that each increasing and decreasing progression is simultaneously compensated for by its reciprocal decreasing and increasing progression. As a quasi-continuous object is elongated it is also thinned; as it is flattened it is also widened; and so on. Compensation is logically entailed in the construction of all progressive series of part–whole deformations within individual objects. The necessary conditions for protoinferential reciprocal ordering are thereby generated every time the subjects produce either an increasing or decreasing series.

III. Direct Decomposing

Breaking quasi-continuous objects is generated by a few subjects but infrequently (Table 5.1, Row 3). It is limited to breaking open ring-shaped objects into strands. Subjects never break Euclidean objects, such as by punching holes through them. Broken rings, that is, strands, are never reconstructed into anything resembling rings again (Table 5.1, Row 4). Breaking is a totally irreversible transformation at its origins.

Decomposing is generated by all subjects and with some frequency (Table 5.1, Row 5, Columns 1, 3, and 5). The frequency does not vary with the number of objects presented nor with the object type, Euclidean or topological-like. The frequency figures given in Table 5.1 for decomposing are necessarily underestimates. The reason is that, when possible, subjects were not permitted to decompose objects by biting pieces off. When subjects nevertheless managed to bite a piece off, it often resulted in premature termination of the condition.

Modeling decomposing during phase II has no effect upon the frequency (Table 5.1, Row 5, Columns 2 and 4). Moreover, subjects never follow the experimenter's decomposing with decomposing as their first form of transforming objects. The first follow-up transformations by subjects are always deforming the objects. The frequency of deformations (Table 5.1, Row 1, Columns 2 and 4) is five times that of decomposing even though deforming was not modeled.

Decomposing is usually a direct intersective result of mappings by objects, for instance, pulling, pinching, or scraping a piece off a ball. Decomposing which is contingent on another object is produced even less frequently than contingent deformation:

47.   *LH raises Ball in air, as looks at it*
48.   *LH hits B twice on table, releasing it after second hit*
48a. *B splits such that a small piece remains in LH*   (6SA, page 34)

Subject 6SA observes the object before decomposing it (Line 47). Other subjects observe the results of their decomposing:

10.   *RH pulls at Ball 1 held in LH*
10a. *the major part of B1 comes off, such that it adheres to the RH thumb*
11.5. *stares at the Large Piece attached to the RH thumb, as slowly moves it a little*   (6AW, page 18)

Prevision and postvision of decomposing indicates that decomposing is beginning to be regulated. Subjects observe themselves decompose one into multiple objects, thereby transforming the part–whole relations between objects. Decomposing changes both the extent and the form (quality) of objects. Most importantly, decomposing changes the quantity, from one into many objects. It constructs many smaller elements out of one bigger element. Thus, decomposing involves simultaneous (*a*) protomultiplication of one element into many elements and (*b*) protodivision of a large extent into smaller magnitudes.

While they do observe their decomposing, subjects never generate two or more temporally consecutive decompositions. Here is the only exception produced by any of the ten subjects throughout all the testing:

24.   *RH repeatedly knocks off little bits with coordinate end of second and third fingers from Ball held by LH*
24a. *two or three little bits fall off onto table*   (6AW, page 22)

As in all other transformations of quasi-continuous objects, 6AW generates the most advanced decomposing. She transforms one object into a set of three or four objects. Even the set she constructs is small in number, and her set is labile. She discards the elements as soon as she creates them. In no way does she preserve the elements together as a collected set of objects.

Simultaneous decomposing is generated rarely. It is limited to the production of the smallest sets possible, two-object sets. Yet the sets may be preserved for some duration:

> 52. *LH fingers rub Ball and grasp at it*
> 52a. *LH thumb and third finger have pieces on them*   (6DF, page 50)

The very structure of decomposing quasi-continuous objects often insures, as it does in the present instance, that the several objects will be preserved together for some time. It is difficult to detach them once they are stuck to the fingers.

In addition to multiplying elements, decomposing divides magnitudes. The resultant new multiple elements are always smaller than the single element out of which they are generated. Inherent, then, in the structure of decomposing quasi-continuous objects is the construction of consecutive orders of decreasing magnitudes. Given the lability and impermanence of decomposing at this stage, these constructions can only establish the barest precursory outlines of progressively decreasing orders. They are limited to the two-step orders ⟨big, smaller⟩.

Most of the time, decomposing divides the initial object into two elements unequal in size:

> 39. *RH taps Ring on table*
> 39a. *R is broken into two, with the Large Piece falling on the table and the Small Piece remaining in the RH*
> 40.5. *RH brings SP toward self*
> 40.5. *LH touches LP*   (6NF, page 25)

Subject 6NF's contingent decomposing (Line 39) results in a big and a small object (Line 39a). Then she simultaneously transacts with both of them (Lines 40.5).

In ways such as this, subjects' simultaneous decomposings construct ordered differences between the magnitudes of two elements. These synchronic orders are limited, at this stage, to two magnitudes, big and small. They are never extended to three magnitudes.

Conditions necessary to coordinating decomposing with deforming are beginning to be generated. One condition is inherent in the structure of decomposing itself. Every time an object is decomposed into two or more objects then the initial object is deformed as well. The internal part-whole relation within the initial object is transformed at the same time as it is multiplied into many objects and divided into smaller sizes.

Coordination is not inherent in the structure of deforming. As we have seen, most transformations of quasi-continuous objects consist of deforming without decomposing them. Yet, as we have also had occasion to see, some deforming is prolonged into decomposing. It may be useful to provide an additional illustration:

85. *LH shakes Ball 3 above table as squeezes and deforms it*
85a. *such that eventually Small Piece of Ball 3 breaks off in LH fingers as Large Piece of B3 falls to table*   (6NF, page 29)

Multiple extended deformations upon a single object are elaborated into decomposing it into two objects, one large and one small.

Decomposing is sometimes elaborated into deforming one of the new objects:

 7. *looks at Strand in RH*
 8. *RH opens and closes a little bit on S*
 8a. *a Little Piece comes off such that it is stuck to fingers*
8aa. *the rest drops to the table*
 9. *pulls RH to body as turns around and looks at mother (first time)*
10. *RH fingers wiggle LP in air a little, slowly (LP still stuck to fingers)*
11.5. *RH opens and closes on LP several times*   (6CB, page 29)

Decomposing is preceded by visual observation of the object (Line 7). It is extended into deforming by prolonging the same mapping form, opening-closing the hand on the Play-Doh (Lines 8 and 11.5).

One other condition necessary to coordinating deforming with decomposing is generated by subjects. One object is simultaneously (*a*) deformed by one organ while (*b*) it is decomposed by another organ:

9.5. *RH pinches Ball between thumb and index finger, making indentations*
9.5. *LH pulls a little piece off B*   (6DF, page 48)

None of these conditions necessary to the development of a coordinated structure of deforming and decomposing is generated frequently. Together, however, they provide a solid foundation for its precursory development. In fact it is the only precursory coordinated structure of protocombinativity manifested with any degree of frequency at this stage. Also, it combines the two main forms of negating the internal part–whole relations within quasi-continuous objects.

IV. Absence of Composing

Decomposing of an initial object is rarely compensated for by recomposing the descendant multiple elements back into one object (Table 5.1,

Row 6). When generated, recomposing never exceeds uniting two descendant objects. As usual, subject 6AW is exceptional. She is the only subject who generated recomposing. One recomposition follows upon the protocol fragment (p. 18, Lines 10–11.5) presented above on page 111:

11.5.   LH *continues to rhythmically squeeze the remaining Small Piece*
13.   LH *grasps back the Larger Piece from RH thumb and rejoins it with the remainder SP that was in LH*
14.5.   LH *continues rhythmic depressing of fingers and squeezing into Combined Piece*
14.5a. *such that it is grossly deformed*   (6AW, page 18)

Recomposition follows immediately after decomposition, but the recomposition prolongs the deformation 6AW is continuously producing with her left hand. Therefore, the extent but not the intensity (form) of the initial object is recomposed.

The other two recompositions generated by 6AW are even more automatic prolongations of ongoing deformation. One recomposition follows upon the protocol fragment (p. 18, Lines 7.5–7.5a) presented on page 106:

7.5aa. *as another result, at some point in the LH fingers' rhythmic squishing, a Little Piece adheres to the thumb, separating from Ball 1*
8.   LH *fingers continue their squeezing such that LP immediately readheres to B1*   (6AW, page 18)

Similarly, the other recomposition is logically entailed by the ongoing mappings:

42.5.   LH *squeezes Ball*
42.5a. *B falls onto the table and a Little Piece remains in LH*
44.7.   LH *grabs onto B*
44.7a. *the LP readheres to B*   (6AW, page 23)

These recompositions do not reconstitute the form of the initial object. They barely begin to reconstitute its extent, both in number and size. Thus, they generate the origins of precursory inverse proto-operations upon quasi-continuous objects. They are nothing more than pragmatic forms of protoreversibility. Decomposing negates the initial extent by breaking it up, that is, by multiplying the number and by dividing the mass. Recomposing affirms the initial extent by putting the broken elements back together again, that is, by adding them together into one object.

Composing, even less than recomposing, is not yet part of the structure of combinativity at this stage. No subjects generate any composition when presented with several quasi-continuous objects (Table 5.1, Row 7,

Column 3). As far as composing is concerned, transactions with three quasi-continuous objects are in no way different from those produced when subjects transact with a single quasi-continuous object. They evidence no signs of composing. Rather, subjects generate an equal amount of deforming and decomposing (Table 5.1, Rows 1 and 5, Column 3) as they do when presented with only one object (Rows 1 and 5, Column 1).

The absence of composition cannot be attributed to any lack of requisite perceptual-motor skills by 6-month-olds. The subjects serve as their own controls in this regard. All the skills necessary for composing quasi-continuous Play-Doh objects are also embodied in the requisite skills for deforming. These include pushing, pressing, and opening–closing the hand or fingers, and 6-month olds generate plenty of deforming. Were this not sufficient, we also have evidence of some recomposing by one subject. Obviously, the same perceptual-motor skills are necessary for recomposing as for composing. Yet, while this subject sometimes recomposes a single object she has taken apart, she never composes two objects into one.

Modeling composing has no effect (Table 5.1, Row 7, Columns 2 and 4). No subjects ever composed after observing the experimenter compose two objects. Rather, they continue to generate about the same rate of deforming and decomposing as they do spontaneously (Table 5.1, Rows 1 and 5, Columns 2 and 4).

The absence of quasi-continuous composing is not compensated by more frequent discrete composing, whether of stabiles or mobiles (Table 5.1, Rows 13 and 14). In fact, quasi-continuous objects have the effect of depressing the rate of discrete composing. Discrete composing productivity is much lower in all quasi-continuous conditions (Table 5.1, Row 14) than in all discrete conditions (Table 3.1, Row 3, Chapter 3, page 53). These differences further indicate that infants at Stage 1 already make appropriate and consistent mapping and combinativity differentiations between the structures of discrete and quasi-continuous objects. They are beginning to be distinguished into separate semantic domains as a function of the differential mapping forms by which they are transformed. They are also beginning to be distinguished into separate physical phenomena by the differential combinativity proto-operations to which they are subjected.

The results are similar in the combined discrete–quasi-continuous condition. No composing is generated in either the spontaneous or the provoked phase (Table 5.1, Row 7, Columns 5 and 6). The rate of decomposing is at least that produced in the purely quasi-continuous conditions (Table 5.1, Row 5, Columns 5 and 6); and recomposing is generated once by one subject (Table 5.1, Row 6, Column 5).

The results on attaching and detaching discrete and quasi-continuous objects consistently round out the picture on protocombinativity. No subjects attach discrete to quasi-continuous objects (Table 5.1, Row 9, Columns 5 and 6). One subject detaches the discrete from the quasi-continuous object during the spontaneous phase (Table 5.1, Row 10, Column 5):

> 23.   *LH pulls Tongue Depressor off TD + Ball, upward*
> 23a. *B becomes detached from TD + B*   (6NF, page 33)

Three subjects detach them during the provoked phase in which the experimenter modeled both attaching and detaching (Table 5.1, Row 10, Column 6):

> 45.   *LH shakes Tongue Depressor + Ball on table*
> 45a. *B becomes dislodged from TD*   (6NF, page 34)
>
> 4.   *RH pulls Ball off Tongue Depressor + Ball held by LH* (6AW, page 24)
>
> 19.   *LH drops Tongue Depressor + Ball to the floor*
> 19a. *TD comes apart from B as LH releases TD + B*   (6TT, page 42)

With one recomposing exception, all combinativity proto-operations generated in the discrete–quasi-continuous conditions negate the initial state of the objects. As in the quasi-continuous conditions, subjects deform, break, and decompose. In addition, they detach combined discrete–quasi-continuous objects. With the exception of the one recomposing, subjects never affirm by composing quasi-continuous objects or attaching discrete and quasi-continuous objects.

II

STAGE 2 AT EIGHT MONTHS: CONSOLIDATION OF ELEMENTARY TRANSFORMATIONS

6

Flexible Unary Transactions

Flexibility in coordination and regulation marks all transformational transactions during this transitional stage. While unary transformations are still the mode, the decided shift is toward their coordination into binary proto-operations. The subset of protosymbolic mappings is elaborated to include the origins of analogical gestures, such as the rudiments of "pretending" to throw an object before actually throwing it.

Progressive regulation applies to all forms of protoinferential transformations generated. Increasingly, subjects reproduce and observe the transformations they are constructing. This applies to (*a*) the initial pretransformational state of affairs, (*b*) the ongoing processes of their transformations, and (*c*) the resultant products of their constructions.

Much effort is put into establishing constant given elements subject to further protoinferential consideration (e.g., as elements of a set). Objects are subjected to a myriad of coordinated inverse transformations and comparative observational methods. While restricted in the main to determining the existential properties of individual objects, these coordinations are becoming sufficiently flexible to begin to be extended in two additional directions. First, they are beginning to be used to differentiate parts from the whole of individual objects. Second, they are increasingly used to compare two individual objects to each other. By themselves, these coordinations provide a progressively regulated proto-operational foundation for constructing constant, given elements out of pragmatic objects. Determining the existential properties of objects is beginning to be augmented by the origins of protoexperimentational operations. They are beginning to be used to determine the causal properties of objects and their physical relations to each other.

Progress in the construction of given elements enhances the consolidation and extension of protoinferential relations. Thus, as we shall see, protocorrespondence relations are becoming progressively extended. This includes the beginnings of regulated three-unit protoequivalences. As we shall also see, subjects generate progressively regulated and extended protoaddition and protosubtraction resulting in ordered quantitative nonequivalence.

I. Regulating Mappings upon Objects

The majority of transactions still consist of successive unary mappings upon singular objects. At the same time, the extent of transformative transactions progress in both their mappings and their objects components.

Binary mappings are becoming more frequent. Two identical mappings are applied simultaneously to the same singular object:

16. *BH slowly move Triangular Column 2 near to face, as looking at it*
17. *RH lets go momentarily and then regrasps while holds TC2 very near mouth, looking closely and making mouthing movements*
    subject: *(quiet vocalizing)*
18. *BH lower and raise TC2 to lap and back in front of face, three times—holds TC2 in front of face after third time*
    (experimenter picks up Triangular Column 1 and holds it up to her own face)
19. *BH lower TC2 to lap as watches experimenter*
    subject: *(vocalizes)*
20. *BH raise and lower TC2 in front of self a few more times, this time not raising it as high as had before—still watching experimenter*
    (experimenter "bounces" TC1 toward subject, then replaces TC1 in array)
21. *BH hold TC2 down near lap*   (8PM, pages 25 and 26)

More frequently, two coordinate but different mappings are applied to the same singular object:

7.3. *while looking closely at Triangular Column 2, LH starts to raise TC2 from lap*
7.7. *RH adjusts grasp, grasping it around middle*
9.3. *RH raises TC2 from lap to table*
9.7. *LH lets go*   (8PM, page 25)

12.3. *LH extends to Triangular Column 2*
12.7. *RH starts to upright TC2*
14.3. *LH touches TC2*
14.7. *RH raises it off table*   (*8PM, page 25*)

At its most advanced, coordination of different mappings takes a reciprocal form:

23. *looks at Triangular Column 2 as RH raises it slowly while LH simultaneously touches end of it*
24. *LH grasps end of TC2*
25.5. *LH turns TC2, such that opposite end moves right and toward subject:*

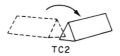

TC2

25.5. *RH releases grasp but continues to touch TC2*
27. *at completion of turn RH grasps opposite end from LH* (*8PM, page 26*)

First, the right hand displaces the object while the left hand touches it. Then the left hand displaces it while the right hand touches it. All the while the subject visually observes the reciprocal binary mappings he is constructing as well as the consequent transformations in the object to which they are applied.

Sequences of consecutive binary mappings are beginning to be generated with some frequency. As evident from the above protocol fragments, these include consecutive binary mappings generated in both partial and total temporal overlap.

Transacting with more than one object at a time is also becoming more frequent. The usual number is two, and the outer limit is three. These usually involve holding at least one object while actively manipulating the others. On the other hand, it is no longer unusual for binary mappings to actively transform both objects when applied to two objects only:

64.3. *RH extends Triangular Column 2 onto table, no release*
64.7. *LH touches Cross Ring 2, moving it a little on table*
66. *LH picks up CR2, displacing Triangular Column 1 to left*
67. *LH lets CR2 go onto table, still touching it*
68.5. *LH slowly picks up CR2*
68.5. *RH turns TC2 on table from diagonal to vertical to diagonal position*
70.5. *looks at CR2 as LH turns CR2 slightly*
70.5. *RH lets go of TC2 and withdraws hand, such that thumb of RH displaces TC2 onto the floor*   (*8PM, pages 28 and 29*)

When both objects are actively transformed the mappings are usually different. The binary mappings may be generated in partial temporal overlap or simultaneously. Yet all subjects[1] generate identical, active binary mappings on two objects at least several times. These active, identical binary forms have special significance for the construction of protoexperiments and protocorrespondences which will be considered in Section III and IV, respectively.

These advances, particularly in the construction of consecutive reciprocal and identical binary mappings, reflect infants' developing capacities to both split and coordinate the constructive transformations which they are generating. Differentiated and integrated binary transformations are progressively regulated. Subjects observe their ongoing process of producing split mappings, relate them to each other with some control, and repeat them with some frequency. These features provide the necessary structural developmental conditions for the creation of regulated protoinferential relations between mappings, such as protocorrespondences.

The change ratio remains substantially constant. Subjects still generate multiple mappings on one object before switching to another; then they generate a sequence of multiple mappings on their new object of transaction; and so on. This is evident from the initial 8PM protocol fragments since all the transactions involved the same object. However, the ratio decreases. More objects are transacted within a given time period. So, the predominance of mappings over objects is reduced. The decrease can only be estimated since, as previously noted in Chapter 2, the boundary between mappings is imprecise.

The three main features of the change ratio found at age 6 months do not change at age 8 months. First, a one-to-one mapping-to-object change ratio is extremely rare. As just noted, the change ratio remains a many-to-one mappings-to-object ratio, although the ratio is decreasing. Second, mapping constancy when changing objects of transaction is still the exception. Usually the mapping changes when the object changes. Third, the majority pattern is one mapping to one object at a time. However, simultaneous or partially overlapping multiple mappings on one object are becoming more frequent. So is single mapping on two or more objects at the same time.

Mapping forms remain compact and repetitive. This transaction constant complements the change ratio, as it did at age 6 months. While remaining compact, mappings progressively differentiate into more specialized and articulate forms:

---

[1] The illustrative protocol fragments are all taken from one subject (8PM) on purpose. This will permit us to make specific longitudinal comparisons (see Chapter 9) with the same subject's (10PM) production of transformative transactions when he is two months older. At the same time, it should be emphasized that the transactions reported in the protocol fragments from 8PM are typical of all the 8-month-old subjects; as are those of 10PM for the 10-month-old subjects.

54. *RH index finger touches Yellow Spoon*
55. *RH index finger scratches the surface of YS*
55a. *displacing YS to left slightly*
56. *RH index finger pushes YS to left*
57. *RH index finger presses onto YS*
58. *RH index finger moves YS back and forth on table*
59. *RH index finger pushes YS to left*   (8PM, page 14)

37. *RH puts Column 2 to mouth*
38. *tongue licks side of C2 held by RH*   (8GP, page 29)

51.5. *LH shakes Receptacle 1*
51.5. *RH waves Column 2 up and down*
53.5. *LH continues shaking R1*
53.5. *RH flings C2*
53.5a. *C2 lands in R1*   (8GP, page 29)

These are but several illustrations of the general progress in differentiating mapping forms. Licking begins to be differentiated from mouthing an object (8GP, Lines 37–38). Throwing an object, such that it becomes an independent missile, is differentiated from waving an object without letting go, in which case it remains a dependent missile (8GP, Lines 51.5–53.5a). Fine movements of individual fingers map touching, scratching, pushing and pressing an object (8PM).

Subjects continue to generate a subset of mappings which have protosymbolic features. No marked general advance was observed in (*a*) anticipatory protogestures, such as opening the mouth prior to bringing something to it; (*b*) reproductive aftergestures, such as continuing to hold the mouth open after removing an object from it; or (*c*) virtual protogestures in which transformations are not consummated. At this stage, however, they are elaborated to include a social dimension. The extension is only precursory and is most evident with respect to virtual protogestures:

45.5. *LH extends Yellow Cross Ring to experimenter*
45.5. *RH extends Green Cross Ring to experimenter*
      (experimenter holds out her hand)
47. *BH withdraw Crosses to self*
48. *turns toward mother*   (8CC, page 17)

By these protocorresponding virtual protogestures of "giving," 8CC draws the experimenter's attention to the objects. Since she does not actually give them to the experimenter, the precursory foundation is laid for symbolic reference to the objects. The reference to the objects is communicative. It is only partially pragmatic because the mappings are not consummated.

One development in protogestural mappings is just beginning to be prepared in rudimentary form. Some analogical protogestures are generated. They are followed up immediately by enactment of the mappings analogized by the protogestures. The protocol fragment (p. 29, Lines 51.5–53.5a) from 8GP presented above provides a good illustration. Subject 8GP repeatedly moves Column 2 up and down without releasing it before flinging it away. The possibility is thereby generated for preparatory gesturing or analogical rehearsal, in this case flinging prior to actually throwing. Indeed, this subject began to visually monitor the process of both his preparatory, gestural, and consequent, enactive mappings:

114.   *RH moves to drop Doll 1 by stretching arm out front, as watching*
114a. *D1 does not drop*
115.   *RH fingers release D1, as watching*
115a. *D1 drops*   (8GP, page 6)

Another frequent early manifestation of analogical pretense is "hesitant" placement of an object. Subjects place an object without releasing it for several seconds before letting go. Often, they visually monitor their protosymbolic constructions, indicating that they are beginning to be regulated. The origins of analogical protosymbolization will be considered further in Section IV because of its potential role as an instrument of protoinferential operations.

II. Constructing Two Objects as Constant Given Elements

Eight-month-olds make marked progress in exploring the existential properties of objects. Comparative exploration has become a well-regulated invariant component in all subjects' constructions of constant given elements. A wide variety of repeated and successive inverse proto-operations are applied to objects. Their application is beginning to be differentiated, such that transformations in particular parts of objects can begin to be selected for special attention and compared with the rest of the object. Subjects use various perceptual modalities to observe both their ongoing proto-operations and the resultant compensatory transformations in the part–whole relations within objects. Moreover, the means of preserving objects in practical memory are becoming more extensive. Developments in means of preserving objects will be reserved for analysis in Section III on causal experimental proto-operations.

Subjects orient more directly toward the objects. Also, they are more likely to inspect them directly. Objects are inspected in advance of, during, and after being transacted with.

Global orientation toward and visual scanning of the whole array of objects when first presented is commonplace:

1. *looks at array* (8DS, page 1)

2. *looks at array* (8NW, page 1)

1. *looks at array as experimenter moves objects toward subject*
2. *looks from left to right of array* (8GP, page 1)

In like manner, so is individualized orientation toward and inspection of single objects as we have already seen in the 8PM protocol fragments presented in Section I. Moreover, different modalities are progressively coordinated with each other in order to carefully examine individual objects:

6.5. *RH holds Brush 1 by bristle end*
6.5. *LH touches and fingers handle end of B1, as looking at it* (8TB, page 8)

12. *RH holds Brush 1 in front of self, vertical in air*
13. *looks at bristle end of B1 for a few seconds, as wiggles RH fingers on bristles, feeling them*
14. *continues to finger B1 bristles with RH, as looks at experimenter* (8TB, page 8)

Split orientation and inspection is just beginning to develop. One modality globally examines the whole array of objects. At the same time another modality individually examines one element within the array:

1. *RH touches Mirror, as looking at array*
2. *RH touching M, as subject looks at experimenter* (8JL, page 1)

Here the subject orients and observes (*a*) the whole set visually and (*b*) one of its elements tactually. This enhances the possibility of differentiating elements from each other. At the same time it makes it possible to coordinate a given element with the set as a whole.

Comparative observation is beginning to be extended toward examining visually one object in relation to a two-object set:

53.5. *RH removes Rectangular Rings 1 and 2 away from mouth, as looks at Square Column 1 and then at RR1 and 2*
53.5. *LH holds SC1* (8NW, page 25)

To the extent that such observations are comparative they are limited to single modal inspection. They do not involve simultaneous transformations of the object and the set. Certainly, they do not involve consecutive inverse transformations necessary to the determination of object identity.

Comparative exploration of part–whole transformations in two singular elements, although still not as frequent as of one object by itself, is no longer unusual. As important, it is becoming semi-systematic and includes repeated inverse transformations:

62.5. *RH holds Circular Ring 3 in air before eyes and rotates CR3 180°, then 180° in other direction, then 180° in initial direction, then 180° reversal*
62.5. *LH holds Circular Ring 2*
64.5. *LH rotates CR2 180°, then 180° reversal, as looks at CR2*
64.5. *RH holds CR3*   (8MM, page 4)

66. *LH rotates Spoon 1 around in mouth, so it's face down in his mouth:*

67. *LH rotates S1 around, so it's face up in his mouth:*

68. *LH rotates S1 around again in mouth to face-down position:*

69. *LH removes S1 from mouth*
70. *looks at S1 held by LH*
71. *RH rotates Cylinder 2 back and forth a few times, as looks at C2*
72. *looks at S1 held by LH*
73. *LH holds S1 in mouth*
74. *RH rotates C2 back and forth, as looks at it*   (8DS, page 16)

These two productions reflect the range of comparing two objects generated at this stage. The first (8MM) involves the same visiomotor coordinations. Inverse part–whole transformations are performed by the hand upon each object and observed visually. The second (8DS) comparison is produced by different coordinations. Inverse part–whole transformations are performed upon one object held by the hand in the mouth and observed tactilokinesthetically by the mouth. Then inverse part–whole transformations are performed by the hand upon the other object and observed visually.

Comparative exploration of transformations in the part–whole structure of single objects has become well-regulated. The essential development is the production of a diversity of reproductive coordinations. This includes subjects observing, at the same time, both (*a*) the ongoing generative process whereby they are constructing inverse protooperations, and (*b*) the successive compensatory transformations through which the object's part–whole states are being related.

Objects are observed visually during repeated inverse rotations by the hand:

112. *RH picks up Doll 1 by head*
113. *RH turns bottom of D1 toward and away from self two times, as watching*
(8GP, page 6)

60.5. *LH rotates Red Hexagonal Column back and forth, about 180° swings, four times, looking at it intently* (8MM, page 34)

Sometimes objects are observed visually in anticipation of, as well as during repeated inverse rotations by the hand:

45. *looks at Circular Ring 2 held by LH*
46. *LH rotates CR2 back and forth several times* (8DS, page 3)

This form of comparative exploration is not only applied repeatedly to one object but repeatedly to two objects in succession:

39.3. *RH holds Yellow Hexagonal Column in front of eyes and rotates it once*
39.7. *LH drops Red Hexagonal Column and grasps YHC along with RH*
39.7a. *RHC falls to lap*
(mother returns RHC upright on table)
41. *BH rotate YHC*
42. *BH drop YHC on the floor to the right*
43. *looks down after YHC on the right*
(experimenter returns YHC upright on table)
44. *RH picks up RHC by clasping its top such that vertical end is projecting in air*
45. *RH rotates RHC 180°*
46. *LH grabs RHC*
47. *BH rotate RHC 180° in other direction*
48. *BH rotate RHC back and forth three times, about 90° swings, looking at it*
(8MM, page 33)

Not only does 8MM engage in manifold inverting the two objects, but he accompanies it with symptoms of practical preservation by searching after one disappearing object (Lines 42–43).

Objects are observed visually during repeated inverse displacements by the hand:

34. *LH moves Blue Brush back and forth, as watching* (8JL, page 31)

Sometimes visual observation of repeated inverse displacements are preceded and succeeded by careful visual inspection of the object. These productions provide all the conditions necessary to compare successive part–whole relations within objects:

16. *BH slowly move Triangular Column 2 near to face, as looking at it*
17. *RH lets go momentarily and then regrasps while LH holds TC2 very near mouth, looking closely and making mouthing movements*
subject: (quiet vocalizing)

18. BH *lower and raise TC2 to lap and back in front of face, three times*
19. BH *hold TC2 in front of face after third time* (8PM, pages 25 and 26)

Objects are observed tactually during repeated rotation:

13. LH *rotates Yellow Clover as touches it with RH*
14. BH *hold YC and looks at it* (8KC, page 12)

8. BH *finger and turn Mirror 1 in front of self, examining it closely*
9. LH *releases momentarily, and RH now holds M1 by mirror end, with the opaque side near his eyes* (8BK, page 15)

It is not unusual for tactilomotor comparative coordination to be followed by visual observation. Objects are explored tactually in between inverse rotations by the hand:

25. LH *rotates Circular Ring 5 over 180°/back 180°*
26. RH *touches CR5*
27. LH *rotates CR5 over 180°* (8DS, page 9)

Objects are observed (*a*) visually during inverse rotations by the hand and (*b*) visually and tactually after inverse rotation:

90. LH *lifts Spoon 2 by rotating it upright and then horizontal in air, as looks at it:*

91.5. *looks at S2*
91.5. RH *touches S2 held by LH* (8TT, page 35)

Objects are observed tactually by the mouth after each transformation in sequences of inverse rotations:

2. LH *brings one end of Green Cylinder to mouth*
3. LH *holds GC down from mouth*
4. LH *inserts second end of GC into mouth*
5. *mouth sucks on GC held by LH*
6. LH *takes GC from mouth*
7. LH *inserts first end of GC in mouth* (8TT, page 8)

Objects are also explored tactilokinesthetically by the mouth during and after each displacement by the hands in a sequence of inverse transformations:

10. *mouths middle of Cylinder 2 held by BH*
11. *looks at experimenter*
12. LH *releases from C2*

13. *RH slides C2 in mouth until has left end in mouth*
14. *looks off to right*
15. *RH slides C2 in mouth until has right end in mouth*
16. *BH hold C2 in mouth*
17. *BH turn C2 in mouth until has left end in mouth*   (8GP, page 20)

Noteworthy in this type of comparative coordination is that both the tactilokinesthetic transformations and observations include back-and-forth inverse displacements of the object. They provide the necessary conditions whereby subjects can (*a*) differentiate the parts (middle, left, and right ends) of an object from each other and (*b*) integrate the parts into a whole object.

Visual and tactual exploration of a differentiated part of an object is coordinated with inverse transformations of the whole object:

26. *BH turn Red Doll in toward self and out away from self, twice, while looking at bottom of doll*   (8BK, page 39)

23. *RH rotates Doll 2 up and down in air as holds the bottom part toward self, while looking at the bottom part:*

24. *inserts RH index finger inside the bottom, partially*   (8AB, page 44)

Occasional subjects are just beginning to coordinate (*a*) inverse proto-operations on the whole object with (*b*) consecutive visual observations of the whole object and particular parts of it:

7. *BH rotate Cup while looking closely at it*
8. *BH rotate C while looking at bottom of cup*
9. *BH rotate C while looking at side of cup*   (8MM, pages 22 and 23)

Subject 8MM repeatedly applies identical inverse transformations to the cup as he successively inspects the whole cup, the bottom of the cup, and finally the side of the cup.

III. Unordered Experimenting with Individual Elements

Causal protoexperimental means of extracting information about discrete elements originate by age 8 months. At this stage the causal proto-operations are precursory, that is, protoexperimental. They develop, over the years, into full-blown experimental means of inducing knowledge about objects and their properties.

At the beginning causal protoexperimentation is limited to single objects, not sets of objects. It consists of nonsystematic and confounded varying of independent variables:

77. *LH picks up Brush 2*
78. *LH drops B2 on the table*
79. *LH picks up B2 and looks at it, while holding Ring 1 in RH*
80. *LH drops B2 on the floor*   (8KC, page 27)

90. *LH picks up Ring 2*
91. *LH drops R2*
92. *watches R2 move on table*   (8KC, page 27)

This protoexperiment is rudimentary in all respects. First 8KC drops Brush 2 on the table (Line 78), then on the floor (Line 80). Then he varies the object from a brush to a ring (Lines 90–91) and the location back to the table (Line 92). Only some causal protoexperimentation is followed by the subject observing the transformational effect upon the object (Line 92). The protoexperimenting is not even sequential with respect to the objects. Many transactions intervene between dropping the brush and the ring. Thus, the conditions are established for linking isolated objects into sets for sequential protoexperiments which develop at the next stage. Then variation begins to be ordered semisystematically.

Even at its origins some causal transformations are preceded by inspection of the instrumental object:

42. *looks down at Circular Ring 3 held by RH*
43. *RH hits CR3 on table twice*   (8MM, page 3)

97. *LH picks up Brush 1*
98. *LH rotates B1 as looks at it, while holding Ring 1 in RH*
99. *LH drops B1*   (8KC, page 28)

There is no indication in the sequence of behaviors that prior inspection, even prior comparative inspection, of the instrumental means determines the subsequent causal transactions. Nevertheless, the necessary conditions for their subsequent coordination are being prepared. Progressively, comparative inspection of the part–whole relations becomes a conceptual means of selecting objects and variables for causal protoexperimental variation in order to determine their effects.

Anticipatory observation of the consequences of causal transformations is just beginning to be generated by a few subjects:

32. *leans over right chair arm and holds the Green Cross over floor with RH, looking down at floor*

33. *RH drops GC onto the floor while looking*
34. *continues to look over right chair arm*
    (as mother retrieves GC)   (8CC, page 16)

49. *leans body over right chair arm as RH holds Green Cross over floor,*
    looking down toward floor
50. *sits up in chair*
51. *leans over right chair arm again, looking toward floor*
52.5. *RH drops GC to floor while looking toward floor* (8CC, pages 17 and 18)

Subject 8CC immediately follows up the last performance with two similar anticipatory causal transformations. It is as though she is just beginning (*a*) to predict and (*b*) to verify the causal effect by both observation and replication.

Cognizance of the dependent variable is not limited to observing what happens:

51. *LH knocks over Doll 1*
51a. *D1 rolls forward*
52. *looks up at experimenter*
    (as experimenter touches D1, rolling it back to place where it fell over)
53. *watches D1's motion*
54. *LH catches D1 on its rebound*   (8GP, page 3)

9. *RH pulls Rectangular Ring 2 toward self*
9a. *RR2 pushes Clover Ring 2 over edge to lap*
10. *LH touches CR2 as it goes over edge*   (8TB, page 31)

This stage, then, marks the origins, however rudimentary, of also manipulating or controlling the effect:

34. *LH picks up Cylinder 2*
35. *LH transfers C2 to RH*
36. *RH holds C2 toward mouth*
37. *looks down*
38. *puts LH on Square Column 1, directly below*
39. *RH hits C2 on SC1*   (8GP, page 35)

By holding Column 1 8GP provides himself with a measure of control over the causal patient; as well as, and simultaneously with, his determination of the causal agent, hitting with Cylinder 2. However, the control is not experimental, and is not yet subjected to ordered variation necessary to differential determination, the hallmark of experimenting. The control is tied to the mappings; it is not part of experimental variation. Thus, what is gained in control is lost in experimental power. This is at the heart of the weakness in protoexperimentational induction during its precursory formation. Protoexperimentation is not yet detached from subjects' mappings. Without it there can be no differentiating of causal contingency from logical entailment. In general, the first stage of proto-experimentation is marked by a lack of differentiation between causal contingency and logical entailment.

Coordination of independent and dependent variables is not limited to simultaneous control, even at this original stage of protoexperimentation. Precursory reciprocity is generated between independent and dependent variables. Usually, reciprocity is limited to coordination between a transformation in the independent variable and a constant dependent variable:

21. *LH throws Rectangular Ring 1 into Receptacle 1 held by RH—it lands around Doll 1*   (8AB, page 48)

29. *LH drops Doll 2 into Receptacle 1*   (8AB, page 48)

3. *LH drops Block 1 in Right Receptacle*   (8KC, page 33)

9. *LH drops Block 1 inside Right Receptacle held by RH* (8KC, page 33)

17. *LH drops Circular Ring 1 in Left Receptacle*   (8KC, page 33)

1. *looks at Receptacle 2 as experimenter places it*
2. *RH takes Cylinder 1 out of mouth*
3. *RH throws C1 in R2*   (8GP, page 27)

61.5. *LH holds Receptacle 1*
61.5. *RH holds Square Column 1 over R1 as looking in R1*
63. *RH drops SC1 in, on top of two blocks in R1*   (8GP, page 30)

127. *RH throws Cylinder 2 toward Receptacle 1 along table*
127a. *C2 hits against side of R1*   (8GP, page 33)

30. *LH flings Triangular Column down such that it hits Cylinder 2*
30a. *C2 rolls to left*   (8GP, page 35)

Some coordinations between independent and constant dependent variables take on a social dimension when the aim is to target the object toward another person:

58. *RH drops Doll 2 in experimenter's RH*   (8GP, page 14)

80. *LH releases Mirror over experimenter's RH*
80a. *M hits experimenter's fingertips and drops to floor*
                                                          (8GP, pages 15 and 16)

109. *RH raises Doll 1*
110. *RH drops D1 abruptly into experimenter's LH*
111. *looks at D1*   (8GP, page 17)

144. *RH raises Mirror over experimenter's LH*
145. *RH drops M in experimenter's LH, as looking at experimenter's hands*
                                                                (8GP, page 18)

Rarely, both independent and dependent variables are transformed simultaneously such that they are reciprocally related to each other:

51.5.   *LH continues shaking Receptacle 1*
51.5.   *RH waves Square Column 2 up and down*
53.5.   *LH continues shaking R1 while looking at it*
53.5.   *RH flings SC2 into R1*   (8GP, page 29)

Both the missile (Column 2) and the target (Receptacle 1) are varied. Subject 8GP throws the column and shakes the receptacle at the same time. These variations are reciprocal to each other. The consequent product is the column landing in the receptacle.

Varying both variables need not be initiated by the subject. The causal patient may be varied by someone else as long as the subject can vary the causal agent:

    (experimenter rolls Cylinder 2 into Spoon 2)
29. *stops activity, watches what experimenter does and LH drops Cup*
30. *RH picks up S2 by its handle*
    (experimenter pushes Cylinder 1 toward subject—it rolls back and forth in front of subject)
31. *watches experimenter's performance*
32. *RH extends S2 toward C1*
33. *RH knocks S2 against C1*
33a. *C1 rolls away*   (8MM, page 24)

The first time the subject is presented with a rolling cylinder he watches it and picks up a spoon. The second time he not only watches the rolling cylinder but hits it with the spoon. The coordinative result is that he reverses the direction in which the cylinder is rolling.

Causal reciprocity is just beginning to be elaborated by a few subjects into transforming ends into means:

48. *RH hits Circular Ring down on top of Triangular Ring*
49. *RH pushes CR against TR*
49a. *TR is displaced to far right*
50. *RH raises CR*
51. *RH places CR on table near TR*
52. *RH picks up TR*
53. *RH hits TR on top of CR*
53a. *CR is displaced*
54. *RH hits TR on top of CR*   (8AB, page 12)

32. *RH holds Cylinder 1 over Cylinder 2, while looking at C2 on table*
33. *RH drops C1 on C2, while looking at C2*
33a. *C1 rolls toward experimenter*
34. *LH picks up and puts C2 in mouth*

35. LH *releases and RH grasps C2 held in mouth*
     (experimenter rolls C1 back to subject)
36. *watches C1 roll back*
37. LH *grasps C1*
38. RH *takes C2 out of mouth, while looking at C1 held by LH*
39. RH *holds C2 over C1, while looking at C1 held by LH*
40. RH *drops C2 on C1, while looking at C1 held by LH*   (8GP, page 21)

The initial target is transformed into an instrument and the initial instrument is transformed into a target. The limit is one reversal between
causal agent and patient. At this stage subjects rarely reverse the causal
roles back to the initial relation constructed. They rarely construct any
causal protocommutative operations (see Chapter 7, Section V).

At age 6 months babies begin to preserve single-element causal events.
They are limited to looking in the direction in which an object drops (see
Chapter 2). That is, they are restricted to single compensatory transformations of tracking disappearing objects. Some 8-month-olds begin to
construct two simultaneous transformations in order to compensate for
disappearing objects:

18. RH *touches Red Doll*
18a. RD *rolls off table onto floor*
19. *as RD rolls to floor, RH jerkily moves after it, following its path, and*
     when it falls looks down on floor after it   (8BK, page 47)

75. RH *pulls at Rectangular Rings 1 and 2 held by LH such that both RR1*
     and RR2 fly out of LH and RH grasp
75a. *one falls to floor, the other to mother's lap*
76. *looks toward floor as RH reaches toward floor, wiggling fingers*
                                                              (8NW, page 26)

The subjects attempt to preserve objects moving away from them by
compensatory tracking via two modalities. Simultaneously, they reach as
well as look after disappearing objects. In the case of 8NW this includes
the possibility of gestural reference by wiggling her fingers at the object on
the floor.

Coordination of binary compensatory transformations lends added
cognitive solidity to events and the preservation of objects. On this
hypothesis we might well expect 8-month-olds to develop collateral symptoms. This is exactly what happens. Eight-month-olds begin to preserve
two-element causal sequences:

66. BH *push Cylinder 2 into Square Column 1*
66a. SC1 *falls to floor*
67. *looks to floor*   (8GP, page 23)

The dependent element (Column 1) is sufficiently differentiated from the causal instrument (Cylinder 2) for the subject to preserve it (Line 67) despite its kinetic transformation. Sequential event preservation of a differentiated causal effect, however, is very impoverished at age 8 months. It does not extend beyond one highly presentational feature of the causal effect. In this particular case the feature which is preserved is the continuous displacement or movement trajectory in space.

IV. Two-Unit Protocorrespondences between Successive Mappings

Mapping protocorrespondences become more frequent at age 8 months. So do the number of mapping forms in which protocorrespondences are generated, such as roll, flick away, knock over, and open–close fingers on an object; although hitting remains a favorite mapping form for constructing protocorrespondences. Discrete protocorrespondences still predominate over continuous protocorrespondences by a factor of about two-to-one.

Most discrete mapping protocorrespondences still construct single-unit equivalences, and most involve only a single reproduction. However, several single-unit reproductions are becoming quite commonplace. Four distinct reproductions are the apparent upper limit:

82. *drops Circular Ring 2 on the table—it lands in between Circular Ring 1 and Block 1*
83. *RH hits on Block 2 held by LH such that B2 falls out of LH onto table:*

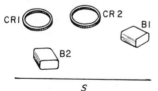

84. *RH hits on table and partially on CR2*
    (experimenter holds up CR2 to subject and drops it on table)
85. *RH lifts CR2 and hits it on table, releasing it*
86. *RH hits on table such that B1 gets pushed to the right and CR2 moves to the left*   (8CC, page 42)

55. *LH hits onto Yellow Clover*
55a. *displacing YC to left*
56. *LH hits on table*
57. *LH touches YC*

58. LH *hits on table*
59. LH *hits onto Green Clover*   (8KC, page 14)

Discrete mapping protocorrespondences which construct multi-unit equivalences are becoming more frequent. Most result in two-unit equivalences:

44. LH *taps Brush 2 on table two times, in front of self, as looks at experi-menter*
45.3. LH *extends B2 to left side of table making contact with table*
45.7. RH *touches Brush 1 to table*
47. LH *taps B2 on table two times, in front of self*   (8TB, page 10)

Discrete mapping protocorrespondences are just beginning to be extended by a few 8-month-olds to the construction of three-unit equivalences:

47. RH *bangs Block 2 on table three times, releasing it after third hit*
48. RH *bangs on top of B2 three times*   (8CC, page 41)

Construction of three-unit equivalences includes rare instances of two distinct protocorresponding reproductions of the initial production:

18. RH *hits Block 2 three times onto table*
19. RH *hits B2 three times onto table*
20. RH *hits B2 three times onto table*   (8TT, page 1)

Thus, the construction of two- and three-unit protoequivalences is just beginning to be regulated.

Simultaneous and partially overlapping discrete protocorrespondences are rarely produced:

63.5. RH *hits Green Clover Ring eight times onto table*
63.5. LH *hits Green Rectangular Ring eight times onto table*
65. RH *and LH alternate in hitting GCR and GRR, respectively, five times onto table*   (8KC, page 14)

Subject 8KC produces a simultaneous eight-unit protocorrespondence followed by an alternating five-unit protocorrespondence. More than likely, however, the protocorrespondences are only between single hitting units reproduced eight times and then five times.

Differentiation possibilities are just beginning to be generated when mappings are generated simultaneously. Not only are the initial protocorrespondences (Lines 63.5) generated by 8KC simultaneous but they are extended both in duration and frequency of repetition. Together these three factors increase the possibilities of focusing upon the part–whole relations within mapping protocorrespondences. This interpretation gains credence from 8KC's next transactions (Line 65). He follows up the initial mapping protocorrespondences with a variant. The first form is simultaneous while the variant is alternating. This reproductive flexibility indicates that these proto-operations are at least partially regulated, that is, involve feedforward with directed modification. As such, they permit increasing control over the protocorresponding products. Controlled variation of the products is an essential ingredient to initially detaching the forms of the resultant protocorrespondences from the forms of the mappings which construct them.

Continuous protocorrespondences are produced a bit more frequently than are discrete protocorrespondences in temporal simultaneity or partial overlap:

70. *LH rotates Doll 1 and Rectangular Ring 1 on table*   (8AB, page 46)

93.5. *RH waves Yellow Hexagonal Column around for 10 seconds*
93.5. *LH waves Red Hexagonal Column around for 10 seconds* (8MM, page 36)

103.3. *RH rotates Yellow Clover*
103.7. *LH rotates Yellow Hexagonal Column*   (8MM, page 36)

Overall, however, there is beginning to develop an apparent temporal lag between the two. Clear construction of discrete protocorrespondences is frequent, varied, and somewhat developed by age 8 months. In comparison, continuous protocorrespondences are relatively rudimentary and infrequent at age 8 months.

The developmental lag is probably due to comparative difficulty in two factors. The first is that it is more difficult to construct and monitor protocorrespondences between continuous than discontinuous phenomena. Discontinuous mapping forms, such as hitting, are already unitized and therefore well-defined by comparison to continuous phenomena. The second is that it is more difficult to determine when subjects are generating continuous than discontinuous protocorrespondences, since it is more difficult to devise operational definitions of continuous protocorrespondences.

Protocorrespondences are often accompanied by visual monitoring of the constructive process. On its surface, visual inspection is directed toward examining the internal part–whole relations in the objects involved. Whether visual observation is also an original step in comparing the unit equivalence relations within mapping protocorrespondences must, for now, remain an open question. What is clearly determinative, however, is that comparative observation is beginning to be directed toward monitoring the productive process, particularly of successive single-unit equivalences:

17. *picks up Red Triangular Column (to right of Blue Brush)*

18. *looking down, RH throws RTC down on table*
18a. *BB is displaced to right*
19. *looks right at BB after RTC lands*
     (experimenter returns RTC)
20. *looks at Red Brush held by LH*
21. *transfers RB to RH*
22. *RH throws RB down onto table in same direction (forward and to left) as*
     RTC was thrown   (8GP, pages 37 and 38)

65. *looks at objects*
66. *LH picks up Blue Brush*
67. *LH jerks BB down*
68. *LH throws BB onto the table, directly down*
69. *looks at BB*
70. *RH picks up BB*
71. *RH jerks BB down, looking down*
72. *RH throws BB down to left*
73. *looks left after BB lands*   (8GP, page 40)

33. *looks down at objects*
34. *RH picks up Blue Triangular Column*
35. *RH jerks BTC up and down, looking straight ahead—not squarely at BTC*
36. *RH throws BTC off to left onto the table*
37. *looks left after it lands*
38. *looks center*
39. *RH picks up Red Triangular Column*
40. *looks down as RH jerks RTC up and down*
41. *RH throws RTC off to the left onto the table*
42. *looks at RTC after it lands*   (8GP, page 42)

Visual monitoring is further evidence that protocorrespondences are becoming progressively regulated protooperations. Entailed is coordination of constructing protocorrespondences while preserving the existential properties of the objects involved. This includes preservation across transformations in the direction of displacement trajectories (e.g., p. 40, Lines 65–73).

Protocorrespondences are just beginning to include analogical protosymbolic features. For instance, 8GP repeatedly precedes throwing an object down by jerking it up and down (p. 40, Lines 65–73; p. 42, Lines 33–42). On other occasions this same subject preceded dropping by its analogical gestural form:

114. *stretches RH arm out front holding Doll 1 in dropping position as*
      watching
115. *RH does not release D1 as continues to hold it outstretched in front*
116. *RH releases D1 outstretched in front as watching*
116a. *D1 falls to table*
117. *looks at D1 hit table*   (8GP, page 6)

In these ways protocorrespondences are beginning to interpenetrate with protosymbolic forms. This augments the process, begun at the previous stage, of detaching protocorrespondences from their mapping forms. It also opens up the possibility of elaborating protosymbolization into a notational instrument for constructing protoinferential relations.

Cooperative correspondences are selectively generated in a fairly regulated manner at this stage. Consider first an extensive sequence of protocorresponding causal displacements or movement trajectories:

46. *RH, holding Car 1, extends index finger to Cylinder 2*
47.5. *RH index finger touches Cyl 2*
47.5a. *Cyl 2 rolls away*
47.5. *LH removes Car 2 from mouth and holds it in air*
  (experimenter rolls Cyl 2 back so that it hits subject's RH)
49. *RH index finger flicks Cyl 2*
49a. *Cyl 2 rolls back toward experimenter*
  (experimenter rolls Cyl 2 back so that it hits subject's RH)
50. *RH index finger flicks Cyl 2*
50a. *Cyl 2 rolls back toward experimenter*
  (experimenter rolls Cyl 2 back so that it hits subject's RH)
51. *LH inserts C2 in mouth and bites on it*
52. *LH removes C2 from mouth and holds it*
53. *RH index finger flicks Cyl 2*
53a. *Cyl 2 rolls toward experimenter*
  (experimenter rolls Cyl 2 back up against RH sitting on table while RH still clutching C1 underneath in palm)
54. *looks at Cyl 2 about 10 seconds*
55. *RH index finger flicks Cyl 2*
55a. *Cyl 2 rolls toward experimenter*
  (experimenter rolls Cyl 2 back)
56. *RH index finger flicks Cyl 2*
56a. *Cyl 2 rolls toward experimenter*
  (experimenter rolls Cyl 2 back against RH)
57. *RH index finger flicks very lightly Cyl 2*
57a. *Cyl 2 oscillates but doesn't roll*   (8MM, pages 13 and 14)

Another series of seven consecutive protocorrespondences between flicking Cylinder 2 so as to roll it away are generated by 8MM a little later in the same test phase. The initial causal production in both sequences is generated by the subject. Corresponding reproductions of his own causal production follow.

These sequences of causal protocorrespondences require the intervention of the experimenter to bring the cylinder back to the subject. The experimenter does it by reproducing the subject's production. Therefore the subject's causal productions necessarily correspond to the experimenter's as well as to his own prior mappings. It is not possible to determine whether the experimenter's reproductive rolling is a necessary ingredient. A plausible hypothesis is that 8MM would have constructed successive protocorrespondences between his own causal productions even if the experimenter had restricted herself to placing back the cylinder in front of the subject without rolling it.

This autogenetic hypothesis is supported by collateral pieces of evidence. The first is ontogenetic: Infants already generate protocorrespondences at the previous stage when they rarely, if ever, engage in cooperative protocorrespondences. Second, the mapping forms are somewhat different. The subject flicks while the experimenter rolls the object. The third is ingredient to the flow of 8MM's transactions. He does not always construct the protocorrespondence as soon as the experimenter rolls the cylinder back to him. At times he interrupts the sequence of protocorrespondences with other mappings on a different object (e.g., Lines 51–53). At other times he interrupts the sequence by visually inspecting the cylinder for about 10 seconds (e.g., Line 54). Finally, at the end of the second series of protocorrespondences (not reproduced here), the subject does not reproduce the experimenter's motions. Instead, he shifts to different transactions. The fourth set of collateral evidence is that most 8-month-old mapping protocorrespondences are still limited, like those of 6-month-olds', to reproducing their own transactions:

24. LH hits once Yellow Clover Ring on the table to right side
25. LH hits once YCR on the table near center, close to objects
26. LH hits once YCR onto Green Rectangular Ring
27. (experimenter picks up Green Clover Ring and hits it down onto table) as subject watches experimenter, while LH holds YCR
28. LH drops YCR   (8KC, page 13)

Three similar sequences follow later on in which 8KC constructs protocorrespondences between his own hitting but desists as soon as the experimenter joins in. Successive protocorrespondences between hitting is already a familiar product of a 6-month-old's transactions. Still, 8-month-olds, such as 8KC, often construct protocorrespondences between their own mappings and not with another person. Thus, when the experimenter reproduces the subject's hitting, 8KC shifts to different mappings and stops forming protocorrespondences.

This is not to gainsay that 8-month-olds can and do selectively construct protocorrespondences together with the mappings produced by others. For instance, subject 8MM was alternately biting on Car 1 held by his right hand and on Car 2 held by his left hand when the experimenter imitated by biting on Cylinder 1. In order to draw the subject's attention, the experimenter first tapped Cylinder 1 on the table a few times. The result was:

66.3. *LH removes Car 2 from mouth and holds it*
66.7. *RH taps Car 1 on table a few times, very clumsily*   (8MM, page 14)

Note that the experimenter reproduces the subject's biting while the subject reproduces the experimenter's tapping. The tapping by the experimenter was incidental; it was used only as a device to make sure that the subject would watch. Thus, it is the subject who selects what aspect of the experimenter's performance he will transform into a cooperative protocorrespondence. The experimenter's behavior is not determinative; it merely provides an occasion from which the subject may or may not select and construct cooperative protocorrespondences. The experimenter constructs a continuous protocorrespondence between "biting" mappings which is not made up of well-defined units. The subject constructs a discrete protocorrespondence of tapping which is made up of well-defined mapping units.

Indeed, some subjects even begin to behave as if they enjoy and are cognizant of the protocorrespondence between their own and another person's mappings:

48. *LH slaps on table*
49. *watches experimenter moving around table to her own side*
      (experimenter slaps her hand on table)
50. *LH slaps on table while smiling at experimenter*
51. *LH thumb raises to mouth*
      (experimenter begins to clear objects)
52. *looks at experimenter while LH and RH slap on table in uneven succession*   (8GP, page 42)

Subject 8GP smiles at the experimenter in the process of generating the protocorrespondence (Line 50). When the experimenter does not continue the protocorrespondence between slapping the table, the subject does while looking at the experimenter (Line 52).

V. Precise Two-Step Additive and Subtractive Mapping Series

Eight-month-old, like 6-month-old, babies continue to generate additive and subtractive variations in mapping frequencies resulting in quantitative protoseries. The rate at which mapping protoseries are generated increases. Most continue to be limited to two-step orders.

When precise, discrete orders are either increased from one to two or two to three units (e.g., from hitting twice to hitting three times), or they are decreased from three to two or two to one units (e.g., from hitting three times to hitting twice). Precise three-step increasing or decreasing orders are still not generated. Imprecise three-step increasing and decreasing discrete orders are generated frequently; for example, hitting ⟨1, 3, many⟩ times and hitting ⟨many, 3, 1⟩ times.

Although more difficult to measure, parallel developments occur in the production of continuous protoseries. Precise increasing and decreasing continuous orders in one mapping form are also limited to two-step protoseries; for example, from hitting to banging or from banging to hitting. Three-step continuous increasing or decreasing orders in one mapping form are generated frequently but remain imprecise; for example, ⟨touching, tapping, banging⟩ or ⟨banging, hitting, touching⟩.

Subjects are just beginning to monitor aspects of the protoorders which they generate. They do not monitor their entire production, only parts. Observing is usually related to a causal component of the construction:

20.5. *LH lowers Cylinder 2 to table*
20.5. *RH hits down one time on C2 while it is being lowered by LH*
22.5. *LH holds C2 on table*
22.5. *RH hits down two times on C2 while it is being held by LH*
24.   *LH raises C2 and looks at it*   (8JL, pages 16 and 17)

It is as though the subjects are trying to determine the results of their ordered causal transformations.

Most precise bidirectional order relations continue to be produced by the minimum of two proto-operations required, one protoaddition and one protosubtraction. Some precise bidirectional order relations are beginning to be extended just beyond the minimum. Three alternating proto-operations of protoaddition and protosubtraction are generated consecutively. Thereby, subject *8TT* generates a ⟨2, 1, 2, 1⟩ bidirectional tapping order:

28.   *subject looks at experimenter*
      (experimenter taps Blue Block 2 on table)
29.   *taps BH onto table*
30.   *taps LH onto table*
31.   *taps BH onto table*
32.   *taps LH onto table*   (8TT, page 6)

Bidirectional proto-orders of this extent mark the main structural developmental advance in coordinating protoaddition with protosubtraction, and, therefore, in constructing proto-orders. The first ⟨2, 1⟩ order is reconstructed to once again form a ⟨2, 1⟩ order. Consecutive reproduction of the same two-step mapping order marks the initial formation of protoidentity between constructed series. Moreover, it marks beginning regulation of bidirectional orderings.

7

Completion of the Precursory Structures of Discrete Combinativity

Progressive suppleness and extension of protoinferential transformations promotes initial diminution in the lability of combinativity proto-operations. Composing, recomposing, and decomposing are becoming less transient and more systematic. While most are still mobiles, their internal part–whole kinetic relations are becoming more complex and regulated. Thus, as we have already seen in Chapter 6, causal mobiles begin to include independent intermediaries or instruments, begin to have directed goals, and begin to be monitored comparatively.

Increasingly, the products of combinativity are preserved beyond their moment of construction. Even when constructions are transformed their successors are more likely to be related to them in protoinferential ways. Uniting elements into a set is more likely to be followed by reuniting them into variant sets. Recomposition constitutes an increasing proportion of combinativity proto-operations. Moreover, consecutive compositions are progressively linked by relational proto-operations, such as protoaddition. They are also progressively conditioned by exchange, correlation, and negation proto-operations.

This progress marks the initial development in and equilibration of combinativity structures. It promotes elaboration of the equivalence, order, and predicate relations which originated at the previous stage. Most importantly, it results in the completion and extension of the precursory, elementary organization of exchange, correlation, and iterative structures. As will be analyzed in some detail below, this includes the origins of coordinated protocommutativity and protosubstitution, many-to-one protocorrespondences, and fully-formed protoreciprocal ordering.

I. Rudimentary Recomposing of Preexistent Groupings

The average rate at which compositions are generated spontaneously during the first test phase is a bit lower than at age 6 months (see Table 7.1 as compared to Table 3.1). The decrease in average rate is general to all conditions. However, the difference does not reach statistical significance (Mann–Whitney $U = 43$, $p > .10$).

If there is an actual tendency to generate fewer compositions at age 8 months it is probably because individual compositions are becoming progressively less labile and less transient. Compositions are beginning to be preserved for longer durations; consequently, fewer overall compositions may be generated within a given time period:

94. *RH picks up three Circular Rings such that CR4 and CR1 remain stacked and CR2 dangles from thumb*
95. *turns body and looks toward Mirror, still clutching the three Circular Rings for 10 seconds such that two are stacked*
96. *mouths back of LH while moving it rhythmically*
97. *turns body toward table*
98. *RH holds and hits CR1, 2, and 4 onto table a few times*
99. *RH inserts stack of CR4 and CR1 in mouth, CR2 dangles nearby off of thumb*
100. *turns body toward mother while mouthing Circular Rings*
101. *turns body back toward table*   (8MM, pages 5 and 6)

Only three consecutive compositions are generated in all this time, a stabile (Line 95) followed by a mobile (Line 98) followed by a replica of the first stabile (Lines 99–101). All three are extended over repeated mappings as well as extended durations.

TABLE 7.1
Spontaneous Phase I: Mean Frequency by 8-Month-Old Subjects of Compositions, Mean Duration of Phase I, and Mean Frequency of Compositions Per Minute

	Class conditions			
	Semicontrol	*Additive*	*Multiplicative*	*Disjoint*
1. Compositions	12.17	11.42	8.17	4.75
2. Time	3 min 24 sec	2 min 33 sec	2 min 42 sec	2 min 13 sec
3. Productivity per minute	3.58	4.48	3.02	2.14

The rate of productivity is less uniform across class conditions than it was at age 6 months (Table 7.1, Row 3 as compared with Table 3.1, Row 3). Composing frequencies range from lows of 2.14 and 3.02 per minute in the disjoint and multiplicative conditions, respectively, to a high of 4.48 per minute in the additive condition. Yet, the variance by ranks between class conditions remains random (Friedman $\chi_r^2 = 6.00$, $df = 3$, $.10 < p < .20$). Lower compositional productivity is a first indication that there may be a tendency toward a developmental lag in level of combinativity proto-operations when 8-month-old subjects transact with multiplicative and disjoint conditions.

Most compositions continue to be generated in the first phase when subjects spontaneously transact with four objects presented in a closely aligned array. Fewer compositions are generated in the second, provoked, and assisted compositions phase, and the third, preexistent compositions phase. However, the differential rate of productivity is narrowing. Eight-month-olds produce more compositions during these latter two test phases than do 6-month-olds.

Decomposing preexistent compositions, set up by the experimenter during the second and third test phases, remain a very subordinate combinativity proto-operation. All decomposing is nonsystematic. It consists mainly of subtracting single elements in isolation.

Recomposing preexistent compositions so that they are related in any way to the presented compositions is rare. It is just beginning, but it is extremely primitive. It usually takes the form of heaping; much like that characterized by Vygotsky (1934) as the original form of classification. It consists of global derangement of the presented arrangements (e.g., shoving most or all objects together into an unorganized configuration).

Precursory coordinate decomposing and recomposing of two preexistent compositions presented simultaneously to subjects originates at this stage:

1. *RH pulls Brush 2 toward center*
2. *RH picks up B2*
3. *RH drops B2 down to left of Circular Ring 1 resulting in:*

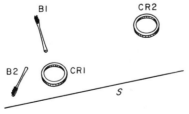

(8KC, page 30)

Subject 8KC recomposes three elements into a new relational structure, but his recomposition is rudimentary in the extreme. It involves transacting with only one element, Brush 2. It is an isolated reunion, and is not followed up by any further reorganization. All his subsequent transactions are with single objects. They do not include the formation of any subsequent compositions or recompositions. As rudimentary as it is, even precursory coordination of decomposing and recomposing is a rare occurrence at age 8 months.

II. Regulated Recomposing of Self-Constructed Groupings

Most compositions generated include only two objects (Table 7.2, Column 10). Three-object compositions are still infrequent and 4-object compositions rare. Compositional size does not vary significantly as a function of class condition (Columns 2, 4, 6, and 8). Yet, if there is any tendency it is to include more objects when composing in the semicontrol conditions and fewer objects in the multiplicative condition. Possibly, this may be a further, but decidedly weak indication that combinativity proto-operations generated in the multiplicative condition lag behind those generated in the other class conditions.

The majority (58%) of compositions are constructed by direct transaction with only one object (Table 7.3, Row 2). Forty-one percent involve direct transaction with two or more objects. This is only a small (5%) increase from age 6 months.

Recomposing their own initial compositions, unlike recomposing preexistent compositions presented by the experimenter, is a well-established combinativity proto-operation. Variants constitute a third of all compositions generated (Table 7.4, Row 5). Only a quarter of the compositions are variants at age 6 months (Table 3.4, page 59).

There is a decided difference in rate of producing variants as a function

TABLE 7.2
Spontaneous Phase I: Mean Frequency and Percentage of Compositional Object Extent Generated by 8-Month-Old Subjects

	Class conditions									
	Semicontrol		Additive		Multiplicative		Disjoint		Total	
	$\bar{x}$	%	$\bar{x}$	%	$\bar{x}$	%	$\bar{x}$	%	$\bar{x}$	%
	1	2	3	4	5	6	7	8	9	10
1. Two-object	9.50	78	9.25	81	7.17	88	4.00	84	7.48	82
2. Three-object	2.50	21	1.50	13	0.83	10	0.50	11	1.33	15
3. Four-object	0.17	1	0.67	6	0.17	2	0.25	5	0.31	3

TABLE 7.3

Spontaneous Phase I: Number of Objects Directly Manipulated by 8-Month-Old Subjects to Produce Compositions in All Class Conditions

	Number of objects				
	1	2	3	4	Total
1. Frequency of compositions	256	158	23	1	438
2. % Compositions	58	36	5	0	99

of class condition. Most variants are generated in the semicontrol and additive conditions (Table 7.4, Rows 1 and 2). These are also the conditions in which subjects generate the most compositions, whether initial or variant. Least variants are generated in the multiplicative and disjoint conditions (Table 7.4, Rows 3 and 4). These are the conditions in which subjects generate the fewest compositions, whether initial or variant.

It would appear that recomposing and composing are becoming related combinativity proto-operations. The more subjects compose, the more they are likely to recompose their own compositions. Differences in variant productivity as a function of class condition is also a second indication that combinativity proto-operations may lag behind in the multiplicative and disjoint conditions.

Recomposing is becoming a progressively regulated combinativity proto-operation. It is no longer unusual for subjects to follow-up their initial compositions with extended series of variants, including some replication between variants. Sometimes the series of recompositions include three-object compositions. Sometimes, they even include several four-object compositions. Most series still involve less than ten recomposings. But the most extended series consisted of an initial composition plus 17 recompositions produced by 8AB in the semicontrol condition. It included 7 two-object, 9 three-object, and 1 four-object variants.

TABLE 7.4

Spontaneous Phase I: Mean Frequency of Composing and Recomposing by 8-Month-Old Subjects

	Thematic	Variant	% Variant
1. Semicontrol	6.42	5.75	47
2. Additive	7.50	3.92	34
3. Multiplicative	6.58	1.58	19
4. Disjoint	4.00	0.75	16
5. All conditions	6.13	3.00	33

III. Continuing Predominance of Mobile Compositions

Continuing compositional lability is underscored by the finding that most constructions (58%) are still mobiles (Table 7.5, Row 8). Thirty-eight percent are stabiles (Row 4) and 4% are combined mobiles and stabiles (Row 9). The ratio between these compositional forms is the same as that generated at age 6 months.

Mobiles are particularly predominant in the multiplicative condition, as they are at age 6 months (Row 8, Column 6). Mobiles no longer predominate in the disjoint condition (Row 8, Column 8). The ratio between mobile and stabile forms in the disjoint approximates that for the semicontrol (Row 8, Column 2) and additive (Row 8, Column 4) conditions. Developmental continuity of mobile predominance in the multiplicative condition is the exception. It is a third indication that composing and recomposing are more labile in the face of multiplicative classes.

Most labiles, regardless of their form, are based upon contact relations. Proximity relations account for less than one-fourth of the compositions. Only 2% are based upon both proximity and contact relations.

Thirty-eight percent of the compositions involve causal relations. All of these are, of course, mobiles. This means that almost two-thirds (65%) of the mobiles are not only kinetic but causal compositions. All of these are, of course, contact mobiles. Consequently 81% of the contact mobiles involve causal relations. Only 19% of the contact mobiles generated are noncausal. Almost all causal mobiles involve asymmetrical placement and displacement relations, such as one object pushing another.

While only 35% of mobiles are noncausal their complexity equals that of any causal mobiles. Most are relatively simple, as are causal mobiles. For instance, two objects are moved around together. Occasional noncausal mobiles are not so simple:

36. *RH brings Car 1 back up in front of eyes, looking at it 5 seconds*
37.3. *RH rotates C1 in front of eyes, looking at it*
37.7. *LH brings Car 2 near C1 in RH and rotates C2*
39. *looks at C1 in RH, looks at C2 in LH, looks at C1, looks at C2*
40. *for next 10 seconds RH rotates C1 and LH rotates C2 near chest and eyes, sometimes alternatively, sometimes simultaneously (rotations made with very elaborate wrist swings), looking back and forth at cars*

(8MM, page 19)

This is among the most complex mobiles constructed by 8-month-olds. It is extended over a long duration, many placements and displacements, and a large spatial expanse. It might have been extended even further if it

TABLE 7.5
Spontaneous Phase I: Mean Frequency and Percentage of Compositional Forms and Dimensions by 8-Month-Old Subjects

| | Class conditions | | | | | | | | | |
| | Semicontrol | | Additive | | Multiplicative | | Disjoint | | Total | |
	$\bar{x}$ 1	% 2	$\bar{x}$ 3	% 4	$\bar{x}$ 5	% 6	$\bar{x}$ 7	% 8	$\bar{x}$ 9	% 10
1. Contact stable	4.25	35	2.58	23	1.83	22	0.50	11	2.29	25
2. Proximity stable	1.25	10	1.42	12	0.50	6	1.25	26	1.10	12
3. Contact–proximity stable	0.17	1	0.25	2	0.00	0	0.00	0	0.10	1
4. Total stable	5.67	47	4.25	37	2.33	29	1.75	37	3.50	38
5. Contact mobile	5.17	42	4.92	43	4.92	60	1.92	40	4.23	46
6. Proximity mobile	0.83	7	1.42	12	0.75	9	0.75	16	0.94	10
7. Contact–proximity mobile	0.33	3	0.00	0	0.08	1	0.08	2	0.13	1
8. Total mobile	6.33	52	6.33	55	5.75	70	2.75	58	5.29	58
9. Mobile–stabile	0.17	1	0.83	7	0.08	1	0.25	5	0.33	4
10. Horizontal[a]	4.50	47	5.67	60	5.50	73	3.00	75	4.67	61
11. Vertical[a]	4.25	45	3.17	33	1.75	23	0.92	23	2.52	33
12. Horizontal–vertical	0.75	8	0.67	7	0.25	3	0.08	2	0.44	6

[a] Compositions whose spatial dimensions are ambiguous are not scored. Consequently, the dimensional means summate to less than the total compositional means.

had not been interrupted by the mother taking the objects away from the subject.

Subject *8MM*'s construction is precursory to complex mobiles in three ways. It includes simultaneous, successive, and alternating symmetrical displacements and placements of two objects. It is preceded (Lines 36–37.3) and accompanied (Lines 37.7–40) by comparative inspection of the objects. It marks the origin of elaborate placement and displacement relations between objects, where the spatial and movement relations are not dependent upon the support of a physical surface.

More compositions are constructed in the vertical dimension. The increase is from one-fourth at age 6 months to one-third of the compositions at age 8 months (Table 7.5, Row 11). The ratio of horizontal to vertical compositions decreases to a high of three-to-one in the multiplicative and disjoint conditions and a low of one-to-one in the semicontrol condition (Table 7.5, Rows 11 and 12).

This is accompanied by a trivial increase (from 4% at age 6 months to 6% at age 8 months) in compositions constructed in both the horizontal and vertical compositions (Row 12). While still infrequent two-dimensional horizontal–vertical compositions, as well as the few two-dimensional horizontal compositions generated, continue to open up possibilities for multiplicative inclusion of one element in two parts of the whole.

Rare instances of horizontal–vertical compositions are just beginning to include precursory prototypes of "bridge" constructions:

13. *RH places Rectangular Ring on top of Circular and Triangular Rings:*

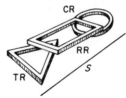

(8AB, page 1)

4. *LH places Yellow Spoon vertically across the two handles of Red Spoons 1 and 2*   (8NW, page 39)

Compositions which bridge two objects with a third involve multiple two-dimensional parts. Consequently, each element is included in two parts of the whole. Bridging, then, opens up another avenue of simultaneous multiplicative inclusion of several elements in two parts of the whole. All three elements of a three-object bridge are included in two of the three parts making up the composition.

IV. Increasing Durability of Compositions

Consecutive compositions continue to predominate (Table 7.6, Column 10). Only one-third are produced in isolation. Partially overlapping compositions are negligible, while simultaneous compositions are never produced.

Consecutive compositions are produced most frequently in the semicontrol and additive conditions (Row 2, Columns 2 and 4). As at age 6 months, isolate compositions are generated most frequently in the multiplicative and disjoint conditions (Row 1, Columns 6 and 8). This is the fourth finding consistent with the hypothesis of a developmental lag in combinativity proto-operations when 8-month-olds transact with multiplicative and, perhaps, disjoint classes. However, the hypothesis of a long-term developmental lag can only be corroborated if the disparity as a function of class condition continues to be manifest at older ages. Testing the hypothesis will therefore have to await analyses of the data for ten-month-olds.

Compositions separated by intervening transactions make it improbable that these constructions are related to each other in any way. Temporally isolated compositions are segregated, fleeting constructions which provide minimal opportunity for reconstruction of and coordination between labiles. As such, the possibilities for cognizing part–whole relations between isolated sets of elements are usually ruled out.

Like all other compositions, however, isolates are increasingly extended in time beyond the moment of their construction. As such they are becoming less labile. This also enhances the possibilities of forming internal part–whole relations within isolate compositions:

46. *RH removes Brush 1 from mouth while LH holds Brush 2 out in front of self, and looks at the two brushes in his hands*
47. *BH put the brushes down between his legs, bending head over to look at them*   (8BK, page 18)

Cognizing part–whole relations internal to an isolated set becomes increasingly probable when the subject not only inspects his composing, but preserves the composition across a spatiotemporal transformation. This pattern of behavior begins to appear in 8BK's construction when he looks at the two brushes in their first separate uncomposed position (Line 46), and then looks at them after displacing them to their second position where they are composed (Line 47).

Extended spatiotemporal isolate labiles accompanied by inspection are no longer unusual. The isolate may be a relatively extended mobile accompanied by inspecting all the elements composed:

TABLE 7.6
Spontaneous Phase I: Temporal Relations between Compositions Generated by 8-Month-Old Subjects

	Class conditions									
	Semicontrol		Additive		Multiplicative		Disjoint		Total	
	$\bar{x}$ 1	% 2	$\bar{x}$ 3	% 4	$\bar{x}$ 5	% 6	$\bar{x}$ 7	% 8	$\bar{x}$ 9	% 10
1. Isolate	2.67	22	3.92	34	4.08	50	2.00	42	3.35	37
2. Consecutive	9.33	77	7.25	64	4.08	50	2.75	58	5.67	62
3. Partially overlapping	0.17	1	0.25	2	0.00	0	0.00	0	0.10	1
4. Simultaneous	0.00	0	0.00	0	0.00	0	0.00	0	0.00	0

2. RH *grasps Blue Brush and Red Triangular Column*
3. RH *slides BB and RTC in arc to right table edge*
4. RH *slides them toward self, lifting BB and RTC while looking at them*
(8GP, page 37)

The isolate may be a somewhat extended stabile accompanied by inspecting individual elements:

41. RH *takes Doll 1 out of mouth, watching the experimenter's moves*
42. RH *holds D1, looking at Doll 2*
43. *looking at D2, RH places D1 near it on side*   (8GP, page 47)

In general, subjects are progressively monitoring their compositional constructions; thereby indicating that composing is becoming a well-regulated combinativity proto-operation.

While protoinferential relations are less likely between isolate compositions they may be beginning to be generated between successive isolates:

23. RH *touches Doll 2 to Doll 1*
23a. *D2 knocks over D1*
    (experimenter pushes the fallen D1 closer)
24. LH *removes Mirror 2 from mouth briefly*
25. *mouths M2 held by LH*
26.5. LH *removes M2 from mouth*
26.5. RH *hits D2 on top of fallen D1*
26.5a. *D1 displaces slightly*   (8CC, page 8)

Some transactions (Lines 24–25) are interpolated between the two compositions (Lines 23–23a and 26.5–26.5a). So, the compositions are segregated temporally from each other. Yet, it does not seem implausible that they may be related to each other by a protoreplacement exchange operation.

V. Introducing the Element of Negation into Exchange Proto-operations

Precursory inferential relations, such as exchange proto-operations, are facilitated by the production of consecutive compositions. Indeed, exchange proto-operations have become commonplace equivalence structures at this stage. Yet, they are all operations upon a single set only. The set is transformed consecutively and recomposed pragmatically. Therefore, the resultant equivalences remain limited to relations between consecutive transforms of the initial single set only.

Replacement proto-operations are generated by all subjects. With one exception (see subject 8AB protocol fragment on page 161), their application is still strictly limited to two-object compositions. Half the protore-placements involve a single exchange of one element. The compositions are usually causal mobiles.

64.7.   *RH pushes Yellow Cylinder across table into Green Triangular Column*
64.7a.   *GTC displaced toward left*
64.7aa. *YC rolls forward to experimenter*
        (experimenter rolls YC toward subject touching subject's RH and rebounding)
66.   *RH touches YC*
66a. *YC rolls toward self slightly*
67.   *RH pushes YC into GTC*
67a. *GTC displaced slightly*   (8TT, page 11)

Protoreplacement is infrequently applied to two consecutive stabile compositions such that a single exchange of only one element is generated:

59.   *LH places Cross Ring 2 partially overlapping Triangular Ring 2*
60.   *LH lifts and drops CR2 in front of TR2*   (8AB, page 34)

Causal replacement is often accompanied by visual monitoring of the dependent effect:

23.   *LH hits Blue Doll onto Red Doll*
23a. *RD rolls toward experimenter*
24.   *watches RD as LH holds BD extended forward just above table*
        (experimenter rolls RD back to subject—it rolls all the way to the table edge)
25.   *eyes follow RD*
26.   *LH hits BD onto RD*
26a. *RD rolls partially over table edge*   (8TB, page 24)

62.   *RH hits Blue Circular Ring onto Red Doll*
62a. *RD rotates 180°*
63.   *looks down at RD*
64.   *RH hits BCR onto RD*
64a. *RD rolls toward table edge*   (8TB, page 25)

Even though these protoreplacements involve only a single exchange they are taking on the form of regulated proto-operations. The subjects observe the results of their initial causal compositions. They immediately follow-up with a composition targeted to take into account what has happened to the causal patient object. The successor causal composition is a direct replication of its predecessor.

Repeated protoreplacements of one element are generated as frequently as single exchanges. Repeated protoreplacements, unlike single exchanges, are applied to stabiles (8GP) as frequently as mobiles (8CC):

42. *LH puts Spoon down in front of Doll 1 as looking down*
43. *looks up at experimenter*
44. *LH picks up and looks at S*
45. *LH touches S down behind and slightly to right of D1*
46. *LH raises S and repeats No. 45*
47. *LH repeats No. 46 several times in rapid succession*   (8GP, page 3)

41. *LH hits Circular Ring 2 on Circular Ring 1*
41a. *CR1 moves to right*
42. *LH taps CR2 on table six times in same place*
43. *LH touches CR2 very lightly on CR1*
44. *LH hits CR2 on CR1*
44a. *CR1 moves about 1 inch away*   (8CC, page 33)

Beyond its purely protoreplacement features 8CC's production is interesting because it simultaneously constructs an alternating ordering relation ⟨ hit, tap, touch, hit ⟩. Analysis of compositional orderings will be deferred to a later section (see pages 166–169). Here it should simply be noted that productions which combine exchange with ordering proto-operations have special significance. They provide the self-generated opportunity to begin to relate equivalence with iterative proto-operations.

While still always limited to two-object compositions, protoreplacement is beginning to be extended beyond direct manipulation and exchange of only one element of the set. One-fourth of 8-month-old subjects begin to generate protoreplacements of both elements composed. Most range from one to three replacements and involve active taking away and replacing of only one object at a time:

48. *RH pulls Block 6 on table in front of self and touches it to Block 5 held by LH on table*
49. *BH separate B6 and B5 about 3 inches*
50. *BH touch B6 and B5 together again*
51. *LH inserts B5 into mouth*
52.5. *mouths B5*
52.5. *RH touches B6 to B5 held in mouth by LH*
54. *RH shakes B6 down in air, rubbing B6 against B5*   (8NW, pages 6 and 7)

Two protoreplacements by 8NW (Lines 52.5 and 54) consist of actively replacing one object, Block 6. A third, however, involves simultaneous replacement of both objects after simultaneously decomposing them (Lines 49–50). Occasional protoreplacements involve more protoreplacements of both objects than of one object:

19. *RH raises Block 1 and LH raises Block 5 touching them together, looking at Blocks and then at ceiling*
20. *turns right to mother (who giggled at him)*

21. *turns back towards table, bringing B1 and B5 up in front of face again such that BH touch, and slightly rotates them together*
22. *lowers arms and LH knocks B5 on B1 held by RH (then glances at experimenter)*
23. *BH hit B5 and B1 lightly together in front of self*
24. *stretches BH out in front of face, moving them apart and rotates B1 and B5 slightly in front of eyes for about 5 seconds*
25. *lowers BH touching B1 and B5 together*   (8BK, page 11)

Four protoreplacements are generated by 8BK. Three involve simultaneous replacement of both objects (Lines 21, 23, and 25). A fifth potential protoreplacement also involves active transformation of both objects (Line 24). However, it is not clear whether this is a protoreplacement or only visiomotor comparison of the two objects in between protoreplacement operations.

Also noteworthy are two additional features; one of which is typical. Almost all protoreplacements of both objects are constructed in the air without any surface support. The other is unusual. This sequence of protoreplacements is exceptional because it intermingles noncausal (Lines 19, 21, and 25) with causal compositions (Lines 22 and 23).

Protosubstitution is generated by 10 of the 12 8-month-old subjects. All protosubstitutions continue to be applied to two-object compositions only. Usually they consist of a single exchange of one element for another in two-object compositions. Like protoreplacements, most protosubstitutions involve causal mobiles, where the exchanged element is the passive recipient:

34. *RH lowers Green Rectangular Ring onto Yellow Rectangular Ring*
35. *RH raises GRR and drops it down onto Yellow Clover Ring*
                                                      (8KC, page 13)

45. *RH hits Block 2 on Block 4 once*
45a. *B4 is displaced a bit*
46. *RH hits B2 on Block 3 once*
46a. *B3 is displaced a bit*   (8TT, page 3)

Exchanging all elements presented except the active object remains exceptional:

84. *RH touches Green Cylinder to Yellow Triangular Column*
85. *RH hits GC on table once*
86. *RH touches GC to Yellow Cylinder*
86a. *YC jiggles slightly*
87. *RH pushes GC against Green Triangular Column*
87a. *GTC falls flat*   (8NW, page 12)

The most advanced protosubstitution is featured by some visual monitoring and directed repetition:

16. *LH brings Block 1 and RH brings Block 2 together, about 4 inches from chin such that the blocks do not quite touch*
17. *looks at B1 and B2 briefly as tilts and holds blocks in front of self*
18. *RH rotates B2 toward self while LH holds B1 in constant position*
19. *RH touches B2 to B1 held by LH, in air*
20.5. *RH rotates B2 to about 2 inches to right of and 1 inch above Block 4 on table*
20.5–28.5. *LH continuously holds B1 in air*
22.5. *looks at Block 3 and B4 as RH holds B2 near B4*
24.5. *RH holds B2 on B3*
26.5. *RH removes B2 from B3 and holds it in air about 2 inches to right of B4*
28.5. *looks at B1 held in air by LH as RH holds B2 near B4*
30.2. *looks towards mother*
30.4. *RH moves B2 to front of self and immediately raises it*
30.4. *LH shakes B1 down onto table and immediately raises it*
30.4a. *B2 and B1 contact on upward motion of B1*   (8TB, pages 1 and 2)

The latter part of this recompositional sequence includes five protosubstitutions (Lines 19, 20.5–22.5, 24.5, 26.5–28.5, and 30.4–30.4a). They form the most extended equivalence structure by protosubstitution generated at this stage:

$$(B2 > B1) \approx (B2 > B4) \approx (B2 > B3) \approx (B2 > B4) \approx (B2 \gtrless B1) \quad (7.1)$$

The first and last compositions involve direct contact by the subject with both objects. Moreover, the last composition is constructed by active reciprocal transformations (symbolized by $\gtrless$) between both objects. Most significantly, the sequence includes precursory inverse relations between some protosubstitutions. While hardly systematic, inverse proto-operations are generated twice in the sequence (i.e., between the first and last compositions and between the second and fourth compositions).

Protocommutative operations are generated by all but 1 of the 12 8-month-old subjects. As with the other two exchange operations, protocommutativity is applied only to single two-object sets. Protocommutativity is applied to all forms of compositions, whether causal mobiles, noncausal mobiles, or stabiles. Almost all involve consecutive binary transformations of both objects. Some involve consecutive transformations of only one object.

Protocommutativity based upon unary transformations usually involves reciprocal transformations:

26. RH *places Yellow Cylinder next to Green Cylinder:*

27. RH *lifts GC by end and drops it on opposite side of* YC (8TT, page 9)

58. *looks at the Yellow Spoon as* RH *brings Orange Spoon over near to it*

59. RH *places OS on top of YS:*

60.   RH *picks up YS*

60a. OS *lifts and replaces on table*

61.   RH *drops YS on table to left of* OS   (8AB, page 17)

Reciprocal binary transformations are also generated to construct protocommutativity, but still infrequently:

30.5. RH *inserts Block 4 into mouth partially*

30.5. LH *raises Block 2 and touches it to B4*

32.5. *mouths B4 held by* RH

32.5. LH *holds B2 touching B4*

34.5. RH *removes B4 from mouth and shakes it down in air once quickly*

34.5. LH *quickly pushes corner of B2 into mouth*

36.5. *mouths B2 held by* LH

36.5. RH *holds B4 touching B2*   (8NW, page 2)

Occasional other protocommutative relations are constructed without any support in the air:

24.   RH *touches Circular Ring 3 to Circular Ring 2 held by* LH *in front of self*

25.   *looks down at CR3 and CR2*

26.   RH *slides CR3 over CR2 held by* LH

27.5. RH *touches CR3 and CR2 symmetrically for an instant*

27.5. LH *holds CR2*   (8MM, page 2)

Most, however, are still constructed with the surface support of the table top.

Both mapping constancy (e.g., 8NW) and visual monitoring (e.g., 8MM) are becoming standard features of protocommutativity. As shown, reciprocal transforming is just beginning to become a feature of protocommutativity. To this extent it is becoming regulated. Still rare, however, is protocommutativity featured by numerous consecutive transformations:

32.   LH *brings Circular Ring 2 stacked on top of Circular Ring 3 to mouth*

33.   *mouths the horizontal stack of CR2 on top of CR3 held by* LH

34. *LH withdraws CR2 and CR3 from mouth and hits both once on table in a vertical position*
35. *LH returns CR2 and CR3 to mouth in a vertical position but does not insert them*   (8MM, page 10)

Like 8MM's production, most are limited to three consecutive transformations.

Even rarer is protocommutativity featured by several consecutive transformations which are conditioned by inverse proto-operations:

20.5. *LH touches Cross Ring 2 to Cross Ring 1*
22.   *LH opens–closes fingers on CR2, twice, as holds it on CR1, such that only CR2 moves*
23.   *LH raises and places CR2 next to CR1, as looks at Triangular Ring 2*
24.   *LH grasps and pushes CR1 against CR2, as looks at this*
24a.   *CR1 moves CR2 about 2 inches to right*
25.   *LH grasps and places CR2 on CR1 without releasing CR2*
26.   *LH raises and places CR2 on CR1*
27.   *LH grasps CR2*
28.   *LH partially raises then lowers CR2 on CR1*
29.   *LH completely raises CR2*
30.   *LH hits CR2 down on CR1*
31.   *LH lifts CR2 and CR1 together*   (8AB, page 41)

The protocommutative series (Lines 23, 24–24a, and 25) constructs equivalence relations between three ordered sets:

$$\langle\; CR2 > CR1 \;\rangle \rightarrow \langle\; CR1 > CR2 \;\rangle \rightarrow \langle\; CR2 > CR1 \;\rangle \qquad (7.2)$$

The first and second and the second and third orders are inverses of each other, thereby resulting in identity between the first and third orders. As at age 6 months, subjects never reproduce inverse protocommutativity.

Subject 8AB's protocommutative operation is embedded in a sequence of multiple protoreplacements. It is preceded by protoreplacement (Lines 20.5 and 22) and it is succeeded by protoreplacements (Lines 26, 28, 30, and 31). Interweaving protoreplacements with protocommutativity expands Eq. (7.2) into

$$(CR2 > CR1) \sim (CR2 > CR1) \sim \langle\; CR2 > CR1 \;\rangle \rightarrow \langle\; CR1 > CR2 \;\rangle$$
$$\rightarrow \langle\; CR2 > CR1 \;\rangle \sim (CR2 > CR1) \sim (CR2 > CR1)$$
$$\sim (CR2 > CR1) \sim (CR2 \gtreqless CR1) \qquad (7.3)$$

Coordination of protoreplacement and protocommutativity began at the previous stage. However, it was rare and was limited to single protoreplacements preceeding and succeeding protocommutativity. At this stage multiple protoreplacements of unordered sets are coordinated with protocommutativity of ordered sets. Although still not generated frequently, such coordinations are no longer exceptional constructions.

Sometimes protoreplacement (Lines 12–18) precedes protocommutativity (Lines 18–22a) without also succeeding it:

12. *LH holds Triangular Ring 1 on Cross Ring 1*
13. *LH lifts TR1*
14. *LH drops TR1 on CR1*
15. *LH lifts TR1*
15a. *LH pulls CR1 closer to self in process of lifting TR1*
16. *LH drops TR1 on CR1*
16a. *CR1 displaces slightly*
17. *LH lifts TR1*
18. *LH places TR1 on table to left of CR1 such that they touch*
19. *LH open–closes on TR1 and CR1 at place where they touch*
19a. *TR1 and CR1 separate and displace away from each other*
20. *LH picks up TR1*
21. *LH puts TR1 down on table behind CR1, without releasing TR1*
22. *LH pulls TR1 against CR1 toward self*
22a. *TR1 pushes CR1 toward subject and partially over edge*

(8AB, pages 31 and 32)

Two other possible forms of coordinating are never generated. Subjects never succeed protocommutativity with protoreplacement without also preceding it with protoreplacement. Subjects never interweave protoreplacement between two series of protocommutativity.

Coordination of protoreplacement with protosubstitution is generated a bit more frequently than at age 6 months. The main advance, however, is in the extent of the coordinations. Series which interweave protoreplacement with protosubstitution are becoming increasingly lengthy:

79. *LH touches Rectangular Ring to Clover Ring*
79a. *RR pushes CR to the right*
80. *LH raises Circular Ring*
81. *LH hits Circ R on top of CR*
81a. *Circ R pushes CR about 2 inches toward experimenter*
82. *LH places Circ R onto table next to CR*
83. *LH raises RR*
84.5. *LH touches RR to Circ R*
84.5. *RH holds Triangular Ring on table*
86. *LH raises Circ R under RR*
87.3. *LH holds Circ R and RR in air, looking at them*
87.7. *RH raises TR*
89. *LH drops Circ R onto table*
90.5. *LH holding RR, raises Circ R to an upright position momentarily, such that RR touches table and Circ R during this*
90.5. *RH releases TR onto table*
92. *LH releases Circ R such that it vibrates to a rest*
93. *LH releases RR on top of Circ R*

94. *LH raises RR*
95. *LH lifts Circ R under RR*
96. *LH drops Circ R onto table*
97. *LH touches RR to Circ R*   (8AB, pages 4 and 5)

This is the most extended series generated. The proto-operations never exceed two-element sets, but the coordination interweaves protosubsitution (Lines 79–79a and 80–81a) with protoreplacement (Lines 81 and 82) with protosubsitution (Lines 82 and 83–86) with multiple protoreplacement (Lines 86, 89–90.5, 92–93, 94–95, and 96–97). The consecutive sequence consists of eight compositions and recompositions plus some monitoring of the transformations:

$$(RR > CR) \approx (Circ\ R > CR) \sim (Circ\ R > CR)$$
$$\approx (RR > Circ\ R) \sim (RR \gtrless Circ\ R) \sim (RR > Circ\ R)$$
$$\sim (RR > Circ\ R) \sim (RR > Circ\ R) \qquad (7.4)$$

Such sequences provide evidence for the hypothesis that a regulated equivalence structure is being constructed.

Precursory coordination between protosubstitution and protocommutativity originates at this stage. However, only single instances are generated and by only 2 of the 12 subjects. One was generated by *8TB* (pp. 1–2, Lines 16–30.4a) and has already been reproduced on page 157. As noted there, the latter part of this recompositional sequence constitutes the most extended equivalence structure by protosubstitution generated at this stage. Now it should be added that it is immediately preceded by the construction of an equivalence structure by protocommutativity (Lines 16, 17, and 18–19). Thus, sequential coordination expands equivalence structure Eq. (7.1) into

$$\langle B1 \gtrless B2 \rangle \rightarrow \langle B1 \gtrless B2 \rangle \rightarrow \langle B2 > B1 \rangle \approx (B2 > B4)$$
$$\approx (B2 > B3) \approx (B2 > B4) \approx (B2 \gtrless B1) \qquad (7.5)$$

The other instance was also limited to a single coordination. That is, protocommutativity was followed immediately by protosubstitution of one of the elements. Thus, in addition to its rarity at this stage, coordinated protocommutativity and protosubstitution does not go beyond the bare minimum linkage. It is not regulated in any way.

Structurally, linking protocommutativity with protosubstitution is the most advanced equivalence coordination that develops at this stage. Combining protocommutativity with protoreplacement is a less complex structural coordination. Neither proto-operation involves exchanging elements for each other. Both involve exchanging orders. Protocommutativity consists of spatial placement exchanges of constant elements. Protoreplacement holds both elements and spatial order constant. The exchange is only in temporal order. Coordinating them, then, only involves combining spatial and temporal order relations between constant elements, and consecutive temporal order is already ingredient in protocommutativity. Therefore, their most rudimentary coordination within a single set already originates at the previous stage.

Protosubstitution consists of exchanging elements. As in protocommutativity, consecutive temporal order is inherent in protosubstitution. Therefore, the most rudimentary coordination between protosubstitution and protoreplacement within consecutive recompositions of a single set already originates at the previous stage. On the other hand, coordinating protocommutativity with protosubstitution requires relating spatial exchanges with object exchanges. Therefore, even their most rudimentary coordination within a single two-element set does not develop until the second stage.

Nevertheless, the origins of even the most rudimentary coordinated protocommutativity and protosubstitution complete the elementary organization of exchange structures. All the direct and coordinated structures of replacement, substitution, and commutative proto-operations necessary to construct part–whole equivalence relations are now in place. However primitive, the precursory foundation has been laid for constructive development of exchange operations.

VI. Completing the Structures of Protocorrespondences within Single Sets

Constructing protocorrespondences within compositions and between recompositions becomes more frequent at age 8 months. This increase complements that of mapping protocorrespondences. In fact, mapping and compositional protocorrespondences are not detached from each other during these early stages. One consequence is that correlations relevant to part–whole relations within compositions and between recompositions of single sets are not differentiated from those relevant to subjects' mappings. Yet, as we shall see, the seeds of detachment are being sown.

Both discrete and continuous protocorrespondences within compositions are becoming more extensive and complex, as well as more frequent. They extend to three objects, accompanied sometimes (8NW) by visual preservation of the compositional result:

55.5. *LH pulls Block 4 over table edge and into lap*
57. *looks down in lap as RH lowers to lap*
58. *looks at Block 2*

59. *LH and arm pull both B2 and Block 3 over table edge and into lap*
60. *looks down in lap*   (8NW, page 3)

98. *RH holds and hits Circular Rings 1, 2, and 3 onto table a few times*
                                                    (8MM, page 6)

They are also becoming more extensive in duration or frequency of reproduction:

27.5.   *RH bangs Doll 1 on top of Mirror five times*
27.5a. *M displaces*   (8CC, page 2)

53. *RH hits Green Rectangular Ring on Yellow Clover Ring 17 times*
                                                    (8KC, page 14)

42. *LH touches Square Column 1 and RH touches Square Column 2 together*
     such that an end of SC1 and a side of SC2 are in contact
     (experimenter wiggles and lightly taps the Triangular Columns 1 and 2
     on the table)
43. *looks at TC1 and TC2 for a moment as BH holding SC1 and SC2 together*
44. *looks down at SC1 and SC2 held together by BH*
                                            (8DS, pages 42 and 43)

Subject 8DS accompanies his construction of an extended spatial protocorrespondence between the square columns with comparative observation.

This stage marks the origins of symmetrical compositional protocorrespondences. Like that produced by 8DS, most are stabile symmetrical protocorrespondences limited to bi-univocal one-to-one matching. Unlike that produced by 8DS, most stabiles are more briefly constructed labile compositions:

38. *RH touches Brush 1 and LH touches Brush 2 together in air* (8TB, page 9)

10. *RH touches Orange Cup and LH touches Yellow Cup together in the air*
     briefly   (8AB, page 14)

Some symmetrical one-to-one protocorrespondences are both stabile and mobile, but predominantly mobile:

42. *LH touches Brush 2 to Brush 1 held by RH and then immediately in*
     succession BH simultaneously make short waving motions in air in
     random manner, keeping hands and objects very close together.
                                                    (8TB, page 10)

This extended mobile is as complex as any within composition protocorrespondences generated at this stage, yet it remains fundamentally labile. While it involves substantial kinetic repetition, the transformations are nonsystematic and they are not monitored except, possibly, kinaesthetically.

Within-labile protocorrespondences are undifferentiated from the mapping protocorrespondences which produce them. Yet, their increased extent generates conditions conducive to their eventual detachment at subsequent stages. The possibilities for detachment are multiplied by the various manifestations that increased extent take (i.e., more elements, longer duration, greater complexity, and more reproductions).

Detachment has special significance for cognitive development. It is a necessary condition for children to consider protoinferential relations as at least partially independent of their own composing transactions. Only then is it possible to cognize compositions as if they are given sets of elements rather than merely actual collections of objects. This is a first step necessary for formal deduction which is differentiated from, yet imposed upon and, ultimately, coordinated with, empirical content.

Extending protocorrespondences beyond their initial moment of construction by consecutive recompositions of single sets is, as we have just seen, no longer rare. The most extended consists of 16 reproductions of the initial hitting composition generated by 8KC. All these correlations between recompositions involve constancy of mapping forms as well as protocorrespondences. The mere extension over time and numerous repetitions supports detachment of the equivalence relations produced from the mappings producing them.

Detachment becomes more likely, however, when (a) the mapping forms vary between recompositions, yet (b) consecutive equivalence relations are preserved within the same set:

92. *LH picks up and rotates Dolls 1 and 2*
93. *LH hits D1 and D2 down onto the table, three times*
94. *LH drops D1 and D2 onto the table*   (8KC, page 4)

The mappings vary from rotation in the initial composition (Line 92) to hitting in the first recomposition (Line 93) to dropping both objects in the second recomposition (Line 94). The first and third mobiles entail continuous protocorrespondences, while the second mobile entails a discrete protocorrespondence.

Throughout, equivalence relations are preserved even though the mapping forms are varied. These conditions promote abstracting of equivalence relations as constants or givens by detaching the processes of construction from their proto-operational products. If the mappings can vary without affecting the proto-operational products then the initial step has been taken toward treating mappings as content. Mappings may remain as necessary embodiments of proto-operations, but they begin to loose their specificity. Any manifestation will do; indeed, any manifestation may be mustered up in the service of producing protocorrelations. If the equivalence relations are nevertheless preserved then the initial step has also been taken toward abstracting of protocorrespondences as forms. While not losing their specificity, the forms begin to acquire protoinferential necessity.

The structural development set into motion at this stage is only the beginning in a long process resulting, during adolescence and adulthood, in fully abstracting quantitative equivalence relations by correlation operations. At its origins, abstracting this, like other proto-operations, from its actual embodiment is entirely rudimentary. Most notably, it only applies pragmatically and specifically to two-element sets.

Protocorrespondences between compositions are just beginning to be extended to two-unit equivalences. For instance, with brief intervening transactions that are not germane and may therefore be omitted, subject 8AB repeated two-unit equivalences:

14. RH hits Circular Ring on top of Triangular Ring, twice
18. RH taps CR next to TR, twice
22. LH hits Clover Ring on CR, twice   (8AB, pages 10 and 11)

Here two-unit equivalence is generated first between consecutive recompositions of a two-element set (Lines 14 and 18). Then it is repeated between two consecutive compositions of two-element sets where the second is not a recomposition of the first (Lines 18 and 22). It should be emphasized, however, that such two-unit equivalences are not generated even once by most of the subjects.

So far the analysis has focused upon bi-univocal (one-to-one) protocorrespondences. Consider now the structural developments in co-univocal (one-to-many) protocorrespondence within single compositions. They, too, are generated more frequently, are becoming more complex, and are featured by greater flexibility and increased regulation.

At the previous stage, all co-univocal protocorrespondences match one-to-many objects in consecutive order. Now they also begin to construct simultaneous one-to-many protocorrespondences:

19. RH throws Rectangular Ring down onto table such that it hits Clover Ring and Circular Ring
19a. Circ R pushed to table edge   (8AB, pages 1 and 2)

5. LH places Cross Ring 1 on top of Triangular Ring 2
6. LH hits Cross Ring 2 on top of stack CR1/TR2   (8AB, page 31)

13. RH drops Green Triangular Column on Yellow Triangular Column and Yellow Cylinder which are sitting next to each other   (8TT, page 8)

Like that produced by 8TT, other simultaneous one-to-many protocorrespondences involve "bridge" constructions, already presented on page 150. Simultaneous one-to-many protocorrespondences, whether or not they form bridge constructions, involve inclusion of one element in relation to two parts. As such they augment the conditions necessary for the formation of multiplicative part–whole proto-operational relations.

While it is the formal isomorph of one-to-many correlations, but in reverse order, many-to-one protocorrespondences does not originate until this stage:

60.5. *RH extends Block 2 toward Block 4 such that B2 is in front of B4*
60.5. *LH extends Block 1 toward B4 and holds B1 on table about 1 inch in front of B4*   (8TB, page 3)

58. *RH pulls by their corners Rectangular Rings 1 and 2 into Square Column 1*
58a. *SC1 is knocked to the floor*   (8NW, page 25)

10. *RH places Rectangular Rings 2 and 3 on top of Triangular Ring 1*
11. *RH raises and immediately lowers RR2 and RR3 on TR1*
                                                                   (8AB, pages 5 and 6)

Subject 8AB's construction is unusual because it is already featured by some regulation. The many-to-one protocorrespondence is reproduced once. Most many-to-one protocorrespondences are extremely labile at their origins. Moreover, their extent is limited to the minimum required. None exceed matching two-to-one objects.

Construction of many-to-one co-univocals completes the elementary organization of protocorrespondence structures. All the direct correlation structures, bi-univocal and co-univocal, necessary to produce part–whole equivalence and multiplicative relations are now available. As primitive as they are, sufficient functional structures have been established for further transformational development of the elements of correlation proto-operations.

VII. Extending Subtractive Iteration within Compositions

The initial organization of direct and coordinated addition and subtraction proto-operations is also completed at this stage. Protosubtraction is generated as frequently as protoaddition. Consequently, decreasing orders within compositions and between consecutive recompositions are now produced as frequently as increasing orders. Reciprocal ordering is just as likely to begin with proto-subtraction as protoaddition. The resultant bidirectional iterative series exceed single alternation between protoaddition and protosubtraction.

The main limitations upon proto-orderings remain twofold. The first is that they are restricted to single series of consecutive compositions. The second is that they are limited to small number series, usually three units, rarely four units, and never five.

Protoaddition continues to be applied within as well as between consecutive compositions. Within composition protoaddition applies to the magnitude of mappings while the number of elements is held constant. The increase may be continuous:

19. *RH rotates Orange Cup into Yellow Cup*
19a. *YC is displaced very slightly away*
20. *LH pushes OC against YC*
20a. *YC slides about 2 inches away*
21. *LH touches OC down on YC*
21a. *YC is pushed further away*   (8AB, page 15)

The increase may be discrete:

44. *RH taps Doll 1 against Spoon held by LH, once, then pauses*
45. *RH taps D1 against S held by LH, twice*   (8CC, page 3)

Protosubtraction begins to be applied within compositions, as well as between consecutive compositions, at this stage. As with protoaddition, the magnitudes of the mappings are ordered while the number of compositional elements is held constant. The decrease may be continuous, for example ⟨hit, tap, touch⟩:

41. *LH hits Circular Ring 2 on Circular Ring 1*
41a. *CR1 moves to right*
42. *LH taps CR2 on table, six times in same place*
43. *LH touches CR2 very lightly on CR1*   (8CC, page 33)

The decrease may be discrete, for example ⟨3, 2, 1⟩:

10. *RH taps Brush 1 just to right of Brush 2, three times*
11. *RH taps B1 on top of B2 twice*
11a. *B2 displaces to left*
12. *pauses as looking at B2*
13. *RH taps B1 on top of B2, once*
13a. *B2 displaces to left, then rotates on table to the right and flips over, so bristles are down*
14. *pauses as looking at B2*   (8CC, page 31)

Alternating protoaddition and protosubtraction begins to be applied to the magnitudes, as well as the set size, of compositions at this stage:

71. *LH hits Red Cross Ring on top of Red Doll*
71a. *RD rolls over table edge into lap*
72. *watches RD roll over edge*
    (experimenter retrieves RD and replaces it upright on table)

73. *looks at RD*
74. *LH hits RCR hard on top of RD*
74a. *RD rolls far to the right*
75. *looks at experimenter*
    (experimenter rolls RD straight toward subject)
76. *Looks down at RD*
77. *LH hits RCR lightly on RD*
77a. *very slight displacement of RD*
78. *LH hits RCR on table 1 inch to left of RD*
79. *LH taps RCR on table 3 inches to left of RD, five times*   (8TB, page 26)

The result is the bidirectional ordering ⟨hit, hit hard, hit lightly, hit, tap⟩. It includes multiple alternation between protoaddition and protosubtraction. It is accompanied by visual monitoring (Lines 72–73 and 76). Perhaps it also includes anticipation that the experimenter will return the patient object (Line 75), thereby permitting the subject to extend the reciprocal ordering relation he is constructing between the magnitudes within a compositional sequence. Together, these features indicate that reciprocal mapping protoseriation within compositions are becoming directed and regulated.

Subjects continue to generate increasing orders between consecutive compositions. Most still consist of single-element protoadditions to form ⟨one-, two-, three-⟩ element consecutive sets. Ordered series of ⟨one-, two-, three-, four-⟩ element consecutive sets are just beginning to be generated, although rarely, as will be discussed.

Protosubtractions producing decreasing series of set sizes are now generated as frequently as protoadditions producing increasing series. Most do not exceed single-element protosubtractions forming ordered decreasing series of ⟨three-, two-, one-⟩ element consecutive sets. Often the constructions are accompanied by perceptual monitoring. Thus, protosubtraction is becoming regulated as well as frequent.

Ordered decreasing series including four-element sets are still generated infrequently by only 25% of the 8-month-old subjects:

1. *LH pushes Yellow Cross Ring to the right into the other three rings*
1a. *Green Circular Ring, Yellow Circular Ring, and Green Cross Ring move in a line to the right*
2.3. *LH slides YCR toward experimenter*
2.7. *RH touches GCR*
4. *LH lifts YCR*
5.5. *mouths YCR held by LH*
5.5. *RH pulls GCR over table edge to floor*   (8CC, page 15)

This sequence of protosubtractions constructs a decreasing order of ⟨four-, three-, two-⟩ element sets.

Usually, protosubtractions from four-element sets are generated in the context of reciprocal bidirectional orderings. It is in these same contexts only that protoadditions are generated which produce increasing orders that include four-element sets:

27. LH *lightly throws down Triangular Ring 1 partially on Triangular Ring 2, which has previously been placed on Cross Ring 2:*

28. LH *lifts Cross Ring 1 and taps it on top of TR1*
28a. CR1 *pushes TR1 flat on table and a little away from TR2, so there is a small separation*
29. LH *raises CR1 and in process LH fingers pull TR2 out from under TR1, so:*

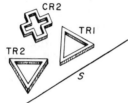

(8AB, page 32)

Alternating protoadditions and protosubractions produce the bidirectional series of ⟨two-, three-, four-, three-⟩ element sets.

It should not be overlooked that most bidirectional series of consecutive sets generated at this stage do not include compositions that exceed three objects. Repeated alternation is just beginning to be generated in this context. Alternation, however, is limited to a single repetition of protoaddition and of protosubtraction. Consequently, the most extended reciprocal orders generated consist of ⟨two-, three-, two-, three-, two-⟩ element consecutive sets. Inherent in these reciprocal orderings, then, is successive reproduction of quantitative iteration. This is the initial opening to forming equivalences between ordering units, albeit entirely limited to consecutive pragmatic series of compositions.

In sum, the elementary organization of protoaddition and protosubtraction is now complete. All the direct and reciprocal ordering relations necessary to produce part–whole ordered nonequivalence relations are available. Sufficient functional structures have been constructed for subsequent developmental elaboration of the elements of iterative structures.

VIII. Random Predication

Predication is still limited to within composition part–whole relations. The reason is that virtually no instances are generated of two partially overlapping or simultaneous compositions (Table 7.6). The structural articulatory features serving to instantiate predicate properties in practical groups are also still limited to order and enclosure. Proximity and separation do not yet mark the compositions generated at this stage.

Order and enclosure continue to be almost perfectly correlated. They stand in one-to-one correspondence in 95% of the compositions where order applies, that is, where two or more objects are directly manipulated in order to compose them. This finding lends developmental corroboration to the hypothesis that these two structural, articulatory features are not differentiated at their origins. They continue to be syncretically fused features of predication in pragmatic set construction.

Predication becomes random at this stage. It should be recalled that the random probability ratio is two-to-one in favor of generating mixed order and enclosure in the semicontrol, additive, and disjoint conditions. The means approximate random probability in all conditions (Table 7.7, Rows 1, 2, and 4). Random predication is corroborated in each instance by the application of sign tests of significance. It should also be recalled that the random probability ratio is two-to-one favoring unmixed order and enclosure in the multiplicative condition. The means approximate random probability (Table 7.7, Row 3). Randomness is corroborated by sign tests of significance.

These findings do not vary as a function of test phase. Attempts to provoke unmixed composing by identities or similarities during phase II were completely unsuccessful. Decomposing and recomposing preexistent, mixed predicate compositions during phase III does originate at this

TABLE 7.7
Spontaneous Phase I: Mean Frequency by 8-Month-Old Subjects Generating Unmixed, Partly Unmixed, and Mixed Compositions

	Order			Enclosure		
	1	2	3	4	5	6
		Partly			Partly	
	Unmixed	unmixed	Mixed	Unmixed	unmixed	Mixed
1. Semicontrol	2.67	0.17	6.17	5.83	0.00	9.50
2. Additive	2.17	0.00	2.25	4.67	0.50	6.25
3. Multiplicative	1.58	0.08	0.75	4.75	0.08	3.33
4. Disjoint	0.83	0.00	0.92	1.50	0.00	3.25

stage (Section I). When generated, decomposing and recomposing neither enhance mixed predication nor construct unmixed predicate grouping, rather, they result in random predicate grouping.

The main and general structural development in predication at this stage is random grouping. During the first stage only semicontrol, ambiguous class structures are grouped randomly. Articulated class structures by negation gives way to random predication. The distinction made at the previous stage in pragmatic predication between ambiguous and class structures is no longer made. All structures are transacted with as if their predicate properties are random or ambiguous.

8

Completion of the Precursory Structures of Quasi-Continuous Combinativity

Composing two quasi-continuous objects into one originates at this stage. While rarely generated, this major development in combinativity proto-operations immediately permits the origins of another set of combinativity structures. Precursory coordinations of composing with deforming, breaking, and decomposing begin to be generated. This ushers in interweaving affirmation (composition) with negation (deforming, breaking, and decomposing) combinativity proto-operations. It complements the interpenetrations between negation operations begun at the previous stage. As such, the elementary coordinative structure of combinativity proto-operations is completed, at least in precursory form. Yet, all combinativity proto-operations remain irreversible. They are never coordinated to produce identity proto-operations such as composing two small balls into a larger ball and then decomposing it back into two small balls.

Deforming and decomposing become more supple and complex. Consecutive sequences of two, and sometimes three, decompositions are generated more frequently. Binary deforming is generated with some frequency, such as pressing both thumbs into one ball. Still, unary deforming remains the mode. Contingent deforming becomes more elaborate, and begins to include protoexperimental deforming. This parallels the origins of protoexperimenting with discrete objects, already analyzed (pages 129–135). More directly relevant to the present considerations is its coordination with the progress made at this stage in monitoring the processes and products of deforming. Together, they extend infants' comparative determination of both the existential properties of quasi-continuous objects and the operational properties of deforming. By itself, progress in monitoring the process and products of consecutive sequences of decomposing reinforces infants' comparative determinations of the part–whole structure of quasi-continuous objects. It also initiates comparative determination of the operational properties of decomposing.

Progress in deforming and decomposing enhances the possibilities for generating and monitoring more advanced protoinferential relations between transformations. Three are particularly significant. The first is the origin of binary protocorresponding deformations of a single object. They produce both single-unit and multiple-unit equivalence relations between part–whole deformations. The second is the beginning detachment of ordering deformations from the protoiterative relations they construct. Detachment is necessary in order to establish order relations as constant givens. Then order relations become subject to further protoinferential consideration, such as precursory coseriated deforming, which also originates at this stage. The third is consecutive decompositions of one object into a single ordered set of three elements preserved for a moment; that is, as the ordered set of ⟨big, medium, small⟩ elements.

I. Flexible Direct Deforming

Deforming continues to predominate transformations of both quasi-continuous objects and combinations of discrete and quasi-continuous objects (Table 8.1). The mean frequency during spontaneous transaction ranges from 3.6 per minute with three objects (Row 1, Column 4), to 6.0 per minute with one object (Row 1, Column 1), to 8.4 per minute with combined discrete–quasi-continuous objects (Row 1, Column 7). While the rate appears highest in the discrete–quasi-continuous condition, the mean is based upon only three subjects. Therefore it is insufficient to determine reliable differences. No significant difference obtains between the one object and three objects conditions (Mann–Whitney $U = 12$, $p = .50$).

The overall frequency of deforming has increased only a little since age 6 months. The main increase is in the frequency of deformations which are multiple and extended over some duration, rather than single and momentary (e.g., repeatedly poking several fingers into a ball of Play-Doh at the same time). About half the deformations are now of this multiple form. The most striking increase in multiple deforming occurs when

TABLE 8.1

Mean Frequency of Combinativity Proto-operations Generated by 8-Month-Old Subjects in Quasi-Continuous and Discrete–Quasi-Continuous Conditions

| | One object | | | Three objects | | | Discrete-quasi-continuous | |
	Phase I 1	Phase II 2	Phase III 3	Phase I 4	Phase II 5	Phase III 6	Phase I 7	Phase II 8
1. Deforming	11.17 (6.67)[a]	3.67 (2.33)	10.40 (8.00)	10.67 (4.17)	2.00 (1.00)	8.40 (6.00)	14.00 (7.33)	6.50 (1.00)
2. Reforming	0.00	0.00	0.00	0.00	0.00	0.00	0.00	0.00
3. Breaking	0.33	0.00	0.60	0.67	0.67	0.20	0.00	0.00
4. Reconstructing	0.00	0.00	0.00	0.00	0.00	0.00	0.00	0.00
5. Decomposing[b]	3.33	0.50	1.40	2.67 (0.17)	0.33	1.20	3.33	2.00
6. Recomposing	0.00	0.00	0.00	0.00	0.00	0.00	0.00	0.00
7. Composing	0.00	0.00	0.40	0.67	0.00	0.20	0.00	0.00
8. Redecomposing	0.00	0.00	0.00	0.00	0.00	0.00	0.00	0.00
9. Attaching	—	—	—	—	—	—	0.00	0.00
10. Detaching	—	—	—	—	—	—	0.00	0.50
11. Number of subjects	6	6	5	6	3	5	3	2
12. Mean duration	1 min 56 sec[c]	1 min 15 sec[c]	1 min 51 sec	2 min 51 sec[c]	1 min 12 sec	1 min 33 sec	1 min 43 sec	1 min 48 sec
13. Discrete compositions	0.00	0.17	4.20	3.17	0.00	2.60	3.00	1.00
14. Rate of productivity	0.00	0.14	2.40	1.20	0.00	1.80	1.80	0.60

[a] Mean frequencies of proto-operations involving multiple transformations are given in parentheses.
[b] The frequencies are necessarily underestimations because, when possible, subjects were not allowed to decompose by biting.
[c] Calculated on the basis of the five subjects for whom duration measures are available.

subjects spontaneously transact with one object; from less than one per minute at age 6 months to almost four per minute at age 8 months.

The deforming rate does not vary as a function of object type (i.e., Euclidean balls or topological rings). It does decrease a little bit during the provoked second phase (Row 1, Columns 2, 5, and 8). However, phase II is designed to provoke composing, decomposing, or attaching and detaching, and not deforming. During phase III, the deforming rate remains constant (Row 1, Column 3) or increases (Row 1, Column 6). The increase is in both overall and multiple deformings. It should be recalled that subjects are presented with two sets of three quasi-continuous objects during phase III.

Deforming remains irreversible. Deforming is never followed by any attempts to generate reciprocal reforming (Row 2). While all objects are deformed several times, they are never reformed to produce intensive protoidentity, thereby preserving the objects' forms. Irreversible deforming is general to all conditions, test phases, and object types.

Deforming continues to be dominated by logically entailed transactions. Most are inherent intersective products of the mappings' and objects' structures (e.g., pressing against Play-Doh necessitates deforming it). Only half of the subjects (6 of 12) generate contingent deforming. All but one of these six subjects generate contingent deforming repeatedly.

Contingent deforming is becoming more elaborate. It includes multiple deformations:

6. *LH pushes Ring 1 down into her lap*
7. *LH pushes R1 down into the arm of the chair*
8. *LH raises R1 up*
9. *LH pushes R1 down into the arm of the chair*
10. *LH pushes R1 into the chair seat*
11. *LH raises R1 up*
11a. *R1 is all squished and no longer in ring shape*
12. *LH touches R1 on her pants*
13. *LH touches R1 further down her leg on her pants*
14. *LH pushes R1 into the chair seat*
15. *LH raises R1 up*
16. *LH puts R1 to mouth and starts to bite it*
   (mother takes it out before subject's teeth close around it)
17. *LH pushes R1 into the arm of the chair*   (8EH, page 7)

48. *RH taps Ball on table a few times*
49. *RH lifts B, holds it in air briefly and looks at it*
50. *RH taps B on table about three times*   (8AB, pages 26 and 27)

Multiple contingent deforming may be continuous in form: Subject 8EH presses the Play-Doh into various surfaces for some time. Or, it may be discrete in form: Subject 8AB taps the Play-Doh in two repeated chunks on the table. In between he monitors the transformation in the part–whole relations internal to the object which is produced by his deforming operations.

The most advanced contingent deformation, generated by one subject, involves multiple objects as well as multiple deformations:

22. RH *hits Ball 4-5 onto table*
23. LH *hits Balls 1 and 2 onto table*   (8JL, page 28)

First, she contingently deforms (Line 22) conglomerate Ball 4-5 which she has just composed and visually inspected. Immediately afterwards she contingently deforms Balls 1 and 2 simultaneously. Shortly afterwards she again deforms Balls 1 and 2 simultaneously, but now the deformations are multiple:

27. LH *hits Ball 1 and Ball 2 onto table twice, as RH holds remainder of Ball 4-5*
28. *looks at B1 and B2 held by LH*   (8JL, page 28)

At this point it is not clear from the videotape whether Balls 1 and 2 have already become composed into a larger conglomerate. They are clearly composed together within the next 5 seconds, after the subject mouths them a bit. In any case, it is apparent that the subject is visually monitoring the transformations, whether deformations or compositions, that she is constructing. The transformations involve repeated contingent deforming of three objects. For the first time, then, one infant deforms simultaneously a set of two objects.

Instrumental contingent deforming, where one object is used to deform another, is generated clearly by only two subjects. Nonrelevant transactions are omitted in the second protocol fragment.

30. LH *hits Large Ball partially on top of Ball 1-2*
31. LH *raises LB*
31a. LB *pushes B1-2 to right as LH raises LB*
32. LH *hits LB down on top of B1-2*   (8AB, page 29)

49. RH *loosely grasps Large Ball by a small part of it, such that the major part of the ball is dangling somewhat*
50. RH *hits LB on top of both Balls 2 and 4*
51. RH *hits LB on top of B2*
52. RH *hits LB on top of B4*
52a. *major part of LB comes off onto table*
53. RH *hits small part of LB, remaining in hand, on top of major part of LB*
59. LH *hits large part of LB on top of Ball 1*
60. LH *hits large part of LB on top of B4*   (8TB, page 22)

Instrumental contingent deforming generated by these two subjects is reciprocal. Both agent and patient objects are deformed simultaneously.

Binary reciprocal deformations result from each instrumental transaction. Both subjects replicate their reciprocal contingent deformations. Subject 8AB's replication is limited to the same two objects. Subject 8TB's replications are extended to five objects. These are initial indications that their reciprocal contingent deformations are becoming regulated.

Subject 8TB's constructions include contingent decomposition of the Large Ball (Lines 52–52a). Contingent decomposition of the Large Ball is a direct simultaneous extension of its instrumental employment to generate contingent deformation. It is immediately extended to continued reciprocal contingent deformation between the two objects resulting from the contingent decomposition (Line 53). After exchanging instrumental objects, from the small to the big part resulting from decomposing the Large Ball, contingent deforming is further extended to one repeat and one new patient object (Lines 59–60). As such, contingent deforming is tightly interwoven with contingent decomposing. The ramifications for the development of coordinated negation proto-operations will be considered in Section III where this topic will be considered further.

Comparative exploration of the part–whole relations internal to quasi-continuous objects is coordinated with deforming them. Individual objects are immediately inspected before (8JL), during (8TB), and after (8PM) being multiply deformed:

1. *RH grasps Ball and lifts it slightly off table by rotating it*
2. *LH touches B held by RH*
3. *LH rotates B, moving B away from RH*
4. *RH moves after B*
5.5. *LH rotates B*
5.5. *RH fingers make multiple indentations in B*   (8JL, page 24)

22. *LH fingers lightly make about four open-squeeze motions on Ball part of Tongue Depressor + Ball as looks closely at what he's doing*
22a. *repeated depressions are made in B*   (8TB, page 39)

91. *LH pulls Ball 1 off RH thumb*
92. *BH grasp B1*
93. *LH removes from B1 held by RH*
93a. *B1 is completely squished by now*
94. *RH moves B1 back and forth as looking at it*   (8PM, page 18)

Comparative exploration is becoming semisystematic. Subject 8JL rotates the ball with her right hand and examines it tactually with her left hand. Then she switches hands and rotates it with her left hand. At this point in her comparative inspection of the ball's surface, 8JL begins to make indentations in the surface with her right hand fingers as she simultaneously rotates it.

Objects are immediately inspected before being contingently deformed:

1. *picks up Ring 1 on LH index finger*
2.5. *rotates LH wrist around*
2.5. *looks at both sides of R1*
4. *RH takes R1 off LH index finger*
5. *RH swishes R1 around*   (8EH, page 7)

These transactions precede consecutive contingent deformations considered on page 176 (8EH, p. 7, Lines 6–17). Comparative exploration includes two important components at this stage. One is differentiated visiomotor inspection of parts of the object (i.e., the ring's two sides). The second is inverse transformations of the objects resulting in identity proto-operations applied to the whole object. In this way, parts are compared in relation to the object's whole identity as a constant given element. Once established, the subject proceeds to contingently deform the object many times.

At the same time, 8-month-olds are becoming progressively accomplished at preserving the existence of quasi-continuous objects when the transformations are limited to presentational transformations:

21. *RH places Ball 4 back on table edge without looking*
21a. *B4 falls to floor*
      (mother returns piece of clay to table)
22. *looks down at B4 after it falls and while mother retrieves it* (8PM, page 23)

This parallels the developments in preserving the existence of discrete objects (pages 124–129). Indeed, 8-month-old subjects repeatedly construct and solve presentational preservation problems of this complexity. In part this may be because they are integral to their protoexperimentation which originates at this stage. Protoexperimenting with discrete objects has already been analyzed (pages 129–135). Protoexperimenting with quasi-continuous objects will be considered shortly; for illustrations of preserving the existence of objects being protoexperimentally deformed see the protocol fragment from 8GP presented on page 181.

Coordinated comparative exploring and deforming is extended to two objects:

1. *RH picks up Ball 3 as looking at it*
2. *looks down at Ball 2, as RH holds B3*
3. *looks at B3 held by RH*
4. *looks at experimenter very quickly*
5. *looks several seconds at B3 held by RH*
6. *RH squeezes B3 between thumb and index*
6a. *B3 is deformed, has indentation marks and is stuck on index finger*
7. *LH removes B3 from RH*

8. *RH touches B3 held by LH*
9. *looks at B2, while LH holds B3*
10. *RH picks up B2, while LH holds B3*
11. *RH pinches B2 between fingers, while LH holds B3*
11a. *B2 is deformed and has indentation marks*
12. *looks at B3 held by LH*
13. *looks at B2 held by RH*
14. *looks back and forth at B2 and B3 briefly, held respectively by RH and LH*
15. *LH releases B3 onto table*
16. *LH takes B2 from RH*
17. *RH touches B3 as looking at it, while LH holds B2*   (8AB, page 25)

Subject 8AB's comparative exploration is exhaustive. To begin with, he immediately looks back and forth between the two objects he is going to deform, while ignoring the third object which he does not deform (Lines 1–4). Thus, his comparative exploration is both selective and directed. He proceeds by visually inspecting Ball 3 which he is about to deform first (Line 5). Deforming is quite differentiated, that is, pinching between two fingers only. It produces multiple reciprocal deformations (Lines 6 and 6a). He tactually observes the resultant changes in Ball 3, as though he is monitoring the transformations he has produced in its part–whole relations and comparing it to its initial predeformed state.

Before switching to deforming Ball 2, 8AB switches to visually monitoring it (Line 9). Again, his deforming is quite differentiated and results in multiple reciprocal deformations (Lines 11 and 11a). He follows up by much visual (Lines 12–14, and 17) and tactual (Line 17) comparative monitoring of the deformations he has produced in both balls. Thereby, he generates all the conditions necessary to comparing the two objects' initial states with their transformed states.

Tactilokinesthetic monitoring inheres in all deforming. Some continue to be monitored visually as well:

48. *RH holds Large Ball up in air and squeezes it as looks at it*
48a. *LB is quite deformed*   (8TB, page 22)

Subjects, then, are monitoring the ongoing processes of their deforming transformations as well as the objects' predeformed and postdeformed states. Monitoring is becoming progressively comparative and systematic. Thereby, infants are progressively constructing sufficient conditions for determining the transformational properties of deforming. This promotes eventual structural development of irreversible into protoreversible deformation.

Comparative determination begins to be buttressed by nonsystematic protoexperimenting which, we have already seen in regard to discrete objects, originates at this stage. Most protoexperimenting with quasi-continuous objects is similar, at least to begin with, to that with discrete objects. It is always applied to only one object; never a set of two or more objects. But it is interspersed with actual or attempted contingent deforming. Consider the following protoexperimental sequence in which minor and irrelevant transactions have been omitted for the sake of clarity:

12. *looks at Ball held by RH*
13. *RH drops B*
14. *RH picks B up and brings it to mouth*
     (experimenter pushes it out of subject's mouth to table)
18. *looks at B*
19. *RH raises B a bit*
21. *RH drops B*
22. *looks at B*
23. *RH touches B*
24. *RH picks B up and brings it to mouth*
     (experimenter and father move subject's hand down—B drops to table)
28. *looks at B*
29. *RH picks B up*
30. *RH drops B*
31. *RH picks up B and brings it to mouth*
     (experimenter and father take B down)
32. *RH picks up B*
33. *RH drops B*   (8GP, pages 58 and 59)

Subject 8GP continues in this vein for several minutes. He drops the ball from different heights, but nonsystematically. In subsequent protoexperimenting, not reproduced here, he also pushes the ball around in different ways, but again nonsystematically. The results are continuous, minor deformations of the ball. They are monitored throughout. In addition, the subject attempts to deform, and perhaps decompose, the ball by mouthing it, but he is not permitted. Thus, the subject drops the ball from different heights and pushes it around in variant but nonsystematic ways in order to observe differential consequences. These include differential, and perhaps even cumulative, deformations.

Recall in this regard 8EH's sequence of transactions (protocol fragment p. 7, Lines 1–5 presented on page 179 and protocol fragment p. 7, Lines 6–17 presented on page 176). After comparatively exploring the ring the subject proceeds to deform it, repeatedly and contingently. These deformations vary as a function of the substance of the surface into which the subject pushes the ring. The substance varies from soft (her own lap) to firm but resilient (the foam rubber seat) to hard (the steel arm of the highchair). Therefore, the effects she produces vary in the order

⟨minor, major, major, intermediate, intermediate, major⟩ deformations. These are the effects of the transformations in Lines 6, 7, 9, 10, 14, and 17, respectively.

Protoexperimenting, even at this precursory level, augments infants' determination of the transformational properties of deforming quasi-continuous objects. Thereby, the subjects begin to provide themselves with an enriched data base for comparative determination of the operation and its results. At this stage, this already includes semisystematic observation by the subjects of (a) the isolated object they are about to transform protoexperimentally, (b) their own ongoing transformational constructions, (c) the ongoing deformations in the object's internal part–whole relations, and (d) the contingent variations in deforming which results.

It should not be overlooked that this data-gathering process is extremely rudimentary. Protoexperimenting is nonsystematic; and the components of comparative observation are semisystematic. Moreover, the components of comparative observation are only beginning to be coordinated with each other, let alone with protoexperimenting. It will therefore be quite a while before infants understand the operational properties of deforming sufficiently for them to begin to transform deforming into a reversible proto-operation. However, the necessary structural foundation has been established.

II. Partial Regulation and Coordination of Equivalence and Order Relations between Deformations

Three forms of protocorresponding deformations are generated. Less advanced manifestations of two are already produced at the previous stage. They are protocorrespondences (a) between multiple synchronic deformations of a single object and (b) between simultaneous deformations of two objects. The third originates at this stage. It consists of binary deformations of a single object.

Multiple synchronic deforming is generated more frequently than before; 75% of the subjects at this stage and 50% at the previous stage. This form of constructing protocorrespondences begins to be regulated. Typically, it is marked by consecutive reproductions on a single object only. Its most advanced manifestation is consecutive multiple application to several objects.

The most advanced production involves consecutive application to three objects. In order to keep the protocol fragment brief some intervening picking up and discarding activity will be omitted:

8. *LH fingers press into Ball 1 twice by opening–closing*
14. *LH fingers press into Ball 2 twice by opening–closing quickly*
16. *LH fingers press into Ball 3 four times by opening–closing* (8BK, page 35)

Repeated multiple synchronic deforming on a single object insures that the resultant protocorresponding traces are recorded and preserved in the object. The protocorresponding deformations are now clearly observable. By itself, regulated synchronic deforming of a single object enhances the possibilities for comparing and determining multiple equivalence relations between single-unit part–whole transformations. These possibilities are augmented when the subjects begin to reproduce multiple synchronic deforming on several objects in succession. Multiple protocorrespondences between single-unit part–whole deformations are recorded and preserved on the several objects. Thereby, the way is opened for comparative determination of (*a*) single-unit equivalences within each object, (*b*) single-unit equivalences between objects, and, potentially, (*c*) equivalences between protocorresponding sets of deformations in as many as three objects.

Missing is any indication that subjects monitor the resultant protocorrespondent deformations in the several objects. Rather, the indications are all in the opposite direction. The subjects still simply discard each object, in turn, after multiply deforming it. On the other hand, subjects are beginning to visually monitor both their transformative activity and the protocorresponding deformations in individual objects:

22. *LH fingers lightly make about four open–squeeze motions on Ball part of Tongue Depressor + Ball as looks closely at what he's doing*
22a. *repeated depressions are made in B*   (8TB, page 39)

Subject 8TB's careful deforming procedure suggests that he may well be monitoring his ongoing transformational activity via tactilokinesthetic as well as visual perception. He certainly monitors visually the resultant equivalence between multiple single-unit deformations. It should not be overlooked, however, that this is as comprehensive visual monitoring as is produced by any subject at this stage. Moreover, not all subjects monitor the deformations they produce, and those that do are still erratic: Sometimes they do and sometimes they do not monitor the resultant protocorresponding deformations.

Protocorresponding deforming of two objects is generated by 3 of the 12 subjects; at the previous stage it was generated by only one subject. With one possible exception, all are limited in application to two objects:

14. *LH hits Balls 1 and 2 onto table, four times*   (8JL, page 28)

The possible exception is a potential three-object set of protocorresponding deformations by *8JL*. The relevant protocol fragment has already been reported on page 177. First, *8JL* contingently deforms conglomerate Ball 4-5 (Line 22). Immediately afterward, she contingently deforms two balls by the same mapping, at the same time (Line 23). The result is equivalent continuous deformations in all three objects. The equivalent deformations are preserved and recorded in all three objects. Therefore, the momentary asynchrony in the constructive process may be relatively unimportant and this construction may foreshadow protocorresponding deformation of three-object sets. Nevertheless, it is not reproduced by this subject, and it is never produced by any other 8-month-old subject. At most, then, it constitutes a nonregulated precursor of equivalence between deformations in three-object sets.

Equivalences between deformations in two-object sets is becoming regulated. It is produced by all three subjects who apply simultaneous deformations to two objects. It is replicated many times. The mapping form is constant (e.g., hitting the balls down onto the table). Deforming is applied simultaneously to both objects. The sequence of protocorresponding deforming is accompanied by subjects visually monitoring the equivalence relations constructed in the part–whole structure of both objects.

Thus, directed equivalences between deformations of two-object sets originate at this stage. It should be recalled that only one subject (6AW) applied simultaneous protocorresponding deformations to two objects at the previous stage (page 109). Her constructions were applied simultaneously to two separate objects which were not united into a set. Each object was deformed in a different hand and the hands were not held together. All three subjects at this stage unite the two objects into a set held by one hand before deforming them simultaneously.

Binary protocorresponding deforming of one object also originates at this stage. This is a direct and particular extension of the general increase in frequency of binary mappings. Binary protocorresponding deforming is generated by 3 of the 12 subjects. One subject generated it only once, while the other two subjects did so repeatedly. The most advanced sequence, omitting nonrelevant intervening transactions, is already fairly extensive:

4.5. *RH fingers squeeze Ball making depressions in it*
4.5. *LH fingers squeeze B making depressions in it*
13.5. *RH thumb presses into B making an indentation in it*
13.5. *LH thumb presses into B making an indentation in it*
14.5. *RH fingers press lightly into B making small depressions in it*
14.5. *LH fingers press lightly into B making small depressions in it*
16. *looks at B as BH raise it*

17. *BH rotate B as looks very intently at it*
20. *looks at B as BH raise it*
21. *LH touches B held by RH*
22. *BH touch B*
23.5. *RH fingers press lightly into B making small indentations*
23.5. *LH fingers press lightly into B making small indentations*

(8TB, pages 15 and 16)

Binary deforming is applied repeatedly to produce multiple synchronic protocorrespondences (Lines 4.5, 14.5, and 23.5). It is also applied by two thumbs only so as to produce a singular synchronic protocorrespondence (Lines 13.5). Reproduction of multiple synchronic binary protocorrespondences plus variation from multiple to singular to multiple synchronic binary protocorrespondences indicates that this is already becoming a regulated proto-operation.

The consecutive and variant equivalence relations produced are monitored extensively by both visiomotor (Lines 16, 17, and 20) and tactilokinesthetic (Lines 21 and 22) perception. Visiomotor inspection includes reversible rotation of the ball. This permits determining protoidentity relations within the part–whole structure of the deformed ball. Applying an identity proto-operation to the ball establishes it as a constant given. This facilitates the subject's comparative determination of the part–whole equivalence deformations which he himself is producing in the ball.

Detaching ordered products of deforming from the ordered process of deforming progresses significantly at this stage. Consider the just quoted protocol (8TB). Five ordered series are involved. First, the continuous magnitude of deforming decreases from fingers squeezing (Lines 4.5) and thumbs pressing (Lines 13.5) to fingers pressing lightly (Lines 14.5 and 23.5). Second, the discrete number of deforming decreases (from fingers to thumbs) and then increases (to fingers). Third, the magnitude of each resultant deformation decreases from big to small indentations. Fourth, since some deformations produced are continuous, they cumulatively increase from deep to deeper indentations. Fifth, since other deformations produced are discrete, they cumulatively increase from some to more indentations.

This sequence, then, generates five ordered part–whole relations within a single object:

1. a continuous decreasing mapping order of ⟨hard, light⟩ pressure;
2. a discrete bidirectional mapping order of ⟨many, few, many⟩ squeezing;
3. a continuous decreasing product order of ⟨big, small⟩ indentations;

4. a continuous increasing product order of ⟨deep, deeper⟩ indentations; and
5. a discrete increasing product order of ⟨some, more⟩ marks.

In this way varied opportunities are generated by subjects within the protocorresponding transformations they are constructing to begin to differentiate their additive and subtractive proto-operations from the orderings produced. Furthermore, the necessary conditions for detaching protoiterative relations, such that they may eventually be considered as constant givens for further protoinferential calculation, are inherent in the subject's own constructions at this stage.

This stage also marks the origins of constructing the necessary conditions to begin to coordinate equivalence with nonequivalence relations in part–whole quasi-continuous objects. Its precursors begin to be formed, as we have just seen, when subjects transact with a single object. Subject 8TB interweaves binary protocorresponding with ordered deformations of one object. Its precursors also begin to be generated when subjects transact with two-object sets. For instance, 8JL (protocol fragment, p. 28, Lines 14, 22–23, and 27, presented on pages 177 and 183) simultaneously generates protocorresponding continuous deformations and protoadditive continuous deformations of Balls 1 and 2. Repeated reproduction by both subjects plus some visual monitoring (e.g., by 8TB), indicates that generating coordinated equivalence with nonequivalence relations is also beginning to be regulated. As such, the precursory conditions necessary to constructing corresponding orderings or protocoseriations are generated. It should not be overlooked, however, that these conditions are so far only generated by one-third of the subjects (4 of 12).

The data discussed reveals another advance in ordered deforming at this stage. Precursory ordered transforming of the part–whole relations in two-object sets originates at this stage. As just noted, 8JL continuously bangs two balls onto the table producing continuous decreasing orders of deformation in both balls; they are progressively flattened.

Precursory ordered deforming of sets is extremely impoverished at this stage. The sets are limited to two objects only. Ordered deforming of sets is generated by only 2 of the 12 8-month-old subjects. Only one of the two subjects produces it more than once. Both subjects generated continuous decreasing orders only. The orders are always continuous, never discrete. The continuous orders are restricted, at least on the surface, to constructing decreasing magnitudes, not increasing magnitudes. Of course, the inherent compensatory structure of continuous objects means that the magnitudes necessarily increase as well; as the balls are increasingly thinned they are also increasingly widened.

One other precursory development originates at this stage. Binary reciprocal mappings begin to be applied to single objects such that ordered deformations are constructed:

  7.5.   LH *hits Ball 1 on RH, twice*
  7.5.   RH *grasps at and immediately releases a part of B1, twice*
  7.5a. *B1 becomes more and more deformed until the major portion of B1 is pulled off and falls to floor*   (8BK, page 34)

Like ordered deforming of two-object sets, however, precursory binary ordered deforming is extremely impoverished at this stage. It is not generated by more than a couple of subjects, etc.

One other, a quantitative increase, marks the development of ordering proto-operations applied to quasi-continuous objects at this stage. While still not generated very frequently, 8-month-olds generate ordering proto-operations much more frequently than 6-month-olds. Otherwise, ordering proto-operations remain much the same. They are rarely the result of contingent deforming. Continuous orderings predominate; discrete orderings are generated rarely. Increasing orders are generated more frequently than decreasing orders. Clear manifestations of alternating increasing with decreasing orders are rarely, if ever, generated. Compensation, as noted above, is inherent in a substantial subset of ordered deformations, as it was at age 6 months.

III. Flexible Decomposing and Its Coordination with Deforming and Breaking

Breaking quasi-continuous objects is still not generated by the majority of subjects. Moreover, it is still generated infrequently (Table 8.1, Row 3). The main advance is that subjects begin to break Euclidean balls, as well as topological rings:

  3.   LH *fingers press into Ball 1 such that thumb pokes through it*
                                      (8BK, page 34)

No attempt is made to reconstruct broken rings or balls (Table 8.1, Row 4). Breaking remains an irreversible transformation at this stage.

Breaking a ball transforms it from a Euclidean-like object into an object which has striking topological features. Breaking a ring transforms it from a topological-like object into an object dominated by Euclidean properties. So, while both remain direct, irreversible proto-operations, the conditions necessary for their transformation into reversible proto-operations originate at this stage. Missing is any integration of the two.

Another development at this stage opens up further avenues for eventually transforming breaking into a reversible proto-operation. It consists of deforming a ring into a mass:

1. *LH takes Large Ring*
2. *RH grabs LR*
3. *BH squish LR together into a large mass*
4. *BH rotate large mass*
5. *LH holds large mass as touches it with RH* (8KC, page 21)

In this way deforming transforms a topological-like into an Euclidean-like object. It is followed up by tactilokinesthetic monitoring (Lines 4 and 5). Missing is any subsequent breaking which would reverse the deformative transformation.

Decomposing frequency does not change significantly from age 6 to 8 months. Most decompositions are still generated during the spontaneous test phase (Table 8.1, Row 5). Frequency of decomposing does not vary as a function of the objects' shape, whether Euclidean or topological. It does vary as a function of the number of objects. Decomposing frequency is inversely related to the number of objects. About twice as many are generated when transacting with one object (Row 5, Column 1) as when transacting with three objects (Row 5, Column 4) or six objects (Row 5, Columns 3 and 6).

Decomposing is generated least frequently during the second, provoked test phase (Table 8.1, Row 5, Columns 2 and 5). Some subjects did not decompose at all, while the rest rarely generate more than one decomposition. It should be recalled that for half of the subjects (6 subjects) this test phase began by presenting them with decompositions of the objects by the experimenter:

1. *watches as experimenter pulls Play-Doh apart*
   (experimenter rolls the Play-Doh, one in each hand; holds them out to subject)
2. *looks at Ball 1 on left*
3. *looks at Ball 2 on right*
4. *(experimenter rotates balls and holds them up) as subject moves towards balls with BH*
5. *LH touches B2*
6. *LH grasps B2*
7. *LH lowers B2 to left side*
   (experimenter puts B1 down)
8. *RH touches B1, while holding B2 in LH*
9. *RH lifts up in air, while B2 in LH*
10. *looks at B2 held in LH*
11. *RH touches B2 held in LH*

    12.   BH *hold B2*
    13.   LH *rotates B2 as RH pulls at it*   (8JL, page 26)

The experimenter's decomposing is observed (Line 1) and the resultant multiplication of objects is comparatively inspected in some detail (Lines 2–10). Yet, the subject does not follow the experimenter by decomposing even though the subject spontaneously decomposed the ball several times during the immediately preceding test phase. Instead, she generates binary deformation of the ball (Line 13), and follows it up with visual and tactual monitoring of the transformation she produces in the ball (not reproduced in the protocol fragment).

The experimenter's decomposing was visible to five subjects. It was not visible to one subject; he was presented with the result of the decomposition only, that is, three smaller objects in the same shape as the single original object. The resultant decrease in decomposing frequency during the second test phase, indeed its extinction for all practical purposes, is therefore significant. It serves to disconfirm the hypothesis that observation of decomposing demonstrated by others may be a cause of decomposing by 8-month-olds. These resuls are continuous with those for 6-month-old subjects presented with modeling of decomposition. They, too, evidenced a marked decrease in rate of decomposing.

Contingent decomposing remains the exception, although it is beginning to be generated more frequently than it was at age 6 months (see, for example, the 8TB protocol fragment, particularly Lines 52–52a, presented on page 177). Most decomposings continue to be direct intersective results of mappings by objects. The prime factors are prior deforming or breaking (8MM) by subjects, lack of structural physical resistance by quasi-continuous objects, subjects' observations of their own decomposing (8NW), and subjects' observations of the object before and after decomposing it (8JL):

    4.   LH *pulls on Large Ring, breaking it immediately*
    5.3. RH *holds dangling Long Piece*
    5.7. LH *grabs LP near RH and pulls*
    5.7a. LH *has a Major Part of LP; RH holds remaining stub*
    7.   LH *inserts end of MP into mouth and bites off a small piece*
                                                    (8MM, page 25)

    50.5. *looks at Piece 3 held by RH*
    50.5. LH *thumb rubs on P3*
    52.   LH *pulls a little piece off from P3*
          (*experimenter continues to hold up single Tongue Depressor to subject*)
    53.   LH *touches Piece 2 and Ball*   (8NW, page 44)

27. *looks at Ball 1*
28. *RH picks up B1, brings B1 to mouth, and takes a bite of B1*
29. *looks down at B1 in RH*
30. *RH brings B1 toward mouth*
     (mother stops her and mother puts B1 down on the table)   (8JL, page 27)

In the main, decomposing still involves only gross unary mappings, such as biting and pinching. Some unary decomposing is becoming a bit differentiated:

123. *RH pulls Ball 1 apart by opposing push of two fingers*
      (experimenter pushes Ball 3 toward subject)
124. *one piece of B1 sticks to RH as lifts RH in air*   (8PM, page 20)

Decomposing by the two fingers is reciprocally related (opposing pushing) to each other (Line 123). This is all the more so when decomposing involves binary mappings; as we have already seen when, for instance, subjects thrust a quasi-continuous object with one hand at another which pulls at the object. Reciprocal binary decomposings are always asymmetrical, never symmetrical. When generated by 8-month-olds, they are usually extensions of deforming. They are rarely reciprocal binary decompositions from the start.

Consecutive multiple decompositions are generated more frequently at age 8 months, but still not by the majority of subjects:

13. *BH split Large Ring into two strands*
14. *RH pulls off a small piece from LH strand; so RH has two pieces and LH one piece*
15. *while holding a strand and the small piece, RH grasps at strand in LH*
16. *drops two of the pieces into lap*
17. *looks toward lap very quickly*   (8NW, page 21)

28. *RH raises Tongue Depressor + Ball by ball part*
29. *LH pulls Piece 1 off the ball of TD + B*
30. *LH pulls Piece 2 off the ball of TD + B releasing it to table*
31. *RH squeezes Piece 3 off the ball of TD + B*   (8NW, page 43)

In the first instance, 8NW decomposes the ring into three elements and, in the second, into four elements. Protomultiplication of one object into a set of many objects is generated twice. So is protodivision of a larger extent into smaller ones. However, the sets remain small. Moreover, no follow-up transactions are generated of the kind that would indicate that the multiple elements are actually related to each other in any way to form collections or sets. Yet, the necessary conditions are being prepared at this stage for subsequent development of multiplying and collecting elements into single sets.

The conditions are also being prepared for constructing ordered sets. As always, the successor elements are smaller than the initial object. So, decreasing orders of ⟨big, smaller⟩ are inherent results of decomposing. These inherent orders are constructed in temporal succession (i.e., first a big object by itself and then only small objects). The orderings are not preserved beyond the moment of construction. They are beginning to be constructed in repeated succession, and they are beginning to be monitored perceptually. While beginning to be regulated orderings, temporal asynchrony between the products means that they are not preserved concretely. Conservation of temporally asynchronous orderings, notwithstanding substantive impermanence, requires representational mappings not yet available during early infancy.

Substantively permanent temporally synchronous ordered two-element sets continue to be generated, as they are at the previous stage. They are becoming less labile. They are also beginning to be extended by a few subjects to ordered three-element sets. This is apparent in the first 8NW protocol fragment (page 190). First, 8NW splits the ring into two, producing two fairly equal halves (Line 13). Then she pulls off a small piece (Line 14). These divisions result in an ordered set of ⟨big, medium, small⟩ elements. The ordered set is preserved in temporal synchrony for a moment in the subject's hands (Lines 14 and 15). When part of the set falls out of her hands, the subject acts to preserve the ordered set by looking after the disappearing elements (Lines 16 and 17).

Coordinated decomposing and deforming is generated at least once by almost all subjects at this stage. Deforming is extended into decomposing:

24. *LH fingers grasp Ball and pull it out of shape*
25. *RH releases grasp as LH takes B and shakes it over left chair arm*
25a. *most of the Play-Doh falls onto the floor*
26. *LH releases the remainder of B onto floor*   (8BK, page 32)

Other productions of deforming extended into decomposing which involve binary mappings have already been presented (e.g., first 8BK protocol fragment on page 187).

Decomposing is extended into deforming:

2. *bites Ball held by LH*
3. *LH pulls B out of mouth*
4. *bites B held by LH*
5. *chews on what she's bitten off*
6. *looks at the deformed B LH pulled out of mouth*
7. *LH pulls at part of B that had been pulled up by teeth*
8. *looks at B*   (8EH, page 5)

Multiple decompositions (Lines 2 and 4) are extended into multiple deformations (Lines 5 and 7). One extension may actually involve composing the two pieces bitten off (Line 5). These coordinations include visual monitoring of the transformations in the ball due to the decompositions (Line 6) and one of the deformations (Line 8).

Coordinations begin to include intertwining deforming and decomposing; see, for instance, the 8TB protocol fragment reproduced on page 177. Subject 8TB's coordination involves consecutive deforming (Lines 49–51), decomposing (Lines 52 and 52a), and deforming (Line 53) of the Large Ball. Moreover, all are contingent transformations. However, intertwined coordinating of deforming and decomposing does not exceed this extent; and it is generated by only a few subjects.

Coordinating breaking with deforming originates at this stage. It is applied to both Euclidean (8BK) and topological objects (8NW):

2. *LH touches Balls 1 and 2*
3. *LH grasps B1 and presses fingers into it*
4. *LH thumb presses through B1*
5. *sits back in chair as opens LH, revealing deformed piece of clay stuck to thumb*
6. *RH grasps B1 with hole from his LH*
7. *LH touches B1 with hole*   (8BK, pages 34 and 35)

33. *LH raises Ring 3 and squeezes it*
34. *LH drops R3 to table*
35. *LH fingers break open R3 into one strand*
36. *RH inserts Ring 1 into mouth*   (8NW, page 18)

Coordinated breaking and deforming is generated by only a minority of subjects. Yet, it is sometimes accompanied by perceptual monitoring. For instance, 8BK tactually examines the ball before and after transforming its internal part–whole relations.

Structural interpenetrations between negation transformations of quasi-continuous objects, then, progress markedly at this stage. Most significant is the origins of coordinating breaking and deforming. Precursory coordinating of breaking with decomposing begins to be generated (see 8MM protocol fragment on page 189). Both forms augment coordination of decomposing and deforming which originates at the previous stage, and which becomes more extensive, complex and regulated at this stage.

Coordinations of negation transformations are not generated in a context of systematic comparative inspection. Consequently, the coordinations achieved remain limited. They exclude directed gauging and modifying of (a) the three forms of negation and (b) their differential products, to accord with each other. At most, the coordinations are limited to treating the three negation forms as though they occupy the same mapping and structural rank, that is, consecutive interweaving.

Still excluded from the coordinative functional structure is differentiation between these three negation forms. There can be no ascription of similarities, differences, or complementarities between deforming, breaking and decomposing. Also excluded are any magnitude or extensity features. Reciprocally, hierarchic integration between these negation forms is excluded. One negation form cannot be subsumed by another, nor can one include another. One negation form can only be extended temporally and materially into another. Excluded, then, are both qualitative or quantitative features of hierarchic integration. Thus, for instance, there can be no question that 8-month-old subjects' constructions evince no symptoms indicating that they are cognizant that decomposing necessarily includes deforming while deforming does not necessarily include decomposing.

These coordinations, in particular, include symptoms of yet another precursory aspect of developing negation. They reveal that 8-month-olds begin to explore spatial, topological properties which make up the part–whole relations within a given object. This includes the continuous relations within an object; between its inside (the contained) and its outside boundary (the container). The subjects begin to effectively examine the inside of quasi-continuous objects, as we have seen, by simply poking their fingers in and out of objects many times, synchronously and asynchronously. Explicit follow-up tactual examination is just beginning:

1. *LH lifts and fingers squeeze into Ball of Tongue Depressor + Ball*
1a. *minor depressions in B*
2. *LH releases B onto table*
3. *LH thumb and finger squeeze into B of TD + B*
3a. *definite indentation in B*
4. *LH releases B onto table*
5. *LH briefly fingers the indentation she made in B*   (8NW, page 42)

Exploring topological part–whole relations also includes the reciprocal continuous property of objects, namely their surround or enclosure. The surroundings of quasi-continuous objects are explored in at least three ways. The first is by deforming (e.g., by pressing fingers in and out of quasi-continuous objects). The second is by decomposing when, for example, in the course of poking, subjects extract bits out of their quasi-continuous surround. The third way is by breaking which splits the object but does not decompose it. Yet, 8-month-olds evince no symptoms of relating the inside (the enclosed) and the surround (the enclosure) of quasi-continuous objects by spatial reciprocity proto-operations (e.g., by alternately exploring the inside hole and the outside surface of ring objects).

IV. Partial Initiation of Direct Composing

Recomposing decomposed elements to reconstitute the original object is never generated (Table 8.1, Row 6). While identity proto-operations are still not produced to reconstruct the initial object, some decomposing begins to have inverse consequences. Inverse results only happen as the combinatorial products of two or more decompositions. Usually, they require decompositions generated in rapid succession. For instance, as previously suggested, 8EH's successive decompositions probably resulted in composing as well as deforming the two pieces bitten off consecutively from the ball (see page 191), but the original ball is not reconstituted. Thus, neither extensive (quantitative) nor intensive (form) identity is produced.

Clearer data are obtained when subjects use their hands, rather than their mouth, to unite decomposed elements. However, they are rarely generated, and do not evidence directedness:

    23.   *RH squeezes small piece*
    24.   *RH pulls away a large piece from long strand in LH*   (8MM, page 26)

The decompositions involved are not generated in rapid succession. Many transactions intervene such that the initial decomposition is well segregated from the second decomposition. It occurs at the outset of the task:

    5.3.   *RH holds dangling long piece*
    5.7.   *LH grabs it near RH and pulls*
    5.7a.   *LH has a large piece of it, RH holds remaining stub*   (8MM, page 25)

The right hand stores the first small piece of Play-Doh decomposed all the while (Lines 5.7–23) until it decomposes the Play-Doh again (Line 24). Eventually the two decomposed pieces are composed into one object. The additive result is union of the pieces into a larger whole.

No further regulative features are manifest, such as repetition. This indicates that inverse compositions (union of decompositions) are anything but deliberate. Nevertheless, they are sufficient to produce the necessary conditions for subsequent inverse compositions by addition of decompositions. Thus, addition of two quasi-continuous negations (in this case, decomposing) proto-operations is an original source of quasi-continuous affirmation (in this case, composing) proto-operations.

These compositions are necessarily preceded by decompositions. They are limited to producing new combinations. They never reconstitute the original object. They always reunite two minor parts previously extracted from a larger whole. They never recombine an extracted part with the object from which it was decomposed. Unlike recomposing, uniting decomposed elements does not reconstruct the original whole, and, as such, does not constitute an identity proto-operation.

These transformations are barely sufficient to begin to relate the structure of quasi-continuous negation to affirmation. Decomposition is a necessary prerequisite to this initial form of composition. By multiplying objects, subjects construct the elements which make uniting them possible. By uniting them, subjects begin to generate the basic extensity conditions of quasi-continuous composing. When one quasi-continuous element is added to another, two results are obtained at the same time. They are different but complementary. First, the number of elements decreases. One quasi-continuous element plus one quasi-continuous element equals one (not two) quasi-continuous element. Second, the magnitude of elements increases. The resultant single element is greater than either of the two single elements which were added together. This ordinal differential is limited to the magnitude relations between each part and the whole. It provides no information about magnitude relations between the part elements. However, babies show no cognizance of these differential products of quasi-continuous composition until they are 18 months old.

Composing originates at this stage. But it remains rare (Table 8.1, Row 7). Only two subjects (of 12) generate direct composing of objects they did not previously decompose. One subject generates composing twice and the other subject three times.

Lack of continuous composing is not compensated by production of discrete compositions; that is, constructing mobiles or stabiles out of the objects as if they are discrete elements. The rate of producing discrete compositions is consistently far below that in any of the discrete conditions (Table 8.1, Rows 13 and 14). The reduced rate of discrete compositions with quasi-continuous objects confirms that proper and consistent combinativity, as well as mapping, distinctions continue to be made between discrete and quasi-continuous objects.

Discrete composing is inherent in continuous composing. Composing two or more quasi-continuous objects into one has as its prerequisite collecting them together into a set. Once collected, composing proto-operations may take into account the continuous properties of the objects and unite the set into an element. The set is protodivided from many into one element. The magnitude of the resultant object is a protomultiplicative product of all the elements.

The most advanced continuous composing, omitting nonrelevant transactions for the sake of brevity, includes temporally overlapping discrete composing:

1. *LH picks up small Balls 1 and 2*
3. *RH picks up small Ball 4, as holds B1 and B2 in LH*
5. *RH picks up small Ball 5 as RH is holding B4, and as LH holds B1 and B2*
6. *RH drops B4 and B5*
7. *RH places on B4 and B5*
8. *RH pushes B4 and B5 together into conglomerate B4-5*
14. *LH hits B1 and B2 on table four times*
17. *looks at RH which has pushed B4 and B5 together into B4-5, as picks it up*
22. *RH hits B4-5 onto table*
23. *LH hits B1 and B2 onto table*
24. *RH moves B4-5 to right in air*
24a. *part of B4-5 falls off to table*
27. *LH hits B1 and B2 onto table twice, as RH holds remainder of B4-5*
28. *looks at B1 and B2 held by LH*
30. *LH brings B1 and B2 to mouth*
31. *LH takes conglomerate B1-2 away from mouth*
     [Note: At some point B1 and B2 squished together, not clear where.]
42. *LH drops part of B1-2 as RH holds remainder of B4-5*   (8JL, pages 27–29)

From the start *8JL* composes Balls 1 and 2 into a discrete labile with contact between the elements (Line 1). Next *8JL* composes a corresponding discrete labile with Balls 4 and 5 in contact with each other (Line 5). This leads immediately into uniting Balls 4 and 5 into one continuous bigger object (Line 8). The continuous composition is preserved across a variety of deformations, only a sample of which is reported here (Line 22). Eventually, it is decomposed into two elements (Line 24a).

The discrete labile composing Balls 1 and 2 is preserved for a long time. The balls are deformed many times (Lines 14, 23, and 27) before they are united into one continuous bigger ball; though precisely when was not visible on the videotape recording (Line 31). In turn, this second continuous composition is preserved until it too is decomposed into two elements (Line 42).

The two sets of quasi-continuous transformations are constructed in overlapping sequences. Thus the subject sequentially: (*a*) composes, deforms, and decomposes elements 4 and 5; and (*b*) deforms, composes, and decomposes elements 1 and 2. Both series of quasi-continuous proto-operations consist of many-to-one and one-to-many asymmetrical part–whole transformations.

This is the first and only instance in which the necessary conditions are being prepared for comparing continuous composing with discrete composing since they overlap temporally. They constitute the original precursory ingredients for determining the similarities and differences between continuous and discrete (*a*) composing and (*b*) correspondences between compositions. They are requisites for constructing partial isomorphisms between the functional structures of continuous and discrete composition. They are also requisites for constructing partial isomorphisms between asymmetrical one-to-many part–whole relations (continuous composing) and symmetrical one-to-one part–whole relations (discrete composing).

Both series intertwine composing, deforming, and decomposing. While not as elaborate, the other subject (8AB) who generated composing also coordinated it with deforming and, perhaps, decomposing. Such transformational series provide the possibility of relating the functional structure of direct affirmation (composition) with those of direct negation (deformation and decomposition). Beyond this there is nothing in the series of transformations which would provide for any coordination more advanced than ascribing affirmation and negation to the same mapping and structural rank. None of the conditions have been generated yet for differentiation and integration between affirmation and negation (see Chapter 14). Thus, there is structural, developmental parallelism between this coordinative organization and that of negation forms discussed in the previous section.

Like decomposing, composing begins as an irreversible proto-operation. Composing is never succeeded by immediate and reciprocal uncoupling of the original elements (Table 8.1, Row 8). Much time elapses and many transactions intervene between subjects' series of composing and decomposing. In addition, the resultant elements produced by decomposing are not equivalent in either extensive (magnitude) or intensive (form) part–whole properties to the objects initially composed. Nevertheless, the precursory constructions necessary to developmental transformation of composing into a reversible proto-operation are generated. These are constituted by the just-analyzed coordinative structures of affirmation and negation.

When generated, composing is accompanied by perceptual monitoring (e.g., 8JL, Line 17). This includes monitoring the transformations in objects' part–whole relations prior to, during and after composing them into a single element:

> 21.   LH holds Balls 2 and 3 as RH touches them and as looking at them
> 22.5. LH squeezes B2 and B3 together into B2-3
> 22.5. RH touches B2-3   (8AB, pages 25 and 26)

The two-object set is inspected tactually by the right hand and visually before continuous composition (Line 21). Continuous composition by the left hand (first Line 22.5) is monitored tactually by the right hand (second Line 22.5). Both the ongoing constructive process and the resultant transformation is monitored tactually. All the necessary ingredients for comparative determination of the properties of composing proto-operations and their resultant part–whole transformations are overtly generated.

Combinativity proto-operations applied to objects in the combined discrete and quasi-continuous condition resemble those applied in both the quasi-continuous and the discrete condition (Table 8.1, Columns 7 and 8, Rows 1–8 and 13–14, respectively). Combinativity proto-operations uniquely applicable to the combined condition are still generated rarely. Discrete and quasi-continuous objects are never attached to each other (Row 9). They are detached only once by one subject (Row 10).

Attaching Play-Doh to and then detaching it from subjects' hands and fingers occurs in all conditions. Attaching often occurs in the course of subjects' transactions with the objects since Play-Doh is a bit sticky. Attachment to an organ tends to provoke attempts to detach the Play-Doh. Some detaching is continuous with that already produced by 6-month-olds. For instance, 8-month-old like 6-month-old subjects shake their hands in order to get rid of Play-Doh stuck to their fingers:

> 32. *Ball 5 sticks to LH thumb*
> 33. *looks at B5*
> 34. *holds LH thumb upside down and shakes it*
> 34a. *B5 falls off and rolls to right*
> 35. *LH picks up Ball 3*
> 36. *B3 sticks to LH thumb*
> 37. *LH shakes vigorously up and down, as looks down*
> 37a. *B3 falls off and rolls to right*   (8GP, page 65)

Eight-month-olds, unlike 6-month-olds, begin to vary, nonsystematically but somewhat experimentally, their procedures for detaching quasi-continuous objects from themselves. Sometimes this follows immediately upon mappings previously used to detach objects, such as opening–closing and shaking the fist. However, when they are not successful in detaching the object other mappings are tried:

> 6. *LH touches and then pulls Ball 1 away from RH*
> 6a. *B1 is stuck to LH thumb*
> 7. *LH shakes down*
> 8. *LH fingers open and close twice on B1, deforming it*
> 9. *RH takes B1 from LH*
> 9a. *deformed B1 is stuck to RH thumb*
> 10. *BH shake up and down four times, with LH banging leg*
> 11. *RH hits onto leg with B1*
> 11a. *B1 comes off into his lap*   (8BK, page 35)

Inherent in Play-Doh attaching to and detaching from subjects' organs is precursory reversibility, always proceeding from attaching to detaching. No signs of precursory combinativity proto-operations uniquely suitable to relating discrete to quasi-continuous objects are generated. All the continuous proto-operations generated at this stage consist of direct negation transformations of deforming, decomposing, and detaching. None are reversed by affirmation transformations of reforming, recomposing, and attaching; nor are any direct affirmation proto-operations of composing and attaching generated.

III

STAGE 3 AT TEN MONTHS: PRECURSORY SECOND-ORDER TRANSFORMATIONS

Binary Transactions

9

Transformational transactions increasingly comprise binary mappings and more than one object but less than four. A small subset of mappings continues to develop protosymbolic properties. Most significant is progress in communicative reference to objects, rare manifestations of semiconventional usage of objects, and much gamelike usage of objects coupled with social anticipation.

Mappings continue to evolve proto-operational properties. Inverse transformations coupled with comparative observation are becoming constants for (a) determining the existential properties of objects and (b) equilibrating them into given elements of protoinferential relations. Three developments are central. The first is the comparative determination of objects from two different spatial perspectives. The second is progress in the comparative determination of individual objects in relation to (a) other single objects and (b) a set of objects, but limited to a few elements. The third is use of ordering proto-operations to systematize experimenting with objects.

Additive and subtractive proto-operations resulting in iterative orders (seriated nonequivalences) and correlation proto-operations resulting in equivalence and multiplicative relations are generated routinely. They are beginning to be used to structure other protoinferential constructions. As just mentioned, for instance, this enables infants to begin to form a precursory logic of experimentation. Iterating and correlating are also beginning to be coordinated with each other. This is the structural cause of the origins of precursory coseriations, that is, the simultaneous construction of two ordered series in one-to-one correspondence with each other.

I. Differentiating and Coordinating Mappings upon Objects

Binary mappings upon singular objects are becoming frequent. Unary mappings upon singular objects are losing their predominance over transactions. To highlight the contrast it is worth considering first a fragment from the age 10-month protocol of the same longitudinal subject described at age 8 months in Chapter 6, pages 120–121:

1.3. *touches Cylinder 1 with LH in grasping way, rotating C1 as fingers C1*
1.3a. *C1 rolls away*
1.7. *bottom of LH touches VW1 as fingers touching C1*
1.7a. *VW1 is slightly displaced*
  3. *LH picks up VW1 as looks down at VW1*
  4. *RH grasps VW1 such that BH fingers rotate VW1 as subject looks at VW1 carefully*
    (experimenter replaces C1 to left of VW2)
  5. *BH lower VW1 near stomach*
  6. *looks at VW1 as BH rotate VW1*
  7. *stops rotating VW1 and looks up*
  8. *turns to look in mirror as RH moves VW1 away from LH*
  9. *RH moves VW1 back to LH while looking in mirror*
10. *LH grasps VW1 held by RH*
11. *looks down at VW1 as BH start rotating VW1*
12. *LH pulls away leaving VW1 in RH, as looks at experimenter*
                                              (10PM, page 22)

Many binary mappings are coordinate. Some consist of active identical mappings (Lines 4–6, and 11). Some do not; even these split transformations are coordinate (Lines 8–10). Though the left hand mappings (release and grasp) are relatively passive, they are reciprocal to the active RH mappings (displace away and back).

Partially overlapping and simultaneous transactions with more than one object are generated frequently. Single-object transactions are also losing their predominance. The usual limit is two objects:

40. *looking at table, LH picks up VW2 while RH holding Cylinder 2*
41. *LH holds VW2 in front of self while RH lowers C2 on right side*
42.3. *LH raises VW2 putting it into mouth, looking at experimenter*

42.7. *RH raises C2*
  [Intervening transactions omitted.]
51.5. *LH raises VW2 putting it in mouth*
51.5. *RH raises C2 to face level*
  [Intervening transactions omitted.]
55.5. *RH lowers C2*
55.5. *LH lowers VW2 from mouth, leaning forward then back as she does so*
              (10PM, pages 24 and 25)

 14. *RH rotates Yellow Cross Ring over horizontally as brings YCR close to LH and touches YCR to Yellow Rectangular Ring in LH, in front of self*
 15. *BH lower objects to table and release*
 15a. *YCR placed on top of Green Rectangular Ring; YRR placed on top of Green Cross Ring*   (10GP, page 11)

Multiple-object transactions increasingly consist of totally active components. Both objects are transformed at the same or partially overlapping times. Different mappings are becoming progressively coordinate with each other, for instance, forming reciprocal relations (e.g., 10GP, Line 14). Identical active mappings on two objects are just beginning to be generated simultaneously to form spatial correspondence relations (e.g., 10GP, Line 15). In like manner reciprocal relations are combined with correspondence relations:

 36. *RH places Yellow Cross Ring 5 on Yellow Cross Ring 3 while pushing both to table edge*
 36a. *YCR3 and 5 fall to floor*   (10JL, page 14)

Asymmetrical placement is generated together with corresponding displacement. All these relational forms will be discussed in subsequent sections.

Transacting with three objects at a time is no longer difficult:

37.5. *mouths Brush 1 held by LH about 5 seconds*
37.5. *RH grasps Brush 2 in lap as looks down toward lap*
39.7. *LH releases B1 and lowers down into lap*
39.7. *mouths B1 held by mouth only*
39.7. *RH holds B2 in lap*
42.7. *LH takes B2 from RH*
42.7. *BH grasp Circular Ring 1*
42.7. *mouths B1 held by mouth only*
45.7. *BH raise CR1 up near face*
45.7. *LH raises B2 up near face*
45.7. *mouths B1 held by mouth only*   (10GP, page 34)

The protocol continues in this vein of two- and three-object transactions for quite a while. It culminates in some four-object transactions:

55.7.   *Brush 2 held in mouth*
55.7.   *LH slides Brush 1 and Circular Ring 1 to the right, touching them to Circular Ring 2*
55.7.   *RH holds CR2*
58.7.   *B2 held in mouth*
58.7.   *LH raises CR1 and B1*
58.7.   *RH raises CR2*
61–63. *holds all objects up a few inches (3 to 4 inches) in front of face very briefly, then lowers BH simultaneously underneath the table, as leans chest against table edge while mouthing B2*   (10GP, page 35)

While remaining in the minority, three-object transactions are generated by almost all subjects at this stage. Even four-object transactions are cropping up with some frequency.

Most 10-month-olds' transactions consist of a mixture of unary and binary mappings upon singular objects:

1. *LH takes Spoon 3*
2. *RH touches S3 held by LH*
3. *BH move S3 to mouth*
4. *LH holds S3 in mouth and RH lets it go*
5. *LH takes S3 out of mouth*
6. *LH holds S3 on legs*
7. *LH drops S3*   (10LL, page 40)

A unary mapping (Line 1) precedes three binary mappings (Lines 2–4) followed by three unary mappings (Lines 5–7).

Two main features of the change ratio remain relatively constant. A one-to-one mapping-to-object change ratio is rare. The basic ratio remains many-to-one mappings-to-objects. Ten-month-olds still generate multiple mappings on one object before switching to another.

Mapping constancy also remains exceptional, but is becoming a bit more frequent. Still, when 10-month-olds switch objects of transaction, they usually switch mappings. This is consistent with the hypothesis that mapping predication during infancy is by negation. In the main, 10-month-olds continue to apply different mappings to successive objects of transaction. Application of the same mapping to successive objects is just beginning to be generated with some frequency (e.g., consecutively dropping several objects).

The third main feature of the change ratio does change substantially. As just noted, the pattern of one mapping per one object at a time is losing its predominance. Increasingly, multiple mappings upon singular objects are generated simultaneously or at partially overlapping times. Unary mappings upon two objects are also becoming more frequent. So are binary mappings upon two objects at the same or partially overlapping times. Consequently, as we shall see, the possibilities for differentiating and integrating transactions are much enhanced.

Mappings remain compact and repetitive. This transaction constant continues to be substantially unchanged from age 6 months. The trend toward differentiating and coordinating mappings begun at age 8 months gathers momentum (e.g., above 10PM, p. 22, Line 4).

Differentiated and integrated compactness coupled with the development in the third main feature of the change ratio has significant implications for cognitive development during infancy. The particular consequences will be pointed to in the appropriate subsequent sections. The general hypothesis may be stated here. Transformations are becoming progressively equilibrated. Equilibration provides a progressively stable foundation for infants to consider their constructions as products as well as ongoing processes. Relatively stable products, or constant givens, provide enriched transactive content on which to construct more advanced protoinferential relations.

All the trends in protosymbolic mappings, initiated during the previous two stages, are augmented during the present stage. Most importantly, analogical protogesturing is being consolidated. Subjects repeatedly pretend or rehearse mappings before acting them out:

49. *RH lifts and almost drops Yellow Cylinder, two times*
50. *RH drops YC*
                                                    (10JC, page 9)

Occasional coordinations of analogical and virtual protosymbols are just beginning to be generated:

25. *LH holds Cylinder 1 over left chair arm as looking down at floor*
26. *LH drops C1 to floor*
27. *turns toward table*
28. *RH picks up Cylinder 2*
29. *turns all the way to left, with RH moving C2 to the left*
30. *leans and looks toward floor as RH holds C2 over floor, but does not release*
                                                    (10CC, page 24)

Analogical protosymbolization (Lines 25 and 26) in which the gesture is consummated is followed immediately by virtual protosymbolization (Lines 29 and 30) in which the gesture is not consummated.

Subjects repeatedly generate social, virtual gestures in which they extend but do not give objects to others. These protoreferential motor gestures are accompanied by vocal gestures by one subject only:

71. *RH holds Clover Ring 2 out toward experimenter as looks at experimenter*
     subject: Iz-zit
     mother: "He's asking 'what is it?'"
                                                    (10DG, page 40)

Whether or not his mother's interpretation is correct, 10DG often accompanied his social virtual gestures by vocal gestures. Together they may well reinforce and extend the precursory foundation for making symbolic reference to objects, albeit still of a quasi-pragmatic and quasi-symbolic character at this stage.

One other personalized yet semiconventional mapping is first manifest at this stage by only one subject. As usual, new developments in proto-symbolization are manifest first and only by 10DG:

1.3. *LH lifts Brush 1 as looking at it*
1.7. *RH lifts Mirror 2*
3.5. *LH strokes handle part of B1 down on left side of hair (near ear)*
(10DG, page 9)

This is the first mapping applied to the brush upon its presentation. Subject 10DG looks at the brush and then strokes it down the side of his hair. Moreover, he repeats this conventional usage later on in the protocol. The usage is still only semiconventional and semiidiosyncratic for two reasons. First, he strokes his hair with the wrong part of the brush. Second, later in the protocol, he performs the same stroking hair gesture three times with a conventionally inappropriate but playfully appropriate object (i.e., a mirror).

The main developments, then, in protosymbolization are threefold. The first is progress in detaching protosymbolic forms from their content by coordinating analogical with virtual gestures. The second is consolidation and extension of protoreference to objects in social communicative contexts. The third is rare formation of pragmatic semiconventions.

Together, these protosymbolic developments provide some foundation for two further structural developments, which will be considered in some detail later in this chapter and in Chapter 10 (pages 254 and 255). The first is to extend the usage of protosymbolization as a notational system in the service of protoinferential constructions, such as correspondence proto-operations (pages 222–225). This structural development originated at the previous stage (see Chapter 6, pages 138–141). The second originates at this stage. Subjects begin to generate gamelike transactions with others (pages 212 and 213).

II. Coordinated Construction of Pairs of Objects as Constant Given Elements

Comparative inspection of the part–whole relations internal to single objects is becoming an extensive procedure:

20. RH holds Block 4 and looks at it
22. RH rotates B4 for some time while looking at it
24. RH lifts up B4 and looks at it
25. LH touches B4 held by RH
34. RH rotates B4 while looking at it
35. LH takes B4 and rotates it while looking at it
61. looks at B4 held by BH
62. RH touches B4 held by LH
63. BH rotate B4
64. BH hold B4 while looking at it
65. BH rotate B4

(10LL, pages 2 and 3)

This is only a partial sample of 10LL's comparative observation of this object (with intervening transactions omitted for the sake of brevity).

Comparative object inspection is becoming progressively differentiated. Ten-month-olds become particularly adept at differentiated inspecting of the internal part–whole relations of single objects by applying inverse transformations, monitoring their transformations, and inspecting the objects:

21. RH holds Green Hexagonal Column
22. looks at GHC
23. RH rotates GHC
24. LH touches GHC held by RH
25. RH rotates GHC

(10LL, pages 25 and 26)

34. RH sticks thumb into bottom part of Doll 1
35. RH thumb rotates D1 over as looks at its face

(10MM, page 57)

10. inserts RH index finger in the bottom of Doll 1 as looks at it
11.5. RH index finger rotates D1 slightly while still looking at it
11.5. vocalizes quietly

(10MM, page 63)

16. LH takes Triangular Column 2 from RH and turns it to flat horizontal position
17. RH takes TC2 from LH and turns it to upright vertical position
18. LH touches TC2 while RH holds it upright on table
19. LH takes TC2 from RH and rotates it 180° so that it is upright with opposite end on top
20. RH grasps TC2 such that BH hold it upright
21. BH rotate TC2 to horizontal position

(10AB, pages 29 and 30)

9. BH hold opposite ends of the Yellow Hexagonal Column and rotate it before her eyes while observing it

(10EH, page 26)

Indeed, some subjects have become exceedingly skilled at single-object comparative inspection involving binary mappings. They are able to carry on a totally different transaction at the same time:

14.5. *LH holds Green Cross Ring while mouth sucks it*
14.5. *RH rotates Yellow Hexagonal Column while looking at it*
(10EH, page 26)

Comparative object inspection is also becoming progressively integrated. At its most overt, integration is manifest by sequential elaboration of successive into alternating inspection:

18. *looks at Green Cross Ring held by RH*
19. *looks at Yellow Hexagonal Column held by LH*
20. *RH inserts GCR into mouth and quickly withdraws it*
21. *LH holds GCR and RH holds YHC as looks back and forth at each twice*
(10EH, pages 26 and 27)

Subject 10EH begins by successively looking once at each object (Lines 18 and 19), held in separate hands. She ends up by looking back and forth at them twice (Line 21).

Progressive integration of comparative observation takes a deeper form as well. Spatial translations, such as inverse displacements or rotations, are becoming invariants of comparative inspection. Objects are carefully observed from all sides:

51. *RH picks up Mirror 2 by round end*
52. *RH rotates M2 once in front of eyes, flipping handle up*
53. *RH inversely rotates M2*   (10EH, page 12)

69. *RH inserts handle of Brush 1 in mouth*
70. *slides mouth along side of B1 until bristles and fingers of RH are in mouth*
71. *withdraws B1 from mouth*
72. *RH rotates B1, holding onto bristles so handle is flipped about while observes closely for about 10 seconds*   (10EH, page 13)

Such transactions constitute skilled advances in previous development of differentiated, inverse comparative observation (Chapter 6, Section II). At this stage differentiated, inverse comparative inspection is also just beginning to be integrated with a second spatial dimension, that of the comparative perspective from which the object is observed. At its origins, constructing projective spatial relations involves reciprocal spatial translations between two dimensions:

37. *RH joins LH in holding round mirror end of Mirror 1*
38. *BH rotate M1 180° a few times by mirror end, as looks at this*
39. *LH grasps handle end of M1 and RH releases M1*
40. *LH rotates M1 180° by handle end, as looks at this*
(10EH, pages 11 and 12)

First, 10EH comparatively sights the part–whole relations internal to the mirror from the mirror end by generating multiple inverse translations (Lines 37 and 38). Then, she sights from the reciprocal perspective of the handle end (Lines 39 and 40).

The scope of comparative inspection expands in other ways as well. It is now fully applicable to alternately inspecting two objects. Sometimes comparative inspection of two objects is generated upon first transacting with the presentation:

1. *RH grabs and draws Green Hexagonal Column toward self*
2. *LH picks up Yellow Hexagonal Column while RH holds GHC in air*
3. *looks back and forth at GHC and YHC*   (10EH, page 26)

Alternate inspection of two objects precedes 10EH's subsequent inspection of one of them, the Yellow Hexagonal Column (Lines 9 and 14.5 presented on pages 209–210). Thus, the subject comparatively inspects the Yellow Hexagonal Column when it is an element of a set of two objects and when it is a singular object. In ways such as these, almost all subjects now compare the structure of individual elements with those of a very small set of objects. Still, this does not include consecutive inverse transformations in the object and the set necessary to complete this observational structure.

Comparatively inspecting two objects is not usually the subjects' initial transaction. Rather, it tends to be embedded in the course of the subjects' transactions:

71. *RH fingers touch top of Green Hexagonal Column held by LH*
72. *RH reaches to Yellow Hexagonal Column as LH holds GHC*
73. *RH holds up YHC and looks at it*
74. *RH rotates YHC and looks at it*
75. *RH places YHC down on table*
76. *looks down at GHC held by LH all this time*
77. *RH touches GHC held by LH*   (10LL, pages 27 and 28)

Progress in differentiated comparative inspection, as just seen, is extended to alternately observing two objects. The first precursory signs of its application to three objects is just beginning to be manifest at this stage. The frequency remains low and the subjects' observational techniques rudimentary:

12. *LH touches Blue Triangular Column*
13. *LH touches bristles of Red Brush*
14. *LH touches bristles of Blue Brush*   (10KC, page 40)

The most extensive sequence of comparative observation includes repeated alternating visual perception of two sets constructed by the experimenter and one object held by the subject:

*(experimenter pulls both stacks of blocks away and then pushes both
stacks toward subject slowly)*
3. *looks at both stacks*
4. *looks at 2-block stack on right*
5. *looks at 3-block stack on left*
6. *turns away to her left*
7. *shakes her head*
   (experimenter pushes the stacks toward subject again)
8. *looks at 3-block stack on left*
9. *looks at 2-block stack on right*
10. *looks at 3-block stack on left*
11. *looks at 2-block stack on right*
12. *looks at 3-block stack on left*
13. *looks at 2-block stack on right*
14. *looks down at Block 6 held by BH all the while*   (10LL, pages 5 and 6)

The scope of comparative observation includes much repeated alternating visual attention. The extent of application includes two sets plus a
singular element. It does not yet, however, include transformational
proto-operations, for example, inverse rotation of both sets. The sets are
constructed by the experimenter, not the subject; and any transformations observed by the subject are also constructed by the experimenter,
not the subject.

The temporal dimension of inspecting objects is just beginning to be
systematically extended into the future. So far, as we have seen, inspecting
has been extended in the present by simultaneously or alternately observing more than one object. It has also been retrospectively extended into
the past by delayed observation (e.g., looking on the floor for an object
which was dropped as long as 10 seconds beforehand). Now it is frequently extended into the future by prevision of what is about to happen:

62. *RH pulls Yellow Clover Ring to her right side*
63.3. *looks down over right chair arm for 5 seconds*
63.7. *RH drops YCR on floor*
   (mother retrieves and gives to experimenter)
65. *watches mother retrieve*   (10PM, pages 53 and 54)

Anticipation of physical effects is coupled with social anticipation:

5. *LH picks up Yellow Clover Ring*
6. *LH drops YCR over left chair arm while looking at experimenter*
7. *sits looking at experimenter with LH dangling over left chair arm*
   *(experimenter places Red Clover Ring flat on table where YCR had been
   and proffers Red Hexagonal Column)*
8. *LH grasps and drops RHC over left chair arm while looking at experimenter*

9. *still looking at experimenter, leans to the left over chair arm*

(*10PM*, page 57)

This is becoming a favorite game of about half the subjects. They frequently project objects to the floor, then look at the experimenter or mother, rather than the floor, as if in anticipation of the objects' retrieval by that person.

Prevision is enhanced by the subjects themselves producing and thereby partly controlling the transformation in the objects. Prevision is readily subject to verification by observing whether the anticipated result occurred. Thus, the conditions are self-generated for predicting the effects of transformations. In order to be used as a prediction and verification structure, anticipatory observation must be coordinated with, at least, semisystematic protoexperimentation. This coordination, as we shall see in Section III, is just beginning to develop during this stage.

III. Semiordered Experimenting with Several Elements

Causal constructions are becoming more varied, differentiated, and integrated. Progressive protoexperimental integration of causal relations will be discussed in a moment. First it should be underlined that subjects engage in a variety of transactions necessary to the refinement of causal transformations and to the determination of their differential effects:

21. *LH grasps end of Cylinder 2, squeezes and releases it fast*
21a. *C2 turns on table*   (*10KC*, page 25)

1. *LH thumb and index finger pinch left end of Red Triangular Column*
1a. *RTC turns on table*   (*10KC*, page 26)

These causal transformations generate differential information about the transmission of force. They do not result in deforming discrete objects. The results are different from when the subjects squeeze or pinch quasi-continuous objects. The results are projecting the objects in space. The movements caused are, however, also different from those the subjects have previously generated and continue to generate by pushing, rolling, or throwing discrete objects. The results are rotational, rather than linear, trajectories.

Protoexperimental means of extracting data on *sets* of objects originate at this stage. Extended sequences of causal transformations applied consecutively to many objects are generated frequently:

23. *LH drops Doll 2 to floor on left while watching this*

24. LH *drags Circular Ring 1 to edge of table and drops* CR1 *to floor*
25. LH *pushes Circular Ring 2 to floor on left*
26. *looks to floor on left after* CR2 *lands*   (10JL, page 21)

39. RH *brushes Yellow Cross Ring 1 off table to right*
40. *looks at floor after* YCR1 *lands*
41. RH *grasps and drags Green Cross Ring and Yellow Cross Ring 3*
42. RH *lifts* YCR3 *to right as releases* GCR
43. *looks at floor*
44. RH *drops* YCR3 *to floor*
45. *looks at floor for 8 seconds*
46. *looks at experimenter*
47. *looks at table area of* GCR
48. RH *draws* GCR *forward and lifts it*
49. RH *drops* GCR *to floor on right while looking at floor*
50. *looks at floor after* GCR *drops on right*
51. *looks at floor on left (nothing there)*
52. LH *drops Yellow Cross Ring 2 on left but it lands on edge of high chair seat*
53. *looks at high chair seat*
54. LH *shakes arm of high chair*
54a. YCR2 *falls to floor*   (10JL, page 14)

In the first instance 10JL protoexperiments with three of the four presented objects; in the second, with four of eight objects. Rare protoexperimental sequences are generated with all objects presented, in this instance four objects:

6. RH *uses Block 1 to push Rectangular Ring 2 off table edge—*RR2 *falls to floor*
7. RH *drops* B1 *over table edge—*B1 *falls to floor*
8. *looks down toward floor, as rests BH on either leg, 3 seconds*
9. *looks quickly at experimenter*
10. *looks at Rectangular Ring 1 and grasps it with LH*
11. LH *holds* RR1 *down just below high chair seat and drops* RR1 *to floor, looking down and up at table briefly, then back down toward floor as* RR1 *hits floor*
12. *looks up as LH grasps Block 2 and slides it to edge of table*
13. LH *holds* B2 *for 2 seconds at table edge as looks down at floor*
14. *looks down as LH extends* B2 *down beneath table edge and drops it to floor*   (10GP, page 42)

To the minor degree to which independent variables are kept separate or not confounded, protoexperimentation is semisystematic. Objects are varied sequentially. Causal transformations are held partially constant. Subject 10JL drops the first two objects and pushes the third in one protoexperiment (p. 21). She brushes the first object and drops the next three objects in a second protoexperiment (p. 14). She does not achieve the same result with the last object; it lands on the highchair instead of the floor (Line 52). So she varies the causal transformation. She changes it from dropping to instrumentally shaking the highchair in order to produce the same result (Lines 54 and 54a). Subject *10GP* instrumentally pushes the first object and drops the next three objects (p. 42).

The most advanced protoexperimenting generated at this stage is the structural developmental product of coordinating (*a*) these just acquired partially systematic causal proto-operations with (*b*) available ordering proto-operations (see pages 225–228). Ordering introduces the crucial element, missing until this stage, necessary to systematize proto-experimental variables. The predominant mode of ordering independent variables involves continuous variation. Usually, this involves ordered variations in causal transformations difficult to measure precisely with the techniques employed in this research. Yet it is evident that they are generated with much frequency at this stage. The most frequent include ordered variations (*a*) ⟨roll, push, swish⟩ in the magnitude of projecting objects on a surface plane, and (*b*) ⟨drop, throw⟩ in the magnitude of projecting objects in the air.

Some ordering of independent variables just begins to involve discrete variation. The number of elements causally transformed are varied:

31. *RH lifts Yellow Circular Ring and drops it over right arm of high chair to*
    floor
32. *transfers Green Circular Ring 1 from LH to RH*
33. *RH picks up Red Circular Ring, so holds GCR1 and RCR in RH*
34. *RH drops GCR1 and RCR over right arm of high chair to floor*
35. *bends over right chair arm, looking toward floor*   (10AB, page 6)

76. *RH lifts and drops Green Cylinder to table*
77.5. *RH lifts and drops GC to table*
77.5. *LH lifts and drops Yellow Cylinder to table*
79. *BH swish back and forth on table, hitting into the cylinders, making*
    them turn and roll away
    (mother pushes cylinders back to subject)
80. *RH lifts GC and LH lifts YC*
81. *LH drops YC to table—it rolls on table*
82. *RH drops GC to table—it rolls on table*
83. *RH lifts and tosses GC to table*   (10JC, page 10)

The second protoexperiment contains elements of both discrete and continuous ordered variation in independent variables. The bidirectionally ordered discrete variation of ⟨one, two, one, one, one⟩ elements projected constitutes the bare minimum required to form a series. Yet, even this precursory discrete ordering is not applied by all subjects to their protoexperimenting. The increasing continuous order ⟨drop, toss⟩ in magnitude of projection is entirely typical of that applied by all subjects to their protoexperimenting. Combined application of rudimentary discrete and continuous ordering to protoexperimenting is sufficient to begin to systematize causal proto-operations. Application of addition and subtraction proto-operations to the way in which independent causal variables are generated is the first stage in constructing a logic of experimentation.

Throughout, the subjects observe the results generated by their protoexperiments, although not consistently. Increasingly, subjects anticipate the results. Sometimes they look to the floor in the direction where the object will land both before and after dropping it (*10JL*, p. 14, Lines 43 and 49). Strikingly, prevision often lasts an extended duration; sometimes as long as 5 to 10 seconds. Repeated coordinated prevision—causal transformation—postvision provides the structural integration necessary to begin to predict, test, and verify results. Indeed, as already noted, subjects may even intervene actively to insure the expected result (*10JL*, p. 14, Lines 51–54a, presented on page 214).

Verification of results seems, then, directed primarily at confirming expectations; even if it requires intervention by the subject to negate disconfirming effects. Accidental results do occur which strikingly disconfirm the subjects' expectations about the existential properties of objects:

7. *RH holding Yellow Cross Ring 2, LH holding Yellow Cross Ring 5, extends both arms between her legs as far as they will go*
8. *knocks Yellow Cross Ring 3 from lap to the floor*
8a. *YCR3 makes a loud sound when it contacts the floor*
9. *immediately brings BH with YCR2 and 5 up to eye level and looks at each one*   (*10EH*, page 29)

Subject *10EH* verifies that she is still holding both objects (Line 9). Verification would not have been necessary if she had not been presented with what she apparently takes to be potential disconfirmation (Line 8a) that both objects are preserved in her hands. Yet, all the time she is in fact holding both objects.

Checking the data of her tactual observations with that of her visual observations is illuminating in one other respect as well. Pseudo-contradictions arise at this stage. In this instance, it is as though objects may be located in two different places at the same time. They may be in one's hand at the same time as they are on the floor, if potentially disconfirming data of the former are observed. "Data" obtained via one observational modality (audition) are potentially disconfirming, regardless of whether the disconfirmation is impossible given observation by another modality (tactile prehension). The apparent contradiction requires checking by a third observational modality (vision). Redundant, two-channel observation is, apparently, adequate at this stage for empirical determination. Logical impossibility is either insufficient or not yet a part of cognitive development at this stage.

Anticipating results facilitates progress in forming causal reciprocity between independent and dependent variables. Protoreciprocity progresses in three ways. The first coordinates transformation in independent variables with constant dependent variables. It began at the previous stage but has become much more extensive and controlled. Subjects direct the trajectory of missiles towards relatively delimited targets.

Targeting missiles into containers, begun at the previous stage, becomes frequent at this stage. Subjects drop, throw, and toss objects into receptacles. Targeting is extended to more challenging goals:

24. *BH drop Triangular Column 2 to floor via lap*
25. *LH takes Square Column 2 from experimenter and drops it to the high chair's footrest*
26. *BH lift Square Column 1*
27. *LH releases SC1 and RH drops it to high chair's footrest* (10AB, page 30)

3. *looking down, LH holds Blue Rectangular Ring over edge of high chair seat and drops BRR to the high chair's footrest*
4. *sits up and looks at other objects*
5. *looks up quickly at experimenter as grasps Rectangular Ring 2*
6. *LH pulls RR2 off table*
7. *looking down, LH holds RR2 over edge of high chair seat and drops it to the high chair's footrest as continues looking down at it for 2 seconds* [Transactions 8–12 are not relevant and are omitted.]
13. *leans forward, as RH extends Rectangular Ring 1 underneath table, looks down and drops RR1 to the high chair's footrest*
14. *remains bent forward and looking down toward floor, 3 seconds more*
15. *sits back in high chair, looking toward objects*
16. *RH grasps Block 2 as LH touches table to left of B2*
16a. *RH action displaces Block 1 toward experimenter*
17. *RH slides B2 off table edge directly to floor as LH withdraws from table and touches B2 at edge of table before it falls, and as looks at experimenter briefly*
18. *looks down on floor for 2 seconds*
19. *looks up at experimenter, laughing* [Transactions 20–22 are not relevant and are omitted.]
23. *LH grasps B1*
24. *LH pulls B1 off table into lap as looking down*
25. *LH extends B1 below high chair seat and drops B1*
25a. *B1 falls to high chair's footrest*
26. *sits up and looks quickly at empty table space (all objects are on floor now)* (10GP, pages 51 and 52)

Two out of three and four out of five objects are successfully targeted toward the footrest by *10AB* and *10GP*, respectively. Subject *10GP*'s series is preceded by two attempts in an earlier task:

8. LH *lowers Green Cross Ring 3 between legs, as looks down in lap*
9. *leaning forward, LH drops GCR3 onto footrest—does this slowly, after locating place under table first*
   [*Transactions 10–13 are not relevant and therefore are omitted.*]
14. LH *holds Green Cross Ring 2 down between legs and drops it to footrest, leaning forward and looking down toward footrest all the while—does it more quickly this time*   (10GP, page 16)

Subject *10GP* rapidly taught himself how to drop objects to the footrest.

The second form of causal protoreciprocity is the complement of the first. Increasingly, subjects calculate the trajectory of missiles in order to stop or catch them. Usually, an organ is displaced such that its trajectory is reciprocal to that of the missile:

   (*experimenter rolls Cylinder 2 back to subject*)
8. LH *touches C2 and stops its roll*
   [*Transactions 9–13 are not relevant and therefore are omitted.*]
   (*experimenter pushes Cylinder 1 back to subject and then pushes C2 back to subject*)
14. *C1 rebounds off of LH*
15. *RH catches and LH touches C2 as it reaches table edge*
                                                         (10KC, pages 27 and 28)

Occasionally, an object is used reciprocally as an instrument to stop a missile:

30. *mouths Yellow Cross Ring 1 for 3 seconds as looks toward experimenter* (*experimenter rolls Yellow Cross Ring 2 toward subject*)
31. LH *removes YCR1 from mouth and touches YCR1 in upright position to YCR2 just as YCR2 is about to roll off table edge*
32. LH *releases YCR1, placing LH flat on YCR2 at edge of table*
                                                              (10GP, page 56)

Calculating results facilitates progress in forming reciprocal compensation. In this third form of causal reciprocity an organ is displaced such that its trajectory is identical to that of the missile. Nonrelevant intervening transactions are omitted in the second protocol fragment:

23. LH *withdraws Cylinder 1 to self and releases it such that it hits table edge and falls toward lap*
24. LH *immediately catches C1*   (10CC, page 24)

43. LH *fingers spread and hit into Cylinder 2—C2 rolls toward experimenter*
44. *as C2 rolls, leans forward a little and LH fingers reach after it* (*experimenter rolls Cylinder 1 to subject—it rolls into subject's LH which is outstretched on table*)

45. *C1 bounces off LH and rolls back to experimenter*
46. *LH reaches after C1, but it's already out of reach*
53. *LH fingers hit C1—it rolls to the right toward experimenter as subject watches it roll*
54. *LH fingers touch C2—it rolls toward experimenter out of subject's reach*
55. *LH fingers reach after C2*
101. *RH pushes C1 to the left*
102. *RH reaches after C1 as it rolls away, looking after it*
105. *pushes Square Column 2 hard to the left—it slides far and fast to the left as watches it*
106. *LH reaches for SC2 and withdraws*
112. *LH reaches C1 as it rolls away but does not catch it, as looking at it*

(*10KC*, pages 17, 18, 22, and 23)

Sometimes the objects' trajectories are generated by *10KC* and sometimes by the experimenter. In all instances, the subject attempts to compensate for the objects' trajectories with that of overtaking trajectories by his hand. As the objects move away, his hand moves after them. Occasionally he is successful; in most instances he is not. Thereby, he obtains some confirmation of his compensations; mainly he receives disconfirmation.

Disconfirmation opens up two new possibilities. The first is the possibility of determining under what conditions it is and is not possible to compensate for a receding trajectory. This becomes a matter of determining under what conditions missiles can and cannot be overtaken (i.e., determining the inclusion and exclusion of causal variables). So, subjects will have to learn to gauge their own movements as compensatory functions of those of receding objects. The second is the possibility of adjusting the trajectories of one's own movements by gauging them against the movements of objects which are potentially susceptible to overtaking. Compensatory calibration increases the rate of successful overtaking (i.e., determining the covariation of causal variables).

IV. Analogical Mapping Protocorrespondences

Mapping protocorrespondences become commonplace at this stage. The mapping forms used include a widening range of placements and displacements (e.g., throw, roll, push, drop, and flatten) and of sound productions (e.g., bang, hit, and tap). The set of objects used is extended to include as many as five elements. The products include the construction of discrete (single-unit and multi-unit) and continuous (spatial, motile, and causal) equivalence.

Most mapping protocorrespondences are still momentary:

1. RH *pushes Doll 2 over*
2. RH *knocks Doll 1 over* (10JL, page 22)

58. LH *grasps end of Square Column 2 and pulls it toward the left a little, hitting into Cylinder 1*
58a. *C1 turns*
59. LH *pushes SC2 around toward left a little more, such that SC2 is in alignment with C1* (10KC, page 18)

A substantial proportion is becoming quite extensive, including long sequences of variant protocorrespondences:

21. RH *lifts up Doll 1 and LH lifts up Doll 2*
22. RH *holds out D1 and LH holds out D2 toward experimenter (experimenter extends hands)*
23. RH *lowers D1 and LH lowers D2, such that D1 touches experimenter's hand*
24.5. LH *releases D2 into experimenter's hand*
24.5. RH *holds D1 touching experimenter's hand*
26.5. LH *picks up D2 out of experimenter's hand*
26.5. RH *pulls D1 toward self, holding it in a semi-inverted position over table (experimenter pulls her hands back)*
28.5. LH *raises D2 toward mouth*
28.5. RH *holds D1 semi-inverted*
30.5. LH *rotates D2 to a semi-inverted position over table*
30.5. RH *holds D1 semi-inverted over table* (10CC, pages 1 and 2)

Most discrete protocorrespondences produce single-unit equivalence. The mappings are still usually successive rather than simultaneous or partially overlapping. However, the reproductive frequency has increased so that the protocorrespondences include many and sometimes all presented objects, as in the second protocol fragment:

4. RH *touches and displaces Doll 1 toward self slightly*
5. RH *displaces Spoon 2 to the right*
6. RH *touches and displaces Doll 2* (10KC, page 48)

41. LH *places Block 2 down on table in front of self, first upright, then turns it so it's flat, and releases it*
42. RH *knocks Rectangular Ring 2 flat*
43. LH *grasps Block 1 and turns it flat such that it hits into Rectangular Ring 1*
43a. *RR1 falls flat* (10GP, page 44)

Multi-unit protocorrespondences are generated, but still less frequently than single-unit protocorrespondences:

10. LH *hits table, twice*

11. *mouths Block 1 held by RH*
12. *LH palm hits table, twice*   (10GP, page 36)

27. *LH hits table, three times*
28. *looks toward floor, experimenter, mother, experimenter, and mirror*
29. *LH hits table, three times*   (10GP, page 43)

Protocorresponding equivalence remains limited to very small numbers. They never exceed 3.

Simultaneous mapping protocorrespondences are still limited to two objects, but they are beginning to generate discrete equivalences as frequently as continuous equivalences. Irrelevant intervening transactions are omitted in the following protocol fragment:

45.5. *RH raises then lowers Green Triangular Column 3 to chair seat*
45.5. *LH raises then lowers Red Block 3 to chair seat*
10.5. *RH drops Green Triangular Column 2*
10.5. *LH drops Red Triangular Column*
86.5. *RH brushes Red Block 2 to floor, right side*
86.5. *LH brushes Red Block 1 to floor, left side* (10PM, pages 72, 73, and 79)

The last two protocorrespondences involve fairly discrete phenomena. The first protocorrespondence involves continuous mappings. But even such continuous mappings (raise then lower) have definable parts and boundaries which are reciprocally related to each other.

Precursors of coordinate continuous and discrete protocorrespondences originate at this stage:

76. *LH raises Yellow Cross Ring and RH raises Yellow Rectangular Ring up before face*
77. *LH thrusts YCR and RH thrusts YRR down toward table, tapping YCR and YRR onto table, one time*   (10GP, page 19)

58.3. *LH raises Orange Spoon up above the table*
58.7. *RH raises Orange Cup*
60.5. *RH taps edge of OC on table*
60.5. *LH waves OS just above the table in motion similar to RH*
62.3. *LH taps OS on table*   (10MM, page 19)

Coordination is facilitated by prolonging continuous into discrete protocorrespondences. It may also be facilitated by the differentiated form of these continuous protocorrespondences. They are articulated into two parts, an upward motion followed by its reciprocal downward motion. Consequently, they have the potential of quasi-discrete protocorrespondences. This potential enhances comparability with their successor discrete protocorrespondence (i.e., simultaneously tapping each object once).

Subjects continue to be highly selective as to whether or not they will engage in cooperative protocorrespondences. Sometimes they do and sometimes they do not. When they do, the cooperative protocorrespondences are still usually initiated by the subjects, rather than by the experimenter. The probability of engagement is highest when subjects first do something to an object which the experimenter reproduces.

Sometimes subjects are willing to engage in cooperative protocorrespondences, but not as extensively as their partner desires:

12. *LH throws Yellow Cross Ring down on table and it bounces across table (experimenter tosses YCR back to subject)*
13. *LH picks up YCR*
14. *LH throws YCR down on the table and it bounces across the table (experimenter picks up YCR and throws it down on the table in front of subject)*
15. *LH knocks over Red Column and Yellow Column*

(10PM, pages 57 and 58)

Thus, the subject determines both whether and how much she will participate in cooperative protocorrespondences. This includes switching to generating an unrelated correspondence, that is, simultaneously knocking two objects over (Line 15).

Analogical protocorrespondences are generated with some frequency by all subjects (e.g., repeatedly jerking an object up and down before throwing it down). Analogizing is also beginning to be applied to cooperative correspondences by half the subjects:

13. *LH holds Green Triangular Column 3 and RH holds Red Square Column 3 in air as turns toward mother*
    (experimenter taps finger on table to draw subject's attention back to task)
14. *looks at experimenter's hand which is on table between objects*
15.5. *LH hits GTC3 on Green Triangular Column 1, twice*
15.5a. *GTC1 rotates, Green Triangular Column 2 is displaced by LH arm*
15.5–23.5. *RH holds RSC3 in air*
    (experimenter taps fingers again)
17.5. *LH extends and holds GTC3 on table near experimenter's hand, arm is covering GTC1 and GTC2, as looks at experimenter's hand*
    (experimenter stops tapping)
19.5. *LH taps GTC3 on table with arm still extended over GTC1 and GTC2*
19.5a. *GTC1 displaced to right*
    (experimenter taps her fingers a few times, then stops)
21.5. *LH holds GTC3 near experimenter's hand and arm is extended over GTC2, as watches experimenter's hand*
23.5. *LH bangs GTC3 half on table and half on experimenter's fingers*

(10PM, pages 69 and 70)

25. *LH pushes end of Yellow Hexagonal Column to left such that it slides and rolls away from subject into Red Clover Ring*
25a. *RCC is displaced slightly*
26. *LH pushes Red Hexagonal Column to left while watching experimenter (experimenter rolls YHC back toward subject and to right of other objects)*
27. *raises LH toward YHC*
28. *stops and looks at YHC with LH raised in air*
29. *LH rolls YHC back and forth, once* (10PM, page 51)

Material "distancing" has been hypothesized as a developmental measure of representational differentiation (Werner & Kaplan, 1963). Less representational distance marks 10PM's first than second sequence. In the first sequence the experimenter is merely trying to keep the subject attending by tapping her fingers on the table between the objects. Subject 10PM looks (Line 14). Then she hits one object with another (Line 15.5). The difference is in the form (tap versus hit) and frequency (many versus two) of the mapping, and in the objects (finger on table versus GTC3 on GTC1). The second time the difference is mainly in mapping frequency and instrumental object (Line 19.5). The third time it is in mapping form and frequency and in instrumental object (Line 23.5).

The second instance is marked by even greater representational distance. The experimenter reproduces the subject's rolling (Lines 25 and 26). The subject does not reproduce the experimenter's transactions directly. Instead she hesitates (Lines 27 and 28), inspects the object (Line 28), and then rolls it back and forth once (Line 29). It is as if she is trying to determine what can be done with the object. This leads her into generating a potential analogical cooperative protocorrespondence. On this interpretation, "rolling the object back and forth in hand" is a relatively distant protosymbol of "rolling the object back and forth between the subject and experimenter."

In addition to its greater representational distance, the second instance is not repeated. The first is repeated three times, albeit in variant forms. On the one hand, greater representational distance and nonrepetition is a technical difficulty in determining whether "distanced" productions, such as the second sequence, constitute analogical protocorrespondences. On the other hand, the hypothesis that representational distance increases with development implies that the greater the representational distance involved the less likely young infants will be to repeat their productions of analogical cooperative protocorrespondence. The finding that the first instance (less "distanced") is and the second instance (more "distanced") is not repeated is consistent with the developmental hypothesis of symbol formation. A corollary expectation is that more distanced analogical protocorrespondences will include repetitions at older ages.

Some infants are just beginning to apply inverse proto-operations, thereby negating the cooperative protocorrespondences initiated by others:

> 16. *RH holds Column 1 in mouth*
>   *(experimenter picks up Spoon 2 and puts it in her mouth)*
> 17. *looks at experimenter*
> 18. *RH takes C1 out of her mouth*
>   *(experimenter takes S2 out of her mouth)*
> 19. *turns away from experimenter laughing, as RH holds C1*   (10LL, page 41)

Subject 10LL watches the experimenter construct a cooperative correspondence (Line 17). Three options are available to her in order to continue the correspondence: preserve the existing object in her mouth, put another additional object in her mouth, or take out and replace the object already in her mouth. She does none of these. Instead, she does the opposite of the experimenter's reproduction of her (Line 18). When the experimenter perseveres by correspondingly taking her object out of her mouth, the subject laughingly turns away and does something else (Line 19). It is as if she appreciates the experimenter's correspondences and/or her own negations of the experimenter's correspondences.

At a later point this same subject further indicates that she appreciates cooperative protocorrespondences:

> 49. *LH puts Yellow Column 2 in mouth*
>   *(experimenter puts Yellow Column 1 on table and puts Orange Spoon 2*
>   *in her mouth)*
> 50. *watches what experimenter does, as LH holds YC2 in mouth*
> 51. *smiles as YC2 is in mouth held by LH*
> 52. *(experimenter puts down OS2) as LH holds YC2 in mouth*
> 53. *LH holds YC2 in mouth*   (10LL, page 45)

Here the subject opts for maintaining the cooperative protocorrespondence. If anything, she would have maintained it longer than the experimenter was willing (Lines 52 and 53).

Cooperative mapping protocorrespondences are progressively elaborated in two other respects. They are extended to include two objects which the participants use interchangeably, and to simultaneous as well as successive mappings by the participants:

> 47. *LH touches Cylinder 2*
> 48. *leans body forward as LH pushes C2 forward—it rolls toward experimenter and to the right—watches it roll*
>   *(experimenter rolls Cylinder 1 back to subject and catches C2)*

49. *LH grasps C1 by right end as it rolls into Square Column 1*
50. *LH raises right end of C1 and releases it*
51. *LH grasps C1 and moves it on table—left to right with jagged motion*
52. *LH fingertips hit C1—it rolls to experimenter*
    (at the same time, experimenter rolls C2 to subject)
53. *LH fingers push C2 to the left—it rolls out of subject's reach*
    (experimenter rolls C1 to subject)
54. *LH fingers hit C1—it rolls to the right, toward experimenter—watches it roll*
    (experimenter rolls C2 back to subject)
55. *LH fingers touch C2—it rolls toward experimenter out of subject's reach—fingers reach after C2*
    (experimenter rolls back C1—it hits into Square Column 2, displacing it)
56. *LH grasps C1*
57. *LH pushes C1 to the left in a circular motion, hard*

                                                   (10KC, pages 17 and 18)

Also included in the sequence is a potential analogical protocorrespondence (Line 50). It is immediately followed by enactment of the direct protocorrespondence (Line 51).

V. Precursory Mapping Coseriation

Protoaddition and protosubtraction resulting in iterative mapping series are now generated almost as frequently as protocorrespondences. Ordered quantitative nonequivalence is constructed, then, almost as readily as quantitative equivalence and multiplicative relations. The differential in rate of production is due to the necessity of generating systematic multi-unit mappings in order to construct ordered nonequivalence. These are still more difficult to construct than single-unit mappings which, as we have just seen, are sufficient to produce the bulk of protocorrespondences generated at this stage.

Protoaddition continues to generate precise two-step increasing orders from one to two and from two to three units. Protosubtraction continues to generate precise two-step decreasing orders from two to one and three to two units. Most mapping iteration is more extended:

83.5. *RH hits cylinder 1 on Cylinder 2 held by LH, six times*
    (experimenter hits Square Column 1 on table, one time)
85.3. *RH hits C1 on table, three times*
85.7. *LH hits C2 on table, one time*   (10CC, page 19)

The decreasing order of ⟨6, 3, 1⟩ hits, like all other three-step series generated, remains imprecise numerically. At a more molar level, the intensity of three-step series continues to be systematized to form quasi-quantitative orders, in this instance ⟨many, some, one⟩ hits. Three-steps remain the limit of undirectional discrete orderings; no four-step uni-directional discrete orderings are generated by any subject.

Protoaddition and protosubtraction continue to be used to generate precise two-step continuous orders, whether of increasing (10AB) or decreasing (10LL) magnitude:

54. *RH hits Yellow Circular Ring onto table, releasing it*
55. *RH lifts and bangs Red Circular Ring onto table* (10AB, page 4)

33. *RH pushes Square Column 1 as watches it roll*
34. *RH slightly pushes C1* (10LL, page 38)

Imprecise continuous orders, particularly of increasing magnitudes, are generated frequently. They may exceed three-step functions, but the techniques used in this research do not allow us to make any determination:

37. *RH slides Block 4 into Block 3, as turns to watch this*
38. *RH slides B4 back and forth, faster, as watches this* (10JC, page 2)

19. *LH taps Doll 2 with back of forefingers*
19a. *D2 rocks a bit in place*
20. *LH grasps D2 and pushes D2 back and forth (←→) on table*
21. *LH increases range of back and forth (←→) sweeping D2*
(10JL, pages 20 and 21)

Subject 10JC generates an increasing speed order; 10JL generates an increasing distance order. Both are reflective of the development at this stage of symmetrical protoseries. Whether the magnitude increase is in extent of speed or distance, the mapping form is symmetrical (i.e., back and forth).

Comparative observation by infants of their protoadditive and pro-tosubtractive mappings and the resultant iterative protoorders is becoming the mode. For instance, 10JC specifically turns in order to visually monitor the ordered speed relations he is constructing. Monitoring the ongoing processes is essential to comparative determinations of the operational properties of protoaddition, protosubtraction, and protoordered nonequivalence. Yet the ongoing processes are made up of mappings which are transformed consecutively. The resultant differential units comprising the iterative series are generated successively rather than simultaneously. Parts of the series are gone as soon as other parts are generated. As long as such pragmatic transience characterizes infants' orderings, so long is it likely that comparative determination of their proto-operational properties will remain precursory.

Comparative determination of the proto-operational properties of ordered nonequivalences is expected to be promoted by specifiable conditions. These are where it is possible for infants to combine monitoring all the parts of and the whole series. Given the pragmatic, nonnotational form of orderings constructed at their origins, this is only possible if infants generate parts of the series in temporal overlap.

This is precisely what begins to develop at this stage. Consider again the 10CC (p. 19) protocol fragment presented above. Parts ⟨3, 1⟩ of the discrete order ⟨6, 3, 1⟩ are generated in partial temporal overlap. This enhances the possibility of comparing the quantitative, but ordered, if imprecise, inequality between these two steps of the three-step series.

On this hypothesis, comparative determination is further enhanced under those conditions where (a) the order is precise and (b) the whole series is constructed simultaneously:

35.5. RH bangs Doll 2 on table, three times
35.5. LH bangs Spoon on table, two times   (10CC, page 45)

   18. RH hits down on top of Red Triangular Column and Cylinder 2, twice—both objects displace
19.5. RH hits down harder on C2—it rolls to experimenter
19.5. LH hits down on Cylinder 1—it rotates and moves a little toward experimenter   (10CC, page 23)

These, like all simultaneous series constructed, are limited to two-step orders. The first is a precise discrete decreasing order of ⟨3, 2⟩ bangs generated simultaneously by two hands. The second is a precise continuous increasing order. It has especially rich potential for comparative determination of the operational properties involved because it includes the construction of both a consecutive and a simultaneous series within a brief temporal frame. The right hand increases its force of hitting (Lines 18 and first 19.5) forming the consecutive proto-order ⟨hit, hit harder⟩. At the same time as the right hand increases its force of hitting, the left hand hits with less force (both Lines 19.5), forming the simultaneous proto-order ⟨hit, hit harder⟩.

The precursory status of these constructions is marked by at least three features. While some infants, such as 10CC, already generate several simultaneous proto-orders, they are in the decided minority. Only a few 10-month-olds generate simultaneous or partially overlapping mapping proto-orders. Those infants who do, never repeat simultaneous proto-orders twice in a row. Visual monitoring of these constructions is haphazard, at best; tactilokinesthetic monitoring is, of course, inherent in constructing the proto-orders; and auditory monitoring, in those series involving sound, depends upon whether the infants focus their attention on the sounds.

Bidirectional orderings remain in the decided minority. However, it is no longer unusual for them to involve both discrete and continuous ordered series:

  5. RH *taps Blue Circular Ring 2 on Green Circular Ring 1, one time*
  5a. *GCR1 moves toward Blue Circular Ring 1*
  6. RH *taps BCR2 onto table in center of the array of objects, eight times*
  6a. *contacts BCR1 once, displacing it very slightly*
  7. RH *hits BCR2 on Red Circular Ring, one time, and releases BCR2*
  8. RH *hits onto BCR2, one time*
  8a. *BCR2 bounces to left of BCR1*
  9. RH *bangs harder and faster onto RCR, one time*
  9a. *RCR moves*
 10. RH *lifts and hits RCR onto table, three times*   (10AB, pages 4 and 5)

The bidirectional continuous ordering ⟨tap, hit, bang, hit⟩ is fairly precise. The bidirectional discrete ordering ⟨1, 1, 8, 1, 1, 3⟩ is imprecise. They do not covary at all. As the continuous order increases, the discrete order decreases, and as the continuous order decreases, the discrete order increases. Thus, reciprocal relations between continuous and discrete orders are being increasingly elaborated.

Finally, and importantly, coseriation originates at this stage:

  7.5. RH *hits Blue Circular Ring on table, one time*
  7.5. LH *hits Yellow Circular Ring on table, one time*
  9.5. RH *taps BCR on table, two times*
  9.5. LH *taps YCR on table, two times*   (10AB, page 7)

Two continuous decreasing ⟨hit, tap⟩ orderings are generated at the same time, one with the right and the other with the left hand. Two discrete increasing ⟨1, 2⟩ orderings are also generated at the same time, one with the right and one with the left hand. Coseriation is generated by only this one 10-month-old subject. Yet it provides the precursory constructions necessary to begin to coordinate ordered nonequivalence with protocorresponding equivalence at each step in continuous and discrete series.

The continuous and discrete orderings generated by 10AB differ in direction. The continuous ordering is the result of protosubtraction, while the discrete ordering is the result of protoaddition. This has become typical at this stage. When generated simultaneously, continuous and discrete orderings are just as likely to differ in directions as to covary. This coincides with the trend noted above for bidirectional orderings which include both continuous and discrete series. It reinforces the possibilities for comparatively determining the reciprocal relations between proto-addition and protosubtraction.

10

Precursors to Second-Order
Discrete Combinativity

Sets of two objects are becoming relatively stable. They are extended temporally and observed comparatively so that they are increasingly preserved. The objects composed begin to be correctively adjusted so that they are in coregulated relations to each other, and the proportion of consecutive compositions increases while that of isolates decreases.

These features of progressively equilibrated two-element sets are conducive to constructing precursory second-order, protoinferential relations. Treating sets as constant givens permits initiation of two central second-order proto-operations. Precursors to protosubstitutions between two two-element sets are generated, as are precursors to protocorrespondences between two two-element sets.

Other advances are still limited to relational and conditional proto-operations upon single sets. They apply to the development of exchange proto-operations. Inverse protosubstitution and inverse protocommutativity becomes more frequent and extensive. Precursory protocommutativity is extended to three-object and rare instances of four-object sets. Coordinated structures of protoreplacement, protosubstitution, and protocommutativity are constructed. They apply to developing correlation proto-operations. Compositional protocorrespondences are progressively detached from the mappings used to produce them. Bi-univocals are beginning to be coordinated with co-univocals. Finally, they apply to the origins of relating ordered nonequivalence with equivalence. Ordered iteration of magnitudes just begins to be coordinated with exchange protooperations.

I. Increasing Composing Productivity

Composing productivity during the spontaneous phase is higher for all conditions at age 10 months than at age 8 months (cf. Table 10.1 and 7.1). Seven of the subjects are longitudinal. The increase for these longitudinal subjects approaches statistical significance (N = 7, x = 1, p = .06, sign test for two related samples).

By themselves these figures probably underestimate the increase in combinativity proto-operations. The reason is that the trend toward generating temporally extended compositions, begun at the previous stage, also progresses at this stage:

11.5.   LH brings Cross Ring 2 in front of face
11.5.   RH raises Triangular Ring 1
   13.   BH rub and tap CR2 and TR1 together for about 15 seconds in front of eyes near face; first half of 15 seconds more symmetrical; second half of 15 seconds RH with TR1 more active in hitting CR2 in LH
   14.   LH holds CR2 and RH holds TR1 apart in front of self, looking at them
   15.   BH touch CR2 and TR1 together briefly   (10MM, page 43)

While still in the minority, increasing temporal expansion indicates that composing is becoming less labile and more stable. This mobile is varied internally from symmetrical to asymmetrical relations (Line 13). Its parts are reproduced numerous times for extensive durations. It is preceded (first Line 11.5) and succeeded (Line 14) by visual, probably comparative, inspection of the elements. It culminates in yet another, much briefer, symmetrical variant composition (Line 15).

TABLE 10.1
Spontaneous Phase I: Mean Frequency by 10-Month-Old Subjects of Compositions, Duration of Phase I, and Mean Frequency of Compositions Per Minute

	Class conditions			
	Semicontrol 1	Additive 2	Multiplicative 3	Disjoint 4
1. Compositions	14.25	14.92	14.18	8.73
2. Time	2 min 56 sec	2 min 36 sec	2 min 20 sec	2 min 28 sec
3. Productivity per min	4.86	5.74	6.09	3.53

The rate of productivity is more uniform across class conditions than it was at age 8 months (Table 10.1, Row 3, as compared to Table 7.1, Row 3). The productivity rate remains relatively low in the disjoint condition; but, this is no longer so for the multiplicative condition. Most compositions are now generated in the multiplicative condition, less in the additive and semi-control conditions, and least in the disjoint condition. These differences are not statistically significant (Friedman $\chi_r^2 = 4.20$, $df = 3$, $p > .20$).

Composing frequency varies as a function of test phase. More compositions are generated during the spontaneous than during the provoked phase; even though the latter is the phase during which the experimenter models and assists the subjects in composing. However, the differential composing productivity between the spontaneous and the provoked phase is greatly reduced from what it was at age 8 months.

Composing productivity is also advancing when the presentation includes prearranged compositions of the elements during the second and third test phase. Still, many transactions with preexistent compositions consist of deforming (e.g., 10KC, Lines 2.7–4) the arrangement and/or subtracting single elements (e.g., 10KC, Line 5):

> 2.7. LH *extends and fingers displace Blue Triangular Column 1 forward, without looking*
> 2.7a. BTC1 *moves into Blue Brush 1, displacing it*
> 2.7aa. BB1 *displaces Red Brush*
> 4. RH *hits Blue Brush 2 which rotates about* 180°
> 5. RH *picks up BB2 by bristles*   (10KC, pages 44 and 45)

Much recomposition still consists of deforming. Often the deformations are more radical; either pushing the objects together into a heap or sweeping them all away. Yet, protosubtraction and protoaddition are applied somewhat more consistently to preexistent compositions. Taking away two elements from two prearranged groupings of two elements each and then composing them into a labile is no longer unusual. Reorganizing both prearranged groupings in this way is, however, still not generated.

Adding some extra elements to prearranged compositions is also generated frequently. Again the limit tends to be one or two objects. Many objects, that is, three or four, are not added to preexistent groupings; except in a gross dumping or heaping mode. Moreover, extra objects are not added on a systematic basis, whether extensive or predicate. Infants do not distribute the extra elements to both prearranged groupings; they add them to one grouping only. They make little, if any, effort to match the extra objects to those in the preexistent sets on the basis of similarities or differences:

(experimenter hands Yellow Cross Rings 2, 3, 4, and 5 in a stack to subject)

1. *BH take YCR2, 3, 4, and 5*
2. *separates them so YCR2 in LH, and YCR3, 4, and 5 stacked loosely in RH*
3. *turns herself from right to left as she arches back*
4. *looks at floor on left*
5. *RH releases YCR3, 4, and 5 next to Green Cross Ring in the prearranged matrix*
5a. *the top two crosses slide away a bit*
6. *RH lifts YCR4*
7. *RH holds it next to YCR2 in her LH on left chair arm as looking at them*
8. *RH throws YCR4 onto table*
8a. *YCR4 slides across Green Rectangular Ring and lands to left of the matrix at some distance*
9. *RH turns YCR3 upright*
10. *RH releases YCR3 such that it turns over*
11. *RH lifts YCR5 slightly off table*
12. *RH pushes YCR5 flat into YCR3 and releases YCR5*   (10JL, page 12)

Indicative of gross compositional addition without attemtion to predicate properties is *10JL's* (Line 5) release of three yellow cross rings near one green cross ring (cf., Section VIII). She does not continue by transacting with all these four cross rings. Instead, she transacts with the extra yellow cross rings only. She pays no attention to the yellow cross ring in the prearranged matrix.

II. Symmetrical Composing without Physical Support

Two-object compositions still predominate. Three-object compositions are infrequent; four-object compositions remain rare (Table 10.2). Compositional size is uniform for all class conditions (Columns 2, 4, 6, and 8).

TABLE 10.2
Spontaneous Phase I: Mean Frequency and Percentage of Compositional Object Extent Generated by 10-Month-Old Subjects

	Class conditions									
	Semicontrol		Additive		Multiplicative		Disjoint		Total	
	$\bar{x}$	%	$\bar{x}$	%	$\bar{x}$	%	$\bar{x}$	%	$\bar{x}$	%
	1	2	3	4	5	6	7	8	9	10
1. Two-object	12.83	90	13.42	90	12.36	87	8.00	92	11.72	90
2. Three-object	1.08	8	1.50	10	1.55	11	0.55	6	1.17	9
3. Four-object	0.33	2	0.00	0	0.27	2	0.18	2	0.20	1

If there is a developmental lag in this feature of combinativity prior to this stage (see Chapter 7, Section II), the disparity is overcome by age 10 months.

There is no increase in the proportion of compositions constructed by direct transactions with two or more objects (Table 10.3). There is a shift, however, in the way infants manipulate the objects when they directly contact two or more objects in order to compose them.

This shift is marked by two features. One is an increase in the proportion of compositions which is the product of symmetrical reciprocity between elements (e.g., banging or touching two or three objects together). The other is an increase in the proportion of compositions constructed in the air:

13. *RH hits Orange Cup on Yellow Cup which is held by LH*
14. *RH hits and brushes OC on the side of YC held by LH and taps bottom of OC on table in one fluid motion*
15. *as looks at the cups, RH puts OC on top of YC held by LH*
15a. *YC taps against the table*
16. *RH bangs OC on the table, 6 seconds, as LH holds YC just above the table on the left side*
17. *RH raises OC and hits it on top of YC* (10MM, pages 16 and 17)

Support by a physical structure, such as the surface of a tabletop, becomes less necessary for composing as babies transact directly with more than one object at a time. As composing becomes increasingly liberated from its dependence upon contingent physical support, chance plays a progressively decreasing role in its determination. To that extent, composing is progressing in its structural development (cf. Langer, 1969a, pp. 178–180). This is a further indication that composing is becoming a progressively equilibrated combinativity proto-operation.

There is no change in the overall frequency of recomposing initial compositions. Variants continue to constitute a third of all compositions (Table 10.4). There is an increase in the rate at which variants are generated in the multiplicative and disjoint conditions; coupled with a

TABLE 10.3

Spontaneous Phase I: Number of Objects Directly Manipulated by 10-Month-Old Subjects to Produce Composition in All Class Conditions

	Number of objects				
	1	2	3	4	Total
1. Frequency of compositions	354	239	6	3	602
2. % Compositions	59	40	1	0	100

TABLE 10.4
Spontaneous Phase I: Mean Frequency of Composing and Recomposing by
10-Month-Old Subjects

	Thematic	Variant	% Variant
1. Semicontrol	8.58	5.67	40
2. Additive	9.50	5.42	36
3. Multiplicative	10.09	4.09	29
4. Disjoint	6.64	2.09	24
5. All conditions	8.72	4.37	33

decrease in the semicontrol condition and no change in the additive condition (cf. Table 10.4, Column 3 and Table 7.4, Column 3). While some disparity in recomposing remains, the developmental gap is closing.

Recomposing continues to form contact, proximity, replacement, and substitution variants. These are becoming progressively extended, structured protoinferentially, regulated, and monitored. Analyses of these structural developmental aspects of recomposing will be deferred to the sections dealing with the development of relational and conditional proto-operations, such as the structures of exchange proto-operations (pages 240–250).

III. Continuing Predominance of Mobile Composition

The pattern of compositional features at age 10 months virtually duplicates that at age 8 months (cf. Table 10.5 and Table 7.5). The overall ratio of 58% mobiles, 38% stabiles, and 4% combined mobiles and stabiles is generated at both ages.

The ratio of mobiles to stabiles continues to vary as a function of class condition. The range is from a low of one-to-one in the semicontrol condition (Rows 4 and 8, Columns 1 and 2) to a high of two-to-one in both the multiplicative (Rows 4 and 8, Columns 5 and 6) and disjoint (Rows 4 and 8, Columns 7 and 8) conditions. The relative sparsity of stabiles in the multiplicative condition is a continuation of the developmental lag found at ages 6 and 8 months. The ratio of mobiles to stabiles in the disjoint condition decreases at age 8 months. At age 10 months it increases again to its 6-month-old level.

Contact between elements accounts for four-fifths of the compositions constructed; proximity accounts for only one-fifth. The ratio does not vary as a function of either class condition or labile form constructed. It remains substantially the same as that generated at age 8 months.

The percentage of compositions involving causal relations increases

TABLE 10.5

Spontaneous Phase I: Mean Frequency and Percentage of Compositional Features at Age 10 Months

	Class conditions									
	Semicontrol		Additive		Multiplicative		Disjoint		Total	
	$\bar{x}$	%	$\bar{x}$	%	$\bar{x}$	%	$\bar{x}$	%	$\bar{x}$	%
	1	2	3	4	5	6	7	8	9	10
1. Contact stabile	5.25	37	3.92	26	3.45	24	1.73	20	3.63	28
2. Proximity stabile	1.42	10	1.83	12	1.00	7	1.00	11	1.33	10
3. Contact–proximity stabile	0.17	1	0.00	0	0.00	0	0.00	0	0.04	0
4. Total stabile	6.83	48	5.75	39	4.45	31	2.73	31	5.00	38
5. Contact mobile	6.33	44	7.58	51	7.91	56	4.73	54	6.65	51
6. Proximity mobile	0.58	4	1.00	7	0.91	6	1.09	13	0.89	7
7. Contact–proximity mobile	0.00	0	0.08	1	0.09	1	0.00	0	0.04	0
8. Total mobile	6.92	49	8.67	58	8.91	63	5.82	67	7.59	58
9. Mobile–stabile	0.50	4	0.58	4	0.82	6	0.18	2	0.50	4
10. Causal	5.08	36	6.75	45	8.27	58	4.36	50	6.11	47
11. Noncausal	9.17	64	8.17	55	5.91	42	4.36	50	6.98	53
12. Horizontal[a]	6.50	55	8.75	65	6.55	61	6.40	78	6.93	63
13. Vertical[a]	5.17	43	4.58	34	3.91	36	1.70	21	3.85	35
14. Horizontal–vertical[a]	0.25	2	0.17	1	0.27	3	0.10	1	0.20	2

[a] Compositions whose spatial dimensions are ambiguous are not scored. Consequently, the dimensional means summate to less than the total compositional means.

from 38% at age 8 months to 47% at age 10 months (Table 10.5, Row 10, Column 10). All causal compositions are mobiles. Eighty-one percent of all mobiles are causal. Ninety-two percent of all contact mobiles are causal. Most causal mobiles are still marked by asymmetrical placement and displacement, such as banging one object on another. Yet, the frequency of causal mobiles marked by symmetrical placement and displacement is becoming substantial; such as banging two objects into each other.

The ratio of causal to noncausal compositions varies as a function of class condition (Rows 10 and 11, Columns 1–8). The range is from a low of one-to-two in the semicontrol condition to one-to-one in the multiplicative and disjoint conditions. This is another indication of compositional disparity generated as a function of class conditions.

Most compositions are still constructed in the horizontal dimension. The range is from a low of 55% in the semicontrol to 78% in the disjoint condition (Table 10.5, Row 12). Only one-third are constructed in the vertical dimension (Row 13); while combined horizontal–vertical constructions remain rare (Row 14).

First attempts are made to construct three-object vertical compositions:

49. *leans forward, RH extends and places Circular Ring 2 on top of Circular Ring 1*
    (experimenter helps straighten it)
50. *RH grasps Brush 2 held in LH*
51. *BH put B2 to mouth*
52. *leans forward, LH releases grasp from B2, RH holding B2 by bristles extends B2 toward stack of CR2/CR1*
53. *RH releases B2 partially on top of stack of CR2/CR1*   (10GP, page 39)

The difficulty seems mainly to be in psychomotor coordination, rather than in conceiving three-object vertical compositions.

Composing objects by spatial containment is just beginning to be generated with any frequency. Subjects begin to drop objects into receptacles, during the second test phase, with some directed proficiency:

22. *RH extends Rectangular Ring 2 to Receptacle 2 and drops it inside, looking as does so*
    (experimenter pushes Block 2 closer to subject)
23. *LH pushes B2 about 2 inches in from table edge*
24. *LH grasps B2 and pulls it off table into lap*
25. *LH extends B2 toward Receptacle 2 and drops it inside*   (10GP, page 47)

Regulated spatial containment is consistent with progress in causal reciprocity already considered (Chapter 9, Section III). It is accompanied by exploring containers. Infants comparatively inspect receptacles:

29. *looks at Receptacle 2, then at Receptacle 1, LH index finger touches Receptacle 1 as looks at it*
30. *LH index finger touches Receptacle 2 as looks at it*
31. *LH index finger touches Receptacle 1 as looks at it*
32. *LH index finger touches Receptable 2 as looks at it*
33. *LH grasps rim of Receptacle 2 and pulls it slightly off table edge toward self, as looking inside (experimenter holds it down) LH releases grasp*
34. *LH grasps rim of Receptacle 1 and pulls it toward self, this time with greater effort, so Receptacle 1 comes further off table edge, as looking inside*
                                                            (10GP, page 48)

Exploration includes spatially inverting receptacles by rotating them:

73. *LH turns Receptacle 2 upside down on table*
74. *LH turns Receptacle 2 right side up*   (10GP, page 50)

Exploring the properties of containers is reciprocal to exploring the possibilities of containing parts of the self within containers:

15.7. *RH palm pushes bottom of Receptacle 2 up toward face so that opening is over her face and the top of her head*
17. *RH removes Receptacle 2 from her head*
18. *RH releases and LH places Receptacle 2 back on table, no release (experimenter helps subject place it flat)*
19. *LH slides Receptacle 2 toward self again*
20. *RH grasps and pushes Receptacle 2 upright over face again as inserts the near rim into her mouth (experimenter holds Cylinder 1 above subject's head)*
21. *looks through the bottom of Receptacle 2 at C1, as maintains position in No. 20*
                                                            (10PM, page 30)

IV. Increasing Frequency of Sequential Composing

Consecutive compositions increase in frequency while compositions generated in isolation decrease (Table 10.6 as compared with Table 7.6). Four-fifths are consecutive and one-fifth are isolates at age 10 months, while two-thirds are consecutive and one-third are isolates at age 8 months. Partially overlapping and simultaneous compositions are rare, although two simultaneous compositions are just beginning to be generated.

The increase in consecutive and decrease in isolate compositions is general. It does not vary as a function of class condition (Rows 1 and 2, Columns 1–8). The developmental lag in generating consecutive compositions in the multiplicative and, perhaps, disjoint conditions manifest at age 8 months is overcome by age 10 months.

TABLE 10.6
Spontaneous Phase I: Temporal Relations between Compositions Generated by 10-Month-Old Subjects

	Class conditions									
	Semicontrol		Additive		Multiplicative		Disjoint		Total	
	$\bar{x}$	%	$\bar{x}$	%	$\bar{x}$	%	$\bar{x}$	%	$\bar{x}$	%
	1	2	3	4	5	6	7	8	9	10
1. Isolate	2.42	17	2.50	17	2.73	19	1.91	22	2.39	18
2. Consecutive	11.50	81	12.08	85	11.09	78	6.45	74	10.35	79
3. Partially overlapping	0.33	2	0.17	1	0.00	0	0.36	4	0.22	2
4. Simultaneous	0.00	0	0.17	1	0.36	3	0.00	0	0.13	1

238

The general increase in consecutive compositions promotes progress in constructing part–whole protoinferential relations between labiles. Precursory construction of some part–whole relations internal to isolated compositions is possible even though the elements and the compositional relations remain constant. Factors enhancing protoinferential relations within isolates which have already developed at earlier stages were outlined in Chapters 4 and 7. Further progress is made at this stage, in part, because isolates, like other compositions, are increasingly extended in duration:

33. *RH moves Circular Ring 4 near to Circular Ring 2 held in mouth by LH*
34. *RH raises CR4 slightly such that RH touches CR2 which LH is still holding in mouth and holds CR2 and CR4 together for 9 seconds*

(10PM, page 5)

Precursory constructions of protoinferential relations between successive isolate compositions are also increasingly probable. Consider a not unusual sequence of three isolate compositions in which the intervening transactions, consisting mainly of mouthing and displacing the spoon, are omitted:

64. *RH touches Spoon next to handle of Mirror*
69.5. *RH holds S a few inches above M*
75. *RH holds S a few inches above M* (10CC, pages 3 and 4)

All three stabiles are featured by proximity. The second stabile is an inexact replacement of the first while the third is an exact replacement of the second. It seems probable, then, that 10CC is structuring equivalence relations between the extent of these three compositions even though she does not generate them consecutively.

This sequence of successive isolate compositions is marked by features requisite to the formation of exchange proto-operations. Others are appropriate to constructing correlation proto-operations. Transactions are interpolated between isolated compositions. Nevertheless they sometimes correspond to each other in remarkable ways:

21. *looks at Brush 2 as LH places Brush 1 on top of it with bristles down such that bristles are matched*
22. *RH grasps handle of B2*
22a. *B1 gets knocked off of B2*
23. *RH raises B2 by handle and inserts bristle end into mouth*
24. *RH removes B2 from mouth, as looking at it*
25. *grasps bristle end of B2 with LH index finger*
26. *LH index rotates bristles of B2 so they are facing down*
27. *RH adjusts grasp on handle end of B2*
28. *RH extends and touches bristle end of B2 to bristles of B1, displacing B1 forward slightly*

(10GP, page 33)

The elements remain constant in *10GP's* compositions, but the relation between them is inverted. This flows from the reciprocal relation between his initial composition (Line 21) and decomposition (Lines 22 and 22a). He places Brush 1 on Brush 2 so the bristles match (Line 21); then he pulls Brush 2 out from under Brush 1 (Lines 22 and 22a). Several transactions with Brush 2 intervene before touching it to Brush 1 so that the bristles match once again (Line 28). These include looking at Brush 2 (Line 24) and adjusting it such that it is in position (Lines 25–27) for matching.

V. Extending Negation to All Exchange Proto-operations upon Two-Element Sets

The increase in the percent of consecutive compositions augments the opportunities for constructing protoinferential relations, such as exchange proto-operations. At this stage, all subjects generate protoreplacements, protosubstitution, and protocommutativity. Coordinations between exchange operations are also generated more frequently.

Two features continue to mark precursory structures of exchange proto-operations. They operate upon consecutive recompositions of a single set; they do not operate upon two sets simultaneously. They operate upon sets composed of two elements; they do not operate upon sets composed of more than two elements. Yet the sets are increasingly extended in duration, and the entire procedure is progressively monitored. This is consistent with the general developments in combinativity proto-operations at this stage. This also promotes progressive development of exchange proto-operations.

Protoreplacements still split between single and repeated exchanges. However, protoreplacements are extended in duration of individual compositions, number of recompositions, and frequency of noncausal exchanges:

37. *RH places Green Circular Ring 1 flat on top of Red Circular Ring such that they overlap*
38. *RH thumb pushes RCR toward self while holding GCR1 on RCR*
39. *RH lifts GCR1 and retouches it to RCR*
40. *RH lifts GCR1 and retouches it to RCR*
41. *RH lifts GCR1*
42. *LH lifts RCR*
43. *RH places GCR1 and LH places RCR together in air, as looks at experimenter*
    subject: (vocalizes)
44. *BH holds Circular Rings together for a few seconds*

> *(experimenter moves her index finger to subject, playing with him)*
> *experimenter: (imitates subject's vocalizations)*
> 45. *BH separate the two Circular Rings several inches apart*
> 46. *BH tap RCR and GCR1 together a few times*
> *subject: (vocalizing and laughing)*
> *(experimenter extends her RH to subject)*
> 47. *RH touches GCR1 to experimenter's hand*
> 48. *RH touches GCR1 to RCR held by LH*   *(10AB, page 6)*

The sequence includes at least five protoreplacements (Lines 39, 40, 43, 44, 46, 48). Noncausal protoreplacements are generated as frequently as causal ones; in this instance four out of five are noncausal. Individual recompositions are extended beyond the moment of their construction. One extended recomposition takes the form of a stabile (Lines 43 and 44). Another takes the form of a mobile (Line 46).

Active prolongation of recompositions beyond their moments of construction marks increasing preservation of the consecutively related sets. They are becoming progressively stable sets or constant given. As such, they are progressively subject to being protoinferentially related to each other by protoreplacement. Protoreplacement within single two-element sets is becoming an equilibrated structure.

Progressive equilibration is corroborated by an increase in frequency of protoreplacements including active exchange of both elements. The number of subjects doubles from one-quarter of age 8 months to one-half at age 10 months. Six of the subjects generate protoreplacements in which both objects are actively replaced. It is no longer unusual for these subjects to intermingle several protoreplacements of one object with several protoreplacements of both objects. For instance, 10AB's first two protoreplacements are applied to one object while his last three are applied to both objects. Protoreplacing both objects may be constructed symmetrically or asymmetrically. Subject 10AB's first two are symmetrical (Lines 43, 44, and 46) while his third is asymmetrical (Line 48).

Typically, replacing both objects is constructed in the air without any surface support. Actively protoreplacing both objects on a surface remains rare. It is also no longer unusual for infants to intermingle noncausal with causal compositions in constructing sequences of protoreplacements. This is apparent in 10AB's production. His first, third, and fifth recompositions are noncausal, while his fourth is causal.

Protosubstitutions are extended to form lengthy sequences, regularly marked by inverse relations between exchanges:

83. *LH touches Rectangular Ring 2 to Clover Ring 1*
83a. *RR2 knocks CR1 flat*

84. *RH places Clover Ring 2 on top of CR1 such that they overlap*
85. *RH lifts CR2—in process, hand pushes CR1 about 4 inches away from self*
86.5. *RH holds CR2 on table*
86.5. *LH extends RR2 toward CR1*
88. *LH touches RR2 to CR1*
89. *LH pulls RR2 on table toward self a little*
89a. *RR2 pushes Rectangular Ring 1 about 1 inch toward subject*
90. *LH touches RR2 to CR1*
90a. *RR2 pulls CR1 a little bit closer to self*
91. *LH raises RR2*
92. *RH raises CR2 off table and drops it about 4 inches in back of CR1*
93. *RH lifts CR1*
    (experimenter pushes CR2 toward subject)
    subject: "Blllleh" (vibrates lips)
94.5. *RH lowers CR1 to table*
    experimenter: (imitates subject's above vocalization)
94.5. *LH lowers RR2 to table*
96. *LH touches RR2 to CR2*   (10DG, page 41)

This sequence forms a semisystematic equivalence structure by six protosubstitutions (Lines 84, 88, 89–89a, 90–90a, 92, 96):

$$(RR2 > CR1) \approx (CR2 > CR1) \approx (RR2 > CR1) \approx (RR1 > RR2)$$
$$\approx (RR2 > CR1) \approx (CR2 > CR1) \approx (RR2 > CR2) \ (10.1)$$

The equivalence structure is semisystematic. It includes many, but not all, possible combinations. Inverse proto-operations are applied to protosubstitutions, but not always. They are applied to the first, third, and fifth compositions. Two repetitions of inverse proto-operations to protosubstitutions originate at this stage. Most, however, consist of only a single inverse proto-operation, such as between the second and sixth composition.

This sequence of protosubstitutions is unusual in one respect. It constructs equivalence relations between all four objects presented. Only one-quarter of the infants (3 of 12 subjects) apply protosubstitution to four objects. The rest apply protosubstitution to only three objects, which is the minimum required to generate this exchange structure.

Alternate unary mappings upon single objects are generated by 10DG to produce the compositions making up this sequence of protosubstitutions. While actively manipulating one object to construct a composition, the other object is not usually discarded, rather, it is stored in the other hand. This facilitates and makes more efficient the formation of equivalence relations by protosubstitution, particularly by inverse protosubstitution.

Alternating procedures of transaction are beginning to be used with some frequency at this stage. So are binary mappings upon both objects composed. They do not appear in 10DG's production, but, they are generated by one-half of the infants. Actively transforming both objects at the same time initiates protosubstitutions which are precursory to the construction of equivalence between two sets:

54. *RH moves Circular Ring 3 toward and touches it to Circular Ring 2 held by LH in front of chest, as looking down at the two circles*
55. *LH turns CR2 and RH turns CR3 slightly, as still looking at them held together*
56.3. *RH extends and touches CR3 to right of and next to Circular Ring 1*
56.7. *leaning forward slightly, LH taps CR2 inside of Circular Ring 4*
58. *RH raises CR3 and LH raises CR2, tapping them together in air above table*
58a. *in process CR2 displaces CR4 nearer to table edge*
59. *LH bounces CR2 up and down in air slightly, near CR3, but not hitting it, as looking at experimenter*
60. *turns left and looks in mirror as holds circles in front of herself, with RH moving CR3 on CR2 held by LH*
61. *BH hold CR2 and CR3 partially overlapped in air as looks in mirror*
62. *BH pull CR2 and CR3 apart*
     subject: "Ooooo—" (smiling)
63. *RH hits CR3 on CR4 a few times, while still looking in mirror*
63a. *CR4 displaces*
64. *RH holds CR3 in air as looks at experimenter*
65. *BH tap CR3 and CR2 together in air*
66. *turns and looks in mirror while BH still tapping CR3 and CR2 together*
     (10MM, page 4)

This forms an equivalence structure by five protosubstitutions (Lines 54, 55, 56.3, 56.7, 58–61, 63 and 63a, 65 and 66):

$$(CR3 \gtrless CR2) \approx (CR3 > CR1) \approx (CR2 > CR4) \approx (CR3 \gtrless CR2)$$
$$\approx (CR3 > CR4) \approx (CR3 \gtrless CR2) \qquad (10.2)$$

The first, fourth, and sixth compositions in Eq. (10.2) are marked by reciprocal active transformations. They are identical to each other as a result of inverse proto-operations. Such constructions, as we have already seen, are typical at this stage. Beyond this, the first four compositions in Eq. (10.2) generate equivalences in which the second and third sets are protosubstitutes of the first and fourth (which are identities), and where the second and third sets are partially overlapping compositions. This forms protocorresponding equivalences between two different but contemporaneous two-object sets; forming a two-to-two correlation. Still missing is the crucial property of exchanging one element from both sets into each other. Instead of following up the second and third compositions by exchanging elements in them, 10MM recombines the two elements she is directly transacting with to reform the initial composition. Thereby, she reconstitutes her initial one-to-one symmetrical protocorrespondence (see Section VI).

Protosubstitution transitional to constructing equivalence between two separately established and preserved sets is rare at this stage; it is generated by only two subjects. Many features of both Eqs. (10.1) and (10.2) are typical of this stage. Binary reciprocal transactions are generated to compose both objects. Some of the transformations and compositions are monitored. Compositions are increasingly preserved over time and transformations such that they can be progressively used as constant givens. Finally, it is no longer unusual for some of the compositions in protosubstitution sequences to take forms other than causal mobiles.

Protocommutativity, like the other two exchange proto-operations, is extended to include numerous recompositions. The most extended protocommutativity generated includes ten order exchanges:

64.5. *RH touches Circular Ring to Triangular Ring*
66. *immediately RH slides CR toward right of self*
67. *RH places and holds CR partially on top of TR*
68. *RH taps CR near TR, once*
69. *RH places and holds CR flat next to and touching TR*
70. *RH slides CR together with TR side by side in front of self*
71. *RH raises CR*
72. *RH index finger inserts into center of TR and pushes it to right, while RH still holds CR such that TR and CR touch each other*
73. *RH lowers CR flat on top of TR*
74. *RH pushes CR such that CR and TR slide toward self*
75. *RH raises CR*
76. *RH index finger inserts into center of TR and pushes it slightly over table edge such that TR tips over edge, while RH still holds CR such that TR and CR touch each other*
77. *RH pushes TR flat onto table*
78. *RH raises CR in air*
79. *RH touches CR to TR*
80. *RH places CR on table 1/2 inch behind TR*   (10TA, pages 3 and 4)

This protocommutative series is marked by a number of typical features. Some of the transformations are unary and some are binary. Reordering is distributed across both elements, singly and together. Reordering begins by being applied to one element; switches to the other element and to both elements. Finally, it reverts to being applied to the initially transformed element. Inverse protocommutativity, initiated at the previous stage and continued during the present, is thereby augmented. The standard form of inverse protocommutativity is becoming

$$\langle\, a > b \,\rangle \rightsquigarrow \langle\, b > a \,\rangle \rightsquigarrow \langle\, a \gtreqless b\rangle \rightsquigarrow \langle\, a > b \,\rangle \qquad (10.3)$$

or

$$\langle\, a > b \,\rangle \rightsquigarrow \langle\, a \gtreqless b \,\rangle \rightsquigarrow \langle\, b > a \,\rangle \rightsquigarrow \langle\, a > b \,\rangle \qquad (10.4)$$

Several central properties are yet to develop before inverse protocommutativity becomes fully reversible. One worth underlining here is that inverse protocommutativity is still not reproduced; that is,

$$\langle\, a > b \,\rangle \rightsquigarrow \langle\, b > a \,\rangle \rightsquigarrow \langle\, a > b \,\rangle \rightsquigarrow \langle\, b > a \,\rangle \qquad (10.5)$$

is never generated.

Reciprocal binary transformations which produce protocommutativity are becoming more frequent, but still remain in the minority. Yet, they are even beginning to be elaborated by a couple of infants so as to include spatial containment relations:

31. *RH holding Blue Circular Ring and LH holding Red Circular Ring touches both rings together for a few seconds*
32. *RH inserts BCR partially through RCR held by LH*
33. *BH lower BCR and RCR together slightly*
36. *RH touches BCR to RCR held by LH*
37. *RH inserts BCR partially through RCR (i.e., repeats No. 32)*
38. *BH hold BCR and RCR together briefly in rough alignment such that both are flat together*   (10DG, page 29)

Minor nonrelevant intervening transactions are omitted. Two reorderings produce reciprocal container–contained relations between the rings (Lines 32 and 37). Replication indicates that protocommutativity which includes reciprocal containment reorderings is beginning to be regulated. Indeed, two test phases later, during the countercondition, this same subject produced another protocommutative series which included an identical, reciprocal containment relation between two rings.

Antecedents to protocommutativity of three-object (*10DG* and *10MM*) and four-object (*10JC*) sets begin to be generated by a few infants:

21.3. *LH thumb slides Block 1 to right until it touches Block 2, so:*

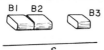

21.7. *RH slides Block 3 to left until it touches B2, so:*

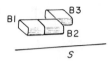

23.5. *LH slides B1 1 inch behind B2, so*
23.5. *LH pushes B2 slightly, in process, so:*

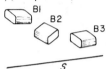

25. *LH slides B1 back to the left about 1 inch from B2, simultaneously flipping it over onto other side by exerting pressure down on a corner*
(10DG, page 2)

13. *RH moves Circular Rings 3 and 1 well aligned together to right toward Circular Ring 4 on table*
14. *RH hits CR3 and CR1 as a unit next to CR4, three times*
15. *LH picks up CR4*
16. *LH brings CR4 and RH brings CR3 and CR1 in front of self*
17. *looks back and forth at circles in BH as LH slides CR4 close to CR1 which is still well aligned against CR3 in RH*
18.3. *RH rotates CR3 and CR1 upside down*
18.3a. *CR1 drops to the floor making noise*
18.7. *looks down, while RH holds CR3 in the air on right side and LH holds CR4 in air on the left*
20. *watches experimenter for 7–8 seconds (as experimenter bends down to retrieve CR1 and replaces it to the right—sits looking at experimenter as holding a ring in each hand)*
21. *LH hits CR4 on table, twice*
22. *LH moves CR4 to front of and touching CR3 held by RH, so:*

23. *RH slides CR3 out from behind CR4 held by LH*
24. *BH touch the edges of CR3 and CR4 together:*

25. *RH moves CR3 back to back of CR4 held by LH, such that No. 22 is reformed*
26. *while holding CR3, RH grasps CR4 taking it under thumb as LH lets go:*

(10MM, pages 1 and 2)

3.5. *RH releases Block 4 on Block 3 which is next to Block 2, as watches*
3.5. *LH holds Block 1 above the other blocks*
5. *BH push all four blocks together, such that they heap up a bit*
6. *BH flatten out the heap with LH on B1 and RH on B4*   (10JC, page 1)

By gross adjustments *10JC* forms a most rudimentary protocommutative structure (Lines 3.5, 5, and 6) with all four objects:

$$\langle\ (B4 > B3,\ B2) < B1\ \rangle \rightsquigarrow \langle\ B1,\ B2,\ B3,\ B4\ \rangle \rightsquigarrow \langle\ B1 > B2,\ B3 < B4\ \rangle$$
$$(10.6)$$

In contrast, *10MM* finely adjusts the objects to each other to form rudimentary protocommutativity between three objects (Lines 13–18.3). Moreover, she comparatively monitors the protocommutative series she is in the process of constructing. The series might well have been extended if *10MM* had not lost one ring (Line 18.3a). Instead, *10MM* continues by generating a protocommutative series with the remaining two objects. It is featured by typical reciprocal binary mappings and one inverse proto-operation (Lines 22 and 26). It is also marked by coregulatory adjustment of two objects to each other which is only generated frequently at the next stage. Coregulation is generated three times in a row when the objects are precisely aligned in parallel (Line 22), edge to edge (Line 24), and back in parallel (Line 25).

Coordinated structures of exchange proto-operations progress and increase. Progress is marked, most centrally, by the origins of coordination between all three exchange operations. Three of the twelve subjects tested generate compositional sequences which interweave protocommutativity, protoreplacement, and protosubstitution. Increase in coordination of protocommutativity with protosubstitution and of protoreplacement with protosubstitution is marked. Eight subjects generate both forms of coordinate exchange proto-operations. Only the frequency of protocommutativity coordinated with protoreplacement does not increase; it is generated by three subjects.

As well as increasing in frequency, coordinated exchange proto-operations are becoming progressively regulated and directed. Directly transforming all the objects exchanged is becoming frequent, exchanged objects are inspected, and sets are preserved for extended periods of time:

1. *LH picks up Blue and Red Circular Rings*
2. *LH holds BCR and RCR*
3. *RH picks up Green Circular Ring*
4. *LH drops RCR into lap while still holding BCR*
5. *LH holds BCR and RH holds GCR together in air*
6. *BH separate BCR and GCR*

7. BH *hold BCR and GCR together again*
8. BH *hold BCR and GCR together for several seconds as fingering them*
(10AB, page 1)

Protosubstitution (Lines 1–5) is followed immediately by reciprocal protoreplacement (Lines 6 and 7). The coordinated series culminates in a
composition which is preserved after it is constructed and which is monitored tactually (Line 8).

Coordinations are also increasingly marked by mapping constancy:

53. RH *slides Triangular Ring 1 left into Cross Ring 2, displacing CR2 to left*
54. RH *slides TR1 right into Cross Ring 1, displacing CR1 to right*
55. RH *slides TR1 left and right into CR1, displacing CR1 to far right*
56. RH *slides TR1 left and right, twice*
(*experimenter slides CR1 back to subject*)
57. RH *slides TR1 left into CR1, displacing CR1 to left*
58. RH *slides TR1 left into CR1, displacing CR1 further left*
(10TA, pages 35 and 36)

The same mapping form, sliding, is used to construct both protosubstitution (Lines 53 and 54) and protocommutativity (Lines 54–58).
One other coordination is also part of this series. It interlaces protocommutativity and protosubstitution with repeated continuous increases in
order of displacements (Lines 54, 55, 57, and 58). Expanded coordinations such as these augment the possibilities for relating equivalence with
ordered nonequivalence extents. They originate at this stage and will be
considered further in Section VII.

While coordinating all three exchange proto-operations just begins at
this stage, the interconnections produced already range from minimal
(10MM) to extensive equivalence structures (10TA):

43.3. LH *turns Cross Ring 2 toward self, from a perpendicular orientation to a
parallel one to self*
43.7. RH *raises Cross Ring 3 as looks down at CR2*
45. RH *moves CR3 in front of self and behind CR2 such that they touch and
are in parallel to each other and self*
46. RH *raises CR3 slightly and then replaces it behind CR2 in same orientation*
(*experimenter replaces Cross Ring 1 down on table*)
47. RH *raises and taps CR3 on table, twice, as LH holds CR2*
48. RH *holds CR3 a couple of inches above table edge and LH holds CR2, as
watches experimenter*
(*experimenter takes CR1 and taps it on table again, then holds it out to
subject*)
49. *watches CR1, as RH turns CR3 towards self and LH turns CR2 slightly*
50. RH *taps CR3 on CR2 held by LH, as turns left and looks in mirror,
smiling*

51. *BH* hold CR3 and CR2 together such that they overlap partially and touch, as smiles at experimenter
    (experimenter replaces CR1 on table)
52. *RH* taps CR3 on CR1, twice, displacing CR1, as LH holds CR2
53. *RH* holds CR3 out slightly above table edge and LH holds CR2 for a few seconds
54. *RH* moves CR3 towards and touches it to CR2 held by LH in front of chest, as looking down at the two circles   (10MM, pages 3 and 4)

50. *RH* touches Orange Spoon to Yellow Cup, displacing YC to far right
    (experimenter moves YC in front of subject)
51. *RH* pushes OS into YC, displacing YC to left
52. *LH* pushes Orange Cup into YC, displacing YC to far right
53. *turns to right and watches YC*
    (experimenter rolls YC back to subject)
54.3. *watches YC roll to self*
54.7. *RH* pushes OS into YC, displacing YC toward experimenter
    (experimenter slides YC in front of subject)
56. *RH* hits OS into YC, displacing YC side to side and away from self
    (experimenter pushes YC in front of subject)
57. *RH* .taps OS on OC, thrice, held by LH
58.5. *LH* raises OC and mouths bottom of OC very briefly
58.5. *RH* touches OS to side of OC
60.5. *LH* lowers and holds OC on table
60.5. *RH* taps OS on OC held by LH
62. *RH* pushes YC to left, such that YC rolls all the way to experimenter
    (experimenter pushes YC to subject)
63. *RH* pushes OS into YC, displacing YC toward experimenter
64. *RH* taps OS on OC held by LH
    (simultaneously with No. 64, experimenter rolls YC back to subject; YC rolls to subject and then starts to roll to the right)
65.5. *LH* presses side of OC against open mouth very briefly
65.5. *RH* hits OS against OC
67.5. *LH* lowers and holds OC on table (at same moment when YC is rolling toward right of subject)
67.5. *RH* pushes OS into YC, displacing YC to far right
    (experimenter returns YC to subject)
69. *RH* hits OS into YC, displacing it to experimenter
    (experimenter pushes YC back to subject; YC comes to a rest against the bottom of OC, as)
70. *RH* touches OS to YC
71.5. *LH* moves OC to the left and forward, away from YC
71.5. *RH* hits OS into YC, twice, displacing YC toward experimenter
73. *RH* hits OS on OC held by LH, once
74.5. *LH* raises OC
74.5. *RH* taps OS on OC, several times
76. *LH* inserts part of bottom of OC into mouth
77.5. *mouths on OC held by LH*

77.5. RH *rubs* OS *against* OC
       (*experimenter rolls YC to subject's left*)
79.5. LH *lowers and holds* OC *on table*
79.5. RH *hits* OS *on* OC, *once*   (*10TA*, pages 14 and 15)

Subject *10MM* interweaves one replacement (Line 46), two commutative (Lines 50 and 51), and two substitution (Lines 52 and 54) exchange proto-operations to form a simple equivalence structure:

$$(CR3 > CR2) \sim (CR3 > CR2) \rightsquigarrow \langle CR3 > CR2 \rangle \rightsquigarrow \langle CR3 \gtrsim CR2 \rangle$$
$$\approx (CR3 > CR1) \approx (CR3 > CR2) \qquad (10.7)$$

Subject *10TA*, on the other hand, already interconnects numerous and repeated exchange proto-operations to form an extensive, regulated and directed equivalence structure:

$$(OS > YC) \sim (OS > YC) \approx (OC > YC) \approx (OS > YC)$$
$$\sim (OS > YC) \approx (OS \gtrsim OC) \rightsquigarrow \langle OS \gtrsim OC \rangle \rightsquigarrow \langle OS \gtrsim OC \rangle$$
$$\approx (OS > YC) \approx (OS \gtrsim OC) \rightsquigarrow \langle OS \gtrsim OC \rangle \approx (OS > YC)$$
$$\sim (OS > YC) \sim (OS > YC) \sim (OS > YC) \approx (OS \gtrsim OC)$$
$$\sim (OS \gtrsim OC) \rightsquigarrow \langle OS \gtrsim OC \rangle \rightsquigarrow \langle OS \gtrsim OC \rangle \qquad (10.8)$$

The consecutive sets in Eq. (10.8) represent, respectively, Lines 50, 51, 52, 54.7, 56, 57, 58.5, 60.5, 63, 64, 65.5, 67.5, 69, 70, 71.5, 73, 74.5, 77.5, and 79.5 of the protocol fragment.

The extended equivalence structure Eq. (10.8) is featured by several inverse proto-operations. They include repeated inverse protosubstitution. Indeed, inverse protosubstitution is generated five times in a row. They also include twice repeated inverse protocommutativity.

While not generated with this frequency by most subjects at this stage, such constructions constitute the origins of regulated inverse exchange proto-operations. They produce stable, that is, relatively equilibrated, identity relations between objects and orders within two-element sets. The structural foundations of constant objects and orders, albeit limited to two-element sets, are thereby established.

VI. Formative Detachment of Composing from Mapping Protocorrespondences

Compositional protocorrespondences become progressively detached from the mappings by which they are produced, but detachment remains infrequent. This indicates that constructing compositional equivalences as abstracted givens remains in its formative stage.

Detaching compositional equivalence from mapping forms is promoted by progress in extended protocorrespondences initiated at the previous stage (see Chapter 7, Section VI). The crucial development, at this stage, is in the origins of protocorrespondences between two contemporaneous two-element sets. They are generated by only one-quarter (three subjects) of the infants. A partially overlapping construction, coordinate with protosubstitution, has already been considered on pages 243–244. Simultaneous (10GP) as well as partially overlapping (10DG) constructions are initiated:

> 7.5. *LH holds Block 1 flat on Block 2 for several seconds*
> 7.7. *looks at self in mirror, smiling*
>   *subject: "hi"*
> 7.8. *RH touches Block 4 to Block 3*   (10DG, page 1)
>
> 15.5. *RH places Yellow Cross Ring on top of Green Rectangular Ring*
> 15.5. *LH places Yellow Rectangular Ring on top of Green Cross Ring*
> 15.5a. *YRR is not placed securely and falls into lap*
> 17. *BH drop into lap as looks down*
> 18. *looks up as LH raises YRR up from lap*
> 19. *LH places YRR on table edge again*
> 19a. *YRR falls into lap again*   (10GP, pages 11 and 12)

Detaching the resultant equivalences from the mapping forms is inherent in the structure of composing protocorrespondences between sets. Single parallel placements correlate two two-element sets to each other. Detachment is constructively enhanced when protocorrespondences are subjected to corrective adjustments, as attempted by 10GP.

Compositional protocorrespondences are constructed by 10GP (Lines 15.5) by placing YCR on top of GRR and YRR on GCR. So the mapping and compositional protocorrespondences are already partially detached from each other. The mappings consist of both hands simultaneously lowering and placing a separate object. Thus, the mappings are in one-to-one correspondence with each other, but they generate two-to-two compositional protocorrespondence.

Elaborated detachment follows rapidly. One composition is unstable; element YRR falls off (Line 15.5a). Subject 10GP tries to reconstruct the composition but he is not fully successful (Lines 17–19a). He tries again and gets a bit closer, almost making it (in the next set of transactions not reproduced). Significantly, the adjustment mappings no longer involve protocorrespondences. Rather, they are initial attempts to correctively reconstruct one of the sets in the two-set protocorrespondence. The result is that the compositional equivalence between sets is further detached from the mapping forms.

Abstracting compositional protocorrespondences from the mappings that construct them is marked by an additional important feature. Reconstructive adjustments originate at this stage. Compositional reconstruction via corrective transactions indicates that sets are taking on durational lives which exceed the processes of their initial construction. Subject 10GP attempts to preserve the YRR-on-GCR composition in the face of its impermanence due to his psychomotor difficulties in balancing objects on top of each other. Thus, labiles are progressively transformed into equilibrated compositions.

The groundwork for progressive detachment at this stage was worked out at the previous stage. In particular, the process of simultaneous construction, of repetitive and reproductive compositions, and of extending the volume and duration of compositions began during the previous stage.

The implication of progressive detachment for part–whole analysis is crucial. It begins to become possible to construct equivalences between two-element extents as "givens," that is, as constructs, rather than merely as "actual." Detachment is only the first step in abstracting constant given quantities from transactive reality. Nevertheless, it permits pragmatic and presentational construction of given quantities. At this stage the extent is small (i.e., two-element sets).

The necessary conditions for correlating two corresponding sets are self-generated by all three infants who construct contemporaneous sets. They correspondingly group two elements together. Simultaneously, they correspondingly group two other elements together. In turn, these two-element correspondence groupings match each other. Thereby, they equate equalities. On this view, then, constructing two-to-two correlations between one-to-one correspondences constitutes the structural origins of second-order equivalence proto-operations.

Corrective compensation, such as that generated by 10GP in order to reconstruct one of his corresponding sets, is part of coregulated composing. It always involves attempted or actual reciprocal adjustment of two objects such that they are in more precise corresponding alignment to each other. Coregulated protocorrespondences by compensation originate at this stage. They are generated by one-half of the infants:

10. *LH brings Cross Ring 1 to right and next to Cross Ring 3 held by RH such that they touch*
11. *RH slides CR3 parallel to CR1 held by LH such that they are well aligned*
12. *LH lets go as RH grasps both together such that they remain well aligned*
(10MM, page 1)

39.3. *LH pushes face of Mirror 2 on table to the right*
39.7. *RH touches face of Mirror 1 to face of M2 held by LH*

41. *LH pulls M2 over table edge toward self, as RH holds M1*
42. *RH touches face of M1 to face of M2 held by LH*   (10DG, page 10)

Subject 10MM preserves the coregulated protocorrespondence beyond the moment of construction (Line 12). Subject 10DG repeats the coregulated protocorrespondence he constructs twice (Lines 39.7 and 42). Preservation and repetition indicate that coregulated compositional protocorrespondences are already directed constructions.

The preponderance of compositional protocorrespondences is still generated sequentially. Consequently, they construct equivalence within one set rather than between two sets. Most also still construct bi-univocal (one-to-one) rather than co-univocal (many-to-one) correlations.

Symmetrical bi-univocal compositional protocorrespondences are generated by all infants. They are becoming almost as frequent as asymmetrical protocorrespondences. Some correlate relatively imprecise continuous magnitudes:

69. *looks at Block 4 and Block 3 as RH sweeps B4 and LH sweeps B3 back and forth across table symmetrically*
70. *looks at experimenter (who is bending over)*   (10JC, page 3)

A little later this same infant generates a variant of the first:

22. *RH pushes Block 1 and LH pushes Block 6 symmetrically right and left many times while looking between them*
23. *continues No. 22 as looks at Block 2*   (10JC, pages 4 and 5)

Both protocorrespondences are extensive, include numerous consecutive repetitions, involve proximity relations between the two elements composed into mobiles, and are monitored while they are being constructed.

Symmetrical bi-univocal compositional protocorrespondences also correlate precise discrete magnitudes:

31. *RH lowers Circular Ring 6 and LH lowers Circular Ring 5 to chest level as taps them together several times*
32. *RH holds CR6 and LH holds Circular Ring 5 touching together as looks at them*
33. *RH taps CR6 and LH taps CR5 together several times as looks at them*
     (10PM, page 13)

24. *RH hits Red Clover Ring and LH hits Yellow Hexagonal Column together, thrice*
25. *RH holds RCR and LH holds YHC touching together for a few seconds*
     (10AB, page 27)

All symmetrical protocorrespondences between discrete magnitudes are limited to single units. They are extensive, include numerous consecutive repetitions, involve contact relations between the two elements composed, and are often monitored while they are being constructed. Some are stabiles (e.g., *10PM*, Line 32, and *10AB*, Line 25). Others are causal mobiles. They are constructed with elements having identical (e.g., *10PM*, Lines 31 and 33) or disjoint (e.g., *10AB*, Line 24) predicate properties. Extensive equivalence is independent of predicate equivalence.

Symmetrical protocorrespondences sometimes begin to take on protosymbolic and social dimensions:

24. *RH extends Cylinder 2 and LH extends Square Column 1 up to experimenter*
   (experimenter extends RH and LH palms on table to subject)
25.3. *RH hits C2 down onto experimenter's LH palm and table*
25.7. *LH lowers and holds SC1 on experimenter's RH*
27. *RH hits C2 onto table*
   (as experimenter withdraws BH)
28. *RH extends C2 and LH extends SC1 up to experimenter*
   (experimenter takes SC1 and taps it onto table)
29. *looks at SC1 as LH reaches for it and RH holds C2*
   (experimenter holds SC1 up to subject)
30. *LH grasps SC1 as RH holds C2*
31. *RH extends C2 and LH extends SC1 up to experimenter*
32. *RH rotates C2 and LH rotates SC1 upside down*   (*10CC*, page 16)

Symmetrical protocorrespondences marked by social and protosymbolic referential features are generated by three subjects. They always involve two objects, one in each hand. Most of the time they involve virtual or actual giving; occasionally they involve hitting on the experimenter's hand. Sometimes, they are also interlaced with nonsocial symmetrical protocorrespondences (e.g., *10CC*, Line 32).

Most asymmetrical discrete compositional protocorrespondences continue to produce single-unit equivalences. Two-unit equivalences are still generated infrequently. Yet, some compositional protocorrespondences are already extended to three units, but by only a couple of infants:

98. *LH hits and bangs Rectangular Ring 2 on Doll 1, thrice*
98a. *D1 falls over*
99. *LH bangs RR2 on table next to D1, thrice*   (*10MM*, pages 60 and 61)

Co-univocal compositional protocorrespondences are generated almost as frequently as bi-univocals. There is no longer a frequency differential between the two major forms of co-univocals. Many-to-one matchings are generated as frequently as one-to-many matchings. Both co-univocal forms are beginning to be repeated with some frequency, and they are monitored by the subjects as they construct them. Thus, co-univocals are becoming regulated, like bi-univocals.

All simultaneous co-univocals are still limited to matching one with two objects (e.g., one object is placed such that it bridges two objects, or two objects are placed such that they form a heap on one object). Successive co-univocals extend to matching one with as many as four or five objects (e.g., one object is consecutively tapped against four objects or four objects are consecutively placed near one object).

Sequences of consecutive compositional protocorrespondences are beginning to be generated which interlace bi-univocals with co-univocals:

> *(experimenter holds Square Column 2 toward subject)*
> 49.5. *RH hits Cylinder 2 against right side of SC2*
> 49.5. *LH hits Square Column 1 against left side of SC2*
> *(experimenter hits SC2 on table and releases it as)*
> 51. *RH holds C2 and LH holds SC1 together*
> 52. *RH brings C2 to mouth as LH holds SC1*
> 53.5. *RH hits C2 onto SC2*
> 53.5. *LH hits SC1 onto SC2*
> 55. *RH extends C2 and LH extends SC1 to experimenter (10CC, page 17)*

Two symmetrical two-to-one co-univocals (Lines 49.5 and 53.5) are interwoven with two symmetrical bi-univocals (Lines 51 and 55). Both co-univocals are targeted with some causal precision. The first bi-univocal only matches the objects to each other. The second bi-univocal adds a social dimension to the protocorrespondence.

Compositional sequences connecting bi-univocals with co-univocals are generated by three subjects. These sequences construct the initial necessary conditions for coordinating the basic structures of correlation proto-operations. This includes differentiating and integrating bi-univocal and co-univocal protocorrespondences. It also includes differentiating and integrating correspondence proto-operations with proto-symbolic and social transactions.

VII. Initial Coordination of Set Equivalence with Ordered Differences

Addition and subtraction of elements producing iteratively ordered set sizes increases in frequency. Magnitude iteration within compositional sequences also progresses. While keeping the number of elements within the compositions constant, magnitude iteration produces unequal continuous and discrete, increasing and decreasing mapping extents. All these developing forms of iteration continue to be generated without regard to the predicate properties (similarities, differences, and complements) of the elements composed and recomposed together or decomposed from each other. This general development furthers the process of differentiating the quantity from the intensity (definition) of sets.

Iterating set size remains limited to small numbers. Most still involve protoadditions which construct ⟨one-, two-, three-⟩ element sets and protosubtractions which construct ⟨three-, two-, one-⟩ element sets. Iteratively ordered sets including four elements necessarily remain rare since four-element compositions are still generated infrequently. A small increase occurs in (a) simultaneously adding two elements to a two-element set resulting in a four-element set and (b) simultaneously subtracting two elements from a four-element set to form two two-element sets. Both adding and subtracting two elements at a time is generated by only one-third of the infants at this stage. Constructing bidirectional iterations increases rapidly. They are generated by three-quarters of the infants. They are also just beginning to be extended to two alternations (e.g., ⟨three-, two-, three-, two-, three-, two-⟩ sets of elements). However, only two infants generate bidirectional series of this extent.

Magnitude protoaddition and protosubtraction within compositional sequences whether continuous or discrete, remain limited to constructing small number series. The usual extent is three-step orders (e.g., ⟨tap, hit, bang⟩ one object on another). Bidirectional magnitude series produced by combined protoaddition and protosubtraction also remain limited to a few steps. The usual extent is one alternation forming reciprocal two-step iterative orders (e.g., hit one object on another ⟨2, 1, 2, 1⟩ times). While longer unidirectional and bidirectional series are increasingly generated, they are usually imprecise.

As noted in Section V, the structures of compositional magnitude iteration begin to be coordinated with those of compositional equivalence. These structural coordinations are produced by infants interweaving exchange with addition and subtraction proto-operations. These include bidirectional orderings, as well as the undirectional orderings presented in Section V:

22.5. *RH taps Orange Spoon against Orange Cup, twice*
24.5. *RH hits OS on top of Yellow Cup, once*
24.5a. *YC rolls to the left*
24.5. *LH grasps and holds OC on the table*
26. *RH taps OS on OC, twice, as watches YC roll*
27. *as YC rolls on top of Yellow Spoon, LH hits OC against YC*
27a. *YC rolls to left* (10TA, page 12)

This is the most complex series of magnitude iterations generated at this stage. Two bidirectional orderings are constructed simultaneously: One is continuous (e.g., ⟨tap, hit, tap, hit⟩ one object against another); the other is discrete (i.e., tap and hit one object against another ⟨2, 1, 2, 1⟩ times). These dual bidirectional orderings do not covary. Rather, they are in inverse relation to each other; that is, as one increases the other decreases. All the magnitude orderings in these series involve causal relations. They include some causal reciprocity. The causal patient in the next to last composition (Line 26) is transformed into the causal instrument in the last composition (Line 27).

These dual bidirectional ordered nonequivalence structures of magnitudes are constructively coordinated with a protosubstitution equivalence structure of elements:

$$(OS \gtrless OC) \approx (OS > YC) \approx (OS \gtrless OC) \approx (OC > YC) \quad (10.9)$$

Together they form a twofold structure of relational (addition and subtraction) and conditional (exchange) proto-operations. The result is to begin to coordinate set equivalence with ordered differences. Thereby, infants continue to construct the precursory structure of units or intervals which remain constant while they are being transformed by ordering proto-operations into iterative series. Of course, the units and series are necessarily small since they are all pragmatic constructions; and, therefore restricted by spatio-temporal or here-and-now limitations which no longer apply when constructions become symbolic.

VIII. Random Predication and Predication by Differences

Predication remains unchanged, with two exceptions to be considered shortly. It is primarily a property of individual compositions since only 3% constitute partially overlapping or simultaneous sets (Table 10.6). It is featured by only order and enclosure. It cannot yet be featured by proximity and separation since this applies only to compositions of four or more objects, and only 1% of the sets compose four objects (Table 10.2). Order and enclosure continue to be almost perfectly correlated. They correspond in 98% of the compositions in which order applies. This trend continues to confirm the hypothesis that they are syncretically fused features of predication at its origins.

Predication is random in both the additive and multiplicative conditions (Table 10.7, Rows 2 and 3). The means approximate the random

TABLE 10.7
Spontaneous Phase I: Mean Frequency by 10-Month-Old Subjects Generating
Unmixed, Partly Unmixed, and Mixed Compositions

	Order			Enclosure		
	Unmixed 1	Partly unmixed 2	Mixed 3	Unmixed 4	Partly unmixed 5	Mixed 6
1. Semicontrol[a]	0.00	0.00	3.50	0.60	0.00	7.00
2. Additive[b]	3.11	0.00	4.44	4.67	0.17	10.08
3. Multiplicative[b]	4.36	0.00	0.91	7.73	0.09	6.36
4. Disjoint[b]	1.88	0.09	2.50	2.82	0.09	5.82

[a] $N = 5$.
[b] $N = 11$.

probability ratio of two-to-one favoring mixed order and enclosure in the additive condition, and of one-to-two favoring unmixed order and enclosure in the multiplicative condition. Randomness is corroborated in each instance by sign tests.

Predication is by disjoint properties in those semicontrol conditions which permit evaluation (Table 10.7, Row 1, Columns 1–3). The distribution of three types of semicontrol conditions was such as to permit evaluation for only five subjects. Yet, the results are disjoint predication for enclosure of compositions ($N = 5$, $x = 0$, $p = .031$, sign test). All five subjects exceeded the random probability ratio of two-to-one favoring mixed enclosure. It is not possible to evaluate statistically the order of predication since it applies to only two of the five subjects. Order of predication is by disjoint properties for these two subjects, as was enclosure for all five subjects. The other three subjects do not generate compositions in which they manipulate more than one object in the semicontrol conditions.

Predication is also by disjoint properties in the disjoint condition (Table 10.7, Row 4). The random probability ratio is two-to-one in favor of mixed predication. The results are predication by disjoint properties for compositional enclosure ($N = 10$, $x = 2$, $p = .055$, sign test). They are in the same direction but not statistically significant for compositional order ($N = 8$, $x = 2$, $p = .14$, sign test).

Together with the results from the previous two stages (Chapter 4, Section V, and Chapter 7, Section VIII), the present findings continue to corroborate the hypothesis that at its origins predication is never by affirmation. Objects are not composed together by similarity. This hypothesis is further corroborated by the present results from phases (II) and (III). As at the previous stages, assisted sorting and counterconditions do not provoke predication by similarity. The thrust of all the findings, then, serve to reinforce the hypothesis that originally predication is by negation, that is, by differences. Gradually, and apparently in a fluctuating manner, predication is progressing toward random grouping, that is, composing which is predicated upon neither identity, nor complementary, nor disjoint properties.

11

Rudiments of Pragmatically Reversible Quasi-Continuous Combinativity

Progress in transforming quasi-continuous objects parallels proto-operational developments with discrete objects described in Chapters 9 and 10. Parallel progress occurs in at least three central structural properties. Mappings are becoming predominantly binary. This includes the origins of binary, coordinate deforming and decomposing one object at the same time. Consequently, decomposing as well as deforming takes binary forms of reciprocity and correspondence. Transformational sequences are featured by semisystematic ordering, including protoexperimental variation. A major consequence is to be found in the origins of genealogical decomposing which produces progressively smaller elements. Part–whole transformations begin to be articulate constructions which are preserved as constant givens. These include decomposing singular objects into preserved two-object sets and generating articulately protocorresponding deformations.

These transformational developments underlie the rudimentary origins of reversible proto-operations. Most notable are the origins of recomposing decomposed elements. Recompositions construct identity proto-operations in the extent (quantity) of individual elements. At this stage they do not yet reconstruct the intensity (form) of individual elements. The antecedents to redecomposing composed elements also originate at this stage. But they are even more rudimentary than recomposing. Redecompositions remain incomplete. Only parts of the composed elements are redecomposed. Therefore redecompositions do not yet quite construct identity proto-operations in either extent or intensity of individual elements.

I. Regulated Direct and Contingent Deforming

Deforming is becoming progressively well-regulated and directed. Infants engage in a two-step process when first presented with quasi-continuous objects. They immediately inspect the objects and then proceed to deform them. One exception occurs when subjects follow inspection with another form of negating, that is, decomposition, to be discussed in Section III. Pragmatic deforming, then, is becoming an applied transformation selectively imposed upon appropriate quasi-continuous substances.

Delay in deforming when presented with quasi-continuous objects is brief. The time is used deliberately to inspect the objects. Thereby infants determine whether they are appropriate objects of deforming or decomposing. Omitting nonrelevant transactions in the second protocol fragment, the following represents the range of initial transactions:

1. *looks at and touches Ring 1 with LH finger*
2. *LH index finger picks up R1, looking at it as holds it in front of face*
3. *LH lowers R1 toward table edge*
3a. *R1 falls onto lap*
4. *looks down as LH lowers to lap and picks up R1*
5. *LH drops R1 to floor as looks after it*
6. *looks up at remaining Rings 2 and 3 on table as LH picks up R2*
7. *looks at R2 briefly while LH holds it just slightly up off table*
   (10GP, page 25)

3. *LH draws Ring to table edge, looking at it*
4. *LH squeezes R between fingers*
13. *RH picks up lower end of R and raises it above LH as looking at it*
14. *BH hold R as looking at it*
15. *RH lowers its end of R as fingers it*
19. *LH raises R as looking at it*   (10PM, page 38)

1. *looks at Ball while holding BH just above it*
2.5. *RH pinches B, pulling a little piece up but not off from B*
2.5. *LH touches B*   (10CC, page 25)

Deforming continues to be the most frequent combinativity proto-operation applied to quasi-continuous objects (Table 11.1). The mean rate of deforming productivity per minute during spontaneous transac-

TABLE 11.1

Mean Frequency of Combinativity Proto-operations Generated by 10-Month-Old Subjects in Quasi-Continuous and Discrete Quasi-Continuous Conditions

	One object			Three objects			Discrete–quasi-continuous	
	Phase I 1	Phase II 2	Phase III 3	Phase I 4	Phase II 5	Phase III 6	Phase I 7	Phase II 8
1. Deforming	11.00 (3.29)[a]	4.71 (1.14)	7.71 (1.00)	13.33 (3.83)	1.83 (0.67)	5.80 (1.20)	5.00 (3.67)	5.33 (2.33)
2. Reforming	0.00	0.00	0.00	0.00	0.00	0.00	0.00	0.00
3. Breaking	0.29	0.14	0.14	0.17	0.33	0.20	0.00	0.00
4. Reconstructing	0.00	0.00	0.00	0.00	0.00	0.00	0.00	0.00
5. Decomposing[b]	5.00	1.57	2.29	2.17	0.83	2.60	1.33	1.67
6. Recomposing	0.29	0.00	0.00	0.17	0.17	0.00	0.00	0.00
7. Composing	0.29	0.14	0.29	0.17	0.00	0.00	0.00	0.00
8. Redecomposing	0.00	0.00	0.00	0.00	0.00	0.00	0.00	0.00
9. Attaching	—	—	—	—	—	—	0.00	0.00
10. Detaching	—	—	—	—	—	—	1.00	0.00
11. Number of subjects	7	7	7	6	6	5	3	3
12. Mean duration	1 min 51 sec	1 min 15 sec[c]	1 min 02 sec	1 min 53 sec	1 min 01 sec	1 min 37 sec	1 min 53 sec	1 min 50 sec
13. Discrete compositions	0.00	0.43	1.86	3.33	1.33	0.60	5.67	1.67
14. Rate of productivity	0.00	0.34	1.81	1.77	1.30	0.37	3.02	0.91

[a] Mean frequencies of proto-operations involving multiple transformations are given in parentheses.
[b] The frequencies are necessarily underestimations because, when possible, subjects were not allowed to decompose by biting.
[c] Calculated on the basis of the six subjects for whom duration measures are available.

tion ranges from a low of 2.66 in the combined discrete–quasi-continuous condition (Row 1, Column 7) to highs of 5.95 in the one-object (Row 1, Column 1) and 7.09 in the three-object (Row 1, Column 4) conditions. Too few subjects were tested in the discrete–quasi-continuous condition to determine whether the relative paucity of deforming in this condition is reliable. The differences between the one- and three-object conditions are minor.

Deforming frequency remains stable with age (cf. Table 8.1, Row 1). It is almost identical in the one-object condition spontaneous test phase; the mean per minute is 6.00 at age 8 months and 5.95 at age 10 months. While the mean per minute almost doubles in the three-object condition, from 3.60 at age 8 months to 7.09 at age 10 months, the variance is large. Thus, the difference does not even approach statistical significance. The frequency of multiple and extended deformations decreases a bit in the one-object condition and increases a bit in the three-object condition. Mean deforming per minute in the combined discrete–quasi-continuous condition decreases from 8.14 at age 8 months to 2.66 at age 10 months. While this is a sharp decrease, its reliability cannot be evaluated since it is based upon only three subjects at each age.

Deforming productivity varies as a function of object type. During the spontaneous phase, the mean frequency per minute of deforming Euclidean solid objects is 7.23 and of deforming topological ring objects is 3.12. The difference is statistically significant (Mann–Whitney $U = 6$, $p = .02$).

Deforming productivity decreases somewhat during the second provoked test phases of the one- and three-object conditions (Table 11.1, Row 1, Columns 2 and 5). However, the decrease is not quite statistically significant ($N = 11$, $x = 3$, $p = .11$, sign test). On the other hand, deforming productivity increases somewhat during the second provoked test phase of the discrete–continuous condition (Row 1, Column 7). Deforming productivity increases a bit during the third test phase of the one-object condition (Row 1, Column 3). It decreases a bit during the third test phase of the three-object condition (Row 1, Column 6). Overall, the rate of deforming productivity is high and, with one possible exception, stable across the three test phases.

Reforming has not yet originated; it is never generated (Row 2). Deforming remains a direct, irreversible proto-operation. It is applied by all subjects, but it is never followed by any inverting transformations that could reform the initial shape and thereby produce an intensive proto-identity operation.

Contingent deforming, such as that resulting from hitting a Play-Doh ring onto the table, is generated by two-thirds of the infants, that is, 8 of the 12 subjects. All eight subjects generate contingent deforming more than once; the range is from 2 to 29 times. Yet, most deformings remain inherent, that is, the logically entailed result of infants' mapping structures in intersection with the structure of quasi-continuous objects (e.g., poking a finger into a ball).

Multiple contingent deforming of single objects is generated frequently. Its structure now includes precursory aspects of semisystematic protoexperimenting:

34. *LH places Ring on chair seat, as watching*
35. *LH raises and drops R onto chair seat, as watching*
36. *LH raises and slaps R onto chair seat two or three times, as watching*
37. *pauses and looks at R*   (10PM, page 39)

The transformations form the ordered variable series ⟨place, drop, slap⟩ the ring onto the chair seat. The infant monitors her variable contingent proto-operations and observes their covarying transformational results, ⟨none, minor, major⟩ deformations of the ring.

This development parallels the progress in protoexperimenting with discrete objects. Infants at this and the previous stage often monitor both their deforming operations and the resultant transformations in the objects. Beginning at this stage they also start to monitor their protoexperimental ordered variations in deforming operations and the resulting differential but covarying transformations in the objects.

Contingent deforming of two objects at the same time is generated by three infants. Some even begin to include three or more objects:

47. *looks at RH holding several pieces (previously decomposed) and at LH holding several pieces (previously decomposed)*
48. *BH bang pieces down on table*
48a. *two little pieces fall out of LH*   (10MM, page 42)

The three infants who generate simultaneous contingent deforming of two or more objects are the only three subjects who generate reciprocal contingent deforming between two objects. These include multiples, indicating that reciprocal contingent deforming is continuing to become regulated:

4. *RH grasps Ring 1/2 (previously composed)*
5. *RH hits R 1/2 onto Large Ring sitting on table, twice*   (10AB, page 21)

Both the instrumental agent (Ring 1/2) and the patient object (Large Ring) are deformed simultaneously and repeatedly.

Reciprocal contingent deforming is also just beginning to be symmetrical, as expected due to the increase of binary mappings at this stage:

8. *RH holds Ring 1 in air and LH holds Ring 2 in air*
9. *BH squeeze R1 and R2 together, lightly*

10. *RH pulls R1 and LH pulls R2 apart*
11. *RH bangs R1 and LH bangs R2 onto table, several times*
11a. *R1 and R2 are deformed*   (*10AB*, page 21)

Subject *10AB* interweaves symmetrical, reciprocal contingent deforming (Line 9) with protocorresponding breaking (Line 10) and, finally, with symmetrical, multiple protocorresponding contingent deforming (Line 11) of the same two objects.

Deforming single objects is increasingly featured by binary mappings. Most of the time this is as simple as one hand holding the object while the other hand deforms it, such as by squeezing and poking. Some involve protocorresponding binary deforming, such as both hands pinching its fingers into one object. Occasionally, binary but different deformations are applied to one object:

17.5. *LH pinches and pulls at one side of Ball*
17.5. *RH squeezes other side of B*
19.3. *LH pinches B*
19.7. *RH pinches B*   (*10KC*, page 32)

All these binary deformations are multiples. They begin by being different but reciprocal to each other (Lines 17.5). They end up being identical (Lines 19.3 and 19.7).

II. Initiating Articulate Equivalence and Order Relations

All three forms of simultaneous protocorresponding deformations generated at the previous stage increase in frequency at this stage (Chapter 8, Section II). Multiple synchronic deformations are generated by almost all infants. Simultaneous protocorresponding deformations of two objects are generated by one-half of the infants (six subjects). Binary deformations of a single object are generated by one-third of the infants (four subjects). One other form of protocorresponding deformations originates at this stage. Consecutive deformations are generated at different positions on a single object. They are fashioned into articulated parts which are preserved while other protocorresponding articulate parts are constructed by additional deformations.

Simultaneous protocorresponding deformations are progressively directed, extended and monitored. This includes multiple synchronic (*10MM*), simultaneous two-object (*10JC*), and binary (*10EH*) protocorrespondences:

4.3. *BH raise Large Ball*
4.7. *LH fingers press LB held by RH*
 6. *LH fingers release LB leaving indentations in LB*
7.3. *RH raises LB over her head*
7.7. *tilts head back looking at LB*   (*10MM*, page 40)

8.3. *RH squeezes Ball 2 between thumb and index finger making dents in it*
8.7. *LH squeezes Ball 1 between thumb and index finger making dents in it,*
     as turns toward B1   (*10JC*, page 14)

 3. *BH pinch Large Ball*
 4. *BH fingers squeeze LB*
 5. *BH fingers sink into LB, as brings it to lap*   (*10EH*, page 21)

Only one infant applies simultaneous protocorresponding deformations to more than two objects:

1.5. *LH bangs down on top of Balls 1 and 2, twice*
1.5. *RH bangs down on Large Ball, twice*
3.5. *LH picks up B2*
3.5. *RH picks up LB*
5.5. *LH fingers squeeze B2 making indentations in it*
5.5. *RH fingers squeeze LB making indentations in it*   (*10CC*, page 29)

The initial protocorrespondences (Lines 1.5) construct both simultaneous discrete mapping equivalence between two units and simultaneous deformation equivalence between three objects. The follow-up protocorrespondences (Lines 5.5) construct both (*a*) multiple synchronic
equivalence within each object and (*b*) simultaneous deformation equivalence between two objects. This elaborate structure of simultaneous
protocorresponding deformations, then, interweaves several forms of
constructing equivalence.
   This infant is also one of the two subjects who begin to generate
deformations in a social context:

2.5. *RH hits on Ball 1 in experimenter's LH, a few times*
2.5. *LH hits on Ball 2 in experimenter's RH, a few times*
 4. *RH lifts B1, squeezing it*
5.5. *RH places deformed B1 in experimenter's RH*
5.5. *LH lifts B2 out of experimenter's RH*
 7. *LH holds B2 above left shoulder and squeezes it*
 8. *LH hits B2 down onto table and then releases it*   (*10CC*, page 27)

Subject *10CC* generates simultaneous protocorresponding deformations of the two balls as soon as the experimenter shows them to her and
before the experimenter has a chance to place them on the table (Lines

2.5). Then she takes Ball 1 from the experimenter and deforms it (Line 4). As she gives deformed Ball 1 back to the experimenter, she takes Ball 2. She deforms Ball 2 both directly (Line 7) and contingently (Line 8).

Most extended protocorrespondences are still limited to single-object deformations. The deformations are reproductions of each other at different locations in the object:

1. *LH touches Ball*
2. *LH index finger pushes B, such that it rolls away a little*
3. *LH grasps B*
4. *RH pinches up little pieces on the top of B*
5. *LH picks up B and squeezes it*
6. *LH puts B down on table*
7. *RH pinches up little bits on the top of B*
8.3. *LH picks B up again*
8.7. *RH digs fingers in B pinching up a portion, as LH lowers B slowly to table*

(10KC, page 31)

Deformation is applied after some tactual examination (Line 1). In rapid succession the subject deforms the object four times by pinching (Line 4), squeezing (Line 5), pinching (Line 7), and digging (Line 8.7). These deformations construct multiple nodules on the surface of the ball without taking any pieces off (Lines 4, 7, and 8.7).

The multiple transformations 10KC produces in the part–whole relations by pinching up little pieces of the ball are rapid and successive reproductions of each other. The internal part–whole deformations correspond to each other. They are preserved by being located at different places on the surface. This means that relatively permanent equivalent part–whole relations are constructed. This facilitates presentational comparison of equivalent internal part–whole transformations.

Rudiments of articulate protocorresponding deformations are generated by about one-fourth of the infants. Precise determination is not possible with the techniques used in this research. It is difficult to always ascertain from videotape records when infants pinch corresponding little parts of an object. The estimate that they are generated by one-fourth of the subjects is therefore conservative and may well be an underestimation.

Articulate discrete protoadditive deformations also originate at this stage. While protoadditions are all consecutive, rare precursors of preserving the resultant ordered differences are generated. Consider further the 10KC protocol fragment just presented. Recall that the infant constructs protocorresponding nodules on the ball. He follows up by constructing a larger nodule on the ball (Line 8.7). Some of the smaller nodules are preserved. Preservation facilitates comparison between the ordered magnitude differences as well as the protocorresponding magnitude equivalence.

Missing entirely is any indication that constructing preserved orders is regulated in any way. Aside from the inherent tactilokinesthetic perception, they are not monitored in any overt perceptual manner. Preserved orders are not replicated by any subjects. Constructively compensating for the magnitude differences is certainly out of the question at this precursory stage; although inherent compensation accompanies all ordered series of deformations (see Chapter 5, Section I).

Articulate consecutive protoaddition resulting in ordered magnitude differences which are not preserved is somewhat regulated. For instance, this same infant *10KC* produced four articulate protoadditive orders. The most extensive comprises six discrete protoadditive transformations:

25. *LH holds Ball as RH adjusts fingers on B and then pulls up (but not off) a piece of Play-Doh*

26 –30. *RH repeats pulling up (but not off) the same piece of Play-Doh, five times, such that the piece becomes progressively elongated*

(*10KC*, page 32)

Unlike *10KC*'s first protoaddition where the ordered difference is preserved, this and his other consecutive orderings produce a single nodule only. Each nodule is continuously increased in magnitude. Thus, each sequence of deformations produces an ordered series of part–whole transformations within the object. The consecutive deformations vary only in the order of their magnitude. Increasing differences ("more and more") are generated in the extent of singular internal part–whole relations.

Articulate discrete protoaddition is generated by 5 of the 12 subjects at this stage. All the increasing orders of part–whole deformations comprise transformations which are consecutively applied on top of each other. Each protoaddition wipes out any trace of its predecessor protoaddition by increasing it. This makes it relatively difficult to compare the progressive steps to each other. Yet, as already noted, some infants already reproduce articulate deformation orderings. This indicates that they are becoming regulated. Yet the reproductions are never replicated twice in a row. As always, orderings are still never constructively compensated; for example, by reciprocal flattening or by inverse reformation.

Discrete decreasing ordered deformation is generated by almost all subjects. Some are direct (e.g., repeatedly banging down on a ball such that it is progressively flattened) and some are contingent (e.g., repeatedly banging down a ball onto the table such that it is progressively flattened). Indeed, they may already be generated protoexperimentally and carefully monitored (e.g., *10PM* protocol fragment presented on page 265). Thus, they are becoming well-regulated, but they are still never constructively compensated by discrete increasing deformations.

Discrete coseriated deformations in sets of two objects are generated by one-half of the subjects. Some are direct (e.g., banging down repeatedly on two objects at the same time) and some are contingent (e.g., banging two objects down onto the table at the same time). One subject already generates discrete coseriated deformations in sets of three objects (Lines 1.5 of the 10CC p. 29 protocol fragment presented on page 267). It is limited to the minimum required to construct a coseriated decreasing order in a set. The three objects are simultaneously flattened, twice in a row.

So far coseriated deformation of sets is dominated by constructing two simultaneous and equivalent discrete decreasing orders. Coseriated increasing orders of deforming sets are not generated except in the most rudimentary form (e.g., plucking up a piece in two objects at the same time). Yet, these coseriated deformations are sufficient to coordinate (*a*) protocorresponding equivalence between part–whole transformations within sets with (*b*) ordered differences in part–whole transformations within sets. They provide a firm constructive basis for establishing the relations between proto-operational magnitude equivalence and iteration applied to sets of two quasi-continuous objects.

III. Small Series of Asymmetrical Geneological Decomposing

Breaking is still produced infrequently and by only three infants (Table 11.1, Row 3). Breaking is limited, in the main, to topological shapes. This is to be expected since Euclidean shapes are more resistant to breaking.

Breaking is not compensated by any attempts to reconstruct the initial form of the object broken (Table 11.1, Row 4). It remains an entirely irreversible form of transforming quasi-continuous objects:

7. *looks at Ring 2 briefly, held by LH just slightly up off table and then on table*
8. *LH raises R2 off table*
9. *LH partially inserts R2 in mouth, takes bite, and then withdraws it from mouth*
9a. *R2 breaks apart*   (10GP, page 25)

1. *RH picks up Large Ring*
2. *RH bounces LR on table three times as moves it to left*
3. *LH grasps LR such that it is held by BH*
4. *BH break LR into one long strand*   (10PM, page 46)

Subject 10GP's breaking is generated by applying a familiar mapping form, biting. Subject 10PM's means of breaking is less familiar, but it follows upon multiple contingent deforming (Line 2). However, the mapping form used to break the Large Ring is different from that used to deform it.

Observation of others does not cause breaking:

2. *watches experimenter decompose one into two rings, looks up, RH extends and grasps Ring 2:*

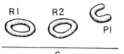

3. *RH slightly raises R2 and replaces it on table*
4. *LH moves in air in front of self, as looks down toward lap*
5. *LH slowly extends and picks up R2 (experimenter points to and touches Piece 1)*
6. *LH drops R2 into lap (experimenter taps P1 again)*
7. *LH raises and shakes R2 back and forth in front of self near seat of chair, dropping it to lap (experimenter picks up Ring 1)*
8. *LH picks up R2 from lap*
9. *BH hold R2, as looks up at experimenter (experimenter holds R1 in front of subject, decomposes it, and places the two pieces on table):*

10. *BH break R2 into a strand, as looks at the two pieces of R1 on table*
11. *looks down at R2 (strand) held by BH*   (10PM, pages 42 and 43)

Subject 10PM observes closely the experimenter's decompositions. The subject does not decompose. Instead, she breaks a ring into a strand (Line 10). Breaking is accompanied by visual comparison of the result with that of the experimenter's decomposing (Lines 10 and 11). Subsequent decompositions by the experimenter also do not cause the subject to either decompose or break objects. Instead, the subject hands pieces of Play-Doh to the experimenter. When experimenter decomposes these two objects, the subject watches and smiles.

Contingent breaking originates at this stage:

19. *LH raises Ring as looks down at it*
20. *LH rubs R up and down on left foot*
20a. *R is broken into one long strand*
21. *LH lets go of R onto seat*
22. *LH touches R (strand)*   (10PM, pages 38 and 39)

Contingent breaking (Line 20) is preceded by visiomotor (Line 19) and followed by tactual inspection. In this way the subject observes the transformation in the object's internal part–whole relation which she has produced by breaking it. The transformation is from a circular topological-like object to an elongated Euclidean-like object.

Deforming rings into a mass increases in frequency:

17. *RH picks up Ring 3*
18. *RH squashes R3 together*   (10JL, page 16)

This is a collateral means of transforming topological-like into Euclidean-like objects. No subjects evidence any attempts to reform the initial topological-like shape of the rings (e.g., by poking holes into the mass).

Decomposing frequency does not change significantly from its rate at age 8 months (cf. Table 11.1, Row 5 and 8.1, Row 5). The only possible increase is in the one-object condition. The mean rate of productivity per minute almost doubles, from 1.45 at age 8 months to 2.70 at age 10 months, but the difference does not achieve statistical significance (Mann–Whitney[1] $U = 11$, $p = .172$).

Decomposing frequency varies as a function of the number of objects with which infants transact (Row 5, Columns 1 and 4). The mean rate of productivity per minute is 2.70 in the one-object condition and 1.15 in the three-object. The difference is statistically significant (Mann–Whitney $U = 6$, $p = .037$). Infants are less likely to multiply objects when they are already presented with multiple objects.

Decomposing frequency also varies as a function of the form of the objects with which the infants transact. More decompositions are generated by infants transacting with Euclidean-like balls than topological-like rings (Mann–Whitney $U = 7$, $p = .077$). The mean rate per minute increases from 1.16 decompositions of rings to 2.55 decompositions of balls.

The mean rate of decomposing frequency decreases during the second, provoked phase (Row 5, Columns 2 and 5). The mean per minute drops from 2.09 in the first, spontaneous phase to 1.24 in the second phase. The drop is statistically significant ($N = 9$, $x = 1$, $p = .02$, sign test). It is also statistically significant for the subset of five subjects presented with modeling of decomposing by the experimenter ($N = 5$, $x = 0$, $p = .031$, sign

---

[1] Even though most of the 8- and 10-month-old subjects were tested longitudinally, a statistical test appropriate for data from independent samples is applied because the research design reversed the object conditions by age. Eight-month-old subjects tested with the one-object condition were tested with the three-object condition at age 10 months, and *vice versa*.

test). Consequently, neither visible nor nonvisible modeling of decomposing constitute direct local causes of the subjects' decomposing, let alone long-term developmental causes.

The organization of decomposing during the second, provoked phase is continuous with that at age 8 months. Some subjects carefully observe the experimenter's performance and then comparatively inspect the resultant objects, but they do not follow by decomposing:

1. *watches experimenter decompose Ball into two balls*
   (experimenter places out two balls—Large Ball on the left, Small Ball on the right)
2. *RH takes LB, displacing SB*
3. *RH holds LB and looks at it*
4. *looks back and forth between the two balls, twice*
   (experimenter holds up SB to subject)
5. *looks at SB while holding LB* (10LL, page 18)

Other subjects do eventually follow up with decompositions, but never immediately. When they do, the mapping forms are always different from that used by the experimenter to decompose (e.g., biting off a piece).

In the face of modeled decomposing three significant factors are becoming constants of infants' subsequent transactions. First, infants may or may not follow up with their own decomposing. Infants determine whether or not they will decompose. Second, when infants decompose, the form of decomposing is their own, not that of the experimenter. Third, when infants decompose, it is always delayed. Taken together, these three findings are consistent with the hypothesis that decomposing, like deforming, is a self-constructed structure of transforming the part–whole relations of quasi-continuous objects.

Decomposing is still mainly the intersective result of direct mappings on objects. Contingent decomposing is not generated more frequently at age 10 months than at age 8 months. The first signs that contingent decomposing is becoming regulated are, however, generated by exceptional subjects:

52. *LH hits Piece 2 down onto the table*
52a. *a large part (LP) of P2 breaks off onto the table while a small part (SP) of P2 remains held by LH*
   (experimenter lightly throws LP in front of subject)
53. *RH grasps LP, pushes it to left and quickly rubs it on the table to right*
53a. *a small piece comes of onto the table* (10TA, page 27)

Successive contingent decomposition of these two objects is followed by much contingent transformation by the same mapping forms. Subject

10TA repeatedly rubs and bangs objects onto the table. The results are mainly contingent deformation. They include at least one additional contingent decomposition:

69.5.   RH *hits Piece 1 onto table*
69.5.   LH *hits Small Piece onto table*
69.5a. *a little bit (LB) comes off SP and falls onto the table*   (*10TA*, page 28)

Long consecutive sequences of contingent transformations, such as that produced by *10TA*, generate variable results. Some result in deformations, others in decompositions. Variable results provide the necessary feedback for progressive modification of contingent transformation; that is, for self-regulation of transformational transactions in order to produce contingent decompositions as well as contingent deformations. This process of elaboration is enhanced when, as is the case with *10TA*, it includes simultaneous contingent transformations. Thus, *10TA* hits both pieces onto the table at the same time. While the mapping forms correspond to each other, the resultant contingent transformations do not because the objects differ. One is deformed and the other is decomposed.

Binary mappings begin to dominate decomposing. Usually binary decompositions take a reciprocal, asymmetric form of split transformations. One organ holds the object while the other decomposes it. Binary symmetrical decomposing just begins:

28.   BH *squeeze Ball, simultaneously pulling it apart*
29.   RH *lets its piece go while LH holds its piece momentarily*
                                                    (*10KC*, page 32)

Both organs hold the object and both organs decompose it.

It is unlikely that *10KC*'s aim in this instance is to go beyond decomposing to constructing a set of two elements. He immediately drops one part while holding on to the other (Line 29). Yet preserving the products of their decompositions as sets is no longer unusual:

24.   RH *raises Ball 2, looking at it*
25.   LH *pulls a piece off of B2 held by RH*
25a. *two equal-sized pieces result*
26.   BH *hold both pieces up and out in air, looking at them and smiling*
                                                    (*10CC*, page 28)

12.   *holds L (large piece) outstretched into one strand between her hands*
13.   LH *pulls off a small piece (L₁) from L held by RH*   (*10JL*, page 19)

25.   LH *pulls off a bit (B) from Large Ball held by RH*
26.   *looks at B held by LH*
27.   *looks at remainder of LB held by RH*   (*10EH*, page 20)

19.3. BH *pull Ball 2 away from her mouth*
19.3a. *one part (P1) comes off in LH while the other part (P2) remains hanging out of her mouth*
19.7. *looks at P1 held by LH*
21.   RH *moves up to her mouth and grasps P2 sticking out of her mouth*
22.   RH *removes P2 from her mouth*
22a.   *P2 is flattened and deformed*
23.   *looks at P1 in LH and P2 in RH which she is holding in front of herself*
(10MM, page 33)

Infants preserve two-object sets long enough to monitor them. Sometimes monitoring includes comparative inspection of the initial single objects and their multiplication by decomposition into sets of two objects (e.g., 10CC).

Multiple decompositions are generated by the majority of infants. Two or more decompositions are generated in sequence. These decompositions multiply one into three or more objects. Some decomposing sequences are becoming fairly extensive. One object is multiplied into several objects. Sets of intermediate size are constructed; that is, no longer small but not yet very large sets:

49.3. RH *squeezes on one side of Ball*
49.7. LH *pulls part that it is grasping off of B to left*
49.7a. *a small, strand-like part (P5) comes off in LH*
51.5.–65.5. RH *grasps remainder of B by continuously squeezing smaller portion of it*
51.5. LH *opens and closes on P5 which sticks to fingers*
53.5. LH *(with P5 stuck to it) grasps B and digs fingers into it*
55.5. LH *pulls off part (P6)*
57.5. LH *opens to left*
59.5. LH *squeezes B and pulls off part (P7)*
61.5. LH *opens to left and P7 falls to table*
63.5. LH *squeezes B and pulls off part (P8)*
65.5. LH *opens to left in air*
67.3. LH *pulls off part (P9)*
67.7. RH *turns B in air slightly such that the smaller portion that it is continuously squeezing is now on top of the weightier portion (whereas before the major part of B was being supported partially by RH grasp)*
69.   LH *moves to left*
70.5. LH *touches major portion of B*
70.5a. *major portion of B (underneath RH) falls onto floor via lap*
70.5. RH *grasps remaining smaller part (P10) of B* (10KC, pages 33 and 34)

While 10KC engages in other operations that will be considered later, here we will focus only on his multiple decompositions. In rapid succession he generates six consecutive decompositions which multiply one into seven objects. These multiple decompositions generate a set of intermediate size, but the set is not preserved. Rather, *10KC* seems merely to discard each piece, in turn, so that he can go on to the next decomposition. Only two-object sets are clearly preserved and monitored at this stage.

Initial indications of ambiguous preservation of sets which include more than two objects begin to be generated:

41. RH *transfers Large Ball to LH, above eye level, as watches LB*
42. LH *hits LB up and down on the table*
42a. *a little part (P3) from LB falls off onto table*
43. LH *moves LB to the left such that it breaks with the main portion (LB) dropping to the table, landing on, and displacing Ball 2, and a small part (P4) remaining in LH*
44. *looks down at LB*
45. RH *(holding Part 2) pulls off a part (P5) from P4 held by LH*
46. RH *pulls off another part (P6) from P4 held by LH*
47. *looks briefly at pieces in BH, then BH bang the table*
48. BH *bang pieces on table*
48a. P4 *splits into two parts (P7 and P8) which fall out of LH onto the table*
                                                     (*10MM*, pages 41 and 42)

Multiple consecutive decompositions, including contingent decompositions, transform one object into a set of six objects. The objects are monitored before and during the sequence of decompositions. To some extent the objects are preserved as a set by the right hand holding onto each part it pulls off from the object held by the left hand.

Multiplication of one into many elements is often generated by protocorresponding decompositions. The result is the construction of a set of objects relatively equivalent in size:

1. LH *picks off a little bit (B1) from Large Ball*
2. LH *opens and closes in air as waves it back and forth*
2a. B1 *falls onto table to the left*
3. LH *grasps LB again and picks off another little bit (B2)*
4. LH *waves off to the left, opening and closing fingers*
5. LH *grasps LB and picks off another little bit (B3)*   (*10KC*, page 36)

Missing is any indication that the identical elements are preserved as an articulate set.

While multiple decompositions do not yet seem directed toward articulate preservation of a set of several elements, they are not limited to constructing many objects out of one. Genealogical, as well as one-to-many, decomposing originates. Subject *10MM*'s sequence begins with genealogical decomposition (Lines 42–45) and ends with one-to-many

decompositions (Lines 46–48a). Other sequences construct only genealogical multiplications:

10. *RH grasps Large Ring (A) held by LH*
11. *RH squishes A into A', then pulls A' apart, pulling off a little piece (B1)*
    while LH holds remainder (B)
12. *RH drops B1 in between legs on seat of high chair*
13. *looks down and picks up B1 with RH*
14. *RH raises B1 up near face*
15. *LH lets go of B*
15a. *B falls to the floor*
16. *leans forward slightly, looking down to floor after B*
17. *RH partially inserts B1 into mouth and bites off larger part (C1)*
18. *puts LH finger to mouth and tastes it as looks at small piece (C2) in RH*
19. *looks down in lap*
20. *leans forward and looks down on floor, extending LH down near edge of*
    seat
21. *sits up in chair, joining LH on C2 held by RH*
22. *BH break C2 into two parts*
22a. *RH holds D2 and LH holds D3*   (10GP, page 30)

The first decomposition of A' into B and B1 prolongs deformation of A
into A' (Line 11). It is followed by multiple decompositions. They give rise
to an asymmetrical genealogy of descendant elements:

Still, the purpose does not seem to go beyond multiple decomposing to
articulate preservation of a set of several elements. Except for the last two
pieces, *10GP* discards each piece. He does look after them (Lines 13, 16,
19, and 20). Preserving the existence of successive elements produced by
multiple decomposing does not construct a constant stable set of multiple
elements. It does produce some of the necessary preconditions for producing and collecting multiple elements into an articulate permanent set.

Genealogical decomposing divides objects into progressively smaller
elements. They construct series of more than two elements ordered by
size. For instance, *10GP* constructs the ordered series of B > C1 > (D2 =
D3) objects. The limit at this stage is constructing sets of three or four
elements ordered by size.

The *10GP* series also includes protocorresponding decompositions which construct equivalent elements (D2 = D3). Thus, ordered differences in magnitude are interwoven with equivalent magnitudes. This enhances the possibility for coordinating iteration with equivalences.

Missing in such extended series, as noted above, is any indication of articulate preservation of the multiple elements as a constant set. Two-object sets, as already noticed, are frequently preserved as constant sets. Preservation includes constructing ordered sets of elements equal or unequal in magnitude.

Negation proto-operations of deforming, breaking, and decomposing continue to be coordinated. Two forms of coordination are continuous with those generated at the previous stage. One consists of sequences which interweave different negation proto-operations (e.g., *10AB* consecutively deforms, breaks, and deforms two objects [pages 265–266]). The other consists of sequences in which different negation proto-operations are prolonged into each other.

Structural interpenetration between two negation proto-operations, particularly between deforming and decomposing, is enhanced by the origins of binary negation. It is a consequence of the general development in binary proto-operations. Subjects begin to generate deforming and decomposing together on the same object and at the same time:

18.5.   *LH pulls a little piece (P1) off of Ball*
18.5.   *RH index finger pushes into B*
18.5a. *leaves indentation mark in B*   (*10CC*, page 25)

Sometimes binary negation includes multiple synchronic deforming and decomposing. For instance, *10KC* deforms and decomposes one object at the same time (see protocol fragment presented on page 275). Moreover, *10KC* repeatedly and consecutively applies binary negation to the object.

The necessary conditions for pragmatic coordination between these two forms of negating part–whole relations are being redundantly self-generated at this stage. Successivity, prolongation, and binary negation all promote elaboration of structural coordination between decomposing and deforming begun at the previous stages. In particular, they promote the elaboration of two facets of structural coordination.

The first is logical. Decomposing always involves deforming, but its resultants are different. Decomposing produces extensive as well as intensive transformations in the part–whole relations between elements. Deforming does not involve decomposing; it only produces intensive transformations in the part–whole relations within elements (e.g., from a ball to a pancake shape).

The second facet of structural coordination is physical. Not only does decomposing produce more elements, but the elements produced are smaller objects. The magnitude decrease transforms the causal physical properties of the objects. In particular it decreases their resistance to infants' psychomotor capacities to transform them. To illustrate, it is much easier to chew or squeeze a small piece decomposed from a ball than to chew or squeeze the whole ball.

IV. Precursory Quantitative Identity by Coordinated Decomposing and Recomposing

Rudimentary recomposing previously decomposed parts originates at this stage (Table 11.1, Row 6). It has two proto-operational properties. All recomposing reconstitutes the initial extent of the whole. Thereby, it constructs an extensity identity proto-operation. Both the initial number and volume are reconstituted. Recomposing may, but need not reconstitute the initial predication of the whole. When it does, recomposing constructs an intensity identity proto-operation. Then the initial form as well as extent is reconstituted.

Intensive protoidentity generated by recomposing is, then, a subset of extensive protoidentity. Reconstituting the initial part–whole extent may or may not also include reconstituting its form. Obversely, intensive protoidentity always includes extensive protoidentity. It is not possible to recompose the initial part–whole intensity of an object without also reconstituting its extent.

Recomposing is generated by only two subjects. Both are limited to constructing extensive protoidentity. Neither construct intensive protoidentity:

10. *RH pulls off a small piece (P1) from Ball held by LH on table*
11. *RH opens and closes in air to right as if unsuccessfully trying to get P1 off of it, as looks at experimenter*
12. *RH fingers squeeze into B with P1, as looking at experimenter*
12a. *P1 is pressed into B*
13. *RH pulls off a small piece (P2)*
14. *looks at RH as RH opens and closes in air*
14a. *P2 falls to table*
15. *RH picks up P2*
16. *RH drops P2 back on table to right*   (10KC, page 31)

19. *BH pull Ball apart in the air*
19a. *RH holds Part 1 and LH holds Part 2*
20. *looks back and forth at P1 and P2*
21. *BH touch P1 and P2 together*

21a. *P1 and P2 are partially composed*
22. *BH pull P1 and P2 apart as RH pulls off Part 3 from P2 held by LH*
22a. *RH holds P1 and P3 while LH holds remainder of P2*
23. *BH put together P1, P3 and P2*
24. *looks at experimenter, as holds P1, P3 and P2 together with BH*
24a. *P1, P3 and P2 are partially composed into one glob*
25. *RH pulls off a part*
25a. *RH holds P1' and LH holds P2'*
26. *RH brushes P1' up and down, contacting P2' held by LH, then waves P1' up and down more vigorously*
        subject: (making sounds)
27. *RH presses P1' against P2' held by LH*
27a. *P1' and P2' become partially composed*
28. *BH pull P1' and P2' apart, as looking at them*
29. *BH touch P1' and P2' together*
30. *RH pulls P1' away*
        subject: "Eeee-"
31. *RH waves P1' around vigorously and LH waves P2' around less vigorously*
32. *BH touch P1' and P2' together, as looking at them*
33. *looks at experimenter, as BH hold P1' and P2' together*
34. *looks at father as BH pull P1' and P2' apart*
34a. *RH holds P1' and LH holds P2'*
35.5. *LH raises P2' toward head*
        subject: [Making excited noises (e.g., "Gee-yeeah")]
35.5. *RH raises P1' behind her head and over her right shoulder*
37. *BH bring P1' and P2' back together in front of self*
38. *BH pull P1' and P2' apart*
38a. *RH holds P1' and LH holds P2'*
39. *RH waves P1' up and down over right chair arm, as leans over right chair arm*
40. *BH touch P1' and P2' together, as sits up again in chair*
41. *BH pull P1' and P2' apart*
42. *RH waves P1' slightly and LH waves P2' slightly*
                                                    (10MM, pages 38 and 39)

Although the 10KC protocol fragment contains only one recomposition, both subjects generate recompositions several times, but all their reconstructions are rudimentary and ambiguous. Subject 10KC's recompositions are always the result of (a) unsuccessful detachment of a decomposed part from the hand doing the decomposing (Lines 10–12), followed by (b) a subsequent protocorresponding decomposition of another part (Lines 12 and 13). The first decomposed part is attached to the hand while it decomposes a second part. Consequently, the first part becomes recomposed with the ball. When 10KC successfully detaches a part he has decomposed from his hand, he never recomposes that part with the ball (Lines 14–16).

Subject 10MM's constructions are featured by binary symmetrical and asymmetrical decompositions and recompositions, protocorresponding decompositions into equivalent parts, monitoring of the constructive process and the two objects preserved as articulate sets, and repeated inverse decomposing and recomposing transformations. As such, these are well-regulated and directed constructions of extensive protoidentities. On the other hand, the recompositions are rudimentary and ambiguous. Subject 10MM barely presses the decomposed parts together. Consequently, it is not always clear whether he is recomposing the parts back into one whole or whether he is merely constructing discrete sets of two elements (e.g., Line 29).

Composing objects not previously decomposed remains infrequent (Table 11.1, Row 7). The number of subjects generating at least one composition increases from 2 of 12 at age 8 months to 4 of 12 at age 10 months. As at age 8 months, the rates of discrete composing in these quasi-continuous conditions stay well below those in the discrete conditions (cf. Table 11.1, Row 14, Columns 1 to 6, and Table 10.1, Row 3).

Composing remains an irreversible combinativity proto-operation. It is never followed up by redecomposition into the original two elements (Row 8). Only one subject follows up by immediately decomposing a piece from the composed objects:

24. BH *lift Ball 1 and Part 2 momentarily squeezing them together such that they become stuck together*
25. RH *pulls off a little bit from P2 of the composed* (B1·P2)

(10DG, page 25)

Other subjects intertwine composing, decomposing, and deforming over longer sequences of transactions, as they do at the previous stage (Chapter 8, Section IV). The psychomotor prerequisites for constructing reversibility between composing and redecomposing are therefore available at both stages. The precursory structural conditions are also prepared by 10DG, if only once. He consecutively (a) composes two elements into one and (b) decomposes the resultant single element into two elements again. Missing is any attempt to construct an identity proto-operation. He does not redecompose the composed single element into the original two elements, rather, he decomposes it into two different elements.

These results continue to support the hypothesis that negation proto-operations applied to quasi-continuous objects are more advanced at their origins than are affirmation proto-operations. Decomposing and deforming continue to be generated much more frequently than composing by all subjects. Only breaking is not generated much more frequently than composing. Furthermore, one form of negation, namely, decomposing, is beginning to be reversible. It is compensated for by follow-up recomposing. At the same time, composing remains irreversible.

This hypothesis gains further credence from the results in the combined discrete quasi-continuous conditions. All three subjects detach the conglomerate object into its discrete and quasi-continuous parts during the spontaneous test phase (Table 11.1, Row 10, Column 7). None of the three subjects attach the discrete and quasi-continuous objects together (Row 9, Column 7).

While detachment is spontaneously generated by all three subjects, it is not successfully provoked by experimenter modeling detachment. None of the three subjects generate detachment during the second test phase (Row 10, Column 8). Nor does the experimenter modeling attachment of discrete to quasi-continuous objects have any effect. Attachment is not generated by any of the three subjects during the second, provoked test phase (Row 9, Column 8). In other respects, combinativity proto-operations in these combined conditions are similar to those generated in the quasi-continuous conditions described in this chapter (Columns 7 and 8, Rows 1–8) and to the discrete conditions described in Chapter 10.

Play-Doh becomes attached to infants' hands in all conditions. The main advance at this stage is in how infants subsequently detach the Play-Doh from their hands. Coordination of organs as instruments of detachment originates at this stage:

14.   *RH lifts Ball 3 which is stuck on the tip of her index finger*
15.   *LH pulls B3 off of RH*   (10CC, page 29)

Infants also monitor their attempts at detachment:

68.   *LH picks up Part 2 which gets stuck to hand*
69.   *looks at LH as moves LH fingers open–close, once*   (10KC, page 34)

Most attachments of quasi-continuous objects to infants' hands are by-products of deforming and decomposing. Some attachments, as well as detachments, begin to be directed products of subjects' transactions:

40.   *RH index finger is placed into center of Ring 3 such that R3 is looped over finger*
41.   *RH index finger slides R3 off table, with finger inserted in center of ring*
42.   *RH and index finger move around very slightly in air with R3 near lap as looks down at this*
42a. *R3 is stuck to RH index finger*
43.   *RH rests on right leg as looks back up at table*

43a.   *R3 falls off onto floor*
 44.   *LH extends and grasps Ring 1 in same manner as before, with index finger inserted into the center*
 45.   *LH and index finger withdraw R1 off table and into lap as looks at this*
 46.   *LH and index finger extend R1 way down between legs, leaning body forward, and release R1*
46a.   *R1 falls to floor*   (10GP, page 27)

Attachment is produced by insertion of a finger inside ring-shaped objects. Subject *10GP's* attachment involves protoexperimental exploration of the internal dimension of objects accompanied by observation (e.g., Lines 41 and 42). Each attachment is followed, in turn, by detachment (e.g., Lines 42a and 43a).

IV

STAGE 4 AT TWELVE MONTHS: EXPANSION OF SECOND-ORDER TRANSFORMATIONS

Ternary Transactions

12

Transactions are becoming progressively complex, differentiated, and integrated. The most extended are ternary transactions in which three mappings are simultaneously applied upon two to four objects. The remainder of infants' transactions are divided about evenly between binary and unary transactions. Increasingly, binary transactions are generated which comprise active mappings that are clearly split from each other (e.g., different) yet are well coordinated (e.g., in reciprocal relations to each other).

Small numbers of objects are readily encompassed. At this stage the outer limit is about six objects. It is not unusual for subjects' transactions to extend immediately to all the elements presented. When not immediate, mappings are extended to all the objects within the course of the test phase in which they are presented. The rule of transaction now is to transform all objects up to about six objects.

Progressive complexity, differentiation, and integration are also manifest in other structural features of protosymbolic and protoinferential constructions. Gestures begin to be generated which combine personalized, idiosyncratic mapping features with quasi-arbitrary rulelike usage of objects. Comparative determination of individual objects and of small sets of objects progressively differentiates and integrates their part–whole relations. Protoexperimentation begins to take into account the predicate properties of classes of objects. Causal transformations are becoming sufficiently controlled to permit rudimentary experimentation with transitive transmission of motion. Combined with advances in iterative ordering applied to causal variables, these developments serve to further systematize infants' precursory logic of experimentation.

Compact mapping continues to characterize transactions. Together with the shifting change ratio, to be detailed subsequently, compactness enhances the trend begun at the previous stage. The developmental trend is toward increasing equilibration and disequilibration of transformations. Transactional and relational constructions are becoming progressively stabilized and regulated. They permit formation of more complex structures. These structures become relatively extended temporally. They are featured by relatively defined spatial and causal dimensions. One illustrative consequence is the elaboration, at this stage, of constructing "bridge" prototypes:

11. *RH places Square Column 3 across Cylinder 4 and Square Column 4:*

12. *RH lifts Cylinder 2*
13. *RH drops C2 on top of SC3*
13a. *C2 rolls off toward experimenter and knocks SC3 off of C4 and SC4, although one end still rests on SC4:*

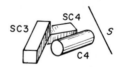

(12DO, page 15)

Inherent in this constructive sequence is progressive equilibrium and disequilibrium. There is marked progress in constructing possibilities and impossibilities. The main implications for the development of physical cognition are the production of more and new: (*a*) independent and dependent variables, (*b*) placement and displacement dimensions, (*c*) causal relations within and between independent and dependent variables, (*d*) spatial relations within and between placement and displacement relations, and (*e*) difficulties in structuring both possible and impossible contingent relations, whether causal or spatial.

Correlative implications are generated for the development of logical cognition. They are the production of more and new: (*a*) order relations, (*b*) part–whole relations, (*c*) reciprocal relations within and between orders, (*d*) inclusion and exclusion relations within and between parts and wholes, and (e) difficulties in structuring both possible and impossible logical relations, whether of orders or of sets.

A consequence manifest in the latter part (Lines 12–13a) of the above protocol fragment is the introduction of uncertainty. The limits of bridge structures are tested, for example, how many bridging elements can be included, beyond which construction is impossible (excluded). At the same time, a new causal targeting relation is elaborated, namely, the possibility of destroying the bridge by "bombing" it with another object.

These developments in physical and logical cognition will be detailed in this chapter and in Chapters 13 and 14. They are indicative of the relatively advanced cognitive structures which have developed by the fourth stage.

I. Constant Mappings upon Successive Objects

Ternary transactions consist of applying three mappings to at least two objects at the same or at partially overlapping times. Ternary mappings are never applied to a singular object, although it is possible in principle. For instance, it is possible to (a) rotate one end of an object with one hand, (b) finger or stroke its middle with another hand, while (c) mouthing the other end. In practice, infant transactions do not exceed binary mappings when only one object is involved (e.g., rotating an object while fingering it).

Three mappings are executed at the same time with as many as three or four objects. Transactions become a bit like three-ring events:

40. *LH holds Square Column 2, as RH picks up Brush 4*
41. *RH brings B4 to mouth and inserts it*
42. *sucks on the bristle end of B4 held by RH*
    (experimenter picks up Brush 3 and holds it in air toward subject)
43. *mouths B4 held by RH*
44. *RH lets go of B4 handle and just leaves it there in her mouth*
45. *LH holds SC2 and mouth holds B4, as RH picks up Brush 1*
46. *RH holding B1, tries to pick up Brush 2, but only displaces B2; cannot quite pick it up, too*
47. *RH brings B1 to mouth, but it falls to her lap, while B4 is held in mouth and SC2 is held by LH*   (12LL, pages 46 and 47)

One, or two, of the three simultaneous transactions are always relatively passive (Line 45). Consequently, the mappings are split but remain relatively noncoordinate. One of the transactions may include constructing compositional relations between two objects (Line 46). Ternary mappings including compositional components are commonplace:

38. *RH inserts Brushes 1 and 2 into mouth for an instant, while LH holds Square Column 2*   (12LL, page 46)

Binary mappings are now generated as frequently as unary mappings. Together, they account for most transactions, while ternary mappings are in the minority. Binary mappings increasingly comprise totally active components. Unary mappings are becoming specialized. They are increasingly applied to initial transactions with novel or unusual objects. Individual differences are beginning to be manifest. While most 12-month-olds generate about equal numbers of unary and binary mappings, some generate one or the other predominantly.

Significant features of the change ratio are altered. A one-to-one mapping-to-object change ratio remains unusual, although it is beginning to occur with some frequency. At the same time, the basic ratio shifts from many-to-1 to many-to-many mappings-to-objects. The reason is that most transactions, as shown, are becoming binary and ternary.

Nevertheless, the ratio remains asymmetrical and, to that extent, constant. Mappings are still changed more frequently than are objects in sequential transactions. However, the degree of asymmetry is decreasing. Parity is increasingly generated between the frequency of changing mappings and objects in sequential transactions.

Mapping constancy is still in the minority, but it is becoming more frequent, especially in protoexperimental activity (Section III). Twelve-month-olds are more likely to apply the same mapping to successive objects, as previously found by Piaget (1951). This development is consistent with the hypothesis that mapping predication, like composing predication, is just beginning to be constructed by affirmation (Chapter 14).

Protosymbolic mappings remain personalized and idiosyncratic. In addition, they are beginning to become partially arbitrary and governed by rulelike usage of objects. The personalized features preserve the meanings for infants, while the arbitrary and rulelike features are necessary for the elaboration of efficient and communicative representation.

Two forms of protoreferential gestures predominate, and are elaborations upon forms generated at the previous stage. One protoreferential form involves sequential coordination of virtual with actual giving of objects to another person. Infants interweave extending objects to others but (a) withdrawing them as soon as the other person starts to take the objects, with (b) not withdrawing them and letting the other person have the objects. This introduces uncertainty into the protoreferential situation and produces a gamelike interaction with chance properties.

The other protoreferential form is also becoming increasingly gamelike. It consists of the often-reported interaction in which infants sequentially drop an object to the floor, then wait for and observe others retrieve the object. They consecutively repeat this sequential interaction many times with the same or different objects. Many other versions of this protoreferential form are also generated. For instance, infants repeatedly roll objects away from themselves across the table top and wait for the other person to give them back.

Both these protoreferential forms remain highly personalized and pragmatic. Yet, they are already acquiring rulelike properties. They are repeated in the same arbitrary manner many times. As such, infants at this stage begin to construct meaningful, reproducible, and codifiable gestural forms of making reference to objects. Rule-governed pragmatic reference culminates in pointing at objects. Deixis becomes a conventional, albeit still gestural, form of reference because it is no longer pragmatic and because it is detached from the specific properties of the objects referred to.

Referential pointing is generated clearly by only one subject:

42. *looks at price sticker on the bottom of Yellow Cup 4 held by RH*
43. *LH points at price sticker on YC4 held by RH*
44. *looks at experimenter and laughs* (12BG, page 30)

Referential pointing is generated one other time as well by 12BG.

Four other infants generate potential rudiments of gestural pointing. These involve aspects or extensions of pushing or reaching after an object:

> *(experimenter puts both VWs 1 and 2 over to subject's left and extends Racer 2 to subject)*
> 10. *RH does not take R2, instead RH makes insistent open–close gestures in the direction of the other nongrouped objects in front of experimenter*
> (12LL, pages 40 and 41)
> 11. *LH index finger pushes Cylinder 1 (against broadside) toward experimenter*
> 11a. *C1 rolls about 4 inches toward experimenter, out of subject's reach*
> 12. *watches C1 roll, as LH on table with index finger extended toward C1*
> 13. *LH fingers open very quickly and reach weakly toward C1 for a moment, but do not reach it* (12JE, page 35)

Such pragmatic behaviors may constitute precursors of referential pointing. For now, however, this remains an untested hypothesis.

Seimconventional usage of objects is still exceptional. It is clearly and repeatedly generated by only three subjects:

> 30. *LH brings Brushes 1 and 2 toward her head (not the bristle ends) and makes about six stroking movements on her head with the two handles*
> 31. *LH transfers B1 and B2 to RH*
> 32. *RH strokes her head about three times with the handle ends of B1 and B2*
> (12LL, page 46)

The idiosyncratic character of 12LL's brushing is revealed by her usage of the handles of two brushes to stroke her hair.

II. Constructing Very Small Single Sets as Constant Given Elements

Comparative inspection becomes progressively varied, differentiated and integrated. This applies to how 12-month-olds determine part–whole relations within objects as well as between objects.

Single objects are explored exhaustively. This facilitates part–whole differentiation and integration:

19. *BH rotate Triangular Ring near eyes*
20. *BH slide fingers up and down TR's sharp edges*
21. *fingers TR all over with BH*   (12LL, page 8)

1. *LH picks up Doll 1*
2. *LH turns D1 around*
3. *looks at D1 held by LH*
4. *LH puts D1 down*
5. *LH picks up D1*
6. *looks at D1 held by LH*   (12AM, page 32)

5. *BH tip Red Cup 2 toward face and looks inside*
6. *BH tip RC2 away from face*   (12RD, page 30)

Differentiated and integrated explorations are coordinated with repeated inverse spatial transformations of objects. Such coordinations strengthen infants' comparative determination of object identity. They are frequently generated in the context of inspecting one or more other objects, thereby furthering comparative determination of objects in relation to each other:

7. *looks back and forth twice at Yellow Hexagonal Column held by LH and Yellow Cross Ring held by RH, as turns YCR over in RH* (12DS, page 8)

1. *RH takes hold of VW1 already in her hands*
2. *LH picks up VW2*
3. *LH rotates VW2 by flipping wrist 180° in one direction, then 180° in other direction, while looking at it*
4. *LH drops VW2*
5. *LH picks up VW2*
6. *LH brings VW2 closer to her eyes as rotates it less than 45°*
7. *looks at VW1 in RH*   (12LL, page 40)

29. *LH picks up Red Car*

30. *LH turns RC up*
31. *looks at bottom of RC*
32. *LH turns RC down*
33. *glances at top of RC*
34.5. *sits back*
34.5. *looks at Yellow Circular Ring and Yellow Car held by RH*
    subject: "Ehhhhhh"   (12RD, page 20)

5.3. *looks at Clover Ring 2, as*
5.7. *LH tips CR2 up and down, two times*
  7. *LH releases CR2*
  8. *LH picks up Rectangular Ring 4*
9.3. *LH turns RR4 around, as*
9.7. *looks at back of RR4*
11.3. *LH turns RR4, as*
11.7. *looks at front of RR4*   (12RD, page 68)

Repeated spatial identity transformations progressively complement protocorresponding inverse transformations when infants make comparative object determinations. Spatial identity transformations take the form of multiple 360° rotations of objects. They are extended and elaborate. They are coupled with visual observation, and they are becoming differentiated and integrated:

18. *BH rotate Car 3 while looking at it for 20 seconds*
19. *spins the wheels of C3 while looking at it*
20. *looks up at experimenter*
21. *looks back down at C3 while BH rotate it*   (12LL, page 41)

Identity transformations in internal part–whole relations are produced and observed by 360° rotations while the subject looks at it (Line 18). Then parts (wheels) of the objects only are protocorrespondingly transformed by 360° rotations while the subject looks at them (Line 19). Finally, 12LL reverts to observing her transformations of the whole object by protocorresponding 360° rotations (Line 21). Thus, she constructs and observes corresponding transformations in part–whole relations within a single object. She does this by successive application of the same identity operation (continuous rotation) to the whole (car), parts (wheels), and the whole again (car).

All objects may be comparatively inspected before the subjects transact with them when the presentation consists of four, but not eight, objects. Comparative inspection is immediate and often repeated. It involves visual back-and-forth scanning of the array. Nonrelevant behaviors are omitted from the following fragment:

1. *looks at array of Cross Rings 1, 2, 3, and 4*

5. *looks at CR1, 2, 3 and 4*
6. *looks from right to left at CR1, 2, 3, and 4*
7. *looks from left to right at CR1, 2, 3, and 4*
8. *looks from right to left at CR1, 2, 3, and 4*
10. *looks from left to right at CR1, 2, 3, and 4*
11. *looks from right to left at CR1, 2, 3, and 4*   (12AM, page 1)

Direct comparative inspection of sets of two or three objects gathered in subjects' hands is frequent and repeated:

23. *looks back and forth, three times, at Green Hexagonal Column held by LH and Yellow Cross Ring held by RH*   (12DS, page 9)

10. *LH picks up Red Spoon 1 and Yellow Spoon 2*
11. *looks at RS1 and YS2 held by LH*
12. *looks at Red Cup 2 held by RH*   (12RD, page 30)

Comparative observation of two objects is extensively elaborated by combining (*a*) differentiated and integrated observation of parts of objects as well as the whole with (*b*) direct and indirect transformations:

15.5. *looks at Yellow Cup 2*
17. *glances back at Yellow Cup 1*
18.5. *looks at YC2*
18.5. *LH picks up YC2*
20. *LH holds up YC2 and RH holds up Red Cup 2, as watches experimenter standing YC1 upright*
21. *looks at RC2 held by RH*
22. *looks at YC2 held by LH*
23. *BH tilt the two cups toward his face*
24. *looks inside YC2 held by LH and inside RC2 held by RH*
25.5. *RH tilts RC2 further toward face*
25.5. *looks inside RC2*
27.5. *RH tilts RC2 away from face*
27.5. *looks at bottom of RC2*   (12RD, pages 30 and 31)

Subject *12RD* begins by direct comparative observation of two whole objects without transforming them (Line 15.5 to first Line 18.5). Then comparative observation (Lines 21 and 22) is combined with corresponding direct displacement transformations of both objects (Line 20). It is followed by corresponding rotation of the two objects (Line 23) combined with comparative observation of the inside part of both cups (Line 24). Comparative observation is continued in simultaneous combination with an ordered increase in the rotation of one object (Lines 25.5). It culminates with an inverse rotation of the same object and observation of its bottom part (Lines 27.5).

Comparative observations of extensive corresponding direct (12DA and

12DS, Lines 11–13) and inverse (*12DS*, Line 14) transformations of two objects are generated regularly and throughout:

9. RH *fingers inside of Green Cross Ring on table*
10. RH *rotates GCR*
11. LH *rotates Yellow Cross Ring*
12. *looks up at mother, turning body to right*
13. *looks down at GCR, then YCR, then back to GCR*   (12DA, page 12)

11. BH *turn Green Cross Ring around while looking at it*
12. RH *picks up the Yellow Cross Ring, as LH holds GCR*
13. RH *turns YCR around by rotating his wrist while looking at it*
14. LH *rotates GCR back and forth and RH rotates YCR back and forth, as looks back and forth, 2 times, for about 15 seconds*   (12DS, page 8)

Consecutive comparative inspection is extended to as many as four objects. This includes extensive protocorresponding identity transformations coupled with visual monitoring (Lines 3 and 5) and extensive inspection of two-object sets (Line 11):

3. RH *brings Doll 3 toward his face and closely looks at it while turning it over and over with BH*
3a. *D3 falls via his lap to the floor*
4. RH *picks up Doll 2*
5. BH *hold D2 in front of face, turning it around while visually examining it in same way as in No. 3, for 15 seconds*
6. LH *holds D2 while RH picks up D4*
7. RH *brings D4 close to his eyes and looks at it*
8. RH *lets D4 go on table in front of self*
9. LH *lets D2 go on table near D4*
10. RH *picks up Circular Ring 4 and LH picks up Circular Ring 3*
11. BH *bring CR4 and CR3 close to face and looks at them about 5 seconds*
    (12DS, page 33)

III. Experimenting with Single Sets of Objects

Causal transformations are becoming subject to fine-grained control. Nonrelevant transactions are omitted in the following fragment:

15. RH *finger pushes down on top of VW1 making it slide across table out of subject's hand toward experimenter*
17. (*experimenter pushes VW1 toward subject*) RH *finger pushes VW1 toward edge of table near self and then back into the center of the table*
20. (*experimenter pushes VW1 toward subject*) RH *finger pushes VW1 toward experimenter*   (12LZ, page 62)

Causal control permits constructing extended "trains," consisting of an instrumental object plus two or more objects:

60. *RH pushes Square Column 1 left*
60a. *SC1 pushes Square Columns 4, 3, and 2 to left*   (12DO, page 20)

"Vehicles" which also require fairly controlled causal coordination of objects are just beginning to be created (Line 80), but they still tend to end up unsuccessful (Line 82a):

80. *BH push Receptacle 2 containing Doll 1 away from self slightly, no release from R2*
81. *LH pushes VW1 away from self*
82. *RH, grasping R2, pushes it away from self and then moves it side to side briefly*
82a. *D1 falls out of R2 onto table*   (12DO, page 51)

Gestural representations of causal mappings are constructed frequently:

4. *opens RH and Yellow Triangular Column 2 falls to floor*
5. *subject's body quakes as if startled*
6. *LH transfers Yellow Triangular Column 1 to RH*
7. *RH flicks wrist throwing YTC1*
7a. *YTC1 falls to lap*
8. *RH pushes YTC1 to floor from lap*
   (mother replaces YTC1 in front of subject)
9. *LH knocks YTC1 to floor*
10. *RH picks up YTC2*
11. *RH throws YTC2 toward floor on right, but does not let go*
12. *RH brings YTC2 down toward her lap*
   (mother replaces YTC1 in front of subject)
13. *looks up at experimenter, smiling, as puts YTC2 in lap*
14. *RH pushes YTC2 to floor*   (12LL, page 9)

After dropping (Line 4) and throwing (Line 7) objects, 12LL gestures throwing another object (Lines 11 and 12) but does not release it and smiles (Line 13). Then the subject pushes it from her lap to the floor (Line 14). This is similar to what she did when she actually threw an object into her lap (Line 7).

Protoexperimenting is still applied to singular objects. Some protoexperimenting sequentially varies the causal mappings (independent variables), while keeping the object constant. This results in differential effects (dependent variables):

35.5. *LH hits VW1 making it spin around on the table*
37. *RH picks up VW1*

38. *transfers VW1 from RH to LH*
39. *LH drops VW1 onto the floor*   (12LZ, page 61)

Other protoexperimenting with single objects holds both the causal mapping and the object constant, thereby replicating the dependent effect which is monitored by the experimenter:

3. *LH drops Cross Ring 4 to the table*
4. *watches CR4 bounce on the table*
5. *LH picks up CR4*
6. *LH drops CR4 to table*
7. *watches CR4 bounce on the table*   (12LZ, page 59)

Surprise is just beginning to be manifest when unexpected results are obtained. Since this research was not designed to measure directly such reactions, the data are necessarily impressionistic:

23. *LH drops Block 4 toward floor as looks at floor*
23a. *B4 lands on table instead*
24. *surprised look on face*
25. *looks back at remaining blocks and cylinders on table*
26. *LH picks up B4*
27. *LH drops B4 to floor*
27a. *B4 lands on floor*   (12BG, page 43)

This sequence is preceded by *12BG* dropping many other objects to the floor. Disconfirmation of his apparent causal expectations is immediately rectified by *12BG* dropping the object to the floor.

By and large protoexperimenting is devoted to investigating the coordinate effects of ordered series of causal transformations with sets of objects. Both the mappings and the objects are varied semisystematically in order to determine or control the differential results:

15. *LH drops Red Block 2 to floor*
16. *LH picks up Red Block 3*
17. *looks at other objects on table*
18. *LH throws RB3 to floor as looks at floor*
19. *LH picks up Blue Cylinder 2*
20. *LH drops BC2 to floor as looks at floor*   (12BG, page 43)

22. *RH holds Green Triangular Column as LH picks up Yellow Triangular Column*
23. *LH throws YTC onto table*
24. *LH picks up YTC again very quickly (as if agitated that it does not roll)*
25. *LH throws YTC back down onto table with more force (experimenter throws YTC back to subject)*
26. *LH picks up YTC*

27. *LH places YTC on table*
    (experimenter rolls Yellow Cylinder toward subject)
28. *LH picks up YC*
29. *LH drops YC*
    subject: "Ahh"
29a. *YC rolls a little*
30. *LH picks up YC*
31. *LH drops YC*
31a. *YC rolls toward experimenter*
    (experimenter rolls YC back toward subject in same manner of dropping it
    so that it makes a loud noise)
32. *LH picks up YC*
33. *LH throws YC hard*
33a. *YC falls to floor*
    subject: "Uhh!"
    (experimenter pushes YTC toward subject)
34. *looks at GTC she has been holding all this time in RH*
35. *RH drops GTC to floor*   (12AM, page 17)

Both (*a*) the ordered variations ⟨drop, throw, throw harder, drop⟩ in causal transformations and (*b*) the unordered variations (block, block, cylinder) and (triangular column, cylinder, triangular column), in objects projected, produce differential results. Infants' aims are twofold and complementary. The first is to monitor and replicate differential results (e.g., 12BG). The second is to monitor and overcome negative results (e.g., 12AM).

Some protoexperimenting holds the causal mapping form constant while varying the objects:

14. *LH flicks fingers against Yellow Cylinder*
14a. *YC rolls away*
15. *LH flicks fingers against Green Triangular Column*
15a. *GTC slides away*   (12LL, page 7)

Differential results are obtained as a function of the objects' forms.

While most protoexperimenting varies the objects, the predicate class properties are often held constant. At this stage, this usually means protoexperimenting with only one of the two presented sets of objects:

1. *LH picks up Doll 2*
2. *LH transfers D2 to RH*
3. *LH picks up Doll 1 while RH holds D2*
4. *LH drops D1 to table*
5. *LH picks up Doll 3*
6. *LH drops D3 to table, next to D1*
7. *LH picks up D3*

8. *LH drops D3 to table*
9. *LH finger taps side of D3, making it roll*
10. *watches D3 roll across table*
11. *LH picks up D1*
12. *LH drops D1 to table, watching it roll*
13. *LH picks up D3, knocking over Half-Columns 1 and 2 and Doll 4*
14. *watches D4 roll toward experimenter*
    (experimenter pushes D4 back toward subject)
15. *LH drops D3 on the table*
16. *watches D3 roll*   (12BG, page 11)

Protoexperimenting is beginning to vary as a coordinate function of both (*a*) unordered class variables (i.e., unary predication), and (*b*) ordered causal variables (i.e., ordered mappings). This is consistent with the origins of unary class composition (Chapter 14) and the developments in iterative ordering (Section V, this chapter). Thus 12BG continues protoexperimenting in the above vein with dolls only for another 21 transactions before he drops an object from the other class of half-columns. This is characteristic of his subsequent transactions which continue for an additional 60 transactions. Protoexperimenting is applied almost exclusively to one class of objects only, dolls, before protoexperimenting with the other class of half-columns.

In part, at least, singular-class protoexperimenting is a result of the effects varying as a function of the predicate properties of the classes. Subject 12BG continuously monitors the differential effects upon the dolls and half-columns; that is, the dolls rolled away and the half-columns did not. In part it may also be a function of progress in verifying the replicability of positive results. Multiple repetition of the rolling effect is continuously monitored by 12BG as if the results might vary even after numerous replications. Little attempt is made to replicate negative results. Three factors may be involved. First, negative effects (not rolling) are less interesting than positive (rolling) effects. Second, protoexperimenting is a function of unary classification at this stage. Third, disconfirming results are to be controlled by elimination.

Replicability requires systematic variation. Indeed, systematic variation has become a frequent, although still highly flawed, feature of protoexperimenting. With relatively infrequent exceptions (e.g., Line 9), 12BG holds both the mappings and class properties constant. He mainly varies the class elements. Often, he replicates the results with a given object before proceeding to another element.

As is fairly typical, 12BG protoexperiments with all the elements of a unary class. He first picks up one doll (Line 1) and then stores it in his right hand (Line 2) while his left hand protoexperiments with the other three dolls, occasionally interspersed with a half-column. Although not within the span of the protocol fragment, he eventually transfers the first doll he picked up in his left hand and protoexperiments with it. Thus, the whole class of dolls is treated as an independent variable.

Rare instances begin to be found in which infants vary both the class and the elements. They protoexperiment exclusively with the elements of each class successively:

32. *RH drops Block 3 to floor*
33. *looks at B3 on the floor*
34. *RH grasps and slides Block 2 across table until it falls off the edge to floor*
35. *LH picks up Block 1*
36. *LH throws B1 to table*
37. *LH picks up Block 4*
38. *LH drops B4 to floor*
39. *LH reaches toward B1 but cannot reach*
40. *(experimenter pushes B1 closer to subject) LH picks up B1*
41. *LH drops B1 to floor*
42. *LH touches Circular Ring 1 and RH touches Circular Ring 2*
43. *LH picks up CR1 and RH picks up CR2*
44. *LH drops CR1 to table*
45.5. *LH picks up CR1*
45.5. *RH drops CR2 to table*
47. *LH drops CR1 to table*
48. *RH picks up CR2 and LH touches CR1*
49. *RH drops CR2 to table*
50. *RH touches CR2*
51. *RH picks up CR2*
52. *RH drops CR2 to table*
53. *RH picks up CR2*
54. *RH picks up and drops CR2 to floor*
55. *LH drops CR1 to floor*
56. *LH picks up Circular Ring 3*
57. *LH drops CR3 to floor*
58. *LH picks up Circular Ring 4*
59. *LH drops CR4 to floor*   (12LZ, page 58)

Protoexperimenting is applied to all elements of the two classes presented. There is no overlap in classes. First, 12LZ projects the square blocks exclusively; then she projects the circular rings exclusively. The causal mapping form, drop, is held constant with two exceptions. These involve variations in the form of motility (i.e., slide and throw) (Lines 34 and 36). The displacement target fluctuates between the floor and the table. Thus, the main variables are class and class elements. Class is varied systematically, in the order of projecting blocks then rings.

The development of causal control, discussed at the beginning of this section, enables infants to begin to construct transitive protoexperiments. These protoexperiments always involve unidirectional transmission of motion from one object to a second object to a third object or to a group of objects. They never include transmission through an intermediary when the objects have not been previously grouped:

3. *RH pushes Square Column 3 into Cylinder 2 and one end of Cylinder 1*
3a. *C2 rolls forward on table and C1 rotates 45° on table*
4. *RH flicks SC3 into C1, several times*
4a. *C1 rotates on table and rolls toward right across table*
5. *RH flicks SC3 on table, several times*
    (experimenter replaces C1 and C2 on table in front of subject)
6. *RH flicks SC3 into C1 and C2*
6a. *C1 rolls toward right across table as C2 rolls toward left into Square Column 1*
7. *RH continues flicking SC3 on table*
    (experimenter rolls C1 back to subject across table)
8. *RH flicks SC3 into C1, several times*
8a. *C1 rotates a little on table*
9. *RH flicks SC3 on top of C1*
9a. *C1 rotates toward left, slightly*
10. *RH flicks SC3 on top of C1, several times*
10a. *C1 rolls toward right across table*
11. *RH pushes SC3 into C1*
11a. *C1 rolls across table toward right*   (12KH, pages 59 and 60)

The square column is used to displace both Cylinders 1 and 2 simultaneously (Lines 3 and 6) and Cylinder 1 alone continuously (Lines 4, 8, 9, 10, and 11). The causal mapping forms are varied from pushing (Line 3) to flicking (Lines 4–10) to pushing (Line 11). Consequently, differential results are produced. The main causal mapping form—flicking one object into another—is continuously increased. Consequently, the main result—transmission of motion—continuously increases in magnitude as *12KH* repeats her flicking motions.

Protoreciprocal covariations between variables are becoming progressively specialized and coordinated. One manifest form is the beginning of directed targeting of missiles toward specific objects causing transitive transmission of motion. Irrelevant intervening transactions are omitted in the second protocol fragment:

81. *LH rolls VW2 on table into and hitting Blue Car, displacing BC*
82. *LH rolls VW2 into Doll 2, knocking D2 over*   (12DA, page 28)

2. *throws Doll 4 at the row of Square Columns 1, 2, and 3*
2a. *D4 rolls on table and knocks over SC2 and SC3*

8. *throws Square Column 4 toward the center of the table*
8a. *SC4 hits SC1, 2, and 3, displacing them*   (12AM, page 34)

Reciprocal containing is becoming well regulated. This is manifest in several ways. One is that subjects hold the container in one hand while using the other to put objects into it (12LZ, Lines 1–9); another is that subjects put the container over the contained object and then take the contained object out from under the container (12LZ, Lines 59 and 60):

1. *RH picks up Receptacle 1*
2. *LH picks up Square Column 1*
3. *LH puts SC1 into R1 held by RH*
4. *LH picks up Cylinder 1*
5. *LH puts C1 into R1 held by RH*
6. *LH picks up Cylinder 2*
7. *LH puts C2 into R1 held by RH*
8. *LH picks up Square Column 2*
9. *LH puts SC2 into R1 held by RH such that all four objects are now in R1 held by RH*   (12LZ, page 50)

59. *BH drop Receptacle 1 over Square Column 1*
60. *RH picks SC1 out from under R1*   (12LZ, page 52)

A complementary form of causal protoreciprocity, controlled catching of missiles, is becoming progressively directed:

23. *looks toward Car 3 held by BH*
    (experimenter uprights all the VWs, then rolls Car 4 to subject)
24. *LH pounces on C4, stopping its motion, while RH holds C3*
                                                                 (12LL, page 42)

The left hand releases Car 3. Its trajectory is reciprocally directed toward catching and stopping Car 4. All the while, the right hand continues holding onto Car 3.

Reciprocal causal compensation is becoming regulated:

42.3. *looks at Yellow Car*
42.7. *LH, holding Yellow Circular Ring, reaches toward YC*
42.7a. *YCR in LH hits into YC and knocks YC off table*
44. *RH reaches toward YC as car goes over side, but does not catch it*
45. *looks at mother*
    subject: "Uuuuhh"
46. *looks down at the floor*
47. *watches mother retrieve YC*
    (mother puts YC on table)
48. *looks at YC on table*
49. *RH picks up YC*   (12RD, pages 20 and 21)

9. *LH's index finger extends to Yellow Cylinder and pushes it so that it rolls about 3 inches*

10.5. *LH comes down with a thud, slamming down on moving YC*

10.5. *RH sets Green Cylinder horizontal and holds it on table*   (12LL, page 7)

On the one hand, *12RD*'s attempted physical compensation for the receding target is unsuccessful (Line 44). His social transaction, looking and vocalizing to his mother followed by looking to the floor (Lines 45 and 46), is successful. On the other hand, *12LL*'s efforts with her left hand are well-regulated and successful, like the beginnings of a cat and mouse game. Indeed, her right hand is simultaneously transacting with another object while all this is going on (second Line 10.5).

IV. Coregulated Protocorrespondences

The contents of mapping protocorrespondences continue to expand. At the same time protocorrespondences are becoming progressively directed and coregulated. This includes a social dimension (*12JM*). Nonrelevant transactions are omitted in the third protocol fragment:

71. *LH holds Blue Hexagonal Column 1 against his forehead and nose for 4 seconds, while RH holds Yellow Circular Ring 2 in air*

72. *LH lowers BHC1*

73. *LH extends BHC1 to experimenter's nose*

74. *LH touches experimenter's nose with one finger*   (12JM, page 45)

6. *bends Plate upward by putting thumb on one side, index and third finger on the other:*

7. *lets go of P*

8. *looks at P*

9. *touches P*

10. *bends P upward as in No. 6*   (12EB, page 1)

17. *RH finger rolls VW1 back and forth on table*

18. *RH holds and rolls VW1 back and forth on table*

21. *RH rolls VW1 back and forth on table*

23. *RH rolls VW1 back and forth on table*   (12LZ, pages 60 and 61)

Discrete protocorrespondences still do not exceed constructing three-unit equivalences. Most discrete protocorrespondences continue to produce single-unit equivalences, but of a more systematic nature:

25. *RH taps Red Spoon on table, once*
26. *RH puts RS back in Red Cup*
27. *RH takes RS out of RC*
28. *RH taps RS on table, once*   (12AM, page 9)

8. *LH picks up and drops Blue Cylinder 1, Blue Cylinder 2, Red Cylinder 1,*
   Red Triangular Column 2, Blue Triangular Column 1, Blue Triangular
   Column 2, one at a time to floor, without looking to locate
                                                                               (12DS, page 14)

115. *RH tosses Spoon 4 onto table to right and behind self, watching it slide to*
     floor
116. *LH transfers Spoon 3 to RH*
117. *repeats No. 115 with S3 as looks at experimenter*
118. *after S3 goes over table edge, turns and looks toward where it went over*
119. *RH lifts Car 4*
120. *RH tosses C4 onto table to right and behind self, not looking*
                                                                               (12JE, pages 63 and 64)

Regulated single-unit bi-univocal protocorrespondences are coordinated with (*a*) causal targeting (e.g., 12DA protocol fragment presented on page 301), (*b*) spatial reciprocity between container and contained, and (*c*) co-univocal protocorrespondences (between one contained object and two containers):

3. *RH taps Cross Ring 2 in Receptacle 1, once*
4. *RH taps CR2 in Receptacle 2, once*
5. *RH taps CR2 in R1, once*   (12AM, page 29)

Simultaneous construction of single-unit protocorrespondences is becoming relatively commonplace:

11.5. *LH holds Yellow Circular Ring over floor on left*
11.5. *RH holds Spoon 1 over floor on right*
13.5. *LH throws YCR to floor*
13.5. *RH throws S1 to floor*
 15. *looks down at the floor to the left*
 16. *hangs way over the left side of the chair, looking down on the floor*
                                                                               (12LL, page 37)

56.5. *LH taps Car 3 on table, once*
56.5. *RH taps Doll 3 on table, once*   (12DA, page 27)

Simultaneous single-unit protocorrespondences are extended to include all the objects when the array consists of a small number, that is, four elements. Nonrelevant transactions are omitted:

24.5. *RH drops Square Column 1 to floor*
24.5. *LH drops Square Column 2 to floor*
29.5. *RH drops SC2 to table*

29.5. LH *drops SC1 to table*
33.5. RH *releases Cylinder 1 on table*
33.5. LH *releases Cylinder 2 on table*
40.5. RH *drops SC2 to floor*
40.5. LH *drops C2 to floor*   (12LZ, pages 48 and 49)

The elements are successively recombined to form single-unit protocorrespondences between two square columns (Lines 24.5 and 29.5), two cylinders (Lines 33.5), and a square column and a cylinder (Lines 40.5). Thus, rudiments of the structural conditions necessary to permute single-unit equivalences begin to be constructed.

As the previous protocol fragment indicates, simultaneous protocorrespondences are becoming elaborate and complex. Potentially, this means that subjects are sometimes constructing both single-unit and multi-unit equivalences within the same performance:

81.5. RH *taps Block 1 on table, sometimes in rhythm and sometimes out of rhythm with LH*
81.5. LH *taps Block 3 on table*   (12DA, page 11)

Alternation between rhythmic and nonrhythmic protocorresponding tapping enhances the possibility of chunking (segmenting) the equivalences by both singular and multiple units.

Second-order correlation protooperations begun at the previous stage (Chapter 10, Section VI) expand rapidly at this stage. They remain limited, however, to constructing no more than two-to-two correspondences between one-to-one matchings. Typically, two test objects are placed in one-to-one correspondence with two social objects as if they "belonged" that way:

51.5. *leaning forward,* RH *places Yellow Spoon 2 on table by experimenter's LH, but does not completely release it*
51.5. LH *places Yellow Spoon 1 by experimenter's RH, without releasing it (experimenter takes hold of handles)*
53.5. RH *picks up YS2*
53.5. LH *picks up YS1, as sits back*
55.5. *leaning forward,* RH *places YS2 near experimenter's LH*
55.5. LH *places YS1 near experimenter's RH*
57.5. RH *picks up YS2 bringing it toward self, as leans back in the chair*
57.5. LH *picks up YS1 pulling it toward self*   (12JM, page 9)

At the same time as each spoon is correlated in one-to-one relationship with each hand, both spoons are correlated in two-to-two relationships with both hands. Moreover, these coordinated bi-univocal protocorrespondences are reproduced twice in succession.

Such sequences clearly meet all the requirements of Frege's definition for correlation operations that construct numerical equivalence (see pages

84 and 85). They could readily substitute for his illustrative example of a waiter matching a knife to each plate on a table. Of course, Frege's hypothetical waiter is not limited to matching knives to plates. He can also match forks, spoons, glasses, place-names, etc., to plates. Moreover, the number of sets the hypothetical waiter can construct is limited only by his resources. Infants are limited to two sets of one-to-one correlation only. Presumably, according to Frege's example, the missing feature in infants' constructions is range of application. This is acceptable if we limit numerical equivalence by correlation operations to pragmatic constructions, whether by waiters or infants. However, we should not lose sight of the fact that constructing formal numerical equivalence requires deductive correlation operations, such as infinite matching, not manifest in Frege's example or by infants. They require hypothetical constructions which do not develop until adolescence and adulthood (Inhelder & Piaget, 1958; Kuhn, Langer, Kohlberg, & Haan, 1977).

The sequence produced by *12JM* terminates in a potential many-to-one co-univocal protocorrespondence when the subject pulls both spoons back to himself (Lines 57.5). Constructing many-to-one correlations in social contexts is no longer unusual:

48. RH *pushes Yellow Cross Ring 3 toward experimenter*
49. LH *holds Yellow Cross Ring 1 out toward experimenter* (12LZ, page 15)

One-to-many co-univocals matching one object to several people are also beginning to be produced:

34. RH *holds VW1 out toward mother*
35. RH *gives VW1 to mother*
     (mother takes VW1 from subject and gives it to experimenter; experimenter puts VW1 back onto the table)
36. LH *picks up VW1*
37. LH *holds VW1 out toward mother*
38. LH *holds VW1 out toward experimenter*
39. *(experimenter takes VW1 and puts out other hand)* looks at experimenter's hand
40. RH *takes VW1 from experimenter*
41. RH *holds VW1 out toward mother, looking at mother*
42. RH *gives VW1 to experimenter*   (12LZ, page 65)

Continuous protocorrespondences are becoming precise. They include paying some attention to maintaining exactly equivalent spatial orientation (*12AM*, Lines 18, 22, and 23; *12LZ*; *12DS*):

18. RH *slides Doll 4 on its head briefly*
19. RH *picks up Doll 2*

20. *RH slides down D2 close to the edge of table*
21. *RH picks up Doll 3*
22. *RH stands D3 on its head*
23. *RH slides D3 around*   (12AM, pages 32 and 33)

95.5. *LH bangs Blue Brush 1 on table, holding it straight down by the handle so that brush head strikes table*
95.5. *watches BB1 as LH bangs it on table*
97. *LH stops banging BB1*
98. *LH bangs BB1 on the table, holding it straight down by the handle so that brush head strikes table*
99. *RH tries but fails to pick up Red Triangular Column 2*
100. *RH picks up Red Brush 2*
101. *RH bangs RB2 on table, holding it straight down by the handle so that brush head strikes table*   (12LZ, page 23)

16. *RH bangs Yellow Hexagonal Column on table, at a tilt*
17. *RH releases YHC on table*
18. *RH picks up Yellow Cross Ring*
19. *RH bangs YCR in same tilted fashion*   (12DS, page 12)

Alternating continuous protocorrespondences are also becoming precise and comparatively observed:

33. *RH bangs Yellow Cross Ring quickly on table, as watches*
34. *LH bangs Green Cross Ring quickly on table, as watches*
35. *RH extends YCR to mother, as watches*
    (mother does not take it)
36. *RH brings YCR back to the table, as watches*
37. *RH bangs YCR on table, as watches*
38. *LH bangs GCR on table, as watches*
39. *RH extends YCR to experimenter, as watches*   (12DS, page 9)

Long nonsequential strings of precise continuous protocorrespondences are also generated. They include application to many objects (e.g., four of the five objects presented to 12DA). They also include some switching between successive and simultaneous equivalences:

6. *RH slides Car 2 back and forth on table*
16. *RH slides C2 back and forth on table*
39. *RH slides Doll 2 back and forth on table*
68. *RH slides C2 back and forth on table*
72. *LH slides Car 1 back and forth on table*
76.5. *RH slides C2 back and forth on table*
76.5. *LH slides C1 back and forth on table*
94.5. *RH slides C1 back and forth on table*
94.5. *LH slides C2 back and forth on table*

102. *LH slides C2 back and forth on table*
104. *RH slides C1 back and forth on table*
110. *LH slides Blue Car back and forth on table*　　　(12DA, pages 25–29)

Progress in coordinating continuous with discrete correlations is marked by infants interweaving precise continuous with precise discrete protocorrespondences:

3.5. *LH flicks Circular Ring 2 up and down*
3.5. *RH flicks Circular Ring 3 up and down*
　5. *RH puts CR3 down on table*
　6. *RH reaches toward right end of object array, knocking over Doll 3*
　7. *RH grasps Doll 4 between thumb and index*
　8. *RH lays D4 on its side*
　9. *RH grasps Doll 2 between thumb and index*
10. *RH lays D2 on its side*
11. *RH grasps Doll 1 between thumb and index*
12. *RH lays D1 on its side*
13. *RH rolls D2, back and forth between thumb and forefingers under palm*
14. *RH rolls D3, back and forth between thumb and forefingers under palm*
　　　　　　　　　　　　　　　　　　　　　　　　　(12EB, page 12)

Subject 12EB begins with a precise and simultaneous continuous protocorrespondence (Lines 3.5). She follows with a precise, discrete protocorrespondence (Lines 7–12, and perhaps 6). She ends with another precise, continuous protocorrespondence (Lines 13 and 14).

Most cooperative protocorrespondences have become compositional at this stage and will be considered in Chapter 14. The remaining cooperative mapping protocorrespondences continue to be produced selectively. They are most likely to occur when the experimenter reproduces an ongoing transaction by the subject. Yet, often reproduction by the experimenter of the subject's protocorrespondence still leads to suppression by the subject:

24. *BH slide Cylinder 1 and Square Column 2 side-to-center, out and in, on table, fast, sometimes hitting them together when pushing them toward center; laughing at experimenter*
　　(experimenter imitates with two cylinders, banging them together)
25. *stops, watches experimenter while BH hold C1 and SC2*　(12DO, page 16)

Apparently, the subject is more interested in watching the experimenter's transaction than in continuing. When the experimenter stops, the subject does not imitate the continuous protocorrespondence. Modeling does sometimes provoke cooperative protocorrespondence:

　　(experimenter taps Rectangular Ring 1 on table)
37. *looks toward experimenter*

38. *RH taps Doll 4 on table*   (*12DA, page 31*)

Cooperative protocorrespondences are just beginning to be coregulated:

> *(experimenter touches Green Square Column to subject's nose, then holds*
> *it out before subject)*
> 1. *laughs, as LH takes GSC from experimenter*
> 2. *LH puts GSC up to his forehead*   (*12JM, page 47*)
>
> 11. *crawls across table to experimenter*
> 12. *touches noses with experimenter*   (*12JM, page 48*)

Precise coregulation by the subject is required to construct these protocorrespondences. He gauges his own mappings in relation to the experimenter's behavior (particularly in Lines 11 and 12). Still, parts of the protocorrespondence are imprecise and transformative (i.e., the forehead is substituted for the nose as the locus for the object) (Line 2). At the same time, the playful social dimension of cooperative protocorrespondences is coming much to the fore.

V. Coordinated Iterative Series

Protoaddition and protosubtraction construct progressively coordinated iterative order relations. Most protoorders are still usually unidirectional increases or decreases, but they are progressively integrated into bidirectional series, and are generated particularly in the context of experimentation. Coordination of ordered variations with protoexperimental and protocorrespondence constructions is consolidated. Some orderings even begin to acquire a cooperative social dimension.

The preponderance of orderings continues to shift to the production of discrete iteration. In part, this progressive shift indicates that the part–whole structure of orders is becoming more directed, differentiated, and coordinated. Iterative series are constructed in which the number increases from one to two to three units:

11. *LH drops Circular Ring 2 to floor*
12. *RH drops Circular Rings 3 and 4 to floor*
13. *looks down at the floor where she dropped the three rings*
23. *RH drops Circular Rings 1, 2, and 3 to table* (*12LZ, pages 55 and 56*)

The time spent in-between dropping two and three objects is devoted to gathering the three objects after the experimenter replaces them on the table.

Shifting to discrete ordering is crucial to infants' developing logic of experimentation. It is perhaps the only pragmatic means infants have available to construct ordered variations in their experimental variables where the differences are precise and quantifiable. Like *12LZ* they can observe the differential results attributable to experimenting with one versus two versus three objects, while holding all other variables constant. Measurement operations can thereby be introduced into the construction of independent variables, at least.

Precise variation already includes reciprocal ordering of the experimental variable (i.e., number of objects). Precise bidirectional discrete orderings are generated in which increasing numbers are followed immediately by decreasing numbers:

46. *RH drops Yellow Rectangular Ring to floor*
47. *LH touches Green Rectangular Ring and Green Circular Ring*
48. *BH pick up GRR and GCR*
49. *BH drop GRR and GCR to floor*
50. *LH picks up Yellow Circular Ring*
51. *LH drops YCR to floor*
52. *looks at floor* (12LZ, pages 12 and 13)

Precise bidirectional discrete orderings are also generated in which decreasing numbers are followed immediately by increasing numbers:

17.5. *LH drops Yellow Rectangular Ring to floor*
17.5. *RH drops Yellow Circular Ring 1 to floor*
19. *RH picks up Yellow Circular Ring 2*
20. *RH drops YCR2 to floor*
21. *RH picks up Green Circular Ring 1 and Green Rectangular Ring*
22. *LH picks up Green Circular Ring 2*
23.5. *RH drops GCR1 and GRR to floor*
23.5. *LH drops GCR2 to floor* (12LZ, page 18)

Continuous protoadditions (e.g., banging increasingly harder) result in ever more extended continuous orderings:

28. *RH bangs Yellow Cross Ring on table about 8 seconds*
29. *RH bangs YCR on table harder and harder*
29a. *the sound gets louder and louder* (12DS, page 9)

Continuous protoaddition begins to be extended to unidirectional transitive transmission of momentum from one object to a set of objects (cf. Section III). This includes co-univocal one-to-many protocorrespondences which are reproduced several times in an ordered series:

12. *looks at Yellow Car 1, Red Car 1 and Yellow Car 2 in a pile*
13. *RH taps Red Rectangular Ring 2 on YC1, RC1, YC2*
13a. *YC1, RC1, YC2 move a little*
14. *RH taps RRR2 on YC1, RC1, YC2*

14a. *YC1, RC1, YC2 move more*
 15. *RH taps RRR2 harder on YC1, RC1, YC2*
15a. *YC1, RC1, YC2 move all the way to further edge of table but do not fall*
 off   (12AM, page 17)

Anticipatory observation of the dependent variable, the pile of cars, precedes the protoexperimental series (Line 12). The results are successively increased in a controlled fashion. The instrumental ring is tapped harder and harder against the pile of cars which, consequently, move farther and father toward the table edge. Thus, ordered covariation begins to mark infants' protoexperiments.

Continuous and discrete orderings continue to be coordinated with each other. They include both mappings and objects:

 70. *RH touches Red Circular Ring to experimenter's LH palm, as leans*
 forward (RH is also holding Yellow Car)
 71. *backs up with RCR (and YC) held by RH*
 72. *RH touches RCR to experimenter's palm, as leans forward*
 73. *RH jerks RCR back, as experimenter begins to curl fingers*
 74. *RH touches RCR to experimenter's palm, as leans forward*
 75. *RH jerks RCR back, as experimenter begins to curl fingers faster*
 76. *RH touches RCR to experimenter's palm, as leans forward*
 77.3. *RH jerks RCR back, as experimenter begins to curl fingers faster*
 77.7. *RH hits RCR on table, once, as backs up*
 (experimenter holds both palms out flat on table)
 79. *RH places RCR and YC into experimenter's LH, as leans forward*
 (experimenter removes objects)
 81.5. *looks at experimenter*
 subject: "Uuuuhh, ahhhh!"
 81.5. *BH hit table, once*   (12RD, page 22)

Such interactions mark the origins of cooperative ordering. Protoseriating speed derives from cooperative "capture and escape" play between the subject and experimenter. The subject extends to and withdraws from the experimenter one object at a faster and faster pace as the experimenter pretends she is trying to capture it faster and faster (Lines 70–77.3). Then, as the experimenter places both hands out to receive the objects, the subject increases the number of objects to two (Line 79). In doing this, the subject also successively constructs two many-to-one protocorrespondences between coupled objects and each of the experimenter's hands. Indeed, the subject finishes with a single-unit mapping correspondence (second Line 81.5).

Not only are continuous orderings coordinated with discrete orderings; but, as we have just seen, they are progressively integrated with discrete protocorrespondences. These integrations are not limited to relating continuous orderings with discrete protocorrespondences:

  42.5. RH *pushes Yellow Rectangular Ring to experimenter and lets it go*
  42.5. LH *pushes Yellow Circular Ring 4 to experimenter and lets it go*
   44. LH *pushes Green Circular Ring, Yellow Circular Ring 1, and Yellow*
        Circular Ring 3 to experimenter and lets them go   (12LZ, page 15)

First, the subject constructs a simultaneous one-to-one protocorrespondence in pushing two objects to the experimenter (Lines 42.5). Then she increases the number of objects she pushes to the experimenter to three (Line 44).

Coordinating ordering with correspondences produces coseriation. While still generated by less than half of the infants, extensive coseriations are generated. These also include bidirectional, albeit imprecise, iterative series:

   9.5. RH *hits on table, three times*
   9.5. LH *hits Green Rectangular Ring 1 on table, three times*
  11.5. RH *hits on Green Rectangular Ring 2, one time*
  11.5a. GRR2 *moves slightly such that it touches Red Clover Ring 2*
  11.5. LH *hits GRR1 on table, one time*
  13.5. RH *hits on table, six times*
  13.5. LH *hits GRR1 on table, six times*
  15.5. RH *hits on Red Clover Ring 1, two times*
  15.5a. RCR1 *moves slightly each time*
  15.5. LH *hits GRR1 on table, two times*
        (*experimenter hits BH on table*)
  17.5. RH *rests on table, as looks at experimenter's performance*
  17.5. LH *holding GRR1 rests on table*
  19.3. RH *hits on GRR2, one time*
  19.3a. GRR2 *displaced away from RCR2*
  19.7. LH *hits GRR1 on table, one time*
  21.3. RH *hits on table, five times*
  21.7. LH *hits GRR1 on table, five times*   (12JM, pages 49 and 50)

Corresponding bidirectional discrete orderings construct the extensive mapping coseries of $\langle 3, 1, 6, 2, 1, 5 \rangle$ hits with each hand. While the discrete magnitudes of all six successive protocorrespondences are quantitatively equivalent, the mappings are analogous. Throughout, the transactions by the left hand remain constant; it uses Green Rectangular Ring 1 as an instrument to hit on the table. The right hand also hits on the table or on an object, but not with an instrument. Analogizing, then, partially detaches the mapping forms of the protocorrespondences from each other, while preserving quantitative equivalence. This is a necessary transitional step toward the formation of symbolic notation of equivalence by one-to-one correspondence.

13

Stable Composing

Composing of discrete objects is becoming an equilibrated combinativity proto-operation. Reciprocally, lability is declining as the central characteristic of infants' compositions. The most significant developments include the following elements: (*a*) preservation of compositions for extended durations, (*b*) increases in the production of more extensive sets (i.e., three- and four-object sets), (*c*) predominance of composing by direct transaction with two or more of the objects composed, (*d*) producing stabiles as frequently as mobiles, (*e*) initial formation of two separate but contemporaneous two-object sets, and (*f*) integration of two small sets to form one larger set.

Compositions are no longer dominated by causality; most become noncausal spatiotemporal static and, occasionally, kinetic structures. These include containment of all presented objects in a single container and embedding objects in each other when possible (e.g., stacking cups in each other). Inverse spatial transformations are also becoming more frequent. Long sequences of putting objects in and out of containers are generated. Some compositional attempts are also made to alternate between stacking and detaching cups.

Subjects carefully observe the compositions they have constructed. This includes examining sets in their initial composed state and then inverting the compositions to form identity proto-operations while continuing to inspect them carefully and in a coordinated fashion:

94. *RH touches Yellow Spoons 1 and 2 held upright in LH*
95. *looking at YS1 and 2 as LH rotates slightly YS1 and 2, held upright in fist, while RH touches and fingers YS1 and 2*   (12JM, page 11)

30. *looks at Brushes 1 and 2 held by handle ends in LH*
31. *LH transfers B1 and 2 to RH by rotating B1 and 2 such that RH grasps bristle ends*
32. *RH transfers B1 and 2 to LH by rotating B1 and 2 such that LH grasps handle ends*   (12RD, page 61)

Internal differentiation and integration is beginning to mark individual compositional structures composed of three or more objects. As noted in Section II, this applies to fairly large compositions as well. Various manifestations will be discussed throughout this chapter and Chapter 14. For now it will suffice to present an illustration of two partially overlapping part compositions (Lines 61.3–61.7) which are integrated with each other (Lines 64.5) to form a symmetrical composition:

61.3. *LH puts handle of Yellow Spoon 1 into middle of Yellow Cross Ring 1, moving YCR1 around on the table*
61.3a. *YCR1 touches Yellow Cross Ring 2*
61.7. *RH touches cup of Yellow Spoon 2 against cup of YS1*
63. *RH pushes cup of YS2 down on cup of YS1, causing handle to come out of center of YCR1*
[Note: *LH did not make any move to raise YS1 out of YCR1.*]
64.5. *LH holds YS1 by cup and places YS1 handle on YCR1*
64.5. *RH holds YS2 by cup and places YS2 handle on YCR1* (12JM, page 9)

Compositional asymmetry decreases in frequency. Compositions are increasingly featured by symmetrical placements on a surface, as in the just cited protocol fragment, as well as in the air. Compositions combining symmetrical with asymmetrical placements and displacements also increase in frequency.

I. Preserving Very Small Single Sets

Composing productivity during the spontaneous phase is higher at age 12 months than at age 10 months in two of the three class conditions for which comparable measures are available (cf. Table 13.1, Row 3, Columns 1, 3, and 5 and Table 10.1, Row 3, Columns 2, 3, and 4). Measures of mean productivity are not available for the semicontrol conditions due to problems in timing the task durations. For the same reason, productivity measures are available for only 6 of the 12 subjects in the three other class conditions. Composing productivity in the four-object additive and

TABLE 13.1

Spontaneous Phase I: Mean Frequency by 12-Month-Old Subjects of Compositions, Duration of Phase I, and Mean Frequency of Compositions per Minute

| | Class conditions | | | | | |
| | Additive | | Multiplicative | | Disjoint | |
	Four-object 1	Eight-object 2	Four-object 3	Eight-object 4	Four-object 5	Eight-object 6
1. Compositions	17.83	16.33	9.33	28.67	10.17	22.17
2. Time	2 min 09 sec	1 min 34 sec	1 min 55 sec	2 min 24 sec	1 min 31 sec	1 min 55 sec
3. Productivity per minute[a]	8.29	10.40	4.86	11.95	6.69	11.55

[a] Based on six subjects per condition.

315

disjoint conditions at age 12 months is almost double that at age 10 months. The differences for the two conditions approach but do not achieve statistical significance (Mann–Whitney U tests). Composing productivity in the four-object multiplicative condition is a bit lower than that at age 10 months.

Composing in the presence of many objects is not a problem. Eight objects evoke more composing than four objects (Table 13.1, Row 3). Increased composing productivity was found in all three class conditions. The increase for all three conditions combined is statistically significant ($N = 6$, $x = 0$, $p = .016$, sign test). A breakdown by conditions reveals that the increase is random in the additive condition ($N = 6$, $x = 4$, $p = .344$), significant in the multiplicative condition ($N = 6$, $x = 0$, $p = .016$), and approaches statistical significance in the disjoint condition ($N = 6$, $x = 1$, $p = .109$).

Composing productivity is less uniform in the four-object than in the eight-object class conditions. The range in the four-object conditions is from a low of 4.86 per minute in the multiplicative to 8.29 per minute in the disjoint condition (Table 13.1, Row 3, Columns 1, 3, and 5). The differences approach but do not achieve statistical significance (Mann–Whitney $U = 4.5$, $.072 < p < .142$). The range in the eight-object conditions is much narrower; from a low of 10.40 per minute in the additive to 11.95 in the multiplicative conditions. The differences are not statistically significant (Mann–Whitney $U = 2.63$, $.252 < p < .43$).

The duration of individual compositions continues to increase in both the four-object (*12JE*) and eight-object (*12AM*) conditions:

12. *RH touches Cylinder 2 to Cylinder 1 held by LH*
13. *RH holds C2 and LH holds C1 together*
14. *BH finger C1 and C2 as holds them together (RH holds C2, LH holds C1) and looks (happily) at experimenter*
15.3. *BH transfer grasps on C1 and C2 such that BH hold both cylinders*
15.7. *looks at C1 and C2*   (12JE, page 27)

2. *LH places Cylinder 4 toward center, below array of objects*
3. *LH reaches all the way to the left and tries to pick up Square Column 1*
3a. *SC1 falls over*
4. *LH stands SC1 upright*
5. *RH picks up Cylinder 3*
6. *RH places C3 toward center near C4*
7. *RH picks up Square Column 2 from the left*
8. *RH places SC2 toward center near C3 and C4*   (12AM, page 37)

Preservation of a set for extended durations enables infants to treat it as a constant given. Then it can be used as content for further protoinferential constructions:

6. *RH picks up Orange Spoon 2 and Yellow Spoon 1, unaligned in hand*

7. *RH knocks OS2 and YS1 into Yellow Cup 2*
7a. *YC2 falls toward self onto table*
   (experimenter picks up YC2 and puts it back into array)
8. *LH holding Orange Spoon 1 and RH holding OS2 and YS1, touches OS1*
   and OS2 together above table
   (experimenter moves Yellow Spoon 2 and Orange Cup 2 back into array)

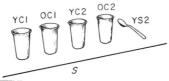

9. *RH touches OS2 onto table briefly while holding YS1 and OS2*
10.3. *RH pushes OS2 and YS1 forward across table, pushing OS2 into OC2*
10.3a. *OC2 displaced across table to right and into YS2*
10.3aa. *YS2 displaced toward right slightly*
10.7. *RH picks up YS2, such that RH holds OS2, YS1, and YS2*
12. *LH transfers OS1 to RH, such that all four spoons are held by RH*
13. *LH picks up YC2*
14. *LH rotates YC2 bottom up above table*
15. *LH knocks bottom of YC2 into top of Orange Cup 1*
15a. *OC1 falls forward onto table*
16. *LH touches bottom of YC2 on table near OC1*
17. *LH sets edge of YC2 on table at 25° angle, somewhat aligned with bottom*
   to top and near OC1:

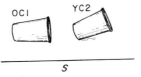

18. *RH places OS1, OS2, YS1, and YS2 in pile on table to right near OC2*
   (12KH, pages 49 and 50)

Here we will only list the protoinferential relations which extended composing permits *12KH* to construct: (*a*) an iterative series of ⟨two, three, three, four, five⟩-element stabile compositions (Lines 6, 8, 10.7, 12, and 18), (*b*) protosubstitution of spoons in the three-element stabiles (Lines 8 and 10.7), (*c*) many-to-one causal relations (Lines 7 and 7a.) as well as causal transmissions (Lines 10.3–10.3aa), and (*d*) binary composition by partial temporal overlap with another two-object composition (Lines 12–17). The structures of these relations will be analyzed in Chapter 14.

Spontaneous transactions in the first test phase are still the source of most composing. Procedures directed toward provoking composing in the second test phase continue to have a negative effect. The result is a decrease in composing productivity, but that decrease is tapering off.

This trend is reflected by several forms of composing that are not generated consistently, but are ever more present. Some involve grouping in receptacles. When the number is small (four objects), all or most are contained. When the number is large (eight objects), many, though usually not more than six, are contained.

Most grouping by containment consists of putting objects one-by-one into only one receptacle, thereby creating a single set. The single grouping is usually impervious to the predicate properties of the elements grouped, that is, whether the elements are identical, complements or disjoints. Grouping by containment is also unaffected by the experimenter's interventions. It does not increase when the experimenter models containing, and does not change the subjects' containing in only one receptacle when the experimenter models containing in two receptacles.

This stage marks the origins of rudimentary grouping into two sets by containing elements one-by-one in two receptacles. To illustrate, one infant used both receptacles to contain six of the eight objects. The order of containment was: square column, square column, cylinder into Receptacle 2; and cylinder, cylinder into Receptacle 1. Then she transferred some objects from one receptacle into the other receptacle, and, finally, contained the fourth cylinder in Receptacle 2. Thus, this infant's one-by-one containing fluctuated between receptacles. Yet, she ended up by grouping equivalent numbers, three objects in each container. While the order of handling is partially class consistent, each receptacle contained a mixture of disjoint objects.

Binary composing by containment in two separate but adjacent receptacles is one way of constructing and preserving two separate but related sets of elements. At most, however, only two sets are constructed by containment. The number of elements within each set is also limited. Rarely, if ever, do the sets compose more than three objects.

Other forms of provoked composing during phase II involve spatial sorting. Individual objects are sometimes added cooperatively:

11. *LH thrusts Rectangular Ring 2 down toward table as if to throw but does not release it*
    (experimenter holds out Clover Ring 2)
12. *LH raises RR2 high in air as fixes eyes on CR2*
13. *while watching CR2, LH extends RR2 toward CR2, such that RR2 nearly touches CR2*
    (experimenter drops CR2 onto Cross Ring 1, just below)
14. *LH drops RR2 onto CR2*
15. *backs up, looking at pile*   (12RD, page 70)

Subject *12RD*'s cooperative composing corresponds to that of the experimenter (Line 14). It is preceded (Lines 12 and 13) by a determined and precise coregulative effort to construct a protocorrespondence with the experimenter (see Chapter 14). In turn, the coregulated protocorrespondence follows upon virtual, perhaps gestural, throwing (Line 11). The subject's cooperative dropping suggests further coregulative elaboration. He modifies virtual throwing without a target into actual dropping onto a target in accordance with the experimenter's composing.

Socially provoked composing requires the experimenter "to fit" her transactions into the subjects' existing forms of composing. A successful fit may be achieved by elaborating on the subjects' immediately preceding transactions via modeling a variant. For instance, in the above protocol fragment, the experimenter elaborates on *12RD*'s virtual throwing by an actual dropping. When the experimenter does not elaborate on the subjects' preceding transactions, provoked composing has no effect:

8.5.   *RH lets VW1 go in front of her*
8.5.   *LH lets VW2 go in front of her*
       (experimenter puts both VWs 1 and 2 over to subject's left and extends Racer 2 to subject)
10.   *does not take it, instead RH makes insistent open–close gesture in the direction of the other nongrouped objects in front of experimenter*
       (experimenter puts R2, the one she tried handing subject, down in front of subject)
       (experimenter hands subject Racer 3)
11.   *RH swats R3 in experimenter's hand*   (12LL, pages 40 and 41)

Instead of cooperating in the experimenter's grouping activity, *12LL* makes gestural reference to the other objects (Line 10). She rejects the object the experimenter is trying to provoke the subject into grouping (Line 11). Subsequent modeling trials are just as ineffective even though the experimenter repeatedly sorts the objects the subject refuses to group. This is the inevitable result with all the subjects at this stage when the experimenter does not model sorting by elaborating or expanding on the subjects' preceding forms of composing.

Modeled forms of composing are particularly ineffective when they conflict with the subjects' forms of composing:

Phase II: experimenter sets up matrix of cups and spoons and alignment of four extra yellow cups in front of subject:

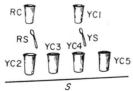

1.   *RH reaches between Yellow Cups 2 and 3 for Yellow Spoon*
2.   *RH bangs YS on table*
3.   *RH puts YS in YC3*
4.   *RH beats YS in YC3*

5. *RH takes YS out*
6. *RH holds YS in Yellow Cup 5*
7. *RH takes YS out*
8. *RH holds YS in Yellow Cup 4*
9. *RH takes YS out*
10. *RH puts YS in YC3*
11. *RH beats YS a few times in YC3*   (12AM, page 11)

Prior to this, in phase I, 12AM generated many protocorresponding compositions by placing and beating one spoon in one cup. Instead of switching to and cooperating in the experimenter's form of composing, 12AM continues to construct a co-univocal protocorresponding composition by placing and beating one spoon in many cups.

Subtracting from preexistent compositions is still generated more frequently than adding, and continues to consist of taking elements away one-by-one. However, now the few elements subtracted are beginning to be taken away systematically and then recomposed. Usually, recomposing does not extend beyond subtracting objects from the preexistent composition and then rejoining them. In addition, a third object (which, in this instance, the experimenter tries to provoke the subject into sorting with one of the preexistent groupings) is sometimes added to the recomposition:

> (*experimenter places two groups in front of subject—one composed of Red Car 1 and Yellow Car 1 and the other composed of Red Rectangular Ring 1 and Yellow Rectangular Ring 1—and hands subject Yellow Car 2*)
> 1. *RH takes YC2*
> 2. *looks at YC2 held by RH on table*
> 3. *RH rotates YC2*
> 4. *looks over to left*
> 5. *LH picks up YC1*
> 6. *LH puts YC1 down in middle of table with YC2*
> 7. *looks over to left*
> 8. *LH picks up RC1*
> 9. *LH puts RC1 in pile in between YC1 and YC2*   (12AM, page 17)

Subject 12AM places the red car between the two yellow cars to form a small symmetrical alignment. Symmetrical compositions are becoming well-regulated, but remain rudimentary. Most symmetrical compositions are limited to three objects.

Addition of objects to preexistent compositions in phase III is always one-by-one, and is still usually limited to a singular object, even when several extras are provided. Moreover, the added singular object is directed toward coupling with a single element of the preexistent composition. This suggests that infants are still adding two objects together rather than adding an element to a set. To illustrate, 12RD is presented with two sorted groupings (three green triangular columns and three yellow circular rings) plus an extra, unsorted green circular ring. After picking up the extra:

3. *RH drops Green Circular Ring near Yellow Circular Ring 3, laughing*
4. *RH picks up GCR*
5. *RH places GCR partially on YCR3*
6. *RH grasps both GCR and YCR3*
7. *RH pushes GCR and YCR3 to meet LH*
8. *LH picks up GCR and YCR3*
9. *LH throws GCR and YCR3 down on table, laughing* (12RD, page 85)

Initially it might appear that 12RD is adding the extra element to one of the preexistent sets. However, he drops it near (Line 3) and places it on (Line 5) a particular element of the set, the third yellow circular ring. Moreover, he continues on to subtract it and the extra element from the set (Line 7). Thereby, he forms a new composition with which he subsequently transacts instead of the preexistent compositions (Lines 8 and 9). This fragment also illustrates that even when the subjects begin by adding, the dominance of subtraction over addition in transacting with preexistent compositions rapidly manifests itself.

Global decomposing is becoming frequent. Preexistent groupings are destroyed in an undifferentiated fashion (e.g., by sweeping the arms back and forth until all the objects are swept off the table). Decomposition of only a part, that is, two or more elements, from larger preexisting whole compositions is just beginning to be generated:

3. *LH picks up and drops Racers 1 and 2 together (out of a preexisting array of four objects)*   (12JM, page 24)

Decomposing, even global, of only one out of two preexistent sets is still not generated.

The most differentiated decomposing of preexistent compositions generated at this stage takes two related forms. One begins with sequential one-by-one subtraction of elements. Then one element is used as a causal instrument to globally decompose the remaining groupings (each of which compose four objects):

1. *RH picks up Racer 4*
2. *RH throws R4 to the right on the table*
3. *RH picks up VW3, next in line*
4. *RH swats VW3 at all the other objects*
4a. *clears the table of both groups of objects*   (12LL, page 42)

The other form begins with protocorresponding subtraction. Each hand successively subtracts an element. Then both hands simultaneously use the held objects as causal instruments for global protocorresponding decomposition.

One-by-one subtracting from preexisting compositions is beginning to be coordinated with global recomposition. Some, but not all, elements of an articulate preexistent composition, such as a grouped matrix, are successively taken away and heaped together. The result is a new but undifferentiated configuration:

1. *RH takes Blue Circular Ring and places it off to the right*
2. *RH takes Red Circular Ring 2 and places it off with BCR*
3. *RH picks up Red Circular Ring 1 and places it with BCR and RCR2 off to right*
4. *RH takes Blue Block 2 and places it with RCR1, BCR, RCR2, such that they form a heap*   (12AM, page 36)

Decomposing parts, globally and in sequence, from preexisting compositions is also beginning to be coordinated with global recompositions. Some, but not all, parts of an articulate preexistent composition are successively taken away and heaped together. Again, the result is a new but undifferentiated configuration:

1. *RH picks up Green Square Column*
2. *RH flings GSC around*
3. *RH shoves GSC into lap*
4. *RH pushes Red Triangular Rings 1 and 2 into lap*
5. *RH pushes Blue Triangular Rings 1 and 2 into lap*   (12EB, page 25)

Deforming parts of (12JM) and whole (12DO) preexisting compositions remains undifferentiated and global, but they are becoming frequent and repeated:

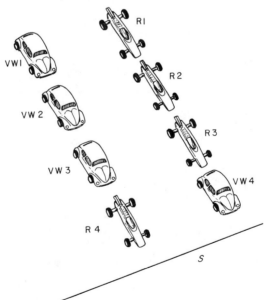

1. *RH picks up VW4*
2. *LH grasps and moves all the VWs on left around together, such that the alignment becomes messed up*

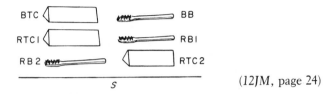

(12JM, page 24)

1. *BH push all the objects toward experimenter with one stroke, smiling*
2. *pulls BH toward self, displacing Red Triangular Column 1*
3. *BH hit down hard on table, displacing more objects*
4. *BH rub side to side on table, displacing objects, laughing*

(12DO, page 32)

Nonarticulate recompositions are produced by global deforming. Both part (12JM) and whole (12DO) nonarticulate recompositions are produced. They begin to be accompanied by symptoms that the subjects are reflecting upon their deforming and recomposing. For instance, 12DO smiles (Line 1) and laughs (Line 4) as he deforms the compositions.

II. Composing by Manipulating All the Objects Composed

Two-object compositions are still the mode (Table 13.2). This is the case in both four- and eight-object conditions (Rows 1 and 4); though one-third of the compositions generated in the eight-object conditions consist of three or more objects. However, even two-object compositions are progressively elaborated. Some are taking on features of conventional relations. In general, this is limited to transactions with relatively familiar objects such as cups and spoons in which, as we have already seen, the subjects begin to stir spoons in cups. Other two-object compositions are becoming coregulated (see Chapter 14, Section III). For instance, two cups are carefully adjusted to each other such that they match spatially, rim-to-rim.

Three and four-object compositions, such as embedding several cups in each other, are becoming more frequent (Table 13.2, Rows 2, 3, 5, and 6). They are generated more than twice as frequently than at age 6 months (Table 3.2). There is little divergence in proportion of three- and four-object compositions as a function of class conditions at age 12 months. They are, however, consistently produced more frequently in the eight-object (Table 13.2, Rows 5 and 6) than in the four-object conditions (Rows 2 and 3). Thus, not only do the eight-object conditions

TABLE 13.2
Spontaneous Phase I: Mean Frequency and Percentage of Compositional Extent Generated by 12-Month-Old Subjects

| | Class conditions | | | | | | | | | |
| | Semicontrol[a] | | Additive | | Multiplicative | | Disjoint | | Total | |
	$\bar{x}$ 1	% 2	$\bar{x}$ 3	% 4	$\bar{x}$ 5	% 6	$\bar{x}$ 7	% 8	$\bar{x}$ 9	% 10
Four-object condition:										
1. Two-object	9.25	85	9.45	80	7.82	86	4.92	80	7.69	83
2. Three-object	1.38	13	1.91	16	1.18	13	0.92	15	1.33	14
3. Four-object	0.25	2	0.45	4	0.09	1	0.33	5	0.29	3
Eight-object condition:										
4. Two-object			7.83	69	11.91	66	10.50	70	10.00	68
5. Three-object			1.92	17	4.45	25	3.10	21	3.12	21
6. Four-object			0.75	7	1.27	7	0.70	5	0.91	6
7. Five-object			0.25	2	0.27	2	0.40	3	0.33	2
8. Six-object			0.25	2	0.18	1	0.20	1	0.21	1
9. Seven-object			0.08	1	0.00	0	0.00	0	0.03	0
10. Eight-object			0.33	3	0.09	1	0.00	0	0.15	1

[a] $N = 8$ in semicontrol, four-object condition.

evoke more frequent composing (Section I), they also elicit more extensive composing than do the four-object conditions.

Five- to eight-object compositions are generated very infrequently (Rows 7–10). Global composing is usually involved when five to eight objects are related to each other:

8.5.   *LH swishes around table*
8.5.   *RH swishes around table*
8.5a. *displaces all the objects*
10.   *puts Red Cylinder 1 in lap*
11.   *shoves Blue Triangular Column 1, Blue Cylinder 1, Blue Cylinder 2, Red Triangular Column 2, Red Cylinder 2 into lap*   (*12EB, page 24*)

Both compositions are labile. The mobile includes all eight objects (Lines 8.5–8.5a). Protocorresponding mapping (swishing) is applied globally without any internal differentiation. It is followed immediately by a stabile which includes six of the eight objects (Lines 10 and 11). The stabile is marked by minor mapping differentiation. One object is placed in the subject's lap, followed by five additional objects which are shoved into the lap.

Articulate composing with five to eight objects is beginning to be produced occasionally:

11.   *RH places Square Column 3 across Cylinder 4 and Square Column 4:*

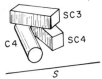

12.   *RH lifts Cylinder 2*
13.   *RH drops C2 on top of SC3*
13a. *C2 knocks SC3 off of C4 and SC4, although one end still rests on SC4, while C2 rolls off toward experimenter:*

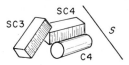

(*Objects on left look like*):

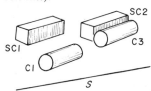

14.   *LH lifts Cylinder 3*
      (*experimenter places C2 a few inches to left to C4*)
15.   *LH touches C3 on top of C4*

16. *LH releases C3 between C4 and C2 such that all are in roughly vertical alignment*
17. *LH lifts Cylinder 1*
18. *LH places C1 between C4 and SC4:*

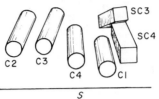

C2   C3   C4   C1

SC3
SC4

S

19. *LH lifts Square Column 2*
20. *LH places SC2 horizontally on C3 and C4*
20a. *SC2 falls down between C2 and C4, with one end resting on C3, vertically:*

C3   C4
C2
SC2

21. *LH places Square Column 1 on top of C4*
21a. *SC1 falls down on table to right of SC2 as LH knocks SC2 off C3 when releasing SC1*
21aa. *SC2 knocks C2 to left and C2 rolls to left*   (12DO, pages 15 and 16)

This eight-object composition includes stabile and mobile parts, combined vertical and horizontal construction, a bridging structure, and placements between objects. At most, these parts are: (*a*) very fleetingly preserved as configurations of internally related elements, (*b*) very roughly disarticulated from each other into different subsets of elements, and (*c*) very loosely coordinated into a composite whole. Yet, the necessary precursory structures marked by differentiation and sequential, but not hierarchic, integration of a set with subsets are generated. Unusual as it still is at this stage, 12DO directly transacts with six of the eight objects making up the composition he has constructed.

The proportion of compositions constructed by direct transactions with two or more objects increases dramatically (Table 13.3). For the first time, direct transaction with only one of the objects composed is less frequent than direct transactions with two or more of the objects composed. This shift is particularly strong in the eight-object conditions. Almost two-thirds of the compositions are constructed by direct transaction with two or more objects. This includes 14% of the compositions which are constructed by direct transaction with three of the objects composed (Table 13.3, Row 4, Column 3).

TABLE 13.3
Spontaneous Phase I: Number of Objects Directly Manipulated by 12-Month-Old Subjects to Produce Compositions in All Class Conditions

| | Number of objects | | | | | | | | |
	1	2	3	4	5	6	7	8	Total
Four-object condition:									
1. Frequency of compositions	167	209	16	3					395
2. % Compositions	42	53	4	1					100
Eight-object condition:									
3. Frequency of compositions	198	265	79	16	8	1	0	2	569
4. % Compositions	35	47	14	3	1	0	0	0	100

Recomposing in the four-object conditions does not increase in overall frequency at age 12 months (Table 13.4, Row 5, Column 3). The rate at which variants are generated does increase in the multiplicative condition, approximating the average for all conditions (Table 13.4, Row 3, Column 3). It remains lowest in the disjoint condition (Table 13.4, Row 4, Column 3), as it is at age 10 months (see Table 10.4).

Recomposing is generated more frequently in some of the eight-object conditions (Table 13.4, Rows 3 and 4). The increase is substantial in the multiplicative and disjoint conditions. The rate is the same in the additive condition (Table 13.4, Row 2). No comparative data are available in the semicontrol condition. This suggests that greater combinativity complexity is elicited by transacting with some eight-object conditions. This complements the already noted increase in frequency and extent of composing in eight- as compared to four-object conditions.

TABLE 13.4
Spontaneous Phase I: Mean Frequency of Composing and Recomposing by 12-Month-Old Subjects

| | Four-object | | | Eight-object | | |
	Thematic 1	Variant 2	% Variant 3	Thematic 4	Variant 5	% Variant 6
1. Semicontrol[a]	5.13	5.75	53			
2. Additive	7.82	4.00	34	7.58	3.83	34
3. Multiplicative	6.09	3.00	33	9.18	9.00	50
4. Disjoint	4.83	1.33	22	9.20	5.70	38
5. All conditions	6.00	3.31	36	8.61	6.12	42

[a] N = 8 in semicontrol, four-object condition.

III. Shift to Stabile Compositions

Compositions are becoming more stable; lability is diminishing. Progressive equilibration of composing is marked by numerous features at this stage. Some have already been considered (i.e., increased frequency, numerical extent, and direct transformational transaction).

The most striking feature is an increase in stabile constructions and a decrease in mobile constructions. Stabiles are now generated as frequently as mobiles. Recall that at age 10 months, 58% of all the compositions are mobiles while only 38% are stabiles (see Table 10.5). Now compositions are split evenly into 47% stabiles and 47% mobiles, with the remainder combinations of mobiles and stabiles. These proportions hold for the four-object conditions (Table 13.5, Rows 4, 8, and 9, Column 10). They are mirrored by the findings for the eight-object conditions (Table 13.6, Rows 4, 8, and 9, Column 10). The replication is exact, with 47% stabiles, 47% mobiles, and the remainder combined mobiles–stabiles. Thus, the two sets of findings corroborate each other and strengthen the hypothesis that composing is becoming equilibrated.

Compare first the distribution of compositional features at ages 10 and 12 months in the four-object conditions (cf. Tables 10.5 and 13.5). At age 12 months there is no longer any effective variance between class conditions in proportion of compositions that are stabiles; the range is from 46 to 48% (Table 13.5, Row 4). The variance ranges from 31 to 48% at age 10 months (Table 10.5, Row 4). The increase in proportion of stabile production from ages 10 to 12 months is general. It increases in all four class conditions. Moreover, the previous developmental lags in generating stabiles in the multiplicative and disjoint conditions have been clearly overcome.

Stabiles continue to be marked primarily by spatial contact. The proportion of contact to proximity to contact–proximity stabiles remains unchanged from what it was at the previous stage (cf. Table 13.5, Rows 1 to 3 and Table 10.5, Rows 1 to 3). The proportion does not vary as a function of class conditions.

While much less frequent than contact stabiles, proximity stabiles are becoming complex and systematic. For instance, they include the construction of two-to-two protocorrespondences:

    26.5.   RH *places Block 1 on right shoulder*
    26.5.   LH *places Block 2 on left shoulder*
     28.   RH *extends B1 to mother*
    29.5.   RH *places B1 to right eye*
    29.5.   LH *places B2 to left eye*   (12DA, page 5)

Two bi-univocal protocorresponding stabiles are generated sequen-

TABLE 13.5
Four-Object Conditions, Spontaneous Phase I: Mean Frequency and Percentage of Compositional Features at Age 12 Months

| | Class conditions | | | | | | | | | |
| | Semicontrol[a] | | Additive | | Multiplicative | | Disjoint | | Total | |
	x̄ 1	% 2	x̄ 3	% 4	x̄ 5	% 6	x̄ 7	% 8	x̄ 9	% 10
1. Contact stabile	4.38	40	4.45	38	3.00	33	2.00	32	3.36	36
2. Proximity stabile	0.88	8	1.00	8	1.18	13	0.67	11	0.93	10
3. Contact–proximity stabile	0.00	0	0.27	2	0.00	0	0.17	3	0.12	1
4. Total stabile	5.25	48	5.73	48	4.18	46	2.83	46	4.40	47
5. Contact mobile	4.25	39	4.73	40	4.00	44	1.83	30	3.62	39
6. Proximity mobile	1.00	9	0.36	3	0.27	3	0.33	5	0.45	5
7. Contact–proximity mobile	0.13	1	0.18	2	0.45	5	0.33	5	0.29	3
8. Total mobile	5.38	49	5.27	45	4.73	52	2.50	41	4.36	47
9. Mobile–stabile	0.25	2	0.82	7	0.18	2	0.83	14	0.55	6
10. Causal	3.63	33	4.09	35	3.00	33	2.00	32	3.12	34
11. Noncausal	7.25	67	7.73	65	6.09	67	4.17	68	6.19	66
12. Horizontal[b]	3.75	38	7.91	72	3.91	64	3.83	74	4.90	63
13. Vertical[b]	5.88	59	2.27	21	2.00	33	1.25	24	2.60	33
14. Horizontal–vertical[b]	0.25	3	0.82	7	0.18	3	0.08	2	0.33	4

[a] N = 8 in the semicontrol condition.
[b] Compositions whose spatial dimensions are ambiguous are not scored. Consequently, the dimensional means summate to less than the total compositional means.

TABLE 13.6
Eight-Object Conditions, Spontaneous Phase I: Mean Frequency and Percentage of Compositional Features at Age 12 Months

	Class Conditions							
	Additive		Multiplicative		Disjoint		Total	
	$\bar{x}$ 1	% 2	$\bar{x}$ 3	% 4	$\bar{x}$ 5	% 6	$\bar{x}$ 7	% 8
1. Contact stabile	3.58	31	5.73	32	5.20	35	4.79	33
2. Proximity stabile	1.42	12	2.00	11	2.20	15	1.85	13
3. Contact–proximity stabile	0.08	1	0.09	1	0.90	6	0.33	2
4. Total stabile	5.08	45	7.82	43	8.30	56	6.97	47
5. Contact mobile	3.67	32	8.00	44	4.80	32	5.45	37
6. Proximity mobile	1.25	11	0.91	5	0.80	5	1.00	7
7. Contact–proximity mobile	0.58	5	0.55	3	0.40	3	0.52	3
8. Total mobile	5.50	48	9.45	52	6.00	40	6.97	47
9. Mobile–stabile	0.83	7	0.91	5	0.60	4	0.79	5
10. Causal	3.42	30	4.36	24	3.40	23	3.73	25
11. Noncausal	8.00	70	13.82	76	11.50	77	11.00	75
12. Horizontal[a]	7.50	77	9.45	65	6.00	51	7.70	64
13. Vertical[a]	1.17	12	3.73	26	3.60	31	2.76	23
14. Horizontal–vertical[a]	1.08	11	1.36	9	2.10	18	1.48	12

[a] Compositions whose spatial dimensions are ambiguous are not scored. Consequently, the dimensional means summate to less than the total compositional means.

tially, with a minor interpolation (Line 28). Both stabiles include belonging relations, two blocks to two shoulders followed by two blocks to two eyes. Both stabiles are featured by parallel proximity, though the spatial distance is obviously minimized when the cubes are placed to the eyes. Thus, proximity stabiles are not only becoming more complex, but some are analogically related to each other (i.e., placement to two shoulders followed by placement to two eyes).

Co-univocal protocorresponding proximity is beginning to be used to construct small two-dimensional compositions:

34.5.   RH *picks up Yellow Spoon 1 and leaning forward drops–places it on the table behind Yellow Cross Ring 2*

34.5.   LH *picks up Yellow Spoon 2 and drops–places it to the left of YCR2*
(12JM, page 8)

The proximal placement of the spoons at two vertices so as to surround the ring forms a symmetrical design. The result is inclusion of the yellow cross ring into a three-object set with two complementary elements, yellow spoons.

Protocorresponding proximity stabiles are extended to include as many as four identical elements.

9.5.   RH *places VW2 in front of VW4 (which is already near to and on the right of VW3)*

9.5.   LH *places VW1 in front of VW3*   (12JM, page 18)

Thus, the VWs form four corners of a squarelike arrangenent.

Proximity stabiles are not only being extended in both time and in number of elements composed but they are also beginning to be integrated with each other:

5.   LH *picks up Doll 1*
6.   *looks at D1 in LH*
7.   LH *places D1 next to and to the left of Doll 2*
8.   RH *picks up Doll 3*
9.   RH *places it below and to the right of Doll 4, which is all the way on the right of the table*
10.   LH *picks up leftmost D1*
11.   LH *places D1 to right of D2*
12.   RH *brings D3 over to the two on the left, D1 and D2, and places D3 next to them*
12a.   *D3 falls on side*
13.   RH *stands up D3*
14.   RH *moves D1 slightly, so D1, D2, and D3 form a loose semicircle, with all dolls upright*
15.   RH *brings D4 over*
15a.   *in doing so, knocks over D3*
16.   RH *places D4*

16a. D4 *falls on its side*
17. RH *picks up D4*   (*12AM*, page 32)

Initially, *12AM* forms two separate proximity stabiles (Lines 5–7 and 8–9). Each composition consists of two identical elements, dolls. The compositions are separate from each other since they are constructed at opposite ends of the table and the other objects. Then the subject integrates the two stabiles she has just constructed by one-by-one integration of two elements from one proximity stabile into the other proximity stabile (Lines 10–17). Thus, the subject ends up constructing a third, integrated proximity stabile composing four identical elements. Moreover, she makes some partially successful coregulative adjustments to establish protocorresponding spatial relations between the elements by standing them up when they fall over.

As already noted, the frequency of stabiles featured by both contact and proximity remains low (Table 13.5, Row 3). Nevertheless, they too are becoming more complex and extended, for example, the configuration constructed by *12DO* (p. 15 and 16, Lines 11–21aa) reported on pages 325–326. Contact–proximity stabiles include constructing two-dimensional structures in the horizontal and the vertical. Thus, bridging structures are becoming regular features of compositions:

7. LH *simultaneously places (a) Spoon 1 on top of and across Spoons 2 and 3, and (b) VW1 in front of and near the three spoons* (*12DO*, page 55)

Mobiles, like stabiles generated in the four-object conditions, continue to be featured by spatial contact between the elements composed (Table 13.5, Row 5). The proportion of proximity mobiles does not change from ages 10 to 12 months (cf. Table 13.5, Row 6 and Table 10.5, Row 6). The proportion of contact to proximity mobiles is relatively constant across class conditions.

While no more frequent, proximity mobiles increasingly involve protocorrespondence operations. For instance, each hand may simultaneously drop objects in parallel and near each other onto the table. A more complex, and difficult to score, version beginning to be generated at this stage occurs when the subjects simultaneously drop objects in parallel to the floor, but to the right and the left of themselves. The scoring difficulty arises over the question of whether the objects are still compositionally related to each other by spatial correspondence or whether they are related only by their parallel, common fate (Wertheimer, 1938). A more complex, but no more difficult to score, version involves protocorresponding compositions which are targeted or include a social belonging dimension (e.g., parallel throwing of two objects toward the experimenter.)

The frequency of mobiles with both contact and proximity features is small but increasing (cf. Table 10.5 and Table 13.5, Row 7). They are typified by multiplicative inclusion of one element in two sets:

27.   RH *rolls Cylinder 2 against Cylinder 1*
27a.   *C1 rolls against Rectangular Ring 1:*

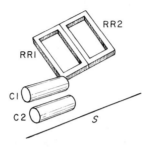

(12DO, page 7)

The mobile begins with contact between Cylinders 1 and 2, and proximity between Cylinder 1 and Rectangular Ring 1 (Line 27). It ends with contact between Cylinder 1 and Rectangular Ring 1, and proximity between Cylinders 1 and 2 (Line 27a). The construction of these successive reciprocal feature relations results in multiplicative inclusion of Cylinder 1. First it is included in a two-object set with another identical cylinder. Immediately following, it is included in a three-object set with two different rectangular ring elements. Multiplicative inclusion in identity and different classes typifies contact–proximity compositions at this stage.

Contact–proximity mobiles are also beginning to be based upon protocorresponding operations:

12.5.   RH *bangs Green Rectangular Ring on Green Cross Ring*
12.5.   LH *bangs Yellow Cross Ring on GCR*   (12LZ, page 11)

The instrumental objects are proximal to and disjoint with each other. At the same time, they are both contacted with and complementary to the same object. Such co-univocal protocorrespondence compositions, then, open the possibility for relating disjoint to complementary class relations.

Only one-third of the compositions are marked by causality at age 12 months (Table 13.5, Rows 10 and 11); while almost one-half are marked by causality at age 10 months (Table 10.5, Rows 10 and 12). The ratio of causal to noncausal compositions no longer varies as a function of class conditions.

All causal compositions are mobiles. The proportion of mobiles marked by causality decreases a bit from what it was at age 10 months (Chapter 10, Section III). Seventy-two percent of all mobiles are causal and 86% of contact mobiles are causal. Mobiles, then, continue to be predominantly causal. The decrease in compositional causality is not as much due to transformations in the structure of mobiles as it is to the overall developmental shift from generating mostly mobiles to producing stabiles as frequently as mobiles.

The overall proportion of compositions constructed in horizontal, vertical, and combined spatial dimensions does not change from age 10 to age 12 months. Almost two-thirds are constructed in the horizontal, one-third in the vertical, and the remainder in combined horizontal–vertical dimensions (Table 13.5, Rows 12–14, Column 10). With one exception, these findings do not vary with class condition. The exception is that the ratio of horizontal to vertical constructions is almost exactly the reverse in the semicontrol condition (Rows 12 and 13, Column 2). Most compositions are constructed in the vertical dimension in the semicontrol condition.

Compositions, then, are still usually single dimensional structures. Most are still horizontal rather than vertical. Vertical forms are expanding, however. They begin to include stacks of as many as four cups embedded in each other. They also include inverse stacking arrangements in which cups are used as upside down tops on each other.

We are now in a position to compare the distribution of compositional features in the four- with the eight-object conditions. Most remarkable is the overall similarities. Already noted is the parallel overall proportion of stabiles to mobiles to combined mobiles–stabiles. The breakdown of these forms of compositions in the eight-object conditions into those marked by contact, proximity and combined features also mirrors that found in the four-object conditions (Tables 13.5 and 13.6, Rows 1–3 and 5–7). They too do not vary as a function of class conditions.

There is a general decrease in causal compositions and a complementary increase in noncausal compositions in the eight-object conditions. While the ratio of causal to noncausal compositions is one-to-two in the four-object conditions, it is one-to-three in the eight-object conditions (Tables 13.5 and 13.6, Rows 10 and 11). The shift is most pronounced in the multiplicative and disjoint conditions. The consequence is a decrease in the proportion of mobiles marked by causality in the eight-object conditions. Only a bare majority (53%) of all mobiles are still causal, and only 68% of contact mobiles are causal. The shift at this stage, then, is to the construction of mobiles marked by noncausal compositional features.

There is no difference in the overall frequency with which compositions are constructed in the horizontal dimension (Tables 13.5 and 13.6, Row 12). The main difference is in the proportion of vertical to combined horizontal–vertical constructions. The frequency of vertical compositions decreases by one-third while that of horizontal–vertical compositions increases threefold (Tables 13.5 and 13.6, Rows 13 and 14). This increase in horizontal–vertical productions significantly enhances the possibilities for constructing multiplicative proto-operations, both in frequency and in complexity.

14

Partial Extension of Second-Order Discrete Combinativity

Consecutive compositions continue to predominate (Table 14.1). They comprise 70% and 78% of the compositions generated in the four- and eight-object conditions, respectively (Rows 2 and 6). Partially overlapping and simultaneous compositions in the four-object conditions increase a bit from age 10 to age 12 months. They now comprise 5% of the compositions (Rows 3 and 4) and are generated by six subjects. The most striking finding, in this regard, is that 10% of the compositions generated in the eight-object conditions comprise two sets constructed in temporal overlap or simultaneity (Rows 7 and 8). They are generated by six subjects. Thus, binary sets are generated almost as frequently as isolate compositions in the eight-object conditions (Row 5). Binary composing is beginning to be a significant factor in infants' cognitive development.

Coupled with the equilibration of individual compositions discussed in Chapter 13, constructing two contemporaneous sets by binary composing opens the way for major developmental transformations in infants' protoinferential structures. Two crucial conditions for constructing protoinferential relations between independent but binary sets are self-generated by infants; although it should not be overlooked that the binary sets are limited to very small numbers of elements. The first condition is the construction of constant given elements comprising the sets. The second is the construction of constant given sets.

TABLE 14.1

Spontaneous Phase I: Temporal Relations between Compositions Generated by 12-Month-Old Subjects

| | Class conditions | | | | | | | | | |
| | Semicontrol[a] | | Additive | | Multiplicative | | Disjoint | | Total | |
	$\bar{x}$ 1	% 2	$\bar{x}$ 3	% 4	$\bar{x}$ 5	% 6	$\bar{x}$ 7	% 8	$\bar{x}$ 9	% 10
Four-object condition:										
1. Isolate	1.88	17	2.64	22	3.09	34	1.58	26	2.31	25
2. Consecutive	9.00	83	8.45	72	5.18	57	4.42	72	6.55	70
3. Partially overlapping	0.00	0	0.18	2	0.64	7	0.17	3	0.26	3
4. Simultaneous	0.00	0	0.55	5	0.18	2	0.00	0	0.19	2
Eight-object condition:										
5. Isolate			1.83	16	1.73	10	1.60	11	1.73	12
6. Consecutive			9.08	80	13.45	74	12.30	83	11.52	78
7. Partially overlapping			0.33	3	2.09	12	0.60	4	1.00	7
8. Simultaneous			0.17	1	0.91	5	0.40	3	0.48	3

[a] N = 8 in semicontrol, four-object condition.

Durable constructions provide the stable constituents necessary for considering and generating more advanced, second-order proto-operational relations (*a*) between elements (parts) and sets (wholes) and (*b*) between binary sets (two wholes). Some of the consequent transformations in proto-operations upon given binary sets develop at this stage. They will be considered in subsequent sections of this chapter, along with the progress in proto-operations on unary sets. Most of the consequent proto-operational progress will not be manifest until the next stages when there is a dramatic increase in binary composing, and will therefore be discussed in Volume II.

I. Transition to Exchange Proto-operations upon Three-Element Sets

Exchange operations are still limited to consecutive recompositions of single sets. The main development is their application to three-element sets, although most still apply to two-element sets. Rudimentary coordination of exchange proto-operations applied to three-element sets is just beginning to be generated by individual infants.

Protoreplacements, like the other exchange proto-operations, are still applied to single sets only, but increased productivity of three or more object compositions provides the necessary condition for extending protoreplacement beyond two-object sets. Five subjects apply protoreplacement to three-object sets.

Sometimes replacement rectifies inadvertent subtraction of an object from a three-element set:

101. *RH extends Brush, Spoon and Car toward mother, but does not give them to her*
102. *RH withdraws B, S, and C*
102a. *C drops out of RH to floor*
103. *watches mother retrieve C as RH holds B and S* *(mother puts C back on the table)*
104. *looks at C as RH holds B and S*
105. *RH picks up C, such that RH holds B, S, and C*   (12RD, page 5)

Protoreplacement reconstitutes this three-object composition which 12RD preserves for an extended duration, that is, for about 2 minutes and over 70 transactions. These transactions include many other proto-inferential relations, such as protocorrespondence with another set. These are only possible when sets are preserved as constant givens. We will examine some of them later on.

This exchange involves only one protoreplacement. Others are marked by regulated protoreplacements:

24. *RH places Blue Doll 2 on table in back of Red Rectangular Ring 2*
25. *RH places Blue Doll 1 upright inside RRR2 such that it is partially on top of the ring's rim and slightly tilted*
26. *RH thumb pushes BD1 flat and out of RRR2*
27. *RH picks up BD1*
28. *RH puts BD1 to his mouth, mouthing the bottom part*
29. *looks at mother as mouths BD1*
30. *RH holds BD1 flat on the table in front of and touching RRR2*
31. *RH pushes BD1 towards RRR2*
31a. *RRR2 moves toward experimenter, slightly*   (12DO, page 49)

66. *RH drops Spoon 4 such that it hits Car 2 and comes to rest about 3 inches to right of and in front of C2*
67. *RH grasps at S4*
67a. *S4 spins around 180° on table*
68. *RH lifts S4*
69. *RH places S4 in same place near C2*
70–71. *repeat of Nos. 68 and 69*
72. *LH raises Spoon 1 about 1 inch above table, as looks at Car 4*
73. *LH transfers S1 to RH*
74. *RH drops S1 behind and to right of C2 which is behind S4*
75. *RH raises C2*
76. *RH drops C2 in about same place*
77. *RH lifts and drops C2 about 4 inches to right of S1 which is behind S4*
                                         (12JE, pages 61 and 62)

While *12DO* only replaces one object, Blue Doll 1, once, he adjusts his replacement (Lines 30 and 31). Subject *12JE*'s replacements are more extensive. First she replaces one object, Spoon 4, twice in a two-object composition (Lines 69–71). She adds another object, Spoon 1, to form a three-object variant composition (Line 74). Then she replaces one object, Car 2, twice in the three-object composition (Lines 76 and 77). Thus, *12JE* also coordinates (*a*) equivalence of two- and of three-object sets by protoreplacement with (*b*) iteration of ⟨two-, three-⟩ object sets by protoaddition. Progress in coordinating extensive equivalence with ordered nonequivalence will be analyzed further in Section III.

Protosubstitution is common and well-regulated when applied to simple two-object compositions in which one object takes the place of another within a single set:

80. *RH places Yellow Clover Ring 1 on Yellow Cross Ring 1 and grasps YCrR1 under YClR1*
81. *RH picks up YClR1/YCrR1*
82. *RH flips and releases YCrR1 such that it flies onto subject's lap and then falls to floor*

83. *RH places YClRl on Green Cross Ring 1 and grasps GCrRl under YClRl*
84. *RH picks up YClR1/GCrR1*   (12DO, page 37)

Protosubstitution is also becoming more complex. Its application is extended by six subjects to three-object compositions. Four of these subjects also apply protoreplacement to three-object sets. Protosubstitution may involve two- as well as one-object exchanges. The composing sequences include numerous, flexible reorganizations of a single three-object set. Shortly before generating the above simple protosubstitution 12DO produced the more advanced form:

54. *RH places Yellow Clover Ring 1 on Green Cross Ring 1 which is touching Yellow Cross Ring 1*
55. *RH picks up YClR1/GCrR1*
56. *RH moves YClR1/GCrR1 close to mouth, but no insertion*
57. *RH places and holds YClR1/GCrR1 on top of Green Clover Ring 1*
58. *RH picks up YClR1/GCrR1/GClR1*
59. *RH touches YClR1/GCrR1/GClR1 to mouth, but no insertion*
60. *RH drops GClR1 which falls to lap, as RH moves YClR1/GCrR1 away from mouth*
    (experimenter slides all the No. 2 objects closer to subject, so):

GClR2   YClR2   YCrRl   YCrR2   GCrR2

                              s

61. *RH places YClR1/GCrR1 on top of YCrR1*
62. *RH releases GCrR1 on top of YCrR1 and lifts YClR1*
    (mother replaces GClR1 to right of YCrR1)
63. *RH transfers YClR1 to LH*
64. *LH transfers YClR1 back to RH*
65. *RH places and holds YClR1 on top of GCrR1 previously placed on YCrR1*
66. *RH grasps YClR1/GCrR1/YCrR1*
67. *RH picks up YClR1/GCrR1, leaving YCrR1 on table*
68. *RH holds YClR1/GCrR1 in front of face, briefly*
69. *RH places YClR1/GCrR1 on YCrR1, such that YClR1 sticks up inside of GCrR1*   (12DO, pages 36 and 37)

This sequence produces equivalences by flexibly combining substitution with replacement proto-operations

$$(YClR1 > GCrR1 \cdot YCrR1) \approx (YClR1 \cdot GCrR1 > GClR1)$$
$$\approx (YClR1 \cdot GCrR1 > YCrR1) \sim (YClR1 > GCrR1 \cdot YCrR1)$$
$$\sim (YClR1 \cdot GCrR1 > YCrR1) \qquad (14.1)$$

From left to right, the sets in Eq. (14.1) represent the compositions found in Lines 54, 57, 61, 65, and 69, respectively. The first two equivalences are the results of actively displacing two objects and substituting one object. First, Green Clover Ring 1 is substituted for Yellow Cross Ring 1. In turn, Yellow Cross Ring 1 is substituted for Green Clover Ring 1. The two exchanges invert each other, thereby constructing an identity set (YC1R1, GCrR1, YCrR1), as well as producing equivalence by substitution.

The last two equivalences are produced by protoreplacements. One involves actively displacing only one object (Line 65), and the other involves actively displacing two objects (Line 69). While coordinated exchange proto-operations will be considered at the end of this section, it should be noted here that both protosubstitutions and protoreplacements are extended to the flexible interchange of as many as two elements in three-object sets. The equivalences generated are limited to consecutive compositions. No equivalences are constructed by exchanging elements between binary sets, that is, two sets composed simultaneously or preserved for at least partially overlapping times.

In the above example two objects are actively manipulated to construct protosubstitution between consecutive three-object sets. In other instances only one object is actively displaced, yet only one object is substituted:

28.5. *LH pushes over Spoon 1 such that it bridges Cars 1 and 3*
30.5. *LH raises and holds S1 upright*
  32. *LH drops S1 such that it bridges Cars 1 and 2*   (12JE, page 59)

Sequential protosubstitution of one element is also used to construct equivalence:

  12. *RH drops Yellow Circular Ring 2 on table as LH continues to push*
       Yellow Circular Rings 1 and 3 into Green Triangular Column 2
 12a. *GTC2 moves forward*
 13.3. *RH picks up YCR2 and rests one edge on table, as LH rests edges of YCR1*
       and 3 on table
 13.7. *RH touches YCR2 to YCR3 of YCR3 and 1 held by LH*
 15.3. *LH transfers YCR3 to RH as RH holds YCR2 such that YCR2 and 3 are*
       held flat and aligned by RH
 15.7. *RH raises YCR3 and 2 off of table, as LH raises YCR1 off table*
  17. *LH drops YCR1 on table*
  18. *RH places and holds edges of YCR2 and 3 on table*
  19. *RH transfers YCR2 and 3 to BH*
  20. *BH place and hold YCR2 and 3 flat and aligned against GTC2*
 20a. *GTC2 is displaced forward, slightly*
  21. *BH transfer YCR2 and 3 to RH*

22.3. *RH picks up YCR2 and 3 off table, as LH picks up YCR1 off table*
22.7. *RH holds YCR2 and 3 and LH holds YCR1 such that YCR3 and 1 touch*
       together
22.7a. *YCR2 and 3 become unaligned but still flat together in RH*
                                              (*12KH*, pages 62 and 63)

Different singular elements are also exchanged sequentially (Lines 13.7, 20, and 22.7) to form an equivalence structure between three-object sets

$$(YCR1 \cdot YCR3 > GTC2) \approx (YCR2 \gtreqless YCR3 \cdot YCR1)$$
$$\approx (YCR2 \cdot YCR3 > GTC2) \approx (YCR2 \cdot YCR3 \gtreqless YCR1) \quad (14.2)$$

The equivalence structure includes an inverse proto-operation which produces identity between the second and fourth sets. They are constructed by reciprocal ternary transactions; all three objects are actively manipulated in order to compose them.

Only one infant protosubstituted two objects in three-element sets:

12. *RH picks up Orange Spoon 2, Orange Spoon 1, and VW2*
13. *RH drops OS2, OS1, and VW2 to table*
14. *RH picks up OS2, Orange Spoon 3, and Orange Spoon 4*
15. *RH drops OS2, OS3, and OS4 to table*   (*12DO*, page55)

Subject 12DO neither inverts his two-element protosubstitution nor generates any other two-element protosubstitutions. It therefore seems most likely that equivalence by two-element protosubstitution will not be actualized until subsequent stages.

Protosubstitution transitional to constructing equivalence between two contemporaneous sets of two elements continues to be generated, as they are at the previous stage (see Chapter 10, Section V). Yet, they are generated by only three subjects, and they never issue in actual exchange of elements between binary sets. Rather, they are always followed by composing one element from each set into a new two-object set.

Protocommutativity between consecutive two-object recompositions is enhanced by progressive equilibrium of combinativity structures; as manifest, for example, by extensive sequences of reciprocal recompositions:

38. *RH bangs Circular Ring 3 on Circular Ring 2*
39. *RH releases CR3*
40. *RH picks up CR2*
41. *RH bangs CR2 on CR3*
42. *RH releases CR2*
43. *RH bangs on CR2 and CR3*
44. *RH picks up CR3*
45. *RH bangs CR3 on CR2*

46. RH *releases* CR3
47. RH *picks up* CR2
48. RH *bangs CR2 on* CR3   (12LZ, page 56)

The sequence of successive recompositions form the protocommutative structure

$$\langle CR3 > CR2 \rangle \ \rightsquigarrow \langle CR2 > CR3 \rangle \ \rightsquigarrow \langle CR2 \cdot CR3 \rangle$$
$$\rightsquigarrow \langle CR3 > CR2 \rangle \ \rightsquigarrow \langle CR2 > CR3 \rangle \quad (14.3)$$

The elements are still not arbitrary nor specified, nor are they classes or sets; they remain collections of individual objects. The relations do not consist of logical constants. Rather, they remain transformational relations of hitting one object against another ($>$) or hitting both objects simultaneously ($\cdot$).

These transformations begin to include both protocommutativity of: (*a*) reciprocal relations between $\langle CR3 > CR2 \rangle$ and $\langle CR2 > CR3 \rangle$; and (*b*) symmetrical and asymmetrical relations (i.e., $\langle CR2 \cdot CR3 \rangle$ with $\langle CR2 > CR3 \rangle$ which precedes it and with $\langle CR3 > CR2 \rangle$ which follows it). After the subject constructs all the asymmetrical and symmetrical relations $\langle CR3 > CR2 \rangle \rightsquigarrow \langle CR2 > CR3 \rangle \rightsquigarrow \langle CR2 \cdot CR3 \rangle$ in sequence, she inverts all the relations to reconstruct identity sets $\langle CR3 > CR2 \rangle \rightsquigarrow \langle CR2 > CR3 \rangle$. Thus, the structures of protoreversible equivalence ($\leftrightsquigarrow$) both between reciprocal, asymmetrical and symmetrical relations

$$\langle CR3 > CR2 \rangle \text{ and } \langle CR2 > CR3 \rangle \leftrightsquigarrow \langle CR2 \cdot CR3 \rangle \quad (14.4)$$

and between identity structures

$$\langle CR3 > CR2 \rangle \text{ and } \langle CR2 > CR3 \rangle$$
$$\leftrightsquigarrow \langle CR3 > CR2 \rangle \text{ and } \langle CR2 > CR3 \rangle \quad (14.5)$$

are constructed for two-object sets at this stage. Note that Eq. (14.5) includes the reproductive feature required to meet the formal criteria of Eq. (10.5) spelled out on page 245.

Protocommutative equivalence between three-element compositions is generated by five infants. Three of these subjects also generate protoreplacement with three-element sets. Three of these five subjects also generate protosubstitution with three-element sets. Only two subjects apply all three exchange proto-operations to three-element sets.

The most advanced protocommutativity applied to three-object sets is generated by 12LZ. She does this just before constructing protocommutativity with a two-object set (presented beginning on page 341):

19. LH *transfers Circular Ring 3 to RH which is already holding Circular Rings 1 and 2, such that RH holds CR1, CR2, and* CR3
20. RH *transfers CR1, CR2, and CR3 to* LH

21. *LH transfers CR1, CR2, and CR3 to BH*
22. *BH transfer CR1, CR2, and CR3 to RH*
23. *RH drops CR1, CR2, and CR3 to table*
24. *LH picks up CR1*
25. *BH push CR1, CR2, and CR3 together on table*
26. *BH pick up CR1, CR2, and CR3, holding them in air*
27. *looks at experimenter, as BH hold CR1, CR2, CR3*
28. *BH drop CR1 to table as RH holds CR2 and LH holds CR3*
29. *RH releases CR2 on table as LH places and holds CR3 on table*
30. *LH picks up CR1*
31. *RH picks up and transfers CR2 to LH, such that LH holds CR1 and CR2*
32. *RH picks up CR3*
33. *LH transfers CR1 and CR2 to RH, such that RH holds CR1, CR2, and CR3*
34. *LH touches Block 1*
35. *RH drops CR1, CR2, and CR3 to floor, as watches them fall to floor*
    (12LZ, pages 55 and 56)

This is the most extensive protocommutative structure generated at this stage. Numerous reorderings of the three-object set are generated by actively manipulating all the objects. Yet, they do not include articulate, repeated inverse transformations resulting in identity sets. This is typical at this stage. Articulate, repeated protoreversible commutativity is applied to two-object sets only, not three-object sets. Protoreversible commutativity is applied only once to three-object sets in any given series; it is never applied consecutively:

37. *RH places Green Cross Ring 1 on Yellow Cross Ring 1*
38. *LH lifts and places Yellow Clover Ring 1 hard, on top of GCrR1, forming YClR1/GCrR1/YCrR1 stack*
39. *LH lifts YClR1/GCrR1, stacked*
39a. *YCrR1 displaces slightly*
40. *LH transfers YClR1/GCrR1 to RH*
41. *RH places YClR1 and GCrR1, not stacked, on top of YCrR1*
42. *RH lifts YClR1; GCrR1 remains partially overlapping YCrR1*
43.5. *RH taps YClR1 on top of GCrR1, and then holds it there*
43.5. *LH grasps GClR1 and YCrR1*
45.5. *LH lifts GCrR1*
45.5. *RH lifts YClR1 and YCrR1*
47. *LH transfers GCrR1 to RH such that it is holding GCrR1, YClR1, and YCrR1*
    (12DO, pages 35 and 36)

The sequence involves four compositions: (*a*) (Lines 37 and 38) stacking three objects on top of each other $\langle$YClR1 > GCR1 > YCrR1$\rangle$, (*b*) (Lines 39–41) taking off the top two objects and then simultaneously placing them unstacked such that they each partially overlap the bottom one $\langle$YClR1 · GCrR1 > YCrR1$\rangle$, (*c*) (Lines 42–43.5) rearranging the objects such that the original stacking order $\langle\text{YC1R1} > \text{GCrR1} > \text{YCrR1}\rangle$ is reconstructed even though the stack is no longer well aligned, and (d) (Lines 45.5–47) separating out the middle object and then bringing it together with the other two into alignment in one hand $\langle\text{YC1R1} \cdot \text{YCrR1} \geqslant \text{GCrR1}\rangle$. This sequence of flexible recompositions forms the three-element protocommutative equivalence structure

$$\langle\text{YC1R1} > \text{GCrR1} > \text{YCrR1}\rangle \rightsquigarrow \langle\text{YC1R1} \cdot \text{GCrR1} > \text{YCrR1}\rangle$$
$$\rightsquigarrow \langle\text{YC1R1} > \text{GCrR1} > \text{YCrR1}\rangle \rightsquigarrow \langle\text{YC1R1} \cdot \text{YCrR1} \geqslant \text{GCrR1}\rangle$$
$$(14.6)$$

The first two reorderings ($\rightsquigarrow$) are unidirectional inverses of each other. Together, they produce a protoreversible relation ($\leftrightsquigarrow$) between the first and the third compositions, resulting in an identity set.

Sequential coordination between exchange operations continues to be applied to two-object sets, but the frequency remains substantially the same as at age 10 months. Rare instances of sequentially coordinate exchange operations applied to three-object sets are just beginning to be generated. As always four coordinations are possible, namely, protoreplacement with protosubstitution, protoreplacement with protocommutativity, protosubstitution with protocommutativity, and protoreplacement with protosubstiution with protocommutativity. Each of these four coordinations is generated by one infant only; moreover, they are all different infants.

Coordinate exchange proto-operations applied to three-object sets, then, barely begin to be structured at this stage. We have already observed an instance of coordinating two exchange operations, protoreplacement with protosubstitution, applied to three-object sets Eq. (14.1) on page 339. The others are of the same limited order. They never exceed minimal coordination. For instance, Eq. (14.1) coordinates protosubstitution followed by protoreplacement. This is the minimum required to form sequential coordination. To exceed it the infant would have had to continue on by reverting to protosubstitution.

II. Initial Protocorrespondences between Two Very Small Sets

Abstracting out compositional from mapping protocorrespondences remains pragmatic at this stage; yet, it clearly progresses. It is generated more frequently than at age 10 months, and it takes four distinct forms. The first and second consist of temporal detachment. The protocorresponding processes are separated in time from their protocorresponding products. The third and fourth involve material disarticulation. Constructive processes which do not protocorrespond to each other produce protocorresponding compositions.

Temporal detachment is enhanced by the small but increased production of four-object compositions made up of two distinct parts. Production of four-object compositions makes it easier to construct parts successively, yet preserve them simultaneously. The successive in-process transactions as well as their ultimate products, coordinate wholes with differentiated yet simultaneous part compositions, may protocorrespond to each other. Still, the consequence is temporal separation of the mapping protocorrespondences, which are successive, from the compositional protocorrespondences, which are simultaneous. The results are two-to-two correlations between distinct parts of a whole set, where the parts are preserved as constant givens beyond their constructive processes:

2. *RH puts Yellow Spoon in Yellow Cup, handle end first*
3. *RH picks up Red Spoon and puts it in Red Cup, cup end first*
(12AM, page 8)

Within compositional protocorrespondences between subsets do not vary as a function of object condition, as is apparent from three constructions by 12LZ which involved realistic, Euclidean, and topological objects:

37.5. *RH places Blue Brush 1 next to Red Brush 1 and uses BB1 to push RB1 toward experimenter*
37.5. *LH places Blue Brush 2 next to Red Brush 2 and uses BB2 to push RB2 toward experimenter*   (12LZ, page 20)

21.5. *LH places Yellow Cross Ring 4 flat on top of Yellow Cross Ring 1*
21.5. *RH puts Green Cross Ring flat on top of Yellow Cross Ring 2*
23. *putting fingers through the centers of these four rings, LH pushes YCR1/YCR4 and RH pushes GCR/YCR2 back and forth across the table between self and experimenter*   (12LZ, page 14)

50.5. *RH picks up Square Column 2 and drops it on Cylinder 2*
50.5. *LH picks up Square Column 1 and drops it on Cylinder 1* (12LZ, page 50)

Two articulate parts of whole compositions are generated simultaneously. The parts correspond bi-univocally to each other. Equivalences are between simultaneous subsets, not successive sets. The protocorrespondences are discrete. They produce precise quantitative equivalences between two subsets. Subsets never include more than two elements at this stage.

Protocorrespondences between subsets of a larger set remain somewhat labile. The mappings tend to be mobile and causal. The compositions are dominated by contact rather than proximal relations. Moreover, they are not preserved much beyond the duration of construction.

The constructive life-span of within-composition protocorrespondences between subsets does become quite extensive in some productions:

> 7.5. *LH holds and pushes Blue Circular Ring 1 and Yellow Circular Ring 1 pushing them forward toward experimenter, back toward self, and forward toward experimenter*
>
> 7.5. *RH covers and pushes Blue Circular Ring 2 and Yellow Hexagonal Column 2 forward toward experimenter, back toward self, and forward toward experimenter*
> *(experimenter pushes Yellow Hexagonal Column 1 back and forth)*
>
> 9. *BH continue pushing their sets back and forth, simultaneously*
>
>   (12LL, page 11)

The constructive duration may have been expanded by the experimenter's cooperative reproduction. The resultant protocorrespondence combines social with subset equivalences for the first time. However, it does not signal any basic change in the causes of protocorrespondences, whether cooperative or not. Subjects remain selective and determinative of their cooperative protocorresponding:

> 24. *RH pushes Cylinder 1 and LH pushes Square Column 2 side-to-center (out and in) on table, fast, sometimes hitting them together when pushing them toward center; laughing at experimenter*
> *(experimenter imitates with two Cylinders, banging them together)*
>
> 25. *stops, watches experimenter, while RH raises and holds C1 and LH raises and holds SC2*
>
> 26. *RH drops C1 to table*
>
> 27. *RH takes SC2 from LH*
>
> 28. *RH drops SC2 to table*   (12DO, page 16)

The experimenter's reproduction results in stopping the subject's simultaneous protocorrespondence. After watching the experimenter, 12DO executes a totally different successive protocorrespondence. Moreover, in doing so he gets rid of the objects.

Most temporal detachment results from the increased production of binary sets of two objects which are preserved contemporaneously. More than half the infants (seven subjects) construct two-to-two correlations between wholes which are preserved beyond their constructive processes as constant givens. Consequently, the compositional protocorrespondences are separated temporally from the mapping protocorrespondences.

Binary sets are constructed at some distance from each other. Some are generated consecutively:

25. *RH lifts and drops Spoon 2 behind and almost touching Spoon 4*
26. *as looks at S2/S4, LH drops Spoon 1 partially on Car 1*   (12JE, page 59)

Others are generated in partial temporal overlap:

8. *RH drops Blue Doll 1 in Red Rectangular Ring 1 such that BD1 lies flat in RRR1*
9.5. *RH lifts BD1*
9.5. *LH places and holds Blue Doll 2 on edge of Red Rectangular Ring 2*
11. *RH places and holds BD1 flat in RRR1*   (12JE, page 44)

43. *LH transfers Spoon to RH*
44. *LH transfers Brush to RH, so RH holds S and B on right chair arm*
45. *looks at array of objects*
46. *LH grasps at Mirror, such that it displaces away*
   (experimenter pushes M back to subject)
47. *LH picks up M and turns it*
48. *looks at array objects from right to left, and then at experimenter*
49. *looks at Car, which is at left end of array*
50.3. *LH picks up C such that LH is holding M and C while RH is holding S and B*
50.7. *rocks back and forth, smiling, and looking at experimenter*
52. *turns around toward mother*
53. *looks at S and B held by RH, while LH is holding M and C*
                                            (12RD, pages 2 and 3)

In all instances the compositions are no longer labile. The two protocorresponding sets are preserved after they are constructed. One construction (12JE, p. 44) involves recomposition by protoreplacement of one set. Another construction (12RD) includes preservation for an extended duration plus comparative observation of the objects.

Yet other constructions begin with consecutive two-object compositions which are recomposed into protocorresponding simultaneous sets:

4. *RH pushes–taps handle of Spoon 2 against Cross Ring 2*
4a. *CR2 pushed away*
5. *LH picks up Spoon 1 and pushes it slightly against Cross Ring 1*
6. *RH taps S2 handle on table, twice*
7. *RH pushes S2 handle against CR2*
7a. *CR2 pushed away further*
8. *looks toward mother*
9.5. *LH places S1 to left of and touching CR1*
9.5. *RH places and holds S2 to right of and next to CR2*   (12JM, page 7)

The sequence of compositions matches repeated sets of equivalent numbers of elements:

$$(S2 > CR2) : (S1 > CR1) : (S2 > CR2) : [(S1 \cdot CR1)] : (S2 \cdot CR2)] \tag{14.7}$$

Reading from left to right, the sets in Eq. (14.7) represent the compositions found in Lines 4 and 4a, 5, 7, 8, 9.5 and 9.5, respectively. Not only are the compositional matchings (:) repeated sequentially but they are elaborated from consecutive mobiles into binary stabile protocorrespondences (Lines 9.5). Simultaneity is represented by bracketing the last two sets in Eq. (14.7). The sets are preserved beyond their production. As such the equivalence between binary sets of two objects is detached from the mapping protocorrespondence, and it is conserved for a while.

Most correlations between binary sets are the products of simultaneous constructions. Some simultaneous constructions are mobiles and these are usually symmetrical mobiles. Thus, little opportunity is provided for detaching the protocorresponding mappings from the protocorresponding compositions:

31.5.   RH slides Green Clover Ring 1 and Yellow Cross Ring 1 side to side a few times, fast
31.5a. other objects hit and displaced
31.5.   LH slides Green Cross Ring 1 and Yellow Clover Ring 1 side to side, a few times, fast
33.5.   RH pulls GClR1 and YCrR1 toward self
33.5.   LH pulls GCrR1 and YClR1 toward self   (12DO, page 35)

Subject 12DO continues by doing different things with the two sets. So the matchings last only as long as the mobiles.

Other simultaneous constructions of binary two-object compositions are already stabiles:

42.5.   RH places Yellow Car 4 partially on Orange Spoon 4
42.5.   LH places Yellow Car 1 partially on Orange Spoon 1   (12JE, page 60)

While such binary stabiles afford clear opportunities for detaching equivalence between sets from mapping protocorrespondences, they are rarely preserved for more than a moment. For instance, 12JE followed up by decomposing and recomposing these two sets into a three-object set and a single object separated from each other.

Correlations between binary two-object stabiles may also be constructed in a social context:

79.   RH places Red Circular Ring and Yellow Car in experimenter's LH (experimenter removes LH with RCR and YC)

80. LH *places Yellow Circular Ring and Red Car into experimenter's RH*
(*12RD*, page 22)

In addition to generating two-to-two matchings between binary sets, such constructions produce two two-to-one matchings between each set and each of experimenter's hands. As such, they provide opportunities for coordinating bi-univocal and co-univocal protocorrespondences. We will return to this development later in this section.

Only one infant constructed binary three-element protocorresponding sets:

132.5. RH *raises Brush, Spoon, and Car, together with*
132.5. LH *raises Doll 1, Doll 2, and Mirror*
132.5a. M *drops out of LH*   (*12RD*, page 7)

Since the hands are held together it is not clear whether *12RD* is constructing (*a*) one integrated six-element whole with two protocorresponding three-element parts or (*b*) two separate but protocorresponding three-element wholes. In any case, the three-to-three correlation is extremely labile. It lasts only as long as the process of raising the objects. Nevertheless, the precursory conditions for extending the numbers in two sets (or subsets) which can be matched are just beginning to be generated by this infant.

Whether the protocorrespondences are constructed consecutively, in partial temporal overlap or simultaneously, binary sets do not tend to compose identical objects. The protocol fragments presented so far are totally representative in this regard (e.g., *12JE* constructs binary sets, each of which comprise a car and a spoon). Such constructions provide the structural conditions necessary to both differentiate and integrate the extensity (quantity) and the intensity (predicate properties) of two small, related sets. On the one hand, they are differentiated when the extent is equivalent but the intensity within and between sets differs (e.g., *12RD's* three-element sets). On the other hand, they are differentiated and integrated when the extent is equivalent while (*a*) the intensity within sets differs but (*b*) the intensity between sets matches (e.g., *12JE's* just noted two-element sets).

Detachment of compositional correlation from the constructive processes of mapping protocorrespondences also results from material disarticulation. One form of material disarticulation is dependent upon progress in physical coregulation:

50.5. LH *holds Red Cup 2 upright on table*
50.5. RH *turns Yellow Cup 1 over on top of RC2, matching them rim-to-rim*
50.5a. RH *motion with YC1 pushes LH and RC2 down, losing match of rims*
(*mother holds RC2 steady, upright*)

52. BH *place YC1 inverted over RC2, rim-to-rim*
52a. *YC1 starts to slip*   (*12RD*, page 32)

96.7. RH *turns Red Cup 2 over as places and holds it rim-to-rim over Yellow Cup 1*
98. RH *begins to lift off RC2*
98a. *RC2 slips*
99. RH *adjusts RC2 on YC1, rim-to-rim*
100. RH *releases RC2*
100a. *RC2 falls off to table*   (*12RD*, page 34)

Precise adjustment in aligning the rim of one cup on top of and against the rim of another cup produces coregulated within composition protocorrespondences. They are produced without the generation of any mapping protocorrespondences. The first composition protocorrespondence is generated by reciprocal transformations (Lines 50.5). The left hand holds one cup stationary and upright while the right hand inverts and places the other cup so that their rims match. Its immediate successor composition protocorrespondence is also generated by reciprocal mappings; only, this coregulation involves social cooperation (Lines 50.5a–52a). The subject's mother holds the bottom cup steady for the subject so that he only has to transact with the top cup. The later protocorrespondences are generated by the subject alone transacting with only the top cup (Lines 96.7–100a). When the coregulation comes undone (Line 98a) the subject readjusts the top cup (Line 99). He is trying to construct precise, or at least successful, coregulation in compositional protocorrespondences.

Another form of material disarticulation originates at this stage. It consists of single mappings which result in composition protocorrespondence:

10. RH *lifts and drops Spoons 2 and 3 on top of Spoons 1 and 4*
                                                             (*12DO*, page 55)

There can be no question of any mapping protocorrespondence since the composition is constructed by only one mapping. The product is a biunivocal protocorrespondence between two subsets (Spoons 2 and 3 on top of Spoons 1 and 4) of a whole set.

These constructions reflect the developing disarticulation of the process of mappings from their transformational products, compositional equivalences. This includes proto-operational detachment. Singular and reciprocal mappings produce protocorresponding compositions. It also includes temporal separation discussed at the outset of this section. Thus, the possibilities for pragmatically abstracting (*a*) equivalences between and within sets from (*b*) the transactions that generated them are greatly enhanced. Abstracting "given" sets and subsets of elements for reconsideration, that is, for part–whole analyses, becomes ever more possible.

We have already remarked upon finding coregulated protocorrespondences when discussing abstracting compositions from the mappings which produce them. Progress in coregulation itself is important and will therefore be considered in additional detail.

Coregulation includes gauging objects in spatial correspondence to each other with some precision. At this stage it already involves continuous compensatory adjustments of objects to each other in order to overcome spatial mismatch. Minimally, fitting things together consists of physical coregulation:

103. *LH touches end of VW4 against end of VW2 held by RH, in air*
(12JM, page 22)

36. *LH pushes Doll 1 on table such that its head touches the head of Doll 2 held upside down above the table by RH*
37. *RH places and holds D2 on table such that it is head-to-head with D1 held by LH* (12KH, pages 10 and 11)

Maximally, fitting involves continuous compensatory adjustment. It may include social coregulation when another person attempts to help. Infants show no signs of requesting social cooperation in their coregulative efforts at this stage even though they use it when it is offered to them. They are distinctly cognizant of the cooperative coregulation, as they are of their own coregulations when they do not involve cooperation:

35. *LH turns over Yellow Cup 2 as raises it*
36. *LH touches and holds YC2 rim-to-rim on Yellow Cup 1*
36a. *YC1 moves in place*
37. *LH removes YC2, turning it upright (a more natural position for subject's wrist)*
(experimenter takes hold of YC1 to hold it in place)
38.3. *watches YC1*
38.7. *LH extends YC2 toward YC1, tipping YC2 toward YC1*
38.7a. *LH drops YC2 to floor*
40. *looks down at the floor*
41. *looks at experimenter as experimenter begins to get YC2 off floor*
(experimenter picks up YC2 and puts it back on the table, first to left of array and then in front of subject)
42. *RH turns Red Cup 2 over and places and holds it on top of YC1 rim-to-rim*
42a. *displaces YC1*
(experimenter holds YC1 in place)
43. *RH replaces RC2 inverted over YC1, rim-to-rim but imperfectly matched*
(experimenter straightens RC2 after subject releases)

44. *during experimenter's maneuver, BH are tensed near the cups, watching*
45. *BH pick up YC1*
45a. *RC2 falls off onto table to right*
46. *BH hold YC1 in position, then looks to right*
47. *BH transfers YC1 to RH*
48. *LH picks up RC2 by bottom*
49. *LH turns RC2 upright*
50.5. *LH holds RC2 upright*
50.5. *RH turns YC1 over on top of it, matching RC2 rim-to-rim*
50.5a. *RH motion with YC1 pushes LH and RC2 down, losing rim-to-rim match*
(mother holds RC2 steady, upright)
52. *BH place YC1 inverted over RC2, rim-to-rim*
52a. *YC1 starts to slip*
53. *BH adjust grip on YC1*
53a. *YC1 steadies inverted on RC2 rim-to-rim and then slips*
54. *BH adjust grip further on YC1*　　　　　　　　(12RD, pages 31 and 32)

109. *RH hits Red Cup 2 on table as experimenter removes Yellow Cup 1 with rim facing subject*
110. *RH raises RC2 to YC1 level*
111. *RH matches RC2 rim to experimenter's YC1 rim:*

112. *as lowers right arm, experimenter keeps her cup matched to subject's; RH pushes RC2 rim-to-rim against YC1 held by experimenter*
　　　　　　　　　　　　　　　　　　　　　　　(12RD, page 35)

The transactions are deliberate and precise. The subject inverts cups so that the rims will match. Protoinverse operations are readjusted, that is, compensate for each other's spatial location in order to overcome mapping perturbation (Line 37) and object resistance (Line 43) in the composition protocorrespondence. When the experimenter helps, the subject watches with tensed hands at the ready near the cups (Line 44). When the experimenter is finished, both hands pick up the bottom cup (Line 45). Perhaps he thinks that he can pick the stack up this way. Instead, he makes the top cup fall off (Line 45a). This leads the subject to reconstruct the coregulative protocorrespondence by applying reciprocal transformations, that is, multiplicative inverse transformations.

These are planned proto-operations since they anticipate each other. He uprights the to-be bottom cup (Line 49). Reciprocally, he inverts the to-be top cup. The product is a union by matching rims (Lines 50.5). Not only is the match precise but it is constructed in the air without the aid of surface support (cf. also *12JM*, p. 22, Line 103). The fit is difficult to preserve due to mapping perturbation and object resistance (Line 50.5a). Attempts to preserve the spatially matched union produce an extensive sequence of cooperative coregulations (Lines 52–54).

Later on it is sufficient for the experimenter to face a cup toward *12RD* (Line 109) to immediately provoke cooperative coregulation (Lines 110 and 111). A protocorrespondence is constructed in the air above the table. The subject maintains arm pressure in a coregulated fashion with the experimenter (Line 112). This permits the subject and the experimenter to lower the cups to the table while preserving the rim-to-rim matched union.

The structure of these successive constructions is becoming integrated; not yet hierarchically, but in pragmatic and presentational succession, and in almost simultaneity. Protoinverse coregulations produce protocorresponding compositions. Decomposition, whether advertent or inadvertent, evokes coordinated protoinverse and protoreciprocal coregulations. This coordinated structural relation between two combinativity protooperations reconstructs the protocorresponding composition. The structure of combinativity proto-operations is protoreversible to the extent that (*a*) they spatially compensate for each other and (*b*) they coregulate protocorrespondences by binary application of inverse transformations.

The structures of the protocorrespondences discussed so far have all been bi-univocal. One-to-one correlations produce equivalences within sets, between subsets of two elements each, and between binary sets of two elements each. Protocorrespondences whose structures are co-univocal are also generated frequently at this stage. Co-univocal protocorrespondences continue to be generated in two basic forms. These are one-to-many correlations and many-to-one correlations.

Many-to-one protocorresponding compositions are now constructed simultaneously (*12LZ* and *12RD*) as well as successively (*12DO*):

12.5. *RH bangs Green Rectangular Ring on Green Cross Ring*
12.5. *LH bangs Yellow Cross Ring on GCR*   (*12LZ*, page 11)

  4. *LH touches Cars 2 and 3 to Yellow Circular Ring 1*   (*12RD*, page 23)

 62. *RH lifts Blue Doll 1*
 63. *RH places BD1 flat inside of Red Rectangular Ring 2, such that BD1 overlaps part of RRR2 rim*
 64. *RH lifts Blue Doll 2*
 65. *RH places BD2 upright on RRR2 rim*   (*12DO*, pages 50 and 51)

One-to-many protocorresponding compositions are now also constructed simultaneously. This is the way in which the subjects generate "bridge" constructions discussed earlier in this chapter. One object is placed in spatial relation to several others forming an arch or bridge between them. Other one-to-many protocorrespondences involve causal rather than spatial relations:

4.5.   *RH taps Green Cross Ring 1 once on Yellow Cross Ring 2, Yellow Clover Ring 1, and table, such that GCR1 touches all three at once*
4.5a. *slightly displaces YCrR1 and YClR1*   (12DO, page 34)

Yet other one-to-many co-univocals involve both spatial and causal relations. Some are successive:

3.   *RH puts Yellow Spoon in Yellow Cup 3*
4.   *RH beats YS in YC3*
5.   *RH takes YS out*
6.   *RH holds YS in Yellow Cup 5*
7.   *RH takes YS out*
8.   *RH holds YS in Yellow Cup 4*
9.   *RH takes YS out*
10. *RH puts YS in YC3*
11. *RH beats YS in YC3, a few times*   (12AM, page 11)

Others are simultaneous:

31. *looks at cluster of Yellow Spoons 1 and 2 and Red Spoon 1 on table*
32. *LH drops Yellow Cup 2 onto cluster of three spoons*
33. *looks at YC2 on YS1, YS2, and RS1*
     subject: "Uh"   (12RD, page 31)

The co-univocal produced by *12RD* relates one cup to three spoons (Line 32). Anticipatory looking at the target dependent variable, the cluster of spoons, precedes the composition (Line 31). It is succeeded by observing the resultant "bridge" structure, plus vocalizing (Line 33).

In formal logic, and at advanced stages of adolescent and adult cognitive development, one-to-many correlations are reciprocal to many-to-one correlations. These two co-univocal forms merely differ in the direction of construction or consideration. At the present stage, however, these two forms of one structure, co-univocal correspondences, are just beginning to be related to each other.

The problem, in part, is relating ascending to descending orders. In itself this is a difficult protoreciprocal operation whose development remains rudimentary at this stage (see Section III). Relating co-univocal forms differing in directional order adds an additional magnitude of complexity. Yet, precursory solutions, limited to consecutive compositions, are generated:

22.5. *LH places Yellow Spoon 1 on top of Yellow Cross Ring 1*
22.5. *RH places and holds Yellow Spoon 2 on YCR1*
24.5. *RH grasps cups of YS1 and 2*

24.5a. *handle of YS1 rotates to the right*
24.5. *LH touches YCR1 and YS1 handle*
26. *BH pick up YS2 and drop it on YCR1 and cup of YS1* (12JM, page 8)

This is as advanced a solution as is produced at this stage. The first co-univocal is many-to-one (Lines 22.5). The second co-univocal is one-to-many (Line 26). It is not exactly clear whether the intervening composition constitutes a bi-univocal two-to-two protocorrespondence (Lines 24.5). If it does, then it would provide evidence not only for initial coordination of the two differing forms of co-univocal structures, but their precursory integration with the differing structure of bi-univocal protocorrespondences as well.

Co-univocal and bi-univocal correlations are only partially isomorphic with each other. Additional operations must be applied to transform or derive one structure into or from the other. Yet abundant evidence is found of progressive coordination between these two different structures.

The most powerful evidence is the pragmatic yet direct transformation of co-univocal into bi-univocal protocorrespondences:

8. *LH places Doll 2 on top of Rectangular Rings 2 and 3*
9. *LH picks up Rectangular Ring 1*
10. *mouths RR1 held by LH, while looking at the array*
11. *LH places RR1 on top of RR2 and RR3*   (12LZ, page 66)

The in-process construction and the products, bridge constructions (Lines 8 and 11), are successive one-to-many co-univocal protocorrespondences. The completed intersective product is a bi-univocal protocorresponding composition. Two elements placed on top bridge two elements underneath. The result is extensive (quantitative) but not intensive (predicate) equivalence. This is a further protological implication of "bridging and bombing" transactions, discussed in Chapter 13. The in-process successive constructions are co-univocal. The final product is bi-univocal.

A collateral source of evidence is alternating construction of co-univocal and bi-univocal protocorrespondences. An unusually long but prototypic sequence is produced by the same subject, 12LZ:

32. *LH holds Green Cross Ring and RH holds Yellow Cross Ring together over the floor*
33. *looks at GCR and YCR*
34. *LH bangs GCR and RH bangs YCR on Green Rectangular Ring once, simultaneously*
35. *LH touches GCR against YCR in RH in mid-air, with GCR slightly above YCR*
36. *mouths YCR held by RH*

37. *RH bangs YCR on the table*
38. *RH bangs YCR and LH bangs GCR on GRR, simultaneously*
39. *LH places GCR on top of GRR*
40. *RH picks up both GRR and YCR but drops both*
41. *RH picks up GRR*
42. *LH touches GCR to GRR in RH, watching what she does*
43. *mouths GRR held by RH*
44. *RH places GRR and LH places GCR on top of YCR*　(12LZ, page 12)

The sequence alternates between bi-univocal and co-univocal protocorrespondences. It proceeds from a bi-univocal protocorrespondence accompanied by observation (Lines 32 and 33), to a co-univocal (Line 34), to a bi-univocal (Line 35), to a co-univocal (Line 38), to bi-univocals (Lines 39–42), to a co-univocal (Line 44).

Two objects are exchanged as substitutes for each other in the last alternation from bi-univocal to co-univocal protocorrespondences. This marks precursory integration of two prime equivalence operations. The last alternation coordinates protocorrespondence with protosubstitution.

Analogical protocorrespondences are produced frequently:

18. *BH hold and hit Circular Rings 2 and 3 onto the table*
18a. *CR2 and CR3 are released and fall to floor*
19. *looks toward floor*
　　 (mother retrieves and places CR2 and 3 on table)
20. *BH hit on top of CR2 and 3*
20a. *CR3 falls to lap*
21. *RH retrieves and places CR3 on table*
22. *BH hit on top of CR2 and 3*　　　　　　　　　(12DA, page 9)

Hitting the rings on the table (Line 18) is analogized by hitting on the rings (Line 20). The well-regulated quality of the protocorrespondence is revealed when one object is displaced to the subject's lap. She reconstructs the placements of the objects as a set (Line 21) so that she can continue to produce the protocorrespondence.

Analogical protocorresponding just begins to acquire conventional features, but only when the subjects transact with familiar realistic objects, such as cups and spoons. Moreover, it may include coregulative protocorrespondences. Some infants become very involved in their productions so that they go on and on. For instance, on one task 12AM's analogical protocorrespondences included more than 50 transactions. A small sampling of her productions will suffice for the present purposes:

8. *RH holds Red Cup in lap*
9. *LH stirs Red Spoon around in (or presses it into) the bottom of RC*
10. *RH puts RC back on table*
11. *LH presses RS into bottom of RC*

12. *LH lifts RS up*
13. *LH taps RS on table*
14. *LH puts RS back in RC*
15. *LH rubs RS around the side of RC*   (12AM, page 8)

62. *RH beats Red Spoon around in Red Cup*
63. *RH takes RS out of RC*
64. *RH touches face of RS to experimenter's finger*
65. *RH puts RS back in RC held by LH*
66. *RH beats RS around in RC held by LH*
67. *RH takes RS out of RC held by LH*
68. *RH taps RS on experimenter's finger*
69. *RH puts RS in RC held by LH*
70. *RH beats RS around lightly in RC*
71. *RH takes RS out of RC held by LH*
72. *RH taps experimenter's finger with face of RS, while LH holds RC*
73. *RH puts RS in RC held by LH*
74. *RH beats RS harder several times in succession on bottom of RC held by LH*   (12AM, pages 10 and 11)

Analogical protocorrespondences are generated between mappings as well as between compositions. Some are becoming conventional when the subject stirs the spoon in the cup (e.g., Line 9). Some are also becoming coregulative when the subject touches or taps the experimenter's finger with the spoon (e.g., Line 64). Moreover, they are extended to the construction of extensive bidirectional magnitude orderings, in this instance ⟨beat, touch, beat, tap, beat lightly, tap, beat harder⟩.

III. Introducing the Element of Associativity to Protoaddition and Protosubtraction

There is a dramatic shift at this stage to generating iterative proto-operations frequently. Protoaddition and protosubtraction are generated as frequently as protocorrespondences. The shift is mainly to constructing iteratively ordered discrete sets, including extensive consecutive series and minimal simultaneous series. Concomitantly, ordered series of continuous and discrete magnitudes are not generated more frequently. Most of the infants' efforts are now directed toward applying protoaddition, protosubtraction, and protoaddition coordinated with protosubtraction to the construction of iterative series of sets.

While magnitude orderings with compositions do not increase, their range of application and their coordinative complexity progresses. They begin to be applied to spatial containment relations (see also the previously discussed 12AM, p. 10 and 11, protocol fragment):

46. *RH holds Yellow Spoon 1 near Yellow Cup 1 and hits YS1 in YC1 lightly one time*
47. *RH raises YS1 higher above YC1 and hits YS1 in YC1 harder, as looking at experimenter*
48. *RH holds YS1 near YC1 and hits YS1 in YC1 lightly (as in Line 46) four times, as looking at spoon in cup*   (12RD, page 44)

Two magnitude orders are increased and then decreased, protocorrespondingly. The series alternates from proximal distance and light hitting (Line 46), to further distance and harder hitting (Line 47), back to proximal distance and light hitting (Line 48). The series forms the bidirectional order (near · light) < (far · hard) > (near · light). Such compositional sequences, then, provide further opportunities for coordinating protoorderings with protocorrespondences. At a general structural level such coordinative constructions augment the already robust repertoire of autogenetic conditions developing at this stage for integrating nonequivalences with equivalences. However, the particular structural result is unique. Coseriation is formed between two bidirectional magnitude orderings. Increases and decreases in magnitude of distance and hitting are directly correlated with each other. Twofold equivalence, by protoreciprocity and by protocorrespondence, is constructed.

Simultaneous series of binary sets originate at this stage. They are generated by four subjects. They are limited to constructing no more than binary sets of ⟨two-, three-⟩ elements, never ⟨three-, four-⟩ elements:

9.5. *LH drops Doll 3 next to Car which is on top of Brush*
9.5. *RH pushes Mirror into Spoon, slightly*   (12KH, page 1)

19.5. *RH roughly touches VW3 and Spoon 4*
19.5a. *VW3 and S4 displace slightly*
19.5. *LH slides Spoon 3, VW2, and Spoon 2 to left*   (12DO, page 55)

17.5. *LH touches bowl end of Spoon 1 to Cars 1 and 3*
17.5a. *C3 tips up on its side a bit*
17.5. *RH lowers Spoon 2 flat on table about 1 1/2 inches behind Car 2*
                                                   (12JE, page 59)

Simultaneous construction of binary sets forming the discrete order ⟨two-, three-⟩ elements makes it possible to observe the whole series at one time. This facilitates further cognition and elaboration of iterative orders. The successive points in a series of consecutive compositions cannot be compared without some representational reconstruction. By themselves consecutive ordered compositions are less conducive to further cognition of iterative series. There is one qualification to this hypothesis which takes on special significance at this stage, namely, successive but coordinated bidirectional orderings. They came as close to simultaneously ordered binary sets as is possible in successive constructions of orders.

Successive coordination of protoaddition and protosubtraction to form bidirectional series of ordered sets is generated as regularly as is either proto-operation by itself. At the previous stage coordinated protoaddition with protosubtraction is generated much less frequently than either protooperation by itself. Furthermore, coordinated bidirectional series are becoming fairly lengthy. Consequently, the sequences involve many protoreciprocal relations between inequalities and equalities.

Most ordered series of sets produced by additive protooperations transform two-element into three-element compositions. Constructing consecutive series of ⟨three-, four-⟩ element sets are becoming more frequent than at age 10 months:

   8.   *RH drops Cylinder 2 next to Rectangular Rings 1 and 2:*

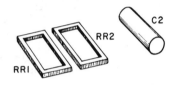

   9.   *LH transfers Cylinder 1 to RH*
  10.   *RH places C1 perpendicularly between RR2 and C2*
  10a. *C1 rolls away*   (12DO, page 6)

One-at-a-time protoadditions of two elements to a composition to form consecutive series of ⟨two-, three-, four-⟩ element sets (e.g., *12DO*, p. 37, Lines 75–78a, on page 363) are generated less frequently than series of ⟨three-, four-⟩ element sets.

A similar pattern obtains for protosubtraction. Most protosubtractions still result in consecutive series of ⟨three-, two-⟩ element sets. Series of ⟨four-, three-⟩ element sets are becoming frequent. One-at-a-time protosubtractions of two elements from a four-element composition to form consecutive series of ⟨four-, three-, two-⟩ element sets are generated less frequently than series of ⟨four-, three-⟩ element sets.

Protoaddition and protosubtraction are detached from their particular enactive mapping processes at this stage, but the detachment remains limited to the construction of very small number series. Consider for illustrative purposes the formation of series of ⟨three-, two-⟩ element sets. They are produced by protosubtraction of one element at a time, two elements at a time, and as in this protocol fragment by reciprocal protosubtraction of one element together with two elements at a time:

  71.3. *RH tilts Red Cup 2 containing Red Spoon 1 and Yellow Spoon 2 toward his face*

71.7.–73.5. *mouths RS1 and YS2, inside of RC2 held by RH*
　73.5. *RH tilts RC2 further*
　75.5. *RH pulls RC2 and RS1 away from mouth a bit*
　75.5. *edge of YS2 handle stays in mouth*
　　77. *RH shakes RC2*
　77a. *RS1 rattles*
　　78. *RH pulls RC2 with RS1 completely away from mouth and YS2 remains*
　　　　dangling from mouth　　　　　　　　　　　　　　(12RD, page 33)

　　The quantitative results of these three orders of protosubtraction are the same. The transactive processes or orders of protosubtracting elements are different. One at a time protosubtraction directly transforms the single element taken away, and not the remaining two-element composition. It results in an ordered series of ⟨three-, two-⟩ element sets. Conversely, two at a time protosubtraction is generated by directly transforming the two-element composition taken away, and not the remaining single element. Yet, it too results in an ordered series of ⟨three-, two-⟩ element sets. Correlatively, one at a time and two at a time protosubtractions directly transform both a singular element and a two-element composition, that is, by reciprocal protosubtractions. And, it too results in an ordered series of ⟨three-, two-⟩ element sets.

　　At this stage, then, all three protosubtractive orders are used by the subjects to produce equivalent quantitative results, that is, to produce ordered series of ⟨three-, two-⟩ element sets. Similar results obtain for three forms of protoaddition. One element at a time, two elements at a time, and reciprocal one together with two elements at a time protoadditions are used to produce ordered series of ⟨two-, three-⟩ element sets. Thus, abstracting protoaddition and protosubtraction out of their mapping forms results in the origins of protological associativity.

　　Protoassociativity is a second-order operation. It produces equivalences between first-order operations, such as protoaddition and protosubtraction, irrespective of their order of application. Protoassociativity applied to protosubtraction produces

$$3 - (1) \approx 3 - (2) \approx 3 - (1 \gtreqless 2) \rightarrow \langle 3\text{-, } 2\text{-}\rangle \text{ elements sets} \quad (14.8)$$

where

$$(a \, \& \, b \, \& \, c) - (a) \approx (a \, \& \, b \, \& \, c) - (a \, \& \, b) \approx (a \, \& \, b \, \& \, c)$$
$$-[(a) \gtreqless (b \, \& \, c)] \rightarrow \langle (a \, \& \, b \, \& \, c), (a \, \& \, b) \rangle \quad (14.9)$$

Reading left to right, Eq. (14.9) states that (*a*) an unordered set composed of three objects **a**, **b**, and **c** from which one of its elements, such as **a**, is subtracted is (*b*) equivalent to the same unordered set from which two elements, such as **a** and **b**, are subtracted is (*c*) equivalent to the same unordered set from which one element, such as **a**, and two elements, such as **b** and **c**, are simultaneously subtracted in (*d*) producing an ordered series beginning with a three-element set, such as **a**, **b**, and **c**, followed by a two-element set, such as **a** and **b**.

Similarly, protoassociativity applied to protoaddition produces

$$1 + (2) \approx 2 + (1) \approx 0 + (1 \gtrless 2) \rightarrow \langle 2\text{-, } 3\text{-} \rangle \text{ element sets} \quad (14.10)$$

where

$$(a) + (b \ \& \ c) \approx (a \ \& \ b) + (c) \approx (0) + [(a) \gtrless (b \ \& \ c)]$$
$$\rightarrow \langle (a \ \& \ b), (a \ \& \ b \ \& \ c) \rangle \quad (14.11)$$

Both Eqs. (14.8) and (14.10) substitute different orders of applying first-order operations to produce equivalently ordered series.

The advance, then, is both structural and functional. Structurally, first-order proto-operations of addition and subtraction are transformed into second-order associative protooperations. It should be stressed that at its origins protoassociativity is precursory. It applies only to the construction of ordered sets of very small numbers.

Functionally, applying first-order proto-operations has become fully flexible; they are used interchangeably. Protoaddition and protosubtraction are becoming abstracted as independent protoinferential structures that can then be applied to a wide variety of apparently dissimilar problems. Thus, they begin to be relatively powerful quantification proto-operations. They are detached from their particular modes of application and from the configuration of elements to which they are applied.

Bidirectional reciprocal iteration is generated by all infants. Most infants extend their bidirectional iteration to as many as four-element sets:

16. RH *places Doll 2 on top of Doll 1*
16a. *D2 immediately rolls off D1 onto table and near edge, flat*
17. RH *lifts and places D2 between Rectangular Rings 1 and 2*
18.5. RH *grasps and slides D1 to left and then in and out of RR2 and onto table*
18.5a. *D1 pushes RR2 to left*
18.5aa. *D1 touches D2*
18.5. LH *touches RR1 and D2, so:*

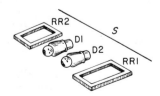

20.5. RH *lifts D1*

20.5. *LH lifts D2 and partially lifts RR1 (with LH pinkie) such that D1 (RH)*
       touches RR1 (LH)
22.5. *RH releases D1 to table in front of RR1*
22.5. *LH releases RR1 flat to table:*

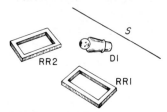

24. *RH lifts D1 and looks at D1 bottom*
24a. *RH slides RR2 to left in process such that RR2 touches RR1*
                                              (*12JE*, pages 44 and 45)

Subject *12JE* generates the reciprocally ordered series of ⟨two-, three-,
four-, three-, two-⟩ element consecutive sets (Lines 16, 17, 18.5, 20.5.–
22.5, and 24, respectively). The reciprocal order is fully symmetrical. This
is still unusual. Most reciprocal orders at this stage are only partially
symmetrical (e.g., ordered series of ⟨two-, three-, four-, three-⟩ and
⟨four-, three-, four-⟩ element consecutive sets).

The most extensive reciprocally ordered series, generated by five subjects, extend to five-element sets. Rare constructions are precise, such as
the ordered series of ⟨four-, five-, four-⟩ element sets generated by one
infant, *12LL*. Usually they are imprecise, such as ordered series of ⟨two-,
three-, five-, two-⟩ and ⟨five-, three-, four-, three-⟩ element sets generated by two other infants, *12JM* and *12DO* respectively.

Protoaddition and protosubtraction are applied to binary sets as well as
objects by eight subjects. Coordinated protoaddition together with protosubtraction applied to binary sets originates at this stage, and is generated by seven subjects. When applied to binary sets, protoaddition produces integration of two smaller sets into one larger set. Protosubtraction
results in differentiating one larger set into two smaller binary sets.
Coordinated protoaddition and protosubtraction constructs protoreciprocity between differentiating and integrating binary sets. Protoreciprocal
composing and decomposing binary sets, in particular, is possible only
because compositions as well as objects have been well-established as
constant givens. As such they can be used as the contents for more
advanced protoinferential forms. They are now subject to precursory
second-order proto-operational constructions, such as protoreciprocal
addition and subtraction. The precursory structure of these second-order
constructions is revealed by at least two major features. First, the consecutive compositions are preserved only momentarily. They are rapidly
transformed into each other. Second, the extent of application is re-

stricted. It never exceeds two sets. It usually applies to a total of four elements, occasionally five to six elements, and rarely to seven to eight elements.

Integrating binary sets already includes reciprocal active transformation of both sets:

62.   *looks at Car and Mirror held by LH*

63.3. *looks at Brush and Spoon held by RH far apart from LH*

63.7. *RH tilts B and S toward LH holding C and M, but there is still some distance between hands*

65.   *LH, holding C and M, grasps B and S*

65a. *C slips to floor from LH holding M, B, and S*

66.   *looks down to floor as C lands*   (12RD, page 3)

Both sets compose two elements and are visually examined before 12RD unites them into one larger set. Integration is only momentary because one of the objects slips out of his grasp. It is clear from 12RD's visual tracing that even it is a stable element.

Integrative constructions are dominated by their correlational form since they produce protocorresponding equivalence between binary sets. Integrative nonequivalence remains asynchronous. Successive integration results in a new whole which is (*a*) more numerous in elements than each of the two sets out of which it was composed and (*b*) composed of only one set. Nevertheless, conditions are now ripe for infants to begin to relate their constructions of protoadditive nonequivalence to protocorresponding equivalence. This complements the subjects' reversible transformations of nonequivalences into equivalences by consecutive protoaddition and protosubtraction which will be analyzed after brief consideration of differentiation of one into two sets.

Dividing a larger set into binary but smaller sets is usually generated by actively transforming only a part of the larger whole:

75.   *RH places Green Cross Ring 1 on top of and bridging Yellow Cross Rings 1 and 2:*

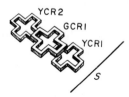

76.   *LH transfers Yellow Clover Ring 1 to RH*

77.   *RH places and holds YClR1 on YCrR1*

78.   *RH lifts YClR1/YCrR1*

78a. *GCrR1 displaces slightly, but still overlaps YCrR2*   (12DO, page 37)

Subject 12DO constructs a four-element composition by one element at a time protoaddition and then divides it into two two-element compositions. Inequalities are generated between the successive four-element and two-element compositions. Equivalences are also produced in these transactions, however. Each successive set comprises two elements. These constructions provide additional possibilities for comparing and coordinating part–whole nonequivalence with part–part equivalence. They directly complement similar opportunities provided by integrating two two-element compositions into one four-element composition, just discussed.

Consecutive transformations of protoadding into protosubtracting sets and vice versa provide minimal conditions for coordinating these two proto-operations applied to binary set. While already generated by seven subjects their constructions are for the most part rudimentary and labile.

The most advanced coordination is generated by one infant, 12RD. Since the protocol fragment is quite lengthy, we will summarize it. He begins by gathering three objects into each hand, thereby forming binary three-element sets. He follows up by twice bringing the binary sets together and then separating them. He finishes by bringing the sets together again, transferring one object from one hand to the other, and then separating the sets. In sequence, then, 12RD: (a) composes two separate three-element sets, (b) integrates the binary sets to form one six-element set, (c) redecomposes the single set back into the same binary three-element sets, (d) reintegrates the binary sets to form the same six-element set; and finally (e) redecomposes the single set into two different binary sets, that is, into a two-element and a four-element set.

Sequential constructions by these seven infants form protoreciprocal structures of adding and subtracting two small sets. Some, such as that by 12RD, also result in structuring identity sets, both of binary but small sets and of one larger set. However, the identity sets are rarely preserved beyond two transformations; thus, for example, 12RD ends by transforming the two small identity sets into two variant sets. Nevertheless, precursory protoreversible structures of adding and subtracting binary but small sets are constructed. These include second-order protoreciprocity between addition and subtraction and second-order identity between integrated and differentiated sets.

IV. Transition to Predication by Similarities

Predication is still primarily a property of single sets since most compositions are generated consecutively or in isolation (Table 14.1). As already noted, six subjects generate two partially overlapping or simultaneous sets. These comprise 5% of the compositions in the four-object conditions and 10% of the compositions in the eight-object conditions. Still, the data base is not sufficiently large to apply statistical tests of significance. Nevertheless, the available data pool conforms to the probabilities for random predication. All three structural articulatory features—order, enclosure, and proximity and separation—mark partially overlapping and simultaneous sets. The distributions for all three features are random. There is no tendency to predicate partially overlapping or simultaneous pairs of sets by either similarities or differences.

Most compositions are still not featured by proximity and separation. Therefore, the rest of the analyses will focus upon order and upon enclosure of all sets treated as individual compositions. The data base is derived from the structured class conditions only, that is, the additive, multiplicative and disjoint conditions. Data on predication were not obtained for the ambiguous, semicontrol class conditions because of a technical difficulty in data collection.

Order and enclosure continue to be strongly correlated. In the four-object conditions they correspond 95% of the time where order applies. The correspondence drops to 90% in the eight-object conditions. These high correspondences in all conditions further confirm the hypothesis that order and enclosure are syncretically fused features of predication at its origins. Yet, the small decrease in percentage of correspondence presages their differentiation at subsequent stages.

Predication is by identical properties in the additive conditions. In the four-object additive condition, the random probability ratio is two-to-one in favor of predicating by complementary rather than identical properties. The mean frequencies for order of composing are over six-to-one in favor of predicating by identical properties (Table 14.2, Row 1, Columns 1–3). The differences are statistically significant ($N = 10, x = 2, p = .055$, sign test). The mean frequencies for enclosure are over three-to-two in favor of identical rather than complementary properties (Row 1, Columns 4–6). The differences are statistically significant ($N = 11, x = 1, p = .006$, sign test).

In the eight-object additive condition, the random probability ratio is four-to-three in favor of predicating by complementary rather than by identical properties. The mean frequencies for order of composing are over three-to-two in favor of identical properties (Row 4, Columns 1–3). The differences approach statistical significance ($N = 12, x = 3, p = .073$, sign test). The mean frequencies for enclosure are almost six-to-five in favor of identical rather than complementary properties (Row 4, Columns 4–6). Again, the differences approach statistical significance ($N = 12, x = 3, p = .073$, sign test).

TABLE 14.2

Spontaneous Phase I: Mean Frequency by 12-Month-Old Subjects Generating Unmixed, Partly Unmixed, and Mixed Compositions

	Order			Enclosure		
	Unmixed 1	Partly unmixed 2	Mixed 3	Unmixed 4	Partly unmixed 5	Mixed 6
Four-object condition:						
1. Additive[a]	6.20	0.00	1.00	7.36	0.00	4.45
2. Multiplicative[a]	6.38	0.00	1.75	6.27	0.00	2.64
3. Disjoint	2.00	0.08	1.33	2.50	0.00	3.67
Eight-object condition:						
4. Additive	4.67	0.00	2.92	5.75	0.75	4.92
5. Multiplicative[a]	3.36	0.00	7.09	4.73	0.25	13.09
6. Disjoint[b]	6.10	0.00	2.50	8.00	0.50	6.20

[a] $N = 11$
[b] $N = 10$

Predication in the multiplicative conditions varies as a function of the number of objects presented. In the four-object condition, the random probability ratio is two-to-one in favor of predicating by complementary rather than by disjoint properties. The mean frequencies for order of composing are over three-to-one in favor of predicating by complementary properties (Row 2, Columns 1–3), but the differences are random ($N = 8$, $x = 3$, $p = .363$, sign test). The mean frequencies for enclosure are slightly over two-to-one in favor of complementary predication (Row 2, Columns 4–6). The differences are random ($N = 11$, $x = 4$, $p = .274$, sign test). Overall, predicating is random in the four-object multiplicative condition.

In the eight-object multiplicative condition, the random probability ratio is five-to-two in favor of unmixed (identical or complementary properties) over mixed (disjoint properties) predication. The mean frequencies for order of composing are over two-to-one in favor of mixed over unmixed predication (Row 5, Columns 1–3). The differences are statistically significant ($N = 11$, $x = 1$, $p = .006$, sign test). The mean frequencies for enclosure are almost three-to-one in favor of mixed predication (Row 5, Columns 4–6). The differences are statistically significant ($N = 11$, $x = 1$, $p = .006$, sign test). Both order and enclosure features of predication are by disjoint properties.

Predicating is random in the disjoint conditions. In the four-object condition, the random probability ratio is two-to-one in favor of predicating by disjoint rather than identical properties. The mean frequencies for

order are less than two-to-one in favor of predicating by identical properties (Row 3, Columns 1–3), but the differences are random ($N = 9$, $x = 3$,
$p = .254$, sign test). The mean frequencies for enclosure are a bit less than
three-to-two favoring disjoint properties (Row 3, Columns 4–6). The
differences are random ($N = 12$, $x = 6$, $p = .613$, sign test).

In the eight-object disjoint condition, the random probability ratio is
four-to-three in favor of predicating by disjoint rather than identical
properties. The mean frequencies for order are more than two-to-one in
favor of predicating by disjoints (Row 6, Columns 1–3). The differences
are random ($N = 9$, $x = 3$, $p = .254$, sign test). The mean frequencies for
enclosure are a bit less than four-to-three in favor of predicating by
identical properties (Row 6, Columns 4–6). The differences are random
($N = 10$, $x = 5$, $p = .623$, sign test).

The major development in predication, then, at this stage is the initiation of affirmation.[1] It is limited to individual compositions generated in
the additive conditions. This includes four- and eight-object additive
conditions. Aside from this development, predication does not change.
Predicating continues to be by negation (in the eight-object multiplicative
condition) or random (in the four-object multiplicative and four- and
eight-object disjoint conditions).

---

[1] Riccuiti (1965) and Nelson (1973) also report sorting by similarities beginning at age 12
months. Missing in these reports are analyses of its complements, sorting by differences and
sorting randomly.

15

Partial Extension of Pragmatically Reversible Quasi-Continuous Combinativity

Two major developments in transacting with quasi-continuous objects mark this stage, and both parallel developments in transacting with discrete objects, analyzed in Chapters 12, 13, and 14. The first is the origin of constructing two contemporaneous but distinct small sets of objects. Decomposing is extended to the formation of binary sets. The result is symmetrical as well as asymmetrical geneological descendants.

The second parallel development is the expansion of protoreversible combinativity operations. Reforming and reconstructing originate at this stage resulting in intensity identity proto-operations, while holding extensity constant. Recomposing continues to be generated at the same rate as at the previous stage, but it is beginning to be regulated. Redecomposing originates at this stage. Both recomposing and redecomposing result in only extensity identity proto-operations at this stage. They do not yet result in intensity identity proto-operations. Thus, while the developments in protoreversible combinativity are wide ranging at this stage, they are only precursory. Most notably, they only result in partial identities.

I. Precursory Form Identity by Coordinated Deforming and Reforming

Deforming is well-regulated and directed. Sometimes it is applied immediately. Other times it is preceded by brief or extensive comparative inspection of the objects. While much deforming is gross, application may also be careful, deliberate, and differentiated:

1. *LH touches Ball*
2. *LH index finger makes a small dent in B*
3. *looks at experimenter*
4. *LH withdraws from B*
5. *LH squeezes B, as looks at experimenter*
6. *LH releases B*
7. *RH pinches B*   (12EB, page 15)

3. *looks down (intently) at Ball with face close to it for 15 seconds*
4. *RH picks up B and squeezes it gently*
5. *RH starts fingering B by exerting pressure with different fingers alter-*
   nately (not simultaneous squeezing of all fingers)   (12DS, page 17)

Subject 12EB's differentiated deformations are preceded by brief tactual examination of the object (Line 1). Subject 12DS's deformations are preceded by lengthy visual inspection of the object (Line 3). Inspection is followed by extended but well-differentiated deforming (Lines 4 and 5). He successively alternates the fingers with which he gently generates multiple deformations. He seems to be tactually comparing the transformations in the internal part–whole relations at the same time as he is generating them.

Deforming has become so well-regulated that symptoms of anticipation are beginning to be manifest:

1. *(as six objects are being brought out) looks at objects as BH extend forward*
   toward objects and make open–close gestures
   subject: (whimpers)
2.3. *RH lifts Small Ball 4*
2.7. *LH lifts Large Ball*
4. *BH depress once into each ball*   (12LL, page 19)

The infant seems so eager that she gestures toward the objects, perhaps making virtual deformations. Her symbolic anticipation is augmented by vocalization. She whimpers with frustrated desire, as if she cannot wait to get her hands on the objects so that she can deform them. As soon as she gets two objects in hand, she immediately deforms them.

Well-regulated deforming is prerequisite to the origins of pragmatic reflection by infants upon their transformations. This is accompanied by either anticipation (12LL) or delight (12JE). Thus, after much deforming and comparative monitoring of three small balls, 12JE

29. *looks at Ball 1 and Ball 2*
30. *looks up at experimenter, laughing*
31. *looks at Ball 3*
32. *RH index finger presses B3*

32a. *makes indentation in and deforms B3 further*
33. *LH index finger presses B1, two times (deeper the second time)*
33a. *two indentations in B1*
34. *looks at experimenter several seconds, making mouthing motions at experimenter*
35. *looks at B3*
36. *looks at B1 and 2*   (12JE, page 54)

Subject *12JE* continues to deform the balls repeatedly with her index fingers. Then she stops transacting with the objects and

41. *claps BH together a few times, laughing, as looks at experimenter*
                                                           (12JE, page 54)

In the next, provoked test phase *12JE* behaves similarly. She continuously deforms objects and comparatively monitors her deformations, with three interruptions of manifest pleasure at what she has wrought. Omitting nonrelevant transactions, these are

16. *claps BH together about five times as laughing at experimenter*
18. *claps BH together three times*
23. *claps BH together a few times, laughing*   (12JE, pages 55 and 56)

These manifestations of delight include rudiments of social communication. Often *12JE* looks at the experimenter while laughing and clapping her hands together. Regulated deformations themselves are beginning to be constructed cooperatively:

8. *(as experimenter extends Ball to subject) leans forward and LH index finger pushes into B*
8a. *pushes B down toward table as simultaneously dents it* (12JE, page 55)

(experimenter extends a piece of Play-Doh to subject)
11. *LH presses Large Ball against piece in experimenter's hand*
                                                           (12RD, page 55)

Both infants cooperate with the experimenter to generate deformations. These include the construction by *12RD* of reciprocal contingent deformations in both the object he is holding and the object the experimenter is extending to him. Cooperative deformation occurs even though the intentions of these partners do not match. While the experimenter's intention is to give the piece of Play-Doh to the subject, *12RD* is intent upon deforming both objects. So, he does not take the object being proffered. Instead he uses the one he is holding as an instrument to deform both.

As is true throughout infancy, deforming is the most frequent combinativity proto-operation applied to quasi-continuous objects (Table 15.1). The mean rate of deforming productivity per minute (for those

TABLE 15.1

Mean Frequency of Combinativity Proto-operations Generated by 12-Month-Old Subjects in Quasi-Continuous and Discrete–Quasi-Continuous Conditions

	One object			Three objects			Discrete–Quasi-continuous	
	Phase I 1	Phase II 2	Phase III 3	Phase I 4	Phase II 5	Phase III 6	Phase I 7	Phase II 8
1. Deforming	8.25 (4.75)[a]	4.70 (2.0)	9.14 (7.29)	5.20 (1.10)	3.44 (1.78)	5.13 (2.38)	10.50 (4.50)	20.00 (10.50)
2. Reforming	0.08	0.00	0.14	0.10	0.00	0.00	0.00	0.00
3. Breaking	0.50	0.00	0.29	0.30	0.11	0.38	0.00	0.50
4. Reconstructing	0.00	0.00	0.00	0.00	0.00	0.13	0.00	0.00
5. Decomposing[b]	2.75	2.00	1.00	0.80	1.22	1.25	0.00	0.00
6. Recomposing	0.08	0.00	0.29	0.10	0.00	0.00	0.00	0.00
7. Composing	0.00	0.10	1.14	0.70	0.22	0.25	0.50	0.00
8. Redecomposing	0.00	0.00	0.43	0.40	0.00	0.12	0.50	0.00
9. Attaching	—	—	—	—	—	—	0.00	0.00
10. Detaching	—	—	—	—	—	—	0.00	1.00
11. Number of subjects	12	10	7	10	9	8	2	2
12. Mean duration	1 min 31 sec[c]	0 min 58 sec[d]	1 min 26 sec[e]	1 min 23 sec[d]	0 min 44 sec[e]	1 min 15 sec[d]	2 min 02 sec	2 min 18 sec
13. Discrete compositions	0.67	1.40	2.86	2.60	0.67	3.63	6.00	9.50
14. Rate of productivity	0.44[c]	2.06[d]	2.80[e]	2.90[d]	1.03[e]	3.20[d]	2.96	4.13

[a] Mean frequencies of proto-operations involving multiple transformations are given in parentheses.
[b] The frequencies are necessarily underestimations because, when possible, subjects were not allowed to decompose by biting.
[c] N = 6 subjects (i.e., calculated on the basis of six subjects for whom duration measures are available).
[d] N = 5 subjects.
[e] N = 4 subjects.

subjects where duration measures are available) in the one-object condition ranges from 4.95 in the provoked to 6.03 in the spontaneous test phase (Row 1, Columns 1–3). In the three-object condition the range is from 3.36 in the countercondition to 5.51 in the spontaneous phase (Row 1, Columns 4–6). In the combined discrete–quasi-continuous condition the range is from 5.17 in the spontaneous phase to 8.73 in the provoked phase (Row 1, Columns 7 and 8), but these figures are based upon only two subjects.

The differences between conditions, then, are minor. Deforming rates do not vary as a function of the number of objects presented, that is, one to six objects. Nor do the rates vary as a function of test condition; the ranges, as we have just seen, are quite moderate. Deforming rates also remain stable with age. They do not differ greatly from what they are at age 10 months (see page 263). The mean rate of deforming Euclidean objects is 6.6 per minute and of deforming topological ring shapes is 4.8 per minute in the one-object condition. In the three-object condition, the means are 5.4 deformations per minute for Euclidean objects and 3.0 per minute for topological objects. These data are based upon too few subjects to permit statistical analyses.

While the frequency of deforming does not increase, its structure changes at this stage. The most significant development is the origins of inverse deforming or reforming (Row 2). The negation relations between deforming and reforming are symmetrical and successive, never asymmetrical or simultaneous. Most important, inverse deforming is a transformation of a transformation. That is, it is a reversible proto-operation which reforms the initial part–whole relations internal to objects. This second-order proto-operation constructs an identity proto-operation which preserves the form of quasi-continuous objects.

The first deformation produces an initial transformation, $+D$. The second deformation negates the first, $-D$. Since the subject combines both transformations, the second cancels out the first. The reversible product is reformation of the original part–whole relation internal to the object. That is, combining consecutive first-order deformations produces the second-order identity proto-operation $+D - D = O$. This proto-operation represents the first stage in the construction of form as a group identity element Eq. (16.5) defined on pages 408 and 409.

At its origins, identity formation is entirely rudimentary. It is generated only once by only three infants. It is limited to the form or internal part–whole relations of a single object. The identity formation is a purely pragmatic reformation of the initial part–whole relation:

1. *BH immediately pick up Large Circular Ring*
2. *BH compress LCR*

2a. *LCR deformed like this: (almost like two parallel lines)*

           LCR

3. *BH rotate deformed LCR close to eyes for about 7 seconds*
4. *BH hook thumbs in between the parallel sides and pull*
4a. *deformed LCR reopens into a circle*   (12LL, page 22)

The subject's first deformation is immediate; both hands close the circular ring into an oval (Line 2). She examines the transformation she produced closely and extensively by inverse rotations coordinated with visual inspection (Line 3). Then both hands reopen the oval into a circular ring (Line 4).

In previous stages, infants establish objects as constant givens and as elements of sets. Identity proto-operations are limited, as we have seen, to spatiotemporal and causal transformations. Form transformations are only irreversible proto-operations. At this stage, identity proto-operations are extended to form transformations. Infants barely begin to compose inverse deformations which preserve the object's initial internal part–whole form relations by first deforming and then reforming it. This requires determination of the resultant, second part–whole state of the object due to direct deforming, such as by paralleling the ring. Determination is manifest in the subjects' careful observations. Reforming the initial part–whole state of the object by circling the ring preserves the object's form. It is manifest in the subjects' well-regulated and carefully controlled second deformations.

Composing inverse deformations construct the conditions necessary to begin to draw the protological inference that pragmatic form identity is a reversible product of negation proto-operations. This inference is prerequisite to the representation of form identity. It relates the three successive states of the object, thereby opening the possibility for representational reconstruction of the first and third states of the object from the second state. This requires drawing the protoinference that the successive states are merely inverse mapping transformations of each other.

Reforming constructs intensive identity by reconstituting the initial predication of the part–whole relations internal to individual elements. The initial extensity remains constant throughout. Neither deforming nor its negation by deforming alters any quantitative properties of objects. Unlike intensive protoidentity by recomposing (see pages 279–281), intensive protoidentity by reforming is not a subset of extensive protoidentity. It is an autonomous proto-operation which reconstitutes the intitial forms of objects. As such, this stage marks the origins, however rudimentary, of constructing predicate identity proto-operations.

Contingent deforming, such as by hitting a ball onto the table, is generated by ten infants. This includes the origins of using a discrete object to deform a quasi-continuous one in the combined discrete-quasi-continuous condition:

20.3. RH *pokes Tongue Depressor 2 into Ball 1*
20.3a. *indentation in B1*   (*12KH*, page 76)

Only one (*12KH*) of the two infants tested in the discrete–quasi-continuous condition generates instrumental deforming with a discrete object. Moreover, *12KH* never repeats instrumental deforming. While too few infants were tested in this condition to make any definitive determination, it seems most likely that instrumental deforming with a discrete object is rudimentary and not regulated at this stage.

Reciprocal contingent deforming entails simultaneous deformations of two quasi-continuous objects. It is generated by seven 12-month-olds, while only three infants did so at age 10 months (page 265). Four of these 12-month-olds generate reciprocal contingent deforming more than once.

Three subjects generate asymmetrical reciprocity. Even though the result is deformation of two objects, only unary mappings are involved (e.g., one object is used to bang upon another). This is typical at the previous stage. Three subjects generate symmetrical reciprocity. Binary mappings are involved since both objects are manipulated (e.g., two objects are banged together). One subject generates both symmetrical and asymmetrical reciprocity, but each only once. His asymmetrical reciprocal contingent deforming is cooperative, and has already been considered on page 371.

Asymmetrical reciprocal contingent deforming is becoming well-regulated, monitored, and systematic:

55. RH *bangs Ball 6 on Ball 4 repeatedly as looks at B4*
56. *looks at Ball 5 while continuing to bang B6 on B4*
57. *looks back at B4, as RH continues to bang B6 on B4*
57a. *B6 and B4 stick together*
58. RH *bangs B6/B4 on table*
59. RH *lets go of B6 part of B6/B4*
60. RH *pulls B4 off B6*
61. RH *picks up B4 and mouths it*
62. RH *bangs B4 on top of B6*
63. RH *drops B4 to table*
64. RH *picks up B6 and bangs B6 on table all around B4 without hitting it*
65. RH *releases B6 next to B4*
66. RH *touches B4*
67. RH *picks up B6*
68. RH *bangs B6 on B4, but hitting the table much of the time also*
69. RH *stops banging B6 on B4 as looks at the other balls on the table*
70. RH *bangs B6 on top of Ball 3*   (*12LZ*, pages 38 and 39)

The sequence begins with reciprocal contingent deforming by banging Ball 6 on 4 (Lines 55–57). The reciprocal deforming is quite extended. It is accompanied by observing the transformation in, at least, Ball 4. It leads into composing and redecomposing (Lines 57a–60) which will be discussed in Section IV. Subject 12LZ continues to generate reciprocal contingent deforming but inverts the objects (Line 62). Ball 4 is used to bang on Ball 6. Then she continues but again inverts the objects (Lines 64–68). Ball 6 is used to bang on Ball 4. Repeated reciprocal contingent deforming is generated but much of the time the target object is missed. Finally, a new target object is selected and reciprocal contingent deforming is applied to it (Lines 69 and 70). Ball 6 is used to bang on Ball 3.

Not only does this infant generate reciprocal contingent deforming but she systematically inverts the objects involved twice in a row. When she tires of inverting her reciprocal contingent deforming, she switches to extending it to a third target object. Thus, she constructs an elaborately coordinate structure of deforming. The structure of part–whole transformations produced includes reciprocal, commutative, and substitution transformations which are related to each other.

II. Equivalence and Order Relations between Sets of Deformations

Protocorresponding deformations of three objects at the same time is generated by only one infant. Protocorresponding deformations of two objects at the same time are still generated by only one-half of the infants. They do begin to include multiple contingent transformations:

51.5.   RH hits Large Ball on table, four times
51.5.   LH hits Ball 1 on table, four times   (12JM, page 30)

At the same time as he generates protocorresponding contingent deformations in two objects, 12JM produces a discrete four-to-four protocorrespondance.

Binary protocorresponding deformations of single objects progress. They become both more frequent, that is, they are generated by six subjects, and are well-regulated:

12.   BH fingers push into Large Ball
12a. indentations made in LB   (12DS, page 17)

18.   BH thumbs depress into Large Ball, as watches
19.   BH thumbs and fingers alternately depress into LB for 15 seconds, as watches
20.   looks up at experimenter, smiles
      subject: "ahere"

21. *BH wrists rotate LB 90° back and forth as subject continues to alternately depress BH thumbs and fingers in LB*   (12LL, page 16)

These constructions are controlled and directed. They are extended and reproduced over a long duration. When altered, the mode of deforming is gradually varied or elaborated as the subjects proceed. Some deformations begin to be enacted in slow motion. This facilitates controlled construction of equivalent deformations. They are preceded, accompanied, and followed by close visiomotor observation of what is happening.

These correlational proto-operations, then, are no longer labile at this stage. The subjects are generating the conditions necessary for both simultaneous and successive comparisons on the same object. They provide optimum conditions for comparing protocorresponding transformations in internal part–whole relations. Stable cognition of continuous equivalence begins to be possible.

Successive but articulate deforming protocorrespondences on a single object continue to be produced by about one-fourth of the infants. They are accompanied, and often preceded, by close examination:

21. *LH places Small Piece 3 on table*
22. *looks at SP3*
23. *LH thumb runs up and down SP3*
24. *looks at SP3*
25. *LH fingers run around SP3*
26. *LH pulls small part up on SP3*
27. *looks at it*
28. *LH pulls another small part up on SP3*   (12AM, pages 21 and 22)

14. *LH places Large Ring on table, looking closely at it*
15. *stares at LR*
16. *RH touches LR*
17. *RH index presses down on LR*
17a. *makes a small dent in LR*
18. *RH presses index into LR two more times in spots next to first dent*
18a. *makes two consecutive dents in LR rim*   (12JE, page 23)

Subject 12AM creates two separate nodules at different places on a ball. Subject 12JE makes three separate dents in a ring. Each deformation is preserved and monitored. These articulate reproductions are therefore conducive to determining unit equivalence in internal part–whole relations.

Consecutive protocorresponding deformations on several objects originate at this stage. Generated by only a few subjects, they are part of the general developing pattern of transacting with all or most objects presented, as long as the set consists of small numbers of elements. For instance, in a fairly short period of time, subject *12EB* transacts with all six objects presented. She deforms four of them, thus generating the possibility for comparing the internal part–whole transformations she has produced in each of a small set of elements. One of the essential ingredients in determining unit equivalence between elements of a set has been self-generated. Still missing is adequate stabilization of the products. The protocorrespondences remain labile. Each object, with the exception of the last, is immediately discarded after the subject deforms it. Lability imposes severe limitations upon the possibilities for comparing protocorresponding deformations, even when applied to separate objects.

Social protocorresponding deformations are progressively regulated. Subjects alter their own deformations in a controlled fashion so as to accord with the mappings used by others:

   36. RH *slowly begins depressing fingers into Large Ball*
   36a. *LB is very deformed*
   37. RH *lifts LB slowly while moving arm to right*
   38. RH *drops LB on the floor to the right*
        (*mother recovers LB, sets it down on table, and squeezes it firmly*)
   39. *watches what mother is doing*
   40. RH *squeezes a corner of the now rather elongated LB*   (*12LL, page 17*)

Subject *12LL* depresses the ball in slow motion so that it becomes very deformed (Line 36). As previously noted, slow motion is one of the symptoms marking controlled deforming which develops at this stage. Her control plus observation of her mother's subsequent deforming by squeezing makes it possible for the subject to calibrate her own deforming procedure. She adjusts it to correspond to her mother's squeezing (Line 40).

Subjects also alter the objects of their deformations in a controlled fashion so as to accord with the objects used by others:

   20. *LH bangs Ball 1 on table*
   21. *looks at B1*
        (*experimenter takes Ball 2 and bangs it on the table*)
   22. *LH bangs B1 on table*
        (*experimenter bangs B2 on table*)
   23. *LH bangs B1 on table*
   24. *LH bangs B1 on table* (*simultaneously with experimenter banging B2 on table*)
        [Pause]
   25. *LH bangs B1 on table*
        (*experimenter bangs B2 on table and then puts it in middle of row*)
   26. RH *picks up B2 and bangs it on table*
   27.5. RH *bangs B2 on table*
   27.5. *LH holds B1 on table*   (*12AM, pages 23 and 24*)

Prior to the protocol fragment reproduced here, *12AM* begins by comprehensive tactual and visiomotor comparative inspection of Balls 1 and 2. She follows up by contingently deforming Ball 1 (Line 20) and then observing its transformation (Line 21). The experimenter imitates the subject. They engage in successive and simultaneous protocorresponding contingent deformation (Lines 22–25). The experimenter disengages by replacing Ball 2 in the middle of the array. The subject immediately selects Ball 2 (Line 26) and continues the protocorresponding contingent deformation with it (Line 27.5). After this, but not reproduced here, *12AM* follows up by visiomotor comparative inspection of deformed Balls 1 and 2, and further extended deformation of both balls.

Protoaddition and protosubtraction producing ordered deformations develop in one way. Ordered series of deforming are becoming increasingly extended, and progressively regulated and monitored:

  1. *RH takes Large Ring and looks at it*
  2. *RH pounds LR on table*
2a. *LR is deformed a bit*
  3. *RH stops pounding LR on table and looks at it*
  4. *RH transfers LR to LH*
  5. *LH pounds LR on table*
5a. *LR shape changes*
  6. *LH pounds LR harder on table*
6a. *LR shape changes further*
  7. *LH bangs LR on table*
7a. *LR flexes slightly*
  8. *LH bangs LR on table*
8a. *LR flexes further*
  9. *LH bangs LR on table*
9a. *LR flexes further*   (12AM, page 20)

Brief observation of the object (Line 1) leads immediately into vigorous contingent deforming (Line 2). The subject observes the resultant part–whole transformation (Line 3). She continues to deform it vigorously (Line 5). Then she deforms it even more vigorously over extended repetitions (Lines 6, 7, 8, and 9). The result is that the shape changes continuously more and more (Lines 6a, 7a, 8a, and 9a).

III. Expanding Asymmetrical Genealogical Decomposing and Constructing Binary Sets

Breaking becomes more frequent at this stage (Table 15.1, Row 3). It is generated by seven infants. Most still break topological ring shapes into strands; six out of these seven subjects break rings. They include binary breaking:

7.5.   RH *holds Large Ring near top*
7.5.   LH *pinches LR near top*
7.5a. LR *eventually splits but does not open out*
9.   RH *transfers LR to LH*
9a.   LR *opens out into long strand*   (12RD, page 48)

Three of these seven subjects break Euclidean balls:

12.   RH *finger pushes through Small Ball 4*
12a.   SB4 *breaks into a doughnut shape*   (12RD, page 57)

One result of breaking Euclidean objects is to give them clearly discernible topological features. This is definitely what another subject, 12LL, does by binary breaking. Then she examines, tactually and visually, the topological transformation in the object's part–whole relation which she has produced:

22.   BH *thumbs press into center of Large Ball*
22a.   LB *has a hole through it*
23.   BH *fingers slide up and press down into this same hole in LB, as looks very intently at LB from about 5 inches from it*
24.   BH *squish LB between fingers, as watches*
24a.   LB *deformed into a lump*
25.   BH *set LB down on table*
26.   BH *withdraw, while maintaining visual regard of deformed LB*
                                                          (12LL, page 17)

After careful examination of the transformed topological part–whole state of the object, 12LL reconstructs it into a Euclidean but deformed shape. Thus, she inversely transforms it back into a Euclidean form, but she does not preserve its form. Moreover, she is the only infant that compensates for breaking with reconstructing (Table 15.1, Row 4).

Nevertheless, this protoreversible construction of object identity is based upon pragmatic combination of breaking with inverse reconstructing. It therefore augments the developing structure of identity formation. Inverse protoreversibility complements, and thereby reinforces, the construction of object identity by inverse protoreversibility presented in Section I. Like reforming, reconstructing produces an intensity identity proto-operation while holding extensity constant.

Precursory protocorresponding breaking is generated by one infant only:

1.5.   LH *picks up Small Ring 1*
1.5.   RH *picks up Small Ring 3*
3.5.   LH *flicks SR1*

3.5a. *SR1 splits open*
3.5.   *RH flicks SR3*
3.5a. *SR3 splits open*   (*12EB*, page 18)

Subject *12EB* splits two rings at the same time by protocorresponding breaking. While she never reproduces protocorresponding breaking, she does construct equivalent breaking transformations in the part–whole relations in a set of two elements. Precursory equivalence in transforming topological into Euclidean forms begins to be possible.

Decomposing frequency does not change significantly from its rate at age 10 months (cf. Table 15.1, Row 5 and Table 11.1, Row 5). The means at age 12 months are lower in both the one-object and three-object conditions, but the differences are not statistically significant (Mann–Whitney tests: one-object condition $U = 10$, $p = .12$; three-object condition $U = 7$, $p = .155$).

The spontaneous rate of decomposing continues to be lower in the three-object ($\bar{x} = 1.53$ per minute) than in the one-object ($\bar{x} = 0.87$ per minute) condition. But the difference is no longer statistically significant ($N = 5$, $x = 2$, $p = .50$, sign test). There no longer is a difference in decomposing rate as a function of the objects' forms, i.e., Euclidean balls and topological rings. However, the data are based upon too few subjects to evaluate statistically.

The rate of decomposing during the second, provoked phase is no longer less than during the first spontaneous phase (Row 5, Columns 1, 2, 4, and 5). It is about the same as that during the first phase. Using decomposing productivity rate during the first phase as the base line indicates that modeling has no effect upon the frequency with which infants generate decomposing. The new development at this stage is that modeling decomposing no linger inhibits its production by infants. However, infants' decompositions during the second phase are no more direct copies of the model, than they are at the previous stages. Rather, their decompositions continue to be selective, transformative, and delayed.

Decomposing has become well-regulated. Sometimes it is preceded by studying the object:

1. *BH finger Large Ball as watches*
2. *BH pick up LB*
3. *BH rotate LB slowly*
4. *BH transfer LB to LH*
5. *LH rotates LB to left and to right*
6. *RH finger touches four to five times LB held by LH, as watches*
7. *looks at experimenter while LH holds LB*
8. *looks down at LB held by LH*
9. *RH finger touches two times LB held by LH*

10. *LH transfers LB to RH*
11. *LH pinches off small piece from LB held by RH*   (12DA, page 19)

Sometimes decomposing is repeated extensively and is accompanied by comparative observation:

22. *BH hold Large Ball, looking at it for about 10 seconds*
23. *bites a little piece (LP1) off LB held to mouth by LH*
24. *RH removes LP1 from mouth and turns it around while staring at it intently, as LH holds LB near mouth*
25. *RH thumb shakes vigorously until LP1 finally falls off*
26. *RH pulls little piece (LP2) off LB held by LH*
27. *LH drops LB to table as RH holds and looks at LP2*
28. *RH lets LP2 go and pulls off four little pieces (LP3, LP4, LP5, LP6) very quickly from LB*
29. *RH puts LP4 into mouth, starts chewing and makes disagreeable expression*
30. *RH picks up remainder of LB and holds it*
31. *RH holds LB over the right side of his chair*
32. *looks down towards the floor as RH holds LB over it*
33. *RH drops LB to floor as watches*
34. *looks toward LP1, LP2, LP3, LP5, and LP6 in front of him on table (experimenter replaces the LB from the floor)*
35. *RH sweeps LB off the table, again to his right*
36. *RH sweeps LP1, LP2, LP3, LP5, and LP6 off table*   (12DS, page 18)

Before decomposing, 12DS carefully examines the object (Line 22). After first decomposing it by mouth (Line 23), the subject carefully examines the piece he bit off (Line 24). He shifts to binary decomposing by hand (Line 26) and examines the piece he pulled off (Line 27). He follows up by rapidly decomposing four more pieces off the ball (Line 28).

Most decomposing, as the above protocol fragments indicate, is binary. Yet, most binary decomposings are still intersective results of direct mappings upon objects. Contingent decomposing is not generated more frequently at age 12 months than at age 10 months. Of course, it should be remembered that the test conditions did not provide the subjects with many potential instruments for contingent decomposing. It is therefore possible that we are underestimating contingent decomposing considerably.

Decomposing is beginning to have social consequences. Sometimes, the acts begin by being gestural and end by being consummated:

11. *LH pinches small piece (SP1) off Large Ball held by RH*
12. *LH puts SP1 in mouth, while RH holds LB*
13. *RH transfers LB to LH*
14. *RH removes SP1 from mouth and extends it to experimenter, while LH holds LB*

15. *RH puts SP1 in mouth, while LH holds LB*
16. *RH removes SP1 from mouth, while LH holds LB*
17. *mouth bites a small piece (SP2) off LB held to mouth by LH, while RH holds SP1*
18. *RH extends and gives SP1 to experimenter, while LH holds LB and mouth holds SP2* (12DA, page 19)

At other times, the social acts are entirely gestural:

21. *BH pull Small Ring apart into two pieces (P1 and P2)*
22. *RH extends P1 to mother but does not give it to her*
23. *RH puts P1 into mouth*
24. *RH extends P1 to mother but does not give it to her*
25. *RH puts P1 to mouth*
26. *RH extends P1 to mother but does not give it to her*
27. *RH hits P1 on high chair, four to five times* (12DA, page 24)

Subject 12DA eventually gives the experimenter a piece (in the first protocol fragment), but she never actually gives any to her mother. She always withdraws the Play-Doh before giving it to her mother (in the second fragment).

Most decomposing still generates no more than one two-element set, but many of these are now preserved beyond their construction as articulate durable sets, as least long enough to be monitored by the infant constructing the set:

11. *BH hold Large Ring*
12. *BH pull LR into two pieces (P1 in RH and P2 in LH)*
13. *looks at P1 in RH and P2 in LH* (12AM, page 20)

Some durable sets are beginning to be constructed which include an intermediate number of objects. For instance, 12DS (protocol fragment presented on page 382) divides one object into seven. He preserves five of the elements as an articulate set for some duration before sweeping the set off the table.

Other durable sets remain small but are embedded in extensive sequences of decompositions:

12. *bites off small piece (A2) from long strand (A*) held by BH*
13. *BH pull remainder of long strand (A1) from mouth*
14.3. *RH holds A1 on table*
14.7. *LH pulls A2 out of mouth and drops it to lap*
16. *RH releases A1 and BH pick up A2*
17. *BH pull A1 into two such that RH holds longer piece (A3) and LH holds smaller piece (A4)*
18. *looks at A3 held by RH*
19. *looks at A4 held by LH*
20. *looks at A3 held by RH*

21. *LH puts A4 in mouth which bites off small piece (A5)*
22. *LH pulls out remainder (A6)*
23. *looks at tip of A6 held by LH, smiling*
24.3. *looks at experimenter*
24.7. *mouth spits out A5 to table*
     (mother clears A5 away)
26. *looks down at table during and after mother clears it*
     subject: "Aaa"
27. *LH holds A6 in mouth which bites off small piece (A7)*
28. *LH pulls out remainder (A8)*
29. *looks up at experimenter*
     (mother takes A7 from subject's mouth)
30. *watches mother put A7 on table*
31.3. *looks at A3 held by RH*
31.7. *RH turns A3 upward a bit as watches*
33. *looks up and smiles at experimenter*
34. *looks at A8 held by LH*
35. *LH puts A8 in mouth which bites off piece (A9)*
36. *mouth bites off piece (A11) from remainder (A10) such that mouth holds
     A11 and LH holds new remainder (A12)*   (12RD, pages 48 and 49)

Subject *12RD* constructs an articulate durable two-element set of A3 and A4 which he comparatively monitors (Lines 17–20) before continuing to multiply decomposing A4. All together he generates six decompositions, after breaking the initial large ring (protocol fragment presented on page 380):

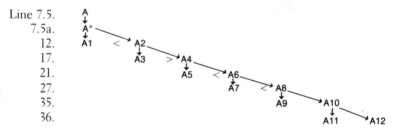

The decomposing sequence begins by producing an asymmetrical genealogy of descendant elements (Lines 12–21). This produces an ordered series of objects decreasing in mass. This includes comparative monitoring of an articulate two-element set (Lines 18–21). It continues on to dividing one into many elements (Lines 27–36). This, too, includes comparative monitoring of the objects (Lines 23, 26, and 30–34). While all the objects constructed are not preserved as an articulate set, they are increasingly monitored. This is consistent with the previous finding that durable sets of intermediate size are beginning to be constructed. Yet, asymmetrical genealogical decomposing remains limited to small numbers at this stage. Moreover, it is generated by only three infants.

Decomposing objects into two sets with symmetrical genealogies originates at this stage. It is rudimentary and generated only once by two infants. Both infants are also among the three subjects who generate asymmetrical genealogical decomposing:

5.5.   RH *squishes Ball A into two parts*
5.5a.   *two small pieces (A1 and A2) fall to table*
5.5.   LH *squishes Ball B into two parts*
5.5a.   *two small pieces (B1 and B2) separate but stick to LH*
7.   RH *picks up and squishes A1 into two parts (A3 and A4) and then A2 into two parts (A5 and A6)*
7a.   *A3, A4, A5, and A6 are clustered on table*
8.   LH *waves in the air to get B1 and B2 sticking to her fingers to fall to the table*
     (mother helps her out by peeling B1 and B2 off subject's fingers and places them on table)
9.   RH *picks up B1 and BH tear B1 apart into eight pieces (B3–10)*

(12LL, page 18)

Subject *12LL* generates two sets with symmetrical genealogies:

Line 4.

5.5., 5.5.

7., 9.

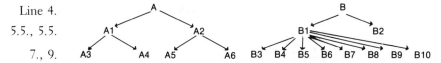

The binary sets constructed by *12LL* are semidifferentiated. On the one hand, the subject generates two separate sets by simultaneous protocorresponding decomposing (Lines 5.5–5.5). The A set (A1, A2) falls to the table; while the B set (B1, B2) remains attached to the subject's hand. The subject continues to decompose the A set into symmetrical genealogical descendants (Line 7). It produces an articulate durable four-element set (A3, A4, A5, A6). The elements of set A continue to be proximal to each other on the table, and, they continue to be separate from the B set which the subject is not successful in detaching from her fingers. On the other hand, as soon as her mother helps the subject detach set B, the subject proceeds to decompose B1 into B3–B10 (Line 9). At this point, she does not make any attempt to keep the elements of the two sets separately collected. So she ends up with a mixed set of eight very small elements and five larger elements.

One result is that the elements become mixed with each other so that the two sets are no longer differentiable from each other as two articulate durable sets. They are fused into a single syncretic set. Though syncretic, the set is relatively durable and includes a large number of elements, about 13. This marks another structural feature of decomposing that originates at this stage. Subjects are just beginning to progress beyond the construction of single sets of small numbers. They begin to generate relatively durable but syncretic single sets of fairly large numbers of elements.

Coordination between decomposing and deforming has become a well-regulated structure:

13. *RH index finger pulls small piece (SP1) off Large Ball held by LH*
14. *RH index finger rubs SP1 into table*
15. *RH index finger pulls small piece (SP2) off LB held by LH*
16. *RH index finger rubs SP2 into table*
    (experimenter extends hand for LB)
17. *RH index finger pulls small piece (SP3) off LB held by LH*
18. *RH index finger rubs SP3 into table*
19. *RH index finger pulls small piece (SP4) off LB held by LH*
20. *RH index finger rubs SP4 into table*
21. *looks at experimenter while experimenter holds hand out for LB held by LH*
22. *turns to mother*
23. *turns back to LB held by LH*
24. *RH index finger pulls small piece (SP5) off LB held by LH*
25. *RH index finger rubs SP5 into table*
26. *RH index finger pulls small piece (SP6) off LB held by LH*
27. *RH index finger rubs SP6 into table*
    (experimenter extends hand for LB held by LH)
28. *RH index finger pulls small piece (SP7) off LB held by LH*
29. *RH index finger rubs SP7 into table*   (12AM, page 26)

Each decomposition (Lines 13, 15, 17, 19, 24, 26, and 28) is followed by contingently deforming (Lines 14, 16, 18, 20, 25, 27, and 29) the smaller piece pulled off. Protocorresponding mappings (pull off) are used in all decompositions, and protocorresponding mappings (rub into table) are used in all deformations. Thus, coordinated decomposing–deforming is extensive, consecutive, and reproductive.

Coordinate structures of decomposing and deforming have become controlled. This makes it possible to comparatively examine (*a*) multiplication of elements by decomposition and (*b*) equivalence of deformation by protocorrespondence, within a delimited spatiotemporal frame. Consider what the same subject does:

15. *LH picks up Small Piece 1 and flicks it back and forth between thumb and index finger*
16. *looks to right as RH reaches to Small Piece 2 and picks it up*
17. *looks at SP2 held by RH*
18. *BH hold SP1 and SP2*
19. *LH runs fingers on SP2 held by RH together with SP1*
20. *LH pulls off small piece (SP3) from top of SP2 held by RH together with SP1*   (12AM, page 21)

The continuation of this protocol fragment has already been presented on page 377. The subject examines the set of two objects (Lines 15–19) before decomposing one of them (Line 20). She preserves the expanded set of three elements long enough to examine the transformation, that is, the new element (Lines 21–25). She proceeds to deform it twice (Lines 26 and 28). The deformations construct articulate protocorresponding equivalent transformations in the part–whole relations internal to the smaller element. They are preserved, like those of the set, long enough to be examined.

IV. Precursory Quantitative Identity by Coordinated Composing and Redecomposing

Recomposing previously decomposed parts is generated as infrequently as at age 10 months (cf. Table 15.1, Row 6 and Table 11.1, Row 6). Moreover, recomposing remains restricted to reconstituting the initial extensity, but not the intensity, of objects. When it is generated, however, extensity protoidentity by protoreversible recomposing is becoming directed and articulate:

50. *RH pulls piece (5A) off Strand 5 and raises 5A above table*
51. *RH presses 5A onto S5 on table*
51a. *S5 and 5A are deformed into one shapeless clump* (12KH, page 35)

Composing objects not previously decomposed increases in frequency (cf. Table 15.1 Row 7 and Table 11.1, Row 7). Composing is now generated by one-half of the infants, that is, six subjects. The most advanced composing, generated by only one infant, unites all six ring objects presented during phase III.

Composing is becoming a directed combinativity proto-operation:

11. *RH places and holds Small Ball 1 on top of Small Ball 2*
12. *RH picks up SB1 and SB2 and squishes them together*
13. *RH wrist flicks composed SB1/SB2 to table* (12LL, page 19)

Subject 12LL takes two of the six objects presented and unites them into a larger mass (Line 12). Although directed, composing is still not always regulated. For instance, 12LL makes no attempt to either observe the product of her composition or follow up with subsequent composing. She immediately discards the new object (Line 13). At other times, as we shall see below, composing is both directed and regulated. This is the case even for subject 12LL. Fluctuation between regulated and nonregulated composing is symptomatic of the transitional structure of this stage of quasi-continuous composition.

The rates of producing discrete compositions in these quasi-continuous conditions continue to stay well below those in the discrete conditions (cf. Table 15.1, Row 14, Columns 1–6 and Table 13.1, Row 3). The rates do increase somewhat over those at age 10 months (cf. Table 11.1, Row 14). Two factors account for the increases. One is the general increase in discrete composing at age 12 months already noted in Chapter 11. Another is the increase in quasi-continuous composing at age 12 months, which we have just noted. Quasi-continuous composing necessarily entails discrete composing to bring the objects together so that they can be united into one. Thus, the increase in rate of quasi-continuous composing increases the rate of discrete composing.

Modeling composing during the second test phase has no effect (Table 15.1, Row 7, Columns 2 and 5). It is often followed by the subject transforming objects. Almost all are deformations and decompositions rather than compositions (Rows 1 and 5, Columns 2 and 5). In fact, only two subjects generate any composing during phase II.

Composing is beginning to take on a directed social dimension. Infants take note of the experimenter's composing. Occasionally, they seem to urge the experimenter on to produce multiple compositions. One infant, 12RD, even initiates cooperative composing. He observes the experimenter's composing throughout, beginning with the experimenter's visible composing, which initiates phase II for this subject. He follows with multiple apparent requests for composing with which the experimenter complies, illustrated in this brief fragment:

11. *LH touches, possibly presses, Large Ball to the piece of Play-Doh in experimenter's hand*
    (experimenter takes LB from subject)
12. *BH hit on table, as bounces and smiles at experimenter*
    (experimenter makes one larger ball in front of subject and puts it on table)   (12RD, page 55)

Notice that 12RD also initiates cooperative composing (Line 11). He does this twice during this test phase. At the end of the test phase 12RD composes two balls on his own.

It would be an error to infer from this description that modeling or social cooperation are even local causes of the origins of composing. As already reported, modeled composing is almost always followed by different forms of transforming, if it is followed by any transforming at all. Furthermore, even in the case of 12RD, this is not the first time he generates composing; 12RD first composed objects during the prior spontaneous test phase:

18.7. *LH picks up Balls 2 and 3 and squeezes them together*
      subject: "Eh—aah—a-deah aaah"

18.7a. *B2 and B3 are composed into a wad (B2/B3)*
  20. *rocks back and forth in seat, as LH holds B2/B3*
  21. *mouths B2/B3 held by LH*
  22. *bites off piece (P1) as LH pulls remainder of B2/B3 from mouth*

                                                           (12RD, page 54)

Second-order reversible coordination between composing and decomposing originates at this stage. Redecomposing is generated by three infants (Table 15.1, Row 8). Subject *12RD*'s constructions are rudimentary in this respect. After composing Balls 2 and 3 into one (Line 18.7), he partially reverses the transformation by redecomposing a piece from the resultant wad (Line 22).

More advanced structural coordination between composing and decomposing is generated occasionally. The inverse transformations are just beginning to be directed and regulated:

  6. *BH raise Rings 1, 2, and 3 and scrunch them together into a blob (B)*
  7. *LH pulls piece (P1) off B held by RH*
  8. *LH transfers P1 to RH which holds remainder of B*
  9. *RH drops P1 while holding onto B*
  10. *LH picks up P1 as RH holds B*
  11. *LH transfers P1 to RH which holds B*
  12. *RH composes B and P1 together as bounces up and down*
  13. *RH transfers recomposed blob (B') to LH*
  14. *RH pulls off a piece (P2) from B' held by LH*
  15. *RH puts P2 in mother's hand*
     (mother puts her hand on the table with P2 in it)
  16. *RH pulls off a piece (P3) from B' held by LH*
  17. *RH puts P3 in mother's hand*
  18. *RH takes P2 and P3 back from mother's hand*
  19. *LH transfers B' to RH which holds P2 and P3*
     (experimenter extends her hand)
  20. *RH touches B', P2, and P3 to experimenter's outstretched hand but does not give them to experimenter*
  21. *RH places down on table in front of her and BH fingers mush B', P2, and P3 together into one recomposed blob (B'')*   (12LL, pages 22 and 23)

Many-to-one composition (Line 6) is followed immediately by one-to-many decomposition (Line 7), followed by composition (Line 12), followed by one-to-many decompositions (Lines 14 and 16), and ends in many-to-one composition (Line 21). The two inverse decompositions or redecompositions are not equivalent to their immediately preceding compositions. Both times the subject pulls off different pieces than she puts together. The two inverse compositions or recompositions are equivalent to their immediately preceding decompositions. Both times the subject puts together the same pieces she pulls off. The successive repetition indicates that this has already become a regulated coordinative structure.

Direct composing and decomposing transformations are beginning to be transformed into each other by an inverse operator. The inverse operator is central to the emergence at this stage of second-order combinativity proto-operations. However, protoreversible redecomposing, like recomposing at this stage, only constructs extensity identity. It never constructs intensity identity. All protoreversible operations at this stage have only partial application. They begin to reconstitute either extensity identity or intensity identity, but never both at the same time.

Once composing is generated fairly frequently, at this stage, redecomposing becomes relatively frequent. That is, redecomposing (Table 15.1, Row 8) becomes more frequent than recomposing (Row 6). This result obtains even though the opportunities for recomposing far exceed those for redecomposing; since decomposing is generated far more frequently than composing. Thus, second-order protoreversible decomposing is generated more frequently than second-order protoreversible composing at their origins. This is consistent with and continues the developmental trend in generating first-order combinativity proto-operations. While all infants generate decomposing frequently (Row 5), only one-half the same infants generate composing and at a much lower rate (Row 7). Negating, then, predominates over affirming reversible combinativity proto-operations as it still does irreversible combinativity proto-operations.

Structural Development during the First Year

16

Protological constructions are extensive. They entail (*a*) combinativity proto-operations of composing, decomposing, and deforming; (*b*) relational proto-operations of adding, subtracting, multiplying, and dividing; and (*c*) conditional proto-operations of exchange, correlation, and negation. They produce precursory equivalence, nonequivalence, and reversible relations. At each stage, then, protological constructions are coherently related into an organization of functional structures. Moreover, the organization of protologic is transformed developmentally stage by stage. These guiding hypotheses are corroborated by the cognitive development of infants from ages 6 to 12 months discovered in this research.

These findings constitute initial evidence for the developmental hypothesis that the origins of logical, mathematical, and experimental cognition are to be found in the organization of transformational operations generated by preverbal infants. The findings also support the structural hypothesis that, from its origins on, the organization of inferential transformations is a threefold foundation composed of combinativity, relational, and conditional proto-operations.

The findings do not support the epistemological views that the origin of logic is an outgrowth of language, particularly of conventionalism and nominalism (e.g., Carnap), of analytic philosophy (e.g., Wittgenstein), and of students of ordinary language (e.g., Strawson). Rather, the findings provide initial confirmation for the hypothesis that protologic precedes language, and, eventually uses protosymbolization as a notational system to facilitate and expand computation. Indeed, we have already discovered some of the precursory development of protosymbolization and its utilization by proto-operations, as in the formation of analogical protocorrespondences. We may therefore well expect that children at intermediate stages of logical cognition will use language as a notational system in the service of their inferential constructions.

These findings, then, provide an empirical base for a structural model of logic at its ontogenetic origins; coupled with a developmental model of logical constructions or operations from infancy to adulthood. Logical cognition is limited to pragmatic and presentational relations of proto-operations throughout the first year. Yet, infants' constructions already produce three basic elements of logic and mathematics. These are extensive and intensive equivalence, iterative ordering, and reversible relations. They also exhibit the basic elements of three operational structures which are necessary elements of even adult logical and mathematical thought. These are combinativity, relational, and conditional operations.

It would be premature to propose a full-scale structural developmental model of logical cognition until we have traced empirically the full course of logical development up to middle childhood. Then systematic comprehensive data begin to be available from other sources in the research literature on cognitive development. The necessary bridging data will be presented in subsequent volumes on our research on logical developments during late infancy and early childhood.

Still, the outlines of a structural developmental model are beginning to unfold. The model accounts for the ontogenetic data reported so far. It conforms to the constraints imposed by our structural developmental theory introduced in the first chapter. Many basic properties of the model have already been considered throughout this work when they were particularly relevant to the analyses of the findings. Here we will draw them together into a preliminary sketch of the model.

The basic, but not exhaustive, defining properties of combinativity structures, as of the two other sets of protological structures which relate and condition them, will be analyzed as a first step toward formulating a structural developmental model. The structural properties of protologic develop stage by stage. Therefore, principles of developmental transformations in these structural properties from the first to the fourth stage will also be analyzed. Together, these analyses are the bases for the initial formulation of our structural developmental model of logical cognition.

In order to keep clear the structural properties that distinguish different stages in the development of protologic the following convention will be adopted. The referenced stage will be marked by the first integer used to number the defining properties. For instance, (1.1) refers to the first structural property defined at the first stage studied here and (4.1) refers to the first structural property defined at the fourth stage.

The constructive picture which emerges is that of original symmetry in the infant's universe. Composing dominates transactions with discrete objects. Deforming, decomposing, and breaking dominate transactions with quasi-continuous objects. Detaching is just beginning to dominate transactions with combinations of discrete and quasi-continuous objects.

There is provisional equilibrium, then, between combinativity operations in intersection with object types. Across the universe of objects, all the fundamental proto-operational structures of combinativity are in place (i.e., composing, deforming, decomposing, breaking, and detaching).

(1.1) *Composition.* Discrete elements are momentarily united to form labile wholes. Compositions have both extensive and intensive structure. They are in initial equilibrium. On the one hand, the extensive structures of combinativity are constructed by affirmation. Objects are composed together into larger wholes simply because they share the common extensive property of being units that can be collected together as elements of a set. On the other hand, the intensive structures of combinativity are constructed by negation. Objects are composed together that differ in their predicate properties. Thus, extensive assimilation of objects to each other by affirmation is symmetrical to intensive accommodation of objects to each other by negation. This supports the theoretical hypothesis that affirmation structures and assimilative functions are balanced by negation structures and accommodative functions from the outset of cognitive development (Langer, in press). There can be no logical or ontogenetic priority of affirmation and assimilation over negation and accommodation.

(1.1.1) *Extensity.* Wholes are constructed in isolation. They are singular collections that are not related to any other collection. They only include very small membership. Usually, only two members belong to a collection. Three-element compositions are rare and four-or-more-element compositions are virtually nonexistent.

(1.1.2) *Intensity.* The properties common to the members belonging to individual compositions vary as a function of class condition. The common property in well-structured class conditions—additive, multiplicative, and disjoint—is differences. In ambiguous class conditions the objects are not collected in terms of their similar or different properties but are random.[1]

---

[1] Claparède's (1918) law of conscious realization or *prise de conscience*, elaborated by Piaget (1976), states that cognizance of differences precedes that of similarities. Noncogni-

(1.2) *Decomposition.* Quasi-continuous objects are partitioned into labile descendant elements. Decompositions have both extensive and intensive structure.

(1.2.1) *Extensity.* Objects are partitioned into very small numbers of descendant elements, which are not collected into even singular labile sets. Inherent in partitioning are two quantitative proto-operations:

(1.2.1.1) *Protomultiplication.* One-to-many decomposition is generated in isolation such that the usual number of descendants are two parts. One-to-three protomultiplication by decomposition is rare and one-to-four-or-more protomultiplication is virtually nonexistent.

(1.2.1.2) *Protodivision.* The descendant parts are smaller than the whole out of which they are generated. With one exception to be specified under (1.9), they remain unordered. In particular, asymmetrical geneological decomposing of a whole into progressively smaller parts is never generated.

(1.2.2) *Intensity.* Descendant parts are different in form from each other and from the whole out of which they are decomposed.

(1.3) *Breaking.* Quasi-continuous objects are broken into different forms. Breaks have intensive structure only. The extensive structure is held constant.

(1.3.1) *Intensity.* Isolated and infrequent breaking is applied to individual quasi-continuous objects. Breaking changes the form and the shape. Solid Euclidean forms are not yet broken into differently shaped topological ring forms. Topological ring forms are broken into differently shaped Euclidean forms.

(1.4) *Deformation.* Quasi-continuous objects are continuously deformed from one shape into another. Deformations have intensive structure only. The extensive structure is held constant.

(1.4.1) *Intensity.* Numerous deformations are applied to individual quasi-continuous objects; sometimes in isolation, sometimes consecutively, and occasionally at the same time. Solid Euclidean forms are shaped

---

zant automatic functioning is based upon similarities. Likewise, the Gestalt "law of equality" states that equal elements are quasi-automatically attracted to each other. This leads Werner (1937) to the hypothesis that the most primitive initial stage of categorizing is by similarities between elements. Differences, according to Claparede and Piaget, disrupt the automaticity of functioning and lead to awareness, including that of similarities. Vygotsky (1962) also claims that advanced classification proceeds from grouping by dissimilarities to sorting by similarities, while young children's initial unorganized congeries or heaps are either randomly constructed or based upon automatic similarities. In this Piaget (1977) concurs. Our findings disconfirm this claim. At first infants compose by differences in structured class conditions and randomly in ambiguous class conditions. Thus, if Claparede's law is valid it applies to the origins of predication as well.

into different solid Euclidean forms only. Topological ring forms are shaped into different topological and Euclidean forms.

(1.5) *Detaching*. Combined objects are partitioned into their constituent discrete and quasi-continuous parts. Detaching has both extensive and intensive structures.

(1.5.1) *Extensity*. Combined objects are partitioned into their constituent discrete and quasi-continuous elements. They are not collected into even labile sets. Inherent in detaching, as in decomposing, are two quantitative proto-operations:

(1.5.1.1) *Protomultiplication*. The combined singular object is multiplied into two objects by detaching one from the other.

(1.5.1.2) *Protodivision*. The descendant parts are smaller than the whole out of which they are generated.

(1.5.2) *Intensity*. As with decomposing, descendant parts are different in form from each other and from the whole out of which they are detached. Unlike decomposing, descendant parts conserve their basic form. This is particularly so for the discrete parts which are not subject to further transformations by infants.

All protologic, including combinativity proto-operations, requires at least minimal constant givens as elements in order to construct protoinferential relations. The elements may be mappings, symbols, objects, collections of objects, or combinations of the preceding list of potential constant givens. Consequently, the level at which phenomena are established as constant givens by infants constrains their stage of protooperational construction of precursory inferential relations.

The hypotheses, here, are twofold. Elements as constant givens are not transmitted to infants, either genetically or environmentally. They are not innate preformed knowledge. Nor are they physical or social preformed knowledge. Constant givens are constructed by infants by their interactions with the phenomena listed above. Constant givens, moreover, are developmental constructions. They are not immutable either before (preformed) or after (constructed) their provisional establishment by infants. They evolve stage by stage of cognitive development.

The construction of constant givens is already in progress during the first stage. It takes many interrelated forms, necessary to detach elements from infants' ongoing processes of construction and experiences. These forms of detachment provide elements with preliminary cognitive independence and logical coherence. This requires determining that individual objects maintain their identity across inverse spatial transformations, comparing the identity of two objects to each other across corresponding inverse transformations, preserving the existence of individual objects by presentational search, and determining the regularities of elementary causal transformations. All these forms of detachment are necessary to establish objects as constant givens notwithstanding their ongoing experienced transformations and their contiguous or contextual relations. Only then is it possible to use them as the given elements for subsequent inferential constructions.

This initial level of constructing constant givens is sufficient to multiply one into many quasi-continuous objects by decomposition. It is not yet adequate as a means of composing a set. As soon as new objects are generated by decomposition they are discarded. They are never collected into even momentary sets.

Such limitations highlight the minimal degree to which experienced objects have been transformed into constant givens at this initial stage. Decomposing transform both the extensive and intensive properties of quasi-continuous objects. These transformations are too radical for infants to detach the new elements they are generating from their ongoing process of decomposing. They immediately discard the new elements, that is, they remain attached to their ongoing constructive experience. This is confirmed by the findings on both breaking and deforming quasi-continuous objects. Both combinativity proto-operations transform the intensive properties of objects while holding their extensive properties constant. Still no effort is made to reform or reconstitute the initial identity of the objects.

Similar but less severe restrictions apply to the composition of discrete objects. They begin by being labile constructions marked by the following features. Compositions are limited to consecutive single sets. Binary sets are not constructed. Sets only include very small numbers of objects. The remainder of the presented objects are not included. Usually, only one of the objects in a set is directly manipulated in order to construct the set. Kinetic compositions or mobiles predominate over static compositions or stabiles. Whether stabiles or mobiles, their life-spans rarely exceed their periods of construction. They are transient sets which do not endure.

This level of constructing constant givens is sufficient to compose discrete objects into labile sets. Composing discrete objects into sets is generated frequently. Recomposing initial into variant sets is a regular characteristic of set construction. Consecutive set construction already predominates over isolate set construction. The rate of producing sets by composition is remarkably constant across class conditions and object types, indicating that the constructions are not fortuitous. Moreover, infants begin to monitor, albeit infrequently, irregularly and briefly, objects before and after composing them. They also begin to monitor their own ongoing combinativity proto-operations upon the objects.

Detaching or abstracting constant elements, whether mappings, protosymbols, objects or sets, from the ongoing flow of infants' constructive processes and interactive experience, then, is minimal. Still it is sufficient to provide the initial givens for further proto-operational constructions. In this regard it is necessary to distinguish between relational and conditional operations applied to mappings and protosymbols from those applied to combinativity proto-operations.

Mappings are abstracted in three main ways so as to provide constant givens for relational and conditional operations (Chapter 2, Section III). First, compactness promotes abstracting the forms of mappings. A very limited set of mapping forms are generated. This insures at least partial transformational consistency and conservation across time and objects of transaction. Second, mapping forms begin, although still rarely during the initial stage, to be repeated consecutively or simultaneously. Then they remain constant regardless of the objects of transaction. Third, a subset of mappings becomes detached from their initial transactive contexts. They begin to acquire protosymbolic features of representing and referring.

These three forms of abstracting mappings as constant givens, then, produce partially stable elements. Some of these are used, even during the first stage, as the given elements of protoinferential relations. Already included are elementary relational proto-operations of addition and subtraction conditioned by reciprocal proto-operations. For instance, bidirectional order relations of $\langle 2, 3, 2 \rangle$ consecutive hits by a hand on an object are generated. They also already include elementary conditional proto-operations which correlate mappings. For instance, single-unit mapping protocorrespondences are generated, such as both hands hitting down once on the table.

These proto-operations upon mappings, as constant given elements, produce pragmatic rudiments of fundamental inferential relations (i.e., equivalence, ordered nonequivalence, and reversibility). They are sufficient to the construction of precursory practical intelligence. This includes those aspects of relational and conditional proto-operations not focally analyzed in this research. For instance, inverse relations may be constructed between mappings, such as inverse displacement mappings.

Still inferential relations upon mappings are severely limited. This is inherent in the limited durability of mappings. They are changed constantly. They are changed much more rapidly than their objects of transaction. This ratio, as we have seen, is a constant of infants' transactions at all four stages; although, importantly, it decreases from the first to the fourth stage. Mappings as compared to objects have limited potential as constant given elements. There is one exception to this rule which becomes increasingly relevant at later stages to be considered in subsequent volumes. This is the subset of mappings which are transformed, structurally and developmentally, into a notational system. Symbols become a powerful pool of constant given elements for operational construction of inferential relations. This is because symbols become a detached and therefore abstract subset of constant given elements.

While still predominantly labile at this stage, objects and compositions of objects are nevertheless powerful sets of constant givens as compared to mappings. The entire spectrum of elementary relational and conditional proto-operations can and are therefore already applied to them.

The original functional structures of constructed relational operations include all the fundamental transformations necessary to generate quantitative relations:

(1.6) *Protoaddition*. Pragmatic additions produce iterative series of ordered increasing magnitudes and numbers. The constructions vary somewhat as a function of the type of objects to which they are applied.

(1.6.1) *Discrete*. Inherent additive iteration predominates. Most compositions generated consist of two-element sets constructed by actively manipulating only one element. Entailed in these compositions is the formation of ⟨one-, two-⟩ element sets. Precursory additive iteration which extends beyond the inherent just begin to be generated. They take three rudimentary yet basic forms.

(1.6.1.1) Three-step ⟨one-, two-, three-⟩ or ⟨one-, two-, many-⟩ element consecutive unary sets are constructed.

(1.6.1.2) Two-point ⟨one, two⟩ or ⟨one, many⟩ discrete magnitude orders are generated within compositions (e.g., hitting one object on another once and then twice).

(1.6.1.3) Two-point continuous magnitude orders are generated within compositions (e.g., hitting one object on another lightly then harder). As compared to discrete iteration, whether of elements or magnitudes, continuous iteration is always imprecisely constructed by practical intelligence. It cannot be constructed precisely until measurement operations are developed during middle and late childhood (Piaget, Inhelder, & Szeminska, 1960). However, these measurement operations are themselves developmental descendants of discrete iteration coordinated with transitivity operations. Thus, the logicomathematical precedence of discrete quantification is maintained throughout cognitive development.

(1.6.2) *Quasi-continuous*. Inherent additive iteration predominates. Most ordered increases are continuous series directly entailed by continuous deformations which produce them (e.g., continuously pulling on a Play-Doh ball such that it is progressively elongated). Some ordered increases form discrete series (e.g., the result of consecutive discrete plucking at a Play-Doh ball). Here the potential for detachment, at least temporally, of the ordered product from the constructive operation begins to be generated.

(1.7) *Protosubtraction.* Pragmatic subtractions produce iterative series of ordered decreasing magnitudes and numbers. These constructions complement those of protoaddition. The level of protosubtraction and the variation due to the differential structures of discrete versus quasi-continuous objects parallels that of protoaddition. The only difference is quantitative, not structural. Protosubtraction is generated less frequently than protoaddition.

(1.8) *Protomultiplication.* Pragmatic multiplications and their products vary as a function of the objects to which they are applied.

(1.8.1) *Discrete.* Two forms are constructed. One will be considered under (1.14), namely, one-to-many correlations which produce multiplicative relations. The other, inclusion relations, produces two-dimensional compositions. Thereby one element is multiplicatively included in two two-element subsets of one three-element set. This is the extent of multiplicative inclusion at its origins. It does not exceed one-by-two multiplications. Even these are generated rarely since most compositions do not exceed one-dimensional two-element sets.

(1.8.2) *Quasi-continuous.* Single objects are decomposed into many objects. Decomposition rarely exceeds minimal multiplication, that is, one-into-two objects transformations. The extent never exceeds one-into-four objects. With rare exceptions the multiple objects are not collected and preserved as a set. The exceptions are always limited to the minimal extent, namely, one two-element set preserved momentarily and monitored. Multiplication never produces binary two-element sets.

(1.9) *Protodivision.* There is no evidence of practical divisibility applied to discrete objects, such as taking out a part (subset) included in a whole (set) to form a composition (set). Pragmatic divisibility is applied to quasi-continuous objects. Single objects are divided into smaller objects by decomposition. This produces order relations. Most are inherent 2-point series. Entailed in the usual fractionating of a larger into two smaller objects is the construction of the consecutively ordered ⟨big, smaller⟩ objects. Synchronic noninherent orders are also beginning to be constructed since the larger object is usually decomposed into unequal fractions (i.e., a small and a big object), but the synchronic order ⟨ small, big⟩ objects is rarely preserved beyond the moment of its construction as a related set.

Both combinativity and relational proto-operations begin to be conditioned from the outset by exchange, correlation, and negation proto-operations. These insure at least minimal integration of the functional structures of logical and mathematical operations into an organized totality at all stages of development.

The original functional structures of constructed exchange include three fundamental equivalence proto-operations. To begin with they are applied only to composing and recomposing single two-element sets. Moreover they are rarely replicated consecutively.

(1.10) *Protoreplacement.* Equivalence between compositions and their recompositions is produced by coordinating protosubtraction of one element **b** from a two-element set (**a, b**) followed by protoaddition of the same single element **b** to reconstitute the initial two-element set (**a, b**). All the elements and the order plus enclosure relations between the elements of set (**a, b**) begin to be kept constant. Thus,

$$(a, b) - (b) + (b) \sim (a, b) \qquad (16.1)$$

(1.11) *Protosubstitution.* Equivalence between consecutive compositions is produced by coordinating protosubtraction of one element **b** from a two-element set (**a, b**) followed by protoaddition of a different element **c** to constitute a variant two-element set (**a, c**). Only one of the elements **a** in the initial two-element set (**a, b**) is kept constant. The order and the enclosure relations begin to be kept constant when the initial set (**a, b**) is transformed into the subsequent (**a, c**) set. Thus,

$$(a, b) - (b) + (c) \approx (a, c) \qquad (16.2)$$

(1.12) *Protocommutativity.* Equivalence between consecutive compositions is produced by coordinating consecutive order and enclosure rearrangements of a two-element set (**a, b**). Both elements of the set are kept constant. The most primitive, that is, precursory, form generated includes only a single rearrangement

$$\langle a, b \rangle \rightsquigarrow \langle b, a \rangle \qquad (16.3)$$

But even at this initial stage two consecutive rearrangements are beginning to be generated which roughly reconstitute the order and enclosure properties of the initial two-element set. Consecutive commutative proto-operations transform Eq. (16.3) into its derivative structure

$$\langle a, b \rangle \rightsquigarrow \langle b, a \rangle \rightsquigarrow \langle a, b \rangle \qquad (16.4)$$

In effect, precursory protoreversibility is applied approximately to protocommutativity.

The original functional structures of constructed correlation include both a fundamental equivalence operation (bi-univocal one-to-one protocorrespondence) and a fundamental multiplicative operation (co-univocal one-to-many protocorrespondences).

(1.13) *Bi-univocal Protocorrespondences.* Equivalence between objects is limited to the minimum of one-to-one matchings between two objects composed into a singular set (e.g., linear spatial alignments between the base of two objects).[2] They are augmented by continuous protocorrespondences (e.g., hit one object *lightly* on another twice in a row). Continuous protocorrespondences are limited to single undifferentiated properties.

(1.14) *Co-univocal Protocorrespondences.* One-to-many multiplicative relations between objects are usually consecutive. They do not usually exceed matching one-to-three objects; although one-to-four matchings are generated rarely. The isomorphic form of many-to-one multiplicative relations between objects is never constructed.

The original functional structures of constructed negation includes two elementary yet fundamental reversible operations (i.e., inverse and reciprocal proto-operations). The proto-operations begin to condition other transformational constructions in rudimentary ways, as shown throughout the analyses of the first stage. As such, they prepare the precursory structures of first-order reversible proto-operations.

(1.15) *Protoinverse.* The application of inverse to direct transformations just begins to create a powerful but incomplete organization of precursory reversible structures. Most important are the following:

(1.15.1) Identity of singular elements and two-element compositions despite spatial transformations begins to be established by compensatory proto-operations, such as combinations of inverting–reverting and displacement–replacement.

(1.15.2) Inverse subtraction and addition (taking away followed by putting back the same element) are ingredient to the formation of equivalence by protoreplacement even when executed in isolation.

(1.15.3) Consecutive decomposing of quasi-continuous objects results in the origins of recomposing by uniting the decomposed parts.

---

[2] This is one of the exceptional instances in which proto-operations are more advanced when applied to mappings than to objects. Equivalence between discrete mappings are already extended to two-to-two matchings by some infants at this stage. These are always consecutive (e.g., bang a hand on the table twice, pause, repeat). When mapping protocorrespondences are constructed simultaneously, then the same minimal limit of one-to-one correlations obtains (e.g., bang each hand on the table once at the same time).

Neither extensive nor intensive identity is produced since the recompositions unite fractional parts of, not the whole of, the initial object.

The lacunae in the organization of protoinverse structures are vast and immediately apparent. Consider some of the properties of the three structures just listed. Inverse protooperations cannot be applied to single sets which contain more than two elements, let alone more than one set, in order to produce identity. They cannot be applied to single sets which contain more than two elements, let alone more than one set, to construct equivalence by protoreplacement or protosubstitution. Moreover, they can only be applied once to single sets. They cannot be used to recompose more than two fractional decompositions of quasi-continuous objects; and they never reconstitute the original whole.

(1.16) *Protoreciprocity*. The application of reciprocal to direct transformations also begins to create a powerful but incomplete organization of precursory reversible structures. Most important are the following:

(1.16.1) Reciprocal variation of order and enclosure is applied to discrete recomposing. The result is equivalence by protocommutativity. Protoreciprocity, then, is ingredient to protocommutativity just as inverting is ingredient to protoreplacement.

(1.16.2) Inherent protoreciprocity accompanies all deformations of quasi-continuous objects. For instance, flattening a ball is necessarily compensated by widening it.

(1.16.3) Reciprocal protoaddition and protosubtraction construct bidirectional orderings. The results are equivalences between increasing and decreasing series. Bidirectional orderings are applied only to discrete objects but not yet to quasi-continuous objects. However, both discrete and continuous magnitudes as well as number of elements are iterated into bidirectional orderings.

The organization of protoreciprocal structures is as incomplete as that of protoinverse structures. Consider some of the properties of the three structures just listed. Protoreciprocity cannot be applied to single sets which include more than two elements, let alone more than one set, in order to produce equivalence. Deforming quasi-continuous objects cannot be compensated by reforming them so as to produce identity by protoreciprocity. Protoreciprocal addition and subtraction cannot be applied to quasi-continuous objects.

Complementing the provisional equilibrium in the organization of first-order protological structures is provisional disequilibrium. Organizational disequilibrium is marked by incompleteness, segregation, and lability. We have already remarked about the incompleteness, segregation, and lability of relational and conditional structures and upon the lability of combinativity structures.

It is necessary to briefly remark upon the segregation between the intensive and extensive properties of protological structures. Throughout this work we have found that they are inversely correlated, at least until the fourth stage. For instance, quantitative equivalence relations within sets by protoexchange or protocorrelational operations are invariably accompanied by random or dissimilar predicate relations between the elements comprising the sets. They are totally uncoordinated. This initial uncoupling provides the inherent structural basis for differentiating quantitative from qualitative or predicate calculations. At the same time segregation between extensive and intensive structural properties is a main source of organizational disequilibrium. This provides the condition necessary to their ultimate coordination, that is, their simultaneous differentiation and integration. This as we already know originates, in small part, at the fourth stage when predication in the additive class conditions begins to be by similarities.

It remains for us to consider the incompleteness of first-order combinativity structures. Disequilibrium in functional structures of combinativity is a fundamental impetus to their progressive developmental reorganization. Let us therefore examine the internal imbalances within the organization of functional structures which are the constructive sources of developing combinativity operations.

Within each subuniverse of objects, combinativity operations are incomplete. Decomposing is lacking in the subuniverse of discrete objects. Composing is missing in the subuniverse of quasi-continuous objects. Attaching is missing in the subuniverse of combined discrete–quasi-continuous objects.

Consequently, combinativity operations are segregated from each other within each subuniverse of objects. Composing is not balanced by decomposing transactions with discrete objects. Deforming and decomposing are not balanced by composing transactions with quasi-continuous objects. Detaching is not balanced by attaching transactions with combined discrete–quasi-continuous objects.

Moreover, the initial functional structures of combinativity are inherent or precursory. They construct only direct and partial transformations of their objects of transaction. With exceptions to be considered later, they are only sufficient to produce first-order inferential proto-operations. These are unrelated to each other. Yet, they are antecedent to second-order proto-operations, or proto-operations on proto-operations, since the fundamental structural elements have been constructed. Their developmental transformation is dependent upon progressively coordinating first-order operations to each other. The balance between combinativity operations across the universe of objects has yet to be applied to each subuniverse of objects.

Aspects of rudimentary coordination between combinativity proto-operations which are beginning to overcome their segregation originate at the first stage. Consider first their applications to discrete objects. Composing sets is followed up fairly often by recomposing; though the relationship is necessarily labile since both initial and variant sets are labile. Combined mobile–stabile compositions are already constructed, although infrequently.

Now consider the coordinate applications of combinativity proto-operations to quasi-continuous objects. Deforming begins to be combined with decomposing. Initially these coordinations are inherent (i. e., deforming is entailed in decomposing). Some are already precursory elaborations (i.e., prolongation of deforming into decomposing, prolongation of decomposing into deforming, and simultaneous but separate application of decomposing and deforming to the same object). As already noted above, one other form of coordination is generated infrequently. It is the inherent entailment of recomposing in some forms of consecutive decompositions.

Rudiments of coordinating some exchange proto-operations which produce equivalence relations also begin to be generated. Protoreplacement and protosubstitution are applied consecutively to the same set, although they are never repeated more than once. Protoreplacement and protocommutativity are also applied consecutively to the same set, although they too are never repeated more than once.

We have already outlined the other major forms of proto-operational coordination which are generated at the first stage under defining properties (1.15) and (1.16). Protoinverse and protoreciprocal negation operations begin to coordinate other proto-operations. Thereby, they initiate reversible relations, such as bidirectional iteration.

The initial equilibrium in the organization of protologic, then, provides the elementary cognitive foundations upon which infants construct progressively advanced cognitions. They provide the organizational integrity and coherence upon which to build the next stage of cognitive development.

The initial disequilibrium in the organization of protologic, particularly its incompleteness, lability and internal segregation, provides the structural and functional impetus for developmental transformation in infants' cognitions. They are directed toward generating progressive organizational equilibrium stage by stage. Progressive equilibrium is marked by increasing completeness, stability and coordinative coherence in the initial organization of protologic. However, as we shall show, these very same developmental transformations are also directed toward generating progressive disequilibrium, stage by stage, in the resultant reorganizations. New potential protoinferential relations, both possible and impossible, and incompleteness, instability and segregation within the more advanced protological organization at each progressive stage again insure that cognition will continue to develop to the next stage.

Throughout this work we have alluded to aspects of the organizational equilibrium and disequilibrium conditions central to cognitive developmental transformations from stage to stage (e.g., pages 288 and 289). The infants' self-generated original logical and mathematical constructions, then, provide the structural developmental mechanisms for their progressive transformations. This, as we have seen, includes constructing, stage by stage, the elementary structures of combinativity. These structures are basic to all part–whole protological constructions, whether of individual elements or sets.

While only partially completed by stage 4, all but one of the structures of combinativity are in place. Decomposing is becoming a regular feature of transactions with sets of discrete objects. Composing is applied to quasi-continuous objects. Only attaching seems to remain inherent. Some quasi-continuous objects become attached to discrete objects, particularly infants' hands, as a necessary consequence of their transacting with such objects. While directed contingent attachment of discrete to quasi-continuous objects is not yet manifest by the few infants tested in this condition, the sample is too small to be definitive. Overall, infants' structural development, even during the first year of life, is already directed towards the construction of progressive symmetry in the universe.

Not only are first-order combinativity structures progressively completed by stage 4, but second-order structures are beginning to be constructed.

(4.1) *Composition.* Composing is partially extended to quasi-continuous as well as discrete objects. The resultant structures are radically different when composing discrete and quasicontinuous objects. Composing discrete elements forms sets or collections. Composing quasi-continuous elements forms single objects.

(4.1.1) *Discrete Extensity.* Binary sets begin to be generated. Unary sets increase in extent, such that they include an intermediate number of members. Some unary sets, of intermediate number, are differentiated into binary subsets of small numbers.

(4.1.2) *Discrete Intensity*. The properties common to the members belonging to a set vary as a function of class condition. Most predication is random in multiplicative and disjoint conditions. Some predication is by differences in these conditions. Predication is by similarities in the additive conditions.

(4.1.3) *Quasi-continuous Extensity*. Many objects are combined into one. Composing is usually limited to small numbers, although intermediate numbers are beginning to be included. The extensive results are twofold. First, the number of elements are divided in the sense that singular objects are abstracted out as the common property of sets. Second, the volume or magnitude of the combined object increases as an additive function of the magnitude of the objects united.

(4.1.4) *Quasi-continuous Intensity*. The predicate properties of the objects composed are negated. The shape of the combined object is different from that of any of the objects it unites.

(4.2) *Decomposition*. Decomposing is partially extended to sets of discrete objects as well as to sets of quasi-continuous objects.

(4.2.1) *Quasi-continuous Extensity*. One, and sometimes two, objects are partitioned into an intermediate number of descendant elements. They begin to be collected into unary, and sometimes binary, durable sets.

(4.2.1.1) *Protomultiplication*. One-to-many decomposition is generated in consecutive sequences. The results are frequent one-to-three and one-to-four protomultiplication and infrequent one-to-five up to one-to-eight protomultiplication. Binary one-to-many decomposition originates. This results in simultaneous construction of two one-to-many protomultiplications.

(4.2.1.2) *Protodivision*. Two forms are generated. The more frequent are asymmetrical geneological decomposing of a single whole object into progressively smaller parts. They construct ordinal divisions. The less frequent are binary symmetrical genealogical decomposing of two whole objects. They result in differentiated, though usually labile binary sets.

(4.2.2) *Quasi-continuous Intensity*. Descendant parts are different in form from the whole out of which they are divided. Most descendant parts are also different in form from each other. Some descendant parts begin to be generated which are roughly similar in form to each other.

(4.2.3) *Discrete Extensity*. Two forms originate, binary sets and binary subsets. Binary sets divide an intermediate number of elements into differentiable, although usually labile collections. Binary subsets divide a constructed whole set, comprising an intermediate number of member elements, into differentiable subsets which are beginning to be stable.

(4.2.4) *Discrete Intensity*. The predicate properties of divisibility into binary sets and subsets could not be fully determined in this research. We can, however, rule out decomposition by affirmation. The elements in each set or subset tend not to be similar to each other. They are either randomly distributed or different from each other.

(4.3) *Breaking*. Binary breaking of two quasi-continuous objects at the same time begins to be generated. Still breaking is relatively infrequent. The extensive properties remain constant while the intensive properties of objects are transformed.

(4.3.1) *Intensity*. Irreversible breaking remains the mode. The forms of the objects broken are permanently changed. Reversibility just begins to be partially applied to breaking. Only Euclidean forms are broken into topological forms and then reconstructed into different shaped Euclidean forms (e.g., a finger is poked through a ball transforming it into a donut-shaped object which is then squished together into a clump). Only the intensive property of form, but not yet shape, of Euclidean objects is becoming reversible.

(4.4) *Deformation*. Deformation is partially extended to preexistent sets of discrete objects as well as to sets of quasi-continuous objects. Deformation has only intensive structures.

(4.4.1) *Quasi-continuous Intensity*. Binary deformations are applied to single objects and to pairs of objects at the same time. The results are binary sets of deformations.

(4.4.2) *Discrete Intensity*. The spatial enclosure properties of preexistent sets are recomposed globally. Sometimes global deformation is applied to the presented whole consisting of well-differentiated binary subsets. Sometimes it is applied to a part (i.e., one of the binary subsets).

(4.5) *Detaching*. Combined objects are partitioned into their constituent discrete and continuous elements. The elements are collected into durable sets.

The alterations in combinativity structures from the first to the fourth stage may be determined by comparing definitional properties (1.1) to (1.5) with (4.1) to (4.5). Developmental alteration is marked by both structural continuity and discontinuity (Langer, 1969a). Consider, for instance, detaching combined objects. With one important exception, both its extensive and intensive structures remain constant from (1.5) to (4.5). One new structural property is constructed. The constituent parts are composed into single, somewhat durable sets.

This represents the kinds of structural developmental transformations in first-order combinativity proto-operations which mark the progress from the first to the fourth stage. There is another important form of structural transformation which develops at the fourth stage. This is the beginning transformation of first-order into second-order combinativity proto-operations. Only some of these have been outlined so far; we have yet to consider most of them. Compare, for instance, properties (1.1) with (4.1) of composing. First-order composing quasi-continuous objects is nonexistent at the first stage. First-order composing is extended, fairly frequently, to quasi-continuous objects by the fourth stage. First-order composing discrete objects into labile unary sets at the first stage is transformed into fairly stable unary sets by the fourth stage. Moreover, first-order discrete composing begins to be transformed into second-order discrete composing. Two major manifestations considered so far are composing binary sets and composing unary sets comprising differentiated binary subsets.

Development of first- and second-order proto-operations are predicated upon advances in the formation of constant given elements. We have traced, in earlier chapters, the transitional stages which issue in abstracting single small sets as well as individual objects as constant givens by the fourth stage. These advances in detaching objects and small sets from infants' ongoing constructive processes and experiences are the cumulative results of progress in all the factors considered in constructing initial constant givens (considered on pages 395–397). The range of inverse spatial transformations used to construct object identity is vastly expanded. It is extended to protocorresponding inverse operations upon small unary sets as well as consecutively to as many as four individual objects coupled with careful comparative observation. Determining the regularities of progressively complex causal transformations is also extended to small sets. This includes the beginnings of a logic of experimentation which is exercised semisystematically.

Sequential stage-by-stage interweaving of these forms of detachment provides individual objects with sufficient cognitive independence and logical coherence such that they can even become the subjects of communication. Protoreferential deixis begins to be generated, but mainly to individual objects. Small sets are also sufficiently detached by stage 4 such that they can be placed in binary inferential relations to each other, such as by protocorrespondence.

While already powerful tools of cognition, the level at which elements and sets are abstracted as constant givens is still vastly different from and weak as compared with their later developments in adolescence and adulthood. They just begin to acquire symbolic features. Yet even these are still embedded in infants' presentational pragmatic transactions. Objects and sets are acquiring temporal durability. Yet the limit is still relatively minor searching for disappearing objects. Only a few objects and small sets can be treated as constant givens at a time. Their durability remains limited to infants' direct transactions with them, although interruptions are less disruptive of this activity than they were previously. Consequently, elements are still not conserved as constant givens across many ordinary transformations. This includes presentational transformations when large numbers of objects or several sets are dealt with. It also includes almost the entire range of representational transformations. Here only minor inroads begin to be made by the application of second-order proto-operations (e.g., inverse deformation of quasi-continuous rings to construct an identity proto-operation).

These are the precursors of representational constant givens. Only when operational identity elements (symbolized in arbitrary notational forms) are constructed during adolescence and adulthood do they become abstracted in full from their constructive processes as constant givens. They become the identity elements of groups of successive operations. When they are combined with any other operation, such as an inverse or exchange operation, the combination leaves these elements unchanged. Thus, these elements acquire the the structure of identity operations. They become given elements which are totally independent of their constructive processes, of their contiguous or contextual relations, and of their embodiment in presentational or representational guises. Call these constant givens the *identity* element **I**. Then, for any universe comprising the set **S** and a binary operation ○ on **S**, there is a unique identity element **I**, such that for any element **a** in **S**,

$$\mathbf{a} \circ \mathbf{I} = \mathbf{I} \circ \mathbf{a} = \mathbf{a} \qquad (16.5)$$

That is, all elements (**a, b, c,** . . . .) of the set **S**, whether they represent the universe of objects, variables, trajectories, quantities, etc., remain unchanged when combined successively with **I** by a binary operation ○, such as an inverse operation. Clearly, this is far from fully realized at the fourth stage. Yet, the necessary precursory foundations, both proto-operational and protosymbolic, have been constructed for postulating the origins of an identity operation.

The two other proto-operations necessary to the precursory foundations of a group of successive transformations or translations are also established in precursory forms by the fourth stage. One of these two other group operations is *associativity* between successive operations. Associativity postulates that if **a, b,** and **c** are any elements in **S**, then

$$(\mathbf{a} \circ \mathbf{b}) \circ \mathbf{c} = \mathbf{a} \circ (\mathbf{b} \circ \mathbf{c}) \qquad (16.6)$$

Protoassociativity of addition Eq. (14.8) and subtraction Eq. (14.9), discovered in the fourth stage and analyzed in Chapter 14, are the initial precursors of Eq. (16.6).

Thus, protoaddition and protosubtraction begin to be detached from their particular constructive processes and from their contiguous or contextual relations. When, and only when, this structural development is fully realized then protoaddition and protosubtraction will be transformed from proto-operations into complete operations. Then addition and subtraction will be fully associative, consequently abstract and representational. Similar structural transformations mark the alteration of all other proto-operations into operations. Of course, this structural developmental process requires many transitional stages, which will be analyzed in subsequent volumes.

The other operation which completes the three postulates comprising a group of operations is *negation*. Whether the binary operation is an inverse or reciprocal operation, negation constructs reversibility. Thus, for any element **a** of **S**, there exists a unique element **a**$^{-1}$, the negation of **a**, such that

$$\mathbf{a} \circ \mathbf{a}^{-1} = \mathbf{a}^{-1} \circ \mathbf{a} = \mathbf{I} \tag{16.7}$$

Identity elements are retrieved by coupling together successive operations which negate each other. We have already noted the developing role of negation proto-operations in the progressive detachment of objects and sets as constant given elements. Their developing role in the progressive construction of precursory reversible relations between first-order operations will be outlined.

By the fourth stage, then, individual objects and small sets of objects are in fairly stable presentational equilibrium. This is the base of constant givens necessary to the completion of the organization of first-order relational and conditional functional structures. In turn, this provides the first-order organizational foundation for the initial construction of second-order relational and conditional functional structures.

In general, structural developments continue to be most advanced when their constant elements are embodied in objects and sets rather than mappings. So the focus will be on relational and conditional proto-operations applied to objects and sets. Protosymbols just begin to constitute constant elements. So, with minor exceptions such as analogical protocorrespondences, they still do not serve as the given elements of proto-operations.

The organization of first-order relational structures is well on its way to completion. Yet it remains precursory for many reasons, such as its limited durability and application to small and intermediate numbers of elements only. Second-order relational structures originate. Most result from coordinative application of conditional proto-operations to relational structures. These will therefore be outlined under conditional structures.

(4.6) *Protoaddition.* The iterative orders produced vary somewhat as a function of the objects to which protoadditions are applied.

(4.6.1) *Discrete.* Directed additive iteration predominates. Most compositions are constructed by actively manipulating two or more objects. The three basic forms of first-order protoaddition develop.

(4.6.1.1) Four-step ⟨one-, two-, three-, four-⟩ element consecutive unary sets are constructed. Binary sets of ⟨two-, three-⟩ elements are constructed simultaneously.

(4.6.1.2) Three-point ⟨ 1, 2, 3 ⟩ discrete magnitude orders are generated.

(4.6.1.3) Many-point continuous magnitude orders are generated (e.g., hitting one object on another increasingly harder, many times).

Second-order protoaddition originates. As already noted, it results from the precursory application of protoassociativity to protoadditivity. Consequently, iteratively ordered sets limited to the minimum of ⟨ one-, two-, three- ⟩ elements, are produced in three possible ways.

(4.6.2) *Quasi-continuous.* Articulate additive iteration takes two forms. One is synchronous (e.g., plucking up nodules of different sizes on a Play-Doh ball); the other is consecutive (e.g., repeatedly pulling up one nodule on a ball such that the nodule becomes longer and longer).

(4.7) *Protosubtraction.* Protosubtractions and the iterative series of ordered decreasing magnitudes and numbers they produce parallel the increasing orders produced by protoaddition. Even the frequency is about the same. Protoassociativity is also applied to subtraction, resulting in the origins of second-order protosubtraction. In addition, as already noted, some protosubtractive decomposition of quasi-continuous objects produces series of objects decreasing in magnitude. At most they form as many as a 5-point decreasing series; though most are limited to 3- and 4-point decreasing series.

(4.8) *Protomultiplication.* Protomultiplication and its products vary as a function of the objects to which they are applied.

(4.8.1) *Discrete.* Two forms are produced. One, co-univocal protocorrespondences, will be considered in (4.14). The other, inclusion relations, in which one element is included in two subsets of one set is produced with some frequency.

(4.8.2) *Quasi-continuous.* Single objects are decomposed into an intermediate number of objects. Eight descendant elements is the maximum. Multiple objects are collected into durable sets, though usually limited to small membership. Multiplication begins to produce binary sets. Usually the membership is small, though intermediate numbers begin to be included.

(4.9) *Protodivision.* Pragmatic divisions and their products vary as a function of the objects to which they are applied.

(4.9.1) *Discrete.* Practical divisibility begins to be applied to sets. A part (subset) included in a larger whole (set) is taken out to form a composition (set). The part taken out includes only small numbers of elements.

(4.9.2) *Quasi-continuous.* Objects are divided into smaller parts. The parts are either roughly equivalent in magnitude or, as already noted, the parts progressively decrease in magnitude.

Combinativity and relational proto-operations are progressively conditioned throughout the four stages by exchange, correlation, and negation proto-operations. The results are progressive integration of the functional structures of logical and mathematical operations. These include the origins of second-order functional structures, which coordinate first-order operations.

Exchange proto-operations continue to apply to single sets only, although transitions to protosubstitution between two sets are evidenced as early as the third stage. Set size is expanded to include three elements, but no more. Exchange proto-operations are frequently replicated consecutively.

(4.10) *Protoreplacement.* Single elements and pairs of elements are repeatedly subtracted from and added back to reconstitute identical three-element sets. All the elements and the order plus enclosure relations between the elements of the set are kept constant. Protoreplacement is becoming co-regulated.

(4.11) *Protosubstitution.* Single elements are repeatedly exchanged in three-element sets. Two elements are held constant, as are the order and enclosure relations. Protosubstitution is becoming coregulated. The structural developmental result is the transformation of irreversible protosubstitution (Eq. 16.2 defined on page 400) into protoreversible substitution, such that

$$(a, b, c) - (c) + (d) - (d) + (c) \approx (a, b, c) \qquad (16.8)$$

(4.12) *Protocommutativity.* Three-element sets are consecutively rearranged where all the member elements are kept constant. Consecutive rearrangements are coregulated such that the initial order and enclosure properties of the set are reconstituted. The result is protoreversible commutativity which conforms to Eq. (16.4), defined on page 400, expanded to three-element sets.

Throughout this investigation we have stressed both the structural developmental continuities and discontinuities between proto-operations and operations, as, for instance, in the transformation of protoaddition into addition and protosubtraction into subtraction considered on page 410. The major structural developmental distinctions between necessary and formal operations, on the one hand, and pragmatic and concrete proto-operations, on the other hand, are worth some further analysis. The major distinctions may be illustrated by contrasting proto-operational with operational exchange structures.

First, exchange proto-operations apply only to finite elements, whether they are made up of objects, mappings, sets, or orders. Exchange operations apply to infinite elements, as well. Second, proto-operations, during the four stages traced here, only exchange very small numbers of finite elements within unary sets. The sets are limited to consecutive recompositions of single collections. Operations exchange small to very large numbers of finite elements between simultaneous n-ary sets. Third, the elements of exchange proto-operations are functional and nonsymbolic. The elements of exchange operations are arbitrary and symbolic. Fourth, the relations between elements of exchange proto-operations are spatiotemporal, causal dynamic, and sociofunctional. The relations between elements of exchange operations are binary conjuncts and disjuncts. Fifth, the embodiments of exchange proto-operations are actual empirical returning transformations. The embodiments of exchange operations are potential reversible calculations. Finally, the products of exchange proto-operations are real and labile equivalence relations. The products of exchange operations are hypothetical and conserved equivalences.

Correlation proto-operations are extended to relating binary sets or subsets to each other. This development, however, occurs only with bi-univocal protocorrespondences. Co-univocal protocorrespondences still apply to single sets only.

(4.13) *Bi-univocal Protocorrespondences.* Equivalence between objects include two-to-two matchings between four objects composed into binary sets or binary subsets.

(4.14) *Co-univocal Protocorrespondences.* One-to-many and many-to-one multiplicative relations match as many as one to four objects. Each form is constructed both consecutively and simultaneously.

Negation proto-operations, both inverse and reciprocal, continue to develop and condition combinativity and relational proto-operations.

The resultant structural developmental transformations are twofold. First-order reversible proto-operations expand and advance. Second-order reversible proto-operations originate in rudimentary forms.

(4.15) *Protoinverse.* The structures of first-order reversibility by inverse proto-operations are progressively, but still not fully, completed.

(4.15.1) Identity by well-regulated compensatory proto-operations is extended to as many as four consecutive objects and two-element sets. The compensatory proto-operations are themselves expanded to include a wide range of inverse transformations, particularly continuous 360° rotations. Identity formation by inverse proto-operations is becoming both differentiated and integrated. Most notable are (*a*) sighting objects from opposite perspectives and (*b*) comparatively rotating part of whole objects.

(4.15.2) Inverse subtraction and addition of the same object in the case of protoreplacement within a set, and different objects, in the case of protosubstitution within a set, is repeated consecutively two or more times. Both produce equivalence within single sets.

(4.15.3) Extensive, but not intensive, identity is produced by recomposing previously decomposed quasi-continuous objects. This form of recomposing begins at the third stage but remains relatively infrequent even at the fourth stage.

The structures of second-order reversibility by inverse protooperations begin to be constructed.

(4.15.4) Consecutive inverse composition and decomposition of binary sets transforms them into single sets, then back into binary sets.

(4.15.5) Consecutive inverse compositions and decompositions of unary sets transforms them into binary subsets, then back into unary sets, and so on.

(4.15.6) Consecutive inverse compositions and decompositions transform single quasi-continuous objects into sets, then back into single objects, and so on. Extensive, but not intensive, identity is produced.

(4.15.7) Inverse deformations and reformations begin to produce intensive (form) identity of singular quasi-continuous objects.

(4.16) *Protoreciprocity.* The structures of first-order reversibility by reciprocal proto-operations are progressively, but still not fully, completed.

(4.16.1) Reciprocal variation of order and enclosure within a set is repeated consecutively two or more times. The result is equivalence by protoreversible commutativity.

(4.16.2) Inherent protoreciprocal deformation of quasi-continuous objects is extended to sets of two objects at the same time (e.g., banging two objects together which produces binary flattening compensated by binary widening of both balls).

(4.16.3) Reciprocal protoaddition and protosubtraction which produce bidirectional orderings are extended to intermediate numbers (i.e., series that compose as many as four-element sets and, rarely, five-element sets).

The structures of second-order reversibility by reciprocal proto-operations just begin to be constructed.

(4.16.4) Reciprocal transformation of one-to-many into many-to-one protocorrespondences begin to be produced consecutively.

(4.16.5) Reciprocal transformations of co-univocal into bi-univocal protocorrespondences begin to be produced consecutively.

(4.16.6) Reciprocal protoadditions and reciprocal protosubtractions produce initial protoassociativity within ordered series of sets. The limit is the minimum of three-unit iterative series.

The organization of first- and second-order proto-operations at the fourth stage is strengthened by their progressive coherence. Two structural developments are of particular importance. First, all the exchange proto-operations are progressively coordinated with each other. They produce complementarity between equivalence relations. Second, protocorrespondences are progressively coordinated with protoadditions and with protosubtractions. They produce coseriation or equivalence between binary increasing orders and equivalence between binary decreasing orders.

The organization of protologic begins to be bidimensional. First- and second-order functional structures coexist at stage 4. Up to stage 4 protologic remains unidimensional, that is, an organization of first-order functional structures at different stages of development. The organization of protologic is transitional between unidimensional and bidimensional functional structures at stage 3, but our data are not sufficiently refined to be complete on this point. While second-order structures are outgrowths of first-order structures, they immediately condition the development of first-order structures.

Each stage is the necessary potential progenitor of a successor stage. The functional structures of progenitor stages are comparatively weak and disequilibrated. Stage 1 is limited to incomplete, segregated, and labile first-order structures. By stage 4 almost all first-order structures are midway to completion, coherent coordination, and conservation. Some second-order structures just originate at stage 4 and are, therefore, comparatively incomplete, segregated, and labile. Associated with developmental progress, then, is equilibration and enrichment of functional structures. This very equilibration and enrichment opens up new cognitive possibilities and impossibilities. Thus, structural development also increases the probability of incompleteness and disequilibrium at successor stages.

Disequilibrium is apparent in at least two ways at stage 4 as compared with its predecessor stages. The first is the rudimentary state of second-order structures when they first evolve at stage 4. The second is the disparity between the two dimensions of protologic which overlap at stage 4. The first dimension of functional structures is midway to completion. The second dimension of functional structures is only precursory. Developmental increase in disequilibrium, then, is the antithesis of developmental increase in equilibrium.

The organization of protologic is an intricate network or open grid system of sets of combinativity, relational, and conditional functional structures. Beginning, at least, with stage 4 these functional structures are at varying developmental levels, either first- or second-order. The gridwork becomes bidimensional. Different functional structures are always of varying centrality to the organization of protologic. The gridwork radiates outward and is open on the outside so as to interact with the physical and sociocultural environment. A good part of the relevant environment, we have seen, includes children's own actions and observations of their consequences.

The dynamics of the gridwork at each stage thereby insure constant internal as well as external interaction. Thus, the permanent possibility for integrative disequilibrium within parts and dimensions of the gridwork, coordinative disequilibrium between different parts and dimensions of the gridwork, and transactional disequilibrium between parts and dimensions of the gridwork and the environment. Thus the permanent possibility for structural development.

Appendix

I. Subjects

Twelve subjects, evenly divided by sex, were tested at ages 6, 8, 10, and 12 months; for a total of 48 subjects. Seven of the subjects at ages 8 and 10 months were tested longitudinally. All the subjects tested were drawn from the nursery school enrollment application lists of the Child Study Center, a facility of the Institute of Human Development, University of California, Berkeley. Parents within the East Bay Area apply within the first few weeks of birth of their children. By and large these children are from middle-class families.

II. Discrete Object Tasks

These tasks are designed to study the development of transformations (a), (b), and (c) outlined in Chapter 1, that is, composing, separating and recomposing discrete objects. This section begins by specifying the conditions generating each discrete object task, and concludes by detailing the testing procedures used in each task.

The research design (see Section V), was varied and controlled for: (a) number of objects presented, from four to ten objects; (b) object type, that is, solid geometric, ring shapes, and realistic (e.g., miniature dolls); (c) class conditions, that is, structured (e.g., two circular rings and two rectangular rings) and ambiguous (e.g., four different ring shapes) sets; and (d) conditions of transaction, that is, free play, provoked grouping (e.g., into class consistent sets), and counterconditions (e.g., presentation of groups of objects sorted by class properties but with two errors).

A. FORM CONDITIONS

Three kinds of discrete objects were presented to the subjects. All are of the ordinary kind children play with, and are usually found in toy stores:

1. *Euclidean* objects such as square and circular columns. All these objects are solid, geometric forms.

2. *Topological* objects, that is, objects whose topological form properties are emphasized, such as square and circular rings. All these objects are geometric, ring forms.

3. *Realistic* objects such as miniature cars and dolls.

All three types of objects are made out of nonflexible and nonbreakable materials (at least as far as infants are concerned) such as masonite and wood. Infants take well to all three kinds of objects. They are quite similar in form to standard block, ring, and realistic objects which comprise many infant toys.

Where appropriate (see Table A.1 in Section V), combinations of these form conditions were tested. For instance, in condition **C** (disjoint classes) the presentation may consist of two classes; one comprising Euclidean objects and the other topological objects, such as four red square columns and four blue cars.

As much as possible, all the other properties of the three kinds of objects were held constant. For instance, all the Euclidean objects used in every class condition were made of wood and had similar size dimensions. An important exception occurs in class conditions **B** and **C**. Testing multiplicative and disjoint conditions requires that the objects in the various classes be different on the basis of two properties. The second variable property was therefore that frequently used in classification studies, namely, color.

B. CLASS CONDITIONS

Sets of discrete objects were presented to the subjects which represent six class conditions. Three conditions (**A, B,** and **C**) embody three well-delineated class structures, respectively. These are additive, multiplicative, and disjoint class structures. Three conditions (**D, E,** and **F**) embody ambiguous class structures which serve as semicontrol conditions. Two additional, but subsidiary, class conditions (**G** and **H**) were also embodied in the task designs, where appropriate. These are singular and intersective class conditions.

The three well-structured class conditions are as follows:

A. Two directly *additive* classes of objects are presented. Each class is made up of two or more members. The classes are the same in all respects except for one property, their form. For instance, the presentation may consist of four miniature cars which are the same except that two cars are VWs and two cars are racers. The objects, then, make up different but complimentary sets, VW cars and racer cars. In turn, these sets constitute additive subsets of a more inclusive set, cars.

B. Four fully *multiplicative* classes of objects are presented. Each class is made up of one or more elements. The classes are the same except for their form and color. For instance, the presentation may consist of four rings: one blue circular ring, one red circular ring, one blue square ring, and one red square ring. Otherwise the objects are all the same. The objects, then, make up a 2×2 matrix of form by color.

C. The *disjoint* condition consists of two classes which differ as much as possible, green rectangular rings and red dolls. Each class is made up of two or more members.

The three semicontrol class conditions are the following:

D. One class of *identical* objects is presented. For instance, the presentation may consist of four blue square columns. All objects are identical.

E. All *different* objects, none of which can be classified together on the basis of shape, are presented. For instance, the presentation may consist of four blue realistic objects: one toy car, one girl doll, one toy plate, and one miniature toothbrush. Thus the presentation consists of all different classes with singular membership.

F. *Identical and different* objects are presented together; that is, one multiple-membered assortment is presented together with several singular classes. For instance, the presentation may consist of four blue rings: two square, one circular, and one clover. Half the objects are identical and half are different.

The two subsidiary class conditions were administered in test phase III (see the Procedure section):

G. A *singular* (odd) class is presented in the context of conditions **A** and **B**. In the context of the additive class condition, the presentation consists, for instance, of five blue cars: two VWs, two racers, and one (singular) sedan. In the context of the multiplicative class condition, the presentation consists, for instance, of five rings: one red circular, one blue circular, one red square, one blue square, and one (singular) yellow triangular.

H. *Intersective* (anomalous) classes are presented only in the context of condition **C**, the disjoint class condition. An illustrative example of the procedure used is helpful in understanding this condition. The tester sorts four objects in front of the subject into two disjoint classes, such as two green rectangular rings and two red dolls. Then the subject is presented with intersective objects which are anomalous in this context, such as one red rectangular ring. One property but not the other is shared with each of the disjoint classes.

C. COMPLEXITY CONDITIONS

Two levels of difficulty were built into the discrete tasks. The task levels range from the simplest possible to a slightly more complex version. Level of complexity is defined in terms of the number of classes and objects presented. Successive complexity follows the progressive alternation between additional elements and additional classes. The simplest version of a task is defined as the least possible classes and the fewest possible members of each class; the next level of complexity is defined as the same number of classes with more members in each class. To illustrate, for condition **A** (additive classes): (*a*) the simplest level consists of two classes with two members of each class, such as two VW cars and two racer cars; and (*b*) the next level consists of two classes with four members of each class, such as four VW cars and four racer cars. Up to and including 10-month-olds, infants were presented with the simplest task level. Twelve-month-olds were also presented with the slightly more complex version.

D. PROCEDURE

The procedure consists of three consecutive phases. The first phase focuses upon the subjects' spontaneous activities. The second phase is designed to provoke grouping activity in subjects when they have not fully sorted the objects during the first phase. These first two procedural phases are used in class conditions **A** through **F**. The third phase includes administering: (*a*) the subsidiary class conditions **G** and **H**; and (*b*) specific counterconditions to be described below. The techniques used in all three phases of the procedures consist of nonverbal probes for eliciting manipulatory activities.

1. *Phase I. Spontaneous Condition*

Testing always begins with the procedure for free play since it provides subjects with the least prompting. Presenting subjects with the objects is invariably sufficient to start them interacting with the objects. The experimenter may encourage subjects with uncontaminated support, such as by smiling, nodding her head, and saying "How nice."

No classification-relevant prompting is introduced until the second phase of testing for provoked sorting. The subjects are allowed to do anything they wish with the objects for 2½ minutes. If they are not finished interacting with the objects after 2½ minutes, the subjects are allowed to continue until they complete what they are doing.

In class conditions **A** to **F** the objects are arranged into a horizontal alignment behind a screen which is placed momentarily in front of the subject. The objects are always aligned in a predesignated random order; with the exception of control condition **D** where all the objects are the same. Then the screen is removed and the subjects are allowed to proceed as they wish.

2. *Phase II. Provoked Condition*

All the provoked probes involve nonverbal modes of working with children to compose and decompose sets. Therefore, the experimenter always handles the objects in the ways in which each subject has been treating them most often during the spontaneous, as well as the provoked period. For instance, the subject may have done a lot of banging the objects on the table. Only then is it permissible for the experimenter to use this form of activity to deal with the objects, that is, by banging them on the table in the process of composing or decomposing the objects into a group. In general, the experimenter copies the subjects' preferred ways of handling the objects so as to stay within the subjects' range of manipulatory capacities and, it is hoped, understanding and interest.

Four types of probes are used. Their systematic distribution across tasks is indicated in the second column of Table A.2, in the research design section. It should be noted that some probes are not applicable to the ambiguous class conditions **D**, **E**, and **F** and are therefore not used in these contexts.

The four types of probes are

(a) *Elaboration.* This procedure consists of two parts. During the first part the objects are sorted into their respective classes. During the second part the grouped classes are decomposed into their constituent elements.

Composition always begins with the experimenter continuing any partial or rudimentary classificatory arrangement(s) made by the subject during the spontaneous activity. The experimenter uses objects not sorted by the subject. Objects which are ambiguously clustered by the subject are also treated as residuals for grouping. The experimenter selects single objects, one at a time, as randomly as possible from residual or ambiguously grouped objects. The selection of objects is from all the possible classes, whether or not the classes are nascently formed on the table. The experimenter first indicates the selected object by pointing to it. When this does not evoke a response, the experimenter hands the object to the subject. If the subject places the object in an appropriate place it is left there and the experimenter goes on to the next object. If the subject places the object in an inappropriate spot, from the viewpoint of classification, then the experimenter puts it in the right place. This procedure is continued until all the objects are sorted into distinct classes.

Decomposition begins as soon as the classes have been well-formed. The experimenter selects a single object from one of the classes. In a very clear and distinct fashion the experimenter shows the subject that she is putting it away into a large container. If this is not sufficient to prompt the subject to put away the other objects, then the experimenter makes a global, sweeping gesture of request over all the remaining objects. If this does not work the experimenter tries the verbal instruction, "Let's put them away" or "Can you give me one?" Finally, if all else fails, the experimenter successively repeats this procedure with each of the other objects until they are all removed. The sequence of removal used by the experimenter is systematic. First the experimenter removes all the elements of one class, then the experimenter removes the elements of a complementary class, and so on.

(b) *Initiation.* This form of provoking classification is an alternate for probe (a). It is used in the absence of any, even rudimentary, class sorting of the objects on the part of the subject during the spontaneous phase. The main difference is that the experimenter has to initiate the composition as well as the decomposition. This is done by selecting one object from each of two complementary classes. They are placed, in a well-separated horizontal plane, to the right and to the left of the subject, and directly in front of him. Beyond this initial bid the procedure used in composing and decomposing classes is identical with that for probe (a).

(c) *Placement.* One open, transparent plastic container is placed on the table for each class of objects presented. If the subject has not produced any classificatory sorting of objects during the phase of spontaneous activity then the initiation procedure followed in probe (b) for composition and decomposition is used. If the subject has produced some spontaneous classification then the elaboration procedure followed in probe (a) is used. First, the subject's partial sort(s) are placed in the containers and the subject is prompted to continue with gestures. Beyond this the procedure reverts to elaborations by the experimenter as it is administered in probe (b).

(d) *Matching.* The composition part of this probe begins with the experimenter sorting all the objects into sets in front of the subject. When this is finished, the subject is handed two additional objects. Two kinds of additional objects are used, but in different conditions: (d1) two identical objects belonging to one class; or (d2) two different objects belonging to two different classes. As in all other probes, this is followed by the decomposition part of the probe. The procedure is the same as that in probe (a).

3. *Phase III. Supplementary Conditions*

The two subsidiary class conditions **G** (singular) and **H** (intersective) plus various counterconditions are administered during the third phase. The basic procedural features of conditions **G** and **H** have already been described in Section II,B. What remains to be outlined are the various counterconditions:

(e) *Counterconditions for Conditions A* and *B*. The experimenter makes proper (additive) alignments or a (multiplicative) matrix with all but two of the objects. The experimenter misplaces the last two objects which are from different classes. The misplacements are positioned so as to be the objects closest to the subject. The subject is allowed to do anything he wishes. However, if the subject does not interact with the two misplaced elements then the experimenter encourages the subject to do so by pointing at and touching each of the objects, successively.

(f) *Countercondition for Condition D*. The experimenter arranges the identical objects into two spatially well-separated groups. For instance, the subject is presented with one group of two blue square columns on his right and another group of two blue square columns on his left. The subject is encouraged to interact with the objects in the usual fashion.

(g) *Countercondition for Condition E*. The experimenter arranges the different objects into two spatially well-separated groups. For instance, the subject is presented with one girl doll plus one toy plate in a group on the subject's right and one toy car plus one miniature toothbrush on the subject's left. The subject is encouraged to interact with the objects in the usual fashion.

(h) *Countercondition for Condition F*. The experimenter arranges the identical and different objects into two well-separated groups. For instance, the subject is presented with one square and one circular ring in one group on the subject's right. In another group on the subject's left, the subject is presented with one square and one clover ring. The subject is encouraged to interact with the objects in the usual fashion.

III. Quasi-Continuous Object Tasks

The overall objective in presenting single quasi-continuous objects and sets of quasi-continuous objects to young children is to investigate the developments in their construction of transformations (d), (e), and (f) outlined in Chapter 1. These consist of deforming, decomposing, and uniting malleable Play-Doh objects. This section will specify both the conditions generating each quasi-continuous object condition and the testing procedures.

The research design (see Section V) varied and controlled for: (a) number of objects presented, from one to six objects, (b) object type, (i.e., solid geometric and ring shapes), and (c) conditions of transaction, that is, free play, provoked decomposing or uniting, and counterconditions (e.g., presentation of groups of objects which are all the same except for size).

A. FORM CONDITIONS

The form conditions are the same in all major respects as those used in the discrete object tasks, but with one exception. The exception is that it is not feasible to use realistic forms with Play-Doh material which will hold their form yet be malleable enough for infants to be able to deform, decompose, or unite them. Consequently, only two form conditions were used, Euclidean and topological.

B. SET CONDITIONS

These conditions are designed to investigate developing decomposing, uniting, and deforming relations between objects and sets which are generated by children. Consequently, two conditions were tested:

I. *One* well-formed, big piece of soft Play-Doh is presented, such as a large, circular ring. It is subject to ready deformation into other shapes or to decomposition into one or more sets of small bits.

J. *Many* well-formed identical small bits of Play-Doh are presented. They are subject to ready deformation into other shapes or uniting into one or more bigger objects. One set of three small bits, such as three circular rings, is presented.

C. PROCEDURE

The procedure consists of three consecutive phases. As always, the first phase allows the subjects to engage in spontaneous activity with the presentation. The second phase is designed to provoke either decomposing or uniting activity. The third phase presents supplementary conditions to be described below. The techniques used in all three phases consist of nonverbal probes for eliciting manipulatory activities in infants.

1. Phase I. Spontaneous Condition

Testing began with the procedure for free play in which infants are encouraged by nonverbal means to transact with the objects presented. The procedure is essentially the same as that outlined for the discrete tasks in Section II, D. The only difference is that the big Play-Doh piece in condition **I** and the set of small Play-Doh bits in condition **J** are set up behind a screen. When the condition calls for one set of three identical small Play-Doh objects, they are presented grouped together into an alignment.

2. Phase II. Provoked Conditions

Two provoked probes are used for conditions **G** and **H**. They consist of probes (a) and (b) made appropriate to the quasi-continuous material involved, namely, soft Play-Doh:

(i) *Elaboration.*   The form of the probe depends on the set condition being tested.

In condition **I** the focus is upon decomposing a big piece into a set of smaller bits. If the subject has partially decomposed the big piece during the spontaneous phase then the experimenter mimics the subject's decomposing technique. The experimenter makes one bit at a time. After the experimenter makes each bit, the experimenter hands the big piece to the subject and places the bit with the others which have already been made. This procedure is repeated until the big piece is totally decomposed.

For half the subjects, the experimenter performs this decomposing transformation in full view. The transformational activity is hidden from the other half of the subjects. That is, the experimenter makes the bits under the table. Only the product of the decomposition is shown to these subjects.

In condition J the focus is upon uniting a set of small bits into a single object. Again the experimenter mimics the subject's uniting technique in elaborating upon it. The experimenter molds one bit at a time into the bigger piece. After each addition, the experimenter hands a bit to the subject and places the big piece in front of the subject. This procedure is repeated until the big piece is totally composed.

Uniting is visibly performed by the experimenter for those subjects who do not see the decomposition transformation. Uniting is nonvisibly performed by the experimenter for those subjects who do see the decomposition. These subjects are only shown the product of the composition.

When the experimenter visibly models decomposing or uniting, then everything is presentational. The initial state(s) of the object(s), the transformational process, and the final resultant state(s) of the object(s) are all visible. When the experimenter decomposes or unites objects such that the subject cannot observe the transformational process, then only the initial and final state(s) of the object(s) are presentationally visible. In all conditions, the subjects are encouraged by nonverbal means to transact with the resultant object(s) for at least a minute. The aim is to determine the effects of these four kinds of transformations— visible decomposing, nonvisible decomposing, visible uniting, and nonvisible uniting—upon the subjects' subsequent transactions with the object(s).

(j) *Initiation.* This probe is used only in the absence of any decomposing by the subject in condition I or uniting in condition J. In condition I it requires the experimenter to make the first bit from the big piece. In J it requires the experimenter to mold together two bits into a larger piece. Beyond this, the procedure reverts to that followed in probe (i), including visible and nonvisible transformations by the experimenter.

3. *Phase III. Countercondition*

One basic countercondition was administered:

(k) *Countercondition for Conditions I and J.* Infants are presented with two separate groups of objects at the same time, one on their right and one on their left. One group consists of one big object plus two small objects. The other group consists of three small objects. The form of the objects is kept constant from the first to the third test phase. For instance, phase I may involve one big circular ring or three small rings. In both instances the presentation in phase III consists of two separate alignments. One alignment comprises one big and two small circular rings. The other alignment comprises three small circular rings. Big and small objects are presented at the same time. The subjects are encouraged, by nonverbal means, to transact with the presentation for at least a minute.

IV. Discrete and Quasi-Continuous Object Tasks

As indicated in Chapter 1, the general purpose in presenting children with discrete and quasi-continuous objects at the same time is to begin to investigate the development of transformations (g) and (h), that is, attaching and detaching these two kinds of objects. One main condition was therefore tested:

K. *Combined* sets of discrete, quasi-continuous, and conglomerate discrete–quasi-continuous objects are presented. Three basic objects are involved: a big Play-Doh ball, a wooden tongue depressor, and another identical big Play-Doh ball with an identical wooden tongue depressor firmly stuck into one end of the Play-Doh ball. The third conglomerate object looks very much like a base drum beater.

As always, testing began with a 2½-minute phase I of spontaneous transaction in which the subjects were encouraged to engage in free play with the presentation. Unless the subjects demonstrated systematic attaching and detaching in phase I, it was followed by test phase II designed to provoke attaching and detaching transformations. We will call this probe (1). The experimenter clears away the first set and brings out a duplicate set. Then the experimenter demonstrates both transformations in a visible way: by detaching the conglomerate object into its constituent parts, a tongue depressor and a ball of Play-Doh; and by attaching via inserting the separate tongue depressor into one end of the Play-Doh ball so as to form a conglomerate object. Then the infants were encouraged to transact with the array for another 2½ minutes.

V. Design

The basic properties of the research design were held constant for all ages in order to insure comparability between the performances of all groups of infants. So, for instance, the testing procedures were always nonverbal in all their relevant features. Only the numerical complexity of the objects presented varied with age. The oldest 12-month-old subjects were also presented with more objects than the youngest subjects.

In order to test the major combinations of task, complexity, and object conditions, six groups of subjects at each age were required. Table A.1

TABLE A. 1
Task Design

		Object forms					
Tasks		E	T	R	E & T	E & R	T & R
A1.	Additive	1	2	3	4	5	6
A2.	Additive	4	5	6	1	2	3
B1.	Multiplicative	6	1	2	3	4	5
B2.	Multiplicative	3	4	5	6	1	2
C1.	Disjoint	5	6	1	2	3	4
C2.	Disjoint	2	3	4	5	6	1
D.	Identical	1	2	—	—	—	—
E.	Different	—	4	3	—	—	—
F.	Identical and different	6	—	5	—	—	—
I.	One	1, 3, 6	2, 4, 5	—	—	—	—
J.	Many	2, 4, 5	1, 3, 6	—	—	—	—
K.	Combined	—	—	—	—	1–6	—

presents the task design. It is in the form of a tasks-by-object forms matrix. For the rows in the matrix: A to C represent the three well-structured class conditions with discrete objects; D to F represent the three ambiguous class conditions with discrete objects; I represents the quasi-continuous single object condition; J represents the quasi-continuous set of objects condition; K represents the combined discrete and quasi-continuous condition; and the numerals 1 and 2 designate, respectively, easier and more difficult complexity levels of each well-structured class condition. The letters heading the columns designate object form conditions, where E is Euclidean, T is topological and R is realistic. The numerals 1 to 6 entered in the matrix represent the six groups at each age that were tested. The 6-, 8-, and 10-month-old groups were assigned to the simplest class conditions A1, B1 and C1 only. The 12-month-old groups were also assigned to the more difficult class conditions A2, B2, and C2.

Two orders of testing the class conditions were used for each of the six groups at each age level. Half the subjects in each group were tested in the order: D or E or F, A, I, J, B, C, K. The other half were tested in the order: D or E or F, B, I, J, A, C, K. To facilitate the 12 month-olds' performances, the levels of complexity within the class conditions A, B, and C were always administered in the order of simplest level first, followed by the next difficulty level. Otherwise, the two orders are designed to insure an adequate mix of different tasks and objects to maintain young children's interest in transacting with the presentations.

Table A.2 presents the procedural design. It is in the form of a tasks-by-

TABLE A.2
Procedural Design

	Tasks	\\ Phases I	II	III
A1.	Additive	*	c	G
A2.	Additive	*	a or b	e
B1.	Multiplicative	*	d1	e
B2.	Multiplicative	*	a or b	G
C1.	Disjoint	*	d2	H
C2.	Disjoint	*	c	H
D.	Identical	*	d1	f
E.	Different	*	d1	g
F.	Identical and different	*	d1	h
I.	One	*	i or j	k
J.	Many	*	i or j	k
K.	Combined	*	1	—

procedural conditions matrix. The same designations as in Table A.1 are used in the rows of the matrix for tasks and complexity (which applies only to the 12-month-olds). The columns are marked I, II, and III representing the three sequential procedural phases from spontaneous, to provoked, to supplementary conditions. Since the spontaneous procedure is used in all conditions the entries in column I are simply asterisks. In column II: a stands for the elaboration probe; b stands for the initiation probe; c stands for the placement probe; $d1$ stands for the matching probe with identical elements; $d2$ stands for the matching probe with different elements: i stands for the elaboration probe appropriate to malleable Play-Doh objects; j stands for the initiation probe appropriate to malleable Play-Doh objects; and l stands for the attaching and detaching modeling probe with sets comprising discrete and quasi-continuous objects. In column III: G stands for the singular class condition; H stands for the intersective class condition; and the letters e through h and k designate the counterconditions, described above, which are appropriate, respectively, for the various tasks.

Table A.2 indicates that a fixed procedural sequence was followed for each task. For instance, reading across the first row indicates that when the subjects are presented with the simplest level additive class condition then the task begins with 2½ minutes of spontaneous activity by the subjects. It is followed by placement probes designed to initiate or elaborate grouping and classification by the subjects. The task ends with the subjects being presented with an odd object for grouping and classification.

VI. Transcribing and Coding

While the subjects are being tested in one room, their entire performances are video- and audio-taped from an adjacent room through a one-way mirror. Systematic and comprehensive systems for transcribing the subjects' transactions with the presented objects into sequential logs and for coding the data logs have been developed. The system of transcription is designed to provide a sequential data log of all the transactions. Basically, it therefore records, in spatiotemporal order, the subjects' actions, relations between the subjects' actions, object transformations produced by the subjects' action, relations between object transformations, and relations between the subjects' action and object transformations.

In marking up the final log of each subject's performance and in coding the data prime attention is given to the subject's actions which are directed toward the object(s). The major features of the subject's actions upon discrete, quasi-continuous, and conglomerate objects which are transcribed and coded are: (1) contact (e.g., touch, grasp, release, squeeze), (2) placement (e.g., on, off, together), (3) displacement (e.g., up, down, back and forth), (4) orientation (e.g., vertical, diagonal, upright), (5) repetitions (e.g., number, duration, punctuation), and (6) intensity (e.g., ordered, strength, speed). Also transcribed and coded, to the extent possible, are: (7) visual regard (e.g., focus on one object, scanning the entire array, looking back and forth between two objects), (8) symbolic (e.g., naming, pointing, pretending), and (9) communicating with the experimenter or the subject's mother in the process of interacting with the object(s) (e.g., giving, showing, requesting help).

When the subject is acting upon more than one object at a time, then the main additional features transcribed and coded are: (10) how the subject is handling them (e.g., with the same or different organs), (11) how the subject is treating them (e.g., in the same or different ways), and (12) how the objects are related to each other spatially, temporally, kinetically, and causally.

Prime consideration is also given to what happens to each discrete, quasi-continuous, and conglomerate object, and its relations to the other objects as a result of each action. The major features transcribed and coded are all the transformations in the object(s) which result from the 12 action features just listed.

When the objects are discrete the main features of what happens to each object are twofold. The first consists of the spatiotemporal, kinetic, and causal features of each object's placements and displacements (e.g., when it is picked up, how it is displaced, where it is placed). The second consists of configural features, that is, the relations generated between sets of objects (e.g., pushing two objects against two others, bunching all objects together, waving two objects around each other). These include: the number of objects configurated; the order in which each object becomes part of a configuration; the spatiotemporal, kinetic and causal relations between the objects configurated; and the predicate relations between the objects configurated, that is, whether the objects are from the same or different classes. The transcription and coding also takes into account the spatiotemporal, kinetic and causal relations between configurations (e.g., the order in which configurations are generated, combinations of previously separate configurations, consecutive replication of the same configuration).

When the objects are quasi-continuous, all the above features apply to working up the sequential data log and the sequential coding. In addition, the unique potential transformations possible with quasi-continuous objects are transcribed and coded. These include any deforming, breaking but not splitting into parts, decomposing into parts, and uniting of objects and sets of objects.

When combined sets of discrete, quasi-continuous, and conglomerate discrete–quasi-continuous objects are presented, all the above features apply to marking up the sequential data log and the sequential coding. In addition, the unique potential transformations applicable to conglomerate objects are transcribed and coded. These are attaching together discrete and quasi-continuous objects and detaching conglomerate objects into their components.

References

Boole, G. *An Investigation of the Laws of Thought*. New York: Dover, 1854.

Cantor, G. Beiträge zur Begründung der transfiniten Mengenlehre, i. *Mathematische Annalen*, 1895, xlvi, 481–512. (Reprinted in *Gesammelte Abhandlungen*, ed. Zermelo.)

Claparede, M. Ed. La conscience de la ressemblance et de la différence chez l'enfant. *Archives de Psychologie*, 1918, 17, 67–78.

Flavell, J. H. Concept development. In P. H. Mussen (Ed.), *Carmichael's Manual of Child Psychology* (Vol. I, 3rd ed.). New York: Wiley, 1970.

Frege, G. *The Foundations of Arithmetic*. Oxford: Blackwell, 1974. (Originally published, 1884.)

Gelb, A., & Goldstein, K. Uber farbennamenammnesei. *Psycholigische Forschung*, 1925, 6, 127–186.

Goldstein, K., & Scheerer, M. Abstract and concrete behavior. *Psychological Monographs*, 1941, 53(2).

Halverson, H. M. An experimental study of prehension in infants by means of systematic cinema records. *Genetic Psychology Monographs*, 1931, 10, 107–286.

Hanfmann, E. Analysis of the thinking disorder in a case of schizophrenia. *Archives of Neurology and Psychiatry*, 1939, 41, 568–579.

Inhelder, B., & Piaget, J. *The Growth of Logical Thinking from Childhood to Adolescence*. New York: Basic Books, 1958.

Inhelder, B., & Piaget, J. *The Early Growth of Logic in the Child*. London: Routledge and Kegan Paul, 1964.

Kasanin, J., & Hanfmann, E. An experimental study of concept formation in schizophrenia. I. Quantitative analysis of the results. *American Journal of Psychiatry*, 1938–1939, 95, 35–52.

Kneale, W., & Kneale, M. *The Development of Logic*. Oxford: Oxford University Press, 1962.

Kramer, E. E. *The Nature and Growth of Modern Mathematics*. New York: Hawthorne, 1970.

Kuhn, D., Langer, J., Kohlberg, L., & Haan, N. The development of formal operations in logical and moral judgments. *Genetic Psychology Monographs*, 1977, 95, 97–188.

Langer, J. *Theories of Development*. New York: Holt, Rhinehart and Winston, 1969.(a)

Langer, J. Disequilibrium as a source of development. In P. H. Mussen, J. Langer, & M. Covington (Eds.), *Trends and Issues in Developmental Psychology*. New York: Holt, Rinehart and Winston, 1969.(b)

Langer, J. Interactional aspects of mental structures. *Cognition*, 1974, 3, 9–28.

Langer, J. Dialectics of development. In T. G. Bever (Ed.), *Developmental and Learning Curves*. Hillsdale, N. J.: Erlbaum, in press.

Luria, A. R. *Cognitive Development*. Cambridge: Harvard University Press, 1976.

Nelson, K. Some evidence for the cognitive primacy of categorization and its functional basis. *Merrill-Palmer Quarterly*, 1973, 19, 21–39.

Piaget, J. *Play, Dreams and Imitation in Childhood*. New York: Norton, 1951.

Piaget, J. *The Origins of Intelligence in Children*. New York: International Universities Press, 1952.

Piaget, J. *The Construction of Reality in the Child*. New York: Basic Books, 1954.

Piaget, J. *Essai de Logique Operatoire*. Paris: Dunod, 1972.

Piaget, J. *The Grasp of Consciousness*. Cambridge: Harvard University Press, 1976.

Piaget, J. *Equilibration of Cognitive Structures*. New York: Viking Press, 1977.

Piaget, J., & Inhelder, B. *The Child's Conception of Space*. New York: Norton, 1967.

Piaget, J., Inhelder, B., & Szeminska, A. *The Child's Conception of Geometry*. London: Routledge and Kegan Paul, 1960.

Ricciuti, H. N. Object grouping and selective ordering behavior in infants 12 to 24 months old. *Merrill-Palmer Quarterly*, 1965, 11, 129–148.

Sugarman, S. *Scheme, order, and outcome*. Unpublished doctoral dissertation, University of California, Berkeley, 1979.

Trunnell, T. L. Thought disturbance in schizophrenia: Pilot study utilizing Piaget's theories. *Archives of General Psychiatry*, 1964, 11, 126–136.

Trunnell, T. L. Thought disturbance in schizophrenia: Replication study utilizing Piaget's theories. *Archives of General Psychiatry*, 1965, 13, 1–18.

Vygotsky, L. S. Thought in schizophrenia. *Archives of Neurology and Psychiatry*, 1934, 31, 1063–1077.

Vygotsky, L. S. *Thought and Language*. Cambridge: MIT Press, 1962.

Weigl, E. On the psychology of so-called processes of abstraction. *Journal of Abnormal and Social Psychology*, 1941, 36, 3–34.

Welch, L. A preliminary investigation of some aspects of the hierarchical development of concepts. *Journal of Genetic Psychology*, 1940, 22, 359–378.

Werner, H. Process and achievement. *Harvard Educational Review*, 1937, 7, 353–368.

Werner, H. *Comparative Psychology of Mental Development*. New York: International Universities Press, 1948.

Werner, H., & Kaplan, B. *Symbol Formation*. New York: Wiley, 1963.

Wertheimer, M. Laws of organization in perceptual forms. In W. D. Ellis (Ed.), *A Source Book of Gestalt Psychology*. London: Routledge and Kegan Paul, 1938.

Index